AIR WAR ITALY 1944-45

AIR WAR ITALY 1944-45

The Axis Air Forces from the Liberation of Rome to the Surrender

Nick Beale • Ferdinando D'Amico • Gabriele Valentini

Airlife

To Linda, Patrizia and Alessandra, for their tolerance and support

Copyright © 1996 by Nick Beale, Ferdinando D'Amico, Gabriele Valentini

First published in the UK in 1996
by Airlife Publishing Ltd

British Library Cataloguing in Publication Data
A catalogue record for this book
is available from the British Library

ISBN 1 85310 252 0

All rights reserved. No part of this book may be reproduced or transmitted in any form or by any means, electronic or mechanical including photocopying, recording or by any information storage and retrieval system, without permission from the Publisher in writing.

Printed in Singapore by Kyodo Printing Co. (S'pore) Pte Ltd

Airlife Publishing Ltd
101 Longden Road, Shrewsbury SY3 9EB, England

PREVIOUS PAGE:
Vicenza, May 1945. The Ju 87 D-5 W.Nr 132230 "+AL" of 3./NSGr.9 abandoned on the airfield by the retreating German unit. Particularly interesting is the dark appearance of the camouflage although still the usual brown wave-mirror over green. The whole tail unit appears to be a replacement with no overspraying on it. (NASM)

Contents

Italian Authors' Preface 6
English Author's Preface 7
Abbreviations and Glossary 8
Key to Italian Province Names 11
Comparative Ranks 12
Organisation of Flying Units 13
Chapter 1   Setting the Stage 15
Chapter 2   June 1944 29
                      Operations, 1-30 June 39
Chapter 3   July 1944 55
                      Operations, 1-31 July 61
Chapter 4   August 1944 77
                      Operations, 1-24 August 83
Chapter 5   Operation Phoenix 89
                      Operations, 25-31 August 93
Chapter 6   September 1944 97
                      Operations, 1-30 September 103
Chapter 7   October 1944 107
                      Operations, 1-31 October 111
Chapter 8   November 1944 117
                      Operations, 1-30 November 121
Chapter 9   December 1944 129
                      Operations, 1-31 December 133
Chapter 10   Old Year, New Year 141
Chapter 11   January 1945 143
                      Operations, 1-31 January 147
Chapter 12   February 1945 151
                      Operations, 1-28 February 157
Chapter 13   March 1945 167
                      Operations, 1-31 March 173
Chapter 14   April 1945 181
                      Operations, 1-19 April 185
Chapter 15   Collapse, Capitulation, Clear-Up 199
                      Operations, 20 April-2 May 205
                      Peacetime 208
Appendix   Luftwaffe and ANR Camouflage and Markings in Italy, 1944-45 209
                      Aircraft Found on Italian Airfields by No. 1 Field Intelligence Unit May 1945 213
Acknowledgements, Source Notes and Bibliography 217
Airfield Maps 220
Index 225

Italian Authors' Preface

It is extremely difficult for an historical researcher to avoid becoming emotionally involved in the subject of his researches, but nevertheless embarrassing. The great difficulty he has to face sooner or later is being forced to choose which is the correct road to go down; that of personal memories, handed down, written or related years after the events they deal with, or that of the official and unofficial sources linked by the thin but strong thread of having been set down immediately following the events of which they speak.

Objectivity is a 'mythical' concept. In reality it is nothing more than an abstraction which, like infinity, cannot be measured or reached in practice. It is a sort of feeble light, visible from far away and occasionally brightened by what one is achieving in attempting to recover the truth.

Before beginning this work with our friend and colleague Nick Beale, we had already published two books, works in which we had given, although in slightly different ways, pride of place to all that the Italian documents, and in particular the personal accounts, said. These had been collected over the years from a great number of the men who flew and fought under the colours of the *Aeronautica Nazionale Repubblicana*.

The picture we obtained seemed complete to us, and we thought then that it added up to a more 'balanced' account than the few things written on the subject up to that point, cutting out the padding of much of the rhetoric used by some Italian researchers (as a matter of fact, for most non-Italian researchers this was, and still is, an almost unknown period). That rhetoric had only managed to create a sharp demarcation between 'good guys' and 'bad guys', obviously including in the first category all the members of the *Repubblica Sociale Italiana* and consigning to the second (in various shades of black) all the others, the partisans and the Anglo-Americans – the latter 'guilty' of being militarily stronger.

We had made a mistake, too, in being satisfied with telling the stories of these men just as they wanted, with simple, plain words and (if this could be called a mistake) becoming not only researchers but personal friends of these 'special' people. The only problem was that by doing this we had left the one and only path an historian can follow: objectivity.

Cross-checking and comparison between the Italian sources and those of the 'enemy' were exactly what our work lacked to make it a real piece of historical research. When, a few years ago, we decided to take this long and winding road, we did not know where it would lead us, nor could we have imagined that it would often confront us with real matters of conscience. To find, for example, that in a single aerial combat where the Italian ANR pilots were credited with eight victories but not a single enemy aircraft was shot down, would have put any other serious Italian researcher in a very embarrassing situation, to say the least!

Then, however, two main factors gained (at least in our case) the upper hand: the desire to try and throw light on what really happened 50 years ago, and the need to understand why there were such glaring differences between some accounts and events that it would have been possible to document objectively, but that up to now were not documented at all.

All of this sometimes brought us into written and oral conflicts with some of the Italian pilots who felt (perhaps rightly from their point of view) themselves and their memories 'betrayed' by reconstructions of ours that upset what they had continued (or wanted) to believe for over 50 years was the only possible truth. Despite suffering deeply from this, we believed and continue to believe that it is fairer and more honest – even for the Italian pilots themselves – to tell the whole truth, or at least to try to do so with all our strength, without any emotional or, even worse, merciful restraint.

We do not know if we have made the best possible choice, but we do believe strongly that the truth can no longer do any harm after so many years. This is either because there are always many ways to interpret a truth (and we have made a particular effort to try and give the reader a 'key' to understand many of the controversial episodes in this book), or because if there are persons so malicious or single-minded as to read in these pages or between the lines things that we did not write, nothing we say will change their minds. After all, this was not the reason this book was written, and they are not the people for whom it was written.

Ferdinando D'Amico
Gabriele Valentini

English Author's Preface

This book's concentration on the Axis air forces means no disrespect to those who defeated them. The sheer scale of the Allied effort precludes covering it in the sort of detail we have attempted here. We do hope, though, that we have given the Allied forces a little of their due.

My own interest in the Luftwaffe and its satellites is accounted for partly by the mystique attaching to what, to someone brought up in 1950s Britain, was still 'the other side'. They are interesting as well *because they lost*: looming defeat compelled them to resort to operational expedients and exotic technical 'fixes' of which the winning side simply had no need. Also, for the researcher the sparsity of the surviving Axis records is at once frustrating and an irresistible challenge. This book was not written from any kind of admiration for dictatorial ideologies: Fascism and Nazism failed even their own self-imposed and brutish criteria of superior strength and final victory; their net product was human suffering.

I am acutely aware that writing is a damned sight easier and safer than flying in combat, and we have tried to restrict comments regarding tactics and airmanship to instances in which something went very clearly wrong or right for one side or the other. This book abounds in cases of mistaken aircraft identification and exaggerated victory claims (plus a few *under*estimates). Unlike the participants, we have been able to cross-check both sides' files. When we say 'we have found no evidence' to support a claim, no more and no less is implied, no one's honesty is in question.

Finally, I would like particularly to thank my uncles, John and Jeremy Bright, who showed me as a small boy their wartime scrapbooks and bomb-splinter collections and told me about Spitfires and Messerschmitts – I ended up writing this.

Nick Beale

Abbreviations and Glossary

AA	Anti-aircraft	
AB	Abwurfbehälter	Cluster-bomb canister
AI	Airborne Interception (radar equipment)	
ALG	Advanced Landing Ground	
ASV	Air [to] Surface Vessel (radar equipment)	
ATI	Air Technical Intelligence	
Awol	Absent Without Leave	
BG	Bombardment Group (US)	
BS	Bombardment Squadron (US)	
B4	German 87-octane aircraft fuel	
CoS	Chief of Staff	
CSDIC	Combined Services Detailed Interrogation Centre	
C3	German 96-octane aircraft fuel	
DF	Direction finding	
Düppel	Anti-radar chaff (equivalent of Allied 'Window')	
E/A	Enemy aircraft	
EK	Eisernes Kreuz	Iron Cross (class I & II)
Enigma	German cypher machine	
Erg.	Ergänzungsgruppe	Replacement/Training Unit
(F)	Fern	Long-range
FAGr.	Fernaufklärungsgruppe	Long-range reconnaissance Gruppe
FBG	Fighter-Bomber Group (US)	
FG	Fighter Group (US)	
FIU	Field Intelligence Unit	
FJ	Fallschirmjäger	Paratroops
Fl.Div.	Fliegerdivision	Air Division
Flivo	Fliegerverbindungsoffizier	Luftwaffe Liaison Officer attached to army unit
FS	Fighter Squadron (US)	
FSU	Field Signals Unit	
FuG	Funkgerät	Radio/radar device
FW	Fighter Wing (US)	
GC	Groupe de Chasse	Fighter Group (French)
GCI	Ground Controlled Interception	

G.d.A.	General der Aufklärungsflieger	General of Reconnaissance
G.d.J	” ” Jagdflieger	” ” Fighters
G.d.S.	” ” Schlachtflieger	” ” Ground Attack
GMT	Greenwich Mean Time	
GOC	General Officer Commanding	
Gr.	Gruppe (German), Gruppo (Italian)	
Gr.C.	Gruppo Caccia	Fighter Gruppo
HE	High explosive	
Ia	Operations Officer (Luftwaffe)	
IAS	Indicated Air Speed	
Ic	Intelligence Officer (Luftwaffe)	
IFF	Identification Friend or Foe	
Jafü	Jagdfliegerführer	Fighter Controller
JG	Jagdgeschwader	Fighter Geschwader
J2	German jet aircraft fuel	
Kdo.	Kommando	Detachment
KG	Kampfgeschwader	Bomber Geschwader
Koflug	Kommando Flughafenbereich	Regional Airfield Command
Komm.Gen.	Kommandierender General	General Officer Commanding
Kogen	” ”	” ” ”
KTB	Kriegstagebuch	War Diary
Lfl.	Luftflotte	Air Fleet
LG	Lehrgeschwader	Training/demonstration Geschwader
L/G	Landing Ground	
MG	Maschinengewehr	Machine-gun
MK	Maschinenkanone	Automatic cannon (over 2 cm calibre)
MM	Matricola Militare	Serial Number (Italian military aircraft)
M/T	Motor Transport	
NAGr.	Nahaufklärungsgruppe	Tactical Reconnaissance Gruppe
NCO	Non-Commissioned Officer	
NSGr.	Nachtschlachtgruppe	Night Harassment Gruppe
Ob.	Oberbefehlshaber	Supreme Commander
Ob.d.L	” der Luftwaffe	Göring
ORB	Operations Record Book	
OKL	Oberkommando der Luftwaffe	Luftwaffe Supreme Command
OKW	Oberkommando der Wehrmacht	Armed Forces Supreme Command
PG	Panzer Grenadier	Mechanised Infantry
PR	Photo-reconnaissance	
PRG	Photo Reconnaissance Group	
PoW	Prisoner of War (English abbreviation)	
P/W	” ” ” (American ”)	
Pz.	Panzer	
RAE	Royal Aircraft Establishment	
RATO	Rocket-assisted Take-off	
RCAF	Royal Canadian Air Force	
Revi	Reflexvisier	Reflector gunsight
RK	Ritterkreuz	Knight's Cross
Rotte	Tactical pair formation (Luftwaffe)	

RV	Rendezvous	
SAAF	South African Air Force	
Schwarm	Tactical formation comprising two *Rotten* (q.v.)	
SD	Sicherheitsdienst	SS Security Service
Sigint	Signals Intelligence	
SMAR	Stato Maggiore Aeronautica Repubblicana	ANR General Staff
Sq.	Squadriglia	
Sqn	Squadron (RAF and Dominions)	
St.	Staffel	
TG	Transportfliegergeschwader	Transport Geschwader
TGr.	Transportfliegergruppe	Transport Gruppe
TRS	Tactical Reconnaissancc Squadron	
Ultra	Allied security classification for decrypted Enigma (q.v.) traffic	
U/s	Unserviceable	
Versuchsverband	Trials Unit (Luftwaffe)	
Wekusta	Wettererkundungsstaffel	Weather Scouting Staffel
Westa	(*see* Wekusta)	
W.Nr.	Werk Nummer	Production Serial Number
Y	Allied radio monitoring (hence 'Y-Service')	
z.b.V.	zur besonderen Verwendung	Special purpose

At Maniago (UD), III./JG 53's Messerschmitts prepare to take-off on one of their last missions in Italy. By the end of June 1944 this Gruppe had rejoined the rest of JG 53 in Germany. (Bundesarchiv)

Italian Provinces and Abbreviations

Agrigento	AG	Frosinone	FR	Pistoia	PT
Alessandria	AL	Genova	GE	Pordenone	PN
Ancona	AN	Gorizia	GO	Potenza	PZ
Aosta	AO	Grosseto	GR	Ragusa	RG
Arezzo	AR	Imperia	IM	Ravenna	RA
Ascoli Piceno	AP	Isernia	IS	Reggio Calabria	RC
Asti	AT	L'Aquila	AQ	Reggio Emilia	RE
Avellino	AV	La Spezia	SP	Rieti	RI
Bari	BA	Latina	LT	Roma	ROMA
Belluno	BL	Lecce	LE	Rovigo	RO
Benevento	BN	Livorno	LI	Salerno	SA
Bergamo	BG	Lucca	LU	Sassari	SS
Bologna	BO	Macerata	MC	Savona	SV
Bolzano	BZ	Mantova	MN	Siena	SI
Brescia	BS	Massa Carrara	MS	Siracusa	SR
Brindisi	BR	Matera	MT	Sondrio	SO
Cagliari	CA	Messina	ME	Taranto	TA
Caltanissetta	CL	Milano	MI	Teramo	TE
Campobasso	CB	Modena	MO	Terni	TR
Caserta	CE	Napoli	NA	Torino	TO
Catania	CT	Novara	NO	Trapani	TP
Catanzaro	CZ	Nuoro	NU	Trento	TN
Chieti	CH	Oristano	OR	Treviso	TV
Como	CO	Padova	PD	Trieste	TS
Cosenza	CS	Palermo	PA	Udine	UD
Cremona	CR	Parma	PR	Varese	VA
Cuneo	CN	Pavia	PV	Venezia	VE
Enna	EN	Perugia	PG	Vercelli	VC
Ferrara	FE	Pesaro	PS	Verona	VR
Firenze	FI	Pescara	PE	Vicenza	VI
Foggia	FG	Piacenza	PC	Viterbo	VT
Forlí	FO	Pisa	PI		

Comparative Ranks

Luftwaffe	ANR	RAF	USAAF
Reichsmarschall			
Generalfeldmarschall		Marshal of the RAF	General (Five Star)
Generaloberst		Air Chief Marshal	General (Four Star)
General	Generale di Squadra Aerea	Air Marshal	Lieutenant-General
Generalleutnant	Generale di Divisione Aerea	Air Vice-Marshal	Major-General
Generalmajor	Generale di Brigata Aerea	Air Commodore	Brigadier-General
Oberst	Colonnello	Group Captain	Colonel
Oberstleutnant	Tenente Colonnello	Wing Commander	Lieutenant-Colonel
Major	Maggiore	Squadron Leader	Major
Hauptmann	Capitano	Flight Lieutenant	Captain
Oberleutnant	Tenente	Flying Officer	First Lieutenant
Leutnant	Sottotenente	Pilot Officer	Second Lieutenant
Stabsfeldwebel	Maresciallo di 1ª Classe	Warrant Officer	Flight Officer
Oberfeldwebel	Maresciallo di 2ª Classe	Flight Sergeant	Master Sergeant
Feldwebel	Maresciallo di 3ª Classe	Sergeant	Technical Sergeant
Unterfeldwebel	Sergente Maggiore		Staff Sergeant
Unteroffizier	Sergente	Corporal	Corporal
Hauptgefreiter	Primo Aviere		
Obergefreiter		Leading Aircraftman	
Gefreiter	Aviere Scelto	Aircraftman 1st Class	Private First Class
Flieger	Aviere	Aircraftman 2nd Class	Private Second Class

Notes:

1. Due to the proliferation of non-commissioned ranks in different air forces, equivalences are less precise than among commissioned officers.

2. The Luftwaffe also had three Officer Candidate grades, beginning with Fahnenjunker (prefixed to the normal NCO rank, e.g. Fhj.Uffz.) and continuing through Fähnrich and Oberfähnrich (used as rank designations in their own right).

Organisation of Flying Units

This *ought* to be easy to explain, but what started as a simple system became more and more complicated (and disregarded) under wartime conditions. Although this account is geared solely to Italy and the period covered by this book, some of it may be applicable in other contexts but do not count on it. Translating German or Italian unit names into English 'equivalents' tends to be very misleading, since units of equivalent size could differ markedly as to operational independence and tactical employment. Also, the Germans tended to entrust command to officers of lower rank than the Allies.

Luftwaffe

Bombers, fighters and transports were organised into Geschwader. Units were designated by a functional prefix and a number, e.g. Kampfgeschwader 1 = Bomber Geschwader 1. In its purest form, one of these units was built up in threes:

3 aircraft = 1 Kette (a tactical vic formation, not a unit as such)
3 Ketten = 1 Staffel
3 Staffeln + a Stabskette (HQ flight of 3 aircraft) = 1 Gruppe
3 Gruppen + a Geschwaderstab (HQ flight of 3 aircraft)= 1 Geschwader

Staffeln were designated by Arabic numerals running consecutively through the Geschwader, while Gruppen had Roman numerals:

I. Gruppe	II. Gruppe	III. Gruppe
1. Staffel	4. Staffel	7. Staffel
2. Staffel	5. Staffel	8. Staffel
3. Staffel	6. Staffel	9. Staffel

Hence I./KG 1 = first Gruppe of Kampfgeschwader 1; 7./KG 1 = seventh Staffel of same. These were sometimes abbreviated to I./1 or 7./1, leaving room for confusion with other units such as Stukageschwader 1 or Jagdgeschwader 1.

In practice a Geschwader could have up to five Gruppen; these could have four Staffeln (as did II./TG 1 and, after July 1944, fighter units); a Staffel could number 20 aeroplanes or more (fighters and other small aircraft). HQ flights could grow to Staffel strength or have no aircraft at all.

With a war on it became increasingly rare for a Geschwader's elements all to be in one place, or even for them all to be in existence. Constituent parts were used to form the nucleus of new formations, formally incorporated into other outfits and renamed, disbanded and re-formed as needed. As with the army's battle groups, it was common for elements of several units to be combined into *ad hoc* formations to meet a tactical need. After 1 June 1944 there never was a whole Geschwader in Italy, and what mattered were Gruppen.

Gruppen were generally capable of independent operation and some, like reconnaissance and night attack units, did not belong to a Geschwader at all. In a free-standing Gruppe, the Staffeln (of which there might sometimes be up to six) could enjoy a considerable degree of operational independence – they might even find themselves in different countries. Again, composite units were put together from available Staffeln ('Gruppe Orlowski' in Italy was an example) which might later be renamed to provide a semblance of order.

The reader will also come across Kommandos (detachments of two or three aeroplanes, usually on some special duty and perhaps intended to form the nucleus of an eventual regular Staffel); a Seenotstaffel (an independent air-sea rescue Staffel, at least in name) and an oddity variously termed a Sonderstaffel or Sonderverband, in effect a special independent Staffel from an unusual parent Geschwader.

The Luftwaffe controlled its own flak and signals troops. These were organised on army lines, in divisions, regiments and battalions.

It is particularly important to realise that almost never in the period covered were Luftwaffe units in Italy operating at anything like their established strength, except where amalgamation of two understrength units briefly brought actual numbers up to (or over) paper levels.

Aeronautica Nazionale Repubblicana

Operating under German patronage, the ANR's units were organised much like the Luftwaffe's, in Gruppi composed in turn of three Squadriglie and a staff flight (called Nucleo Comando in II° Gruppo; in I° a Sezione di Gruppo was only formed in February 1945). There were (German) orders issued in June 1944 to form a Geschwaderstab to control the Gruppi Caccia (fighters), and in January 1945 to give them four Squadriglie apiece. The first idea apparently foundered because for much of the time only a single Gruppo was operational and never more than two, the second was probably impeded by shortages of fuel and trained pilots.

The Gruppi were essentially independent entities, even to the extent of their aircraft marking practices (see Appendix) The numbering of Gruppi was simply I°, II° and III° (first, second, third) for the fighters and I° for the torpedo and bomber units. Within each Gruppo the Squadriglie were also numbered 1ª, 2ª, 3ª, although the fighter units went over to the German system in early 1945 and were renumbered 1ª-9ª across the Gruppi.

The ANR had its share of 'autonomous squadrons' at various times, although they play only a minor role in our particular story; it also had one Transport Gruppo, organised on German lines and operating in support of the Luftwaffe on the Eastern Front during 1944. A second transport unit was constituted that year and completed its transfer to Germany, but for a variety of reasons it never progressed beyond the training stage.

A final point to note is that the Germans frequently spoke and wrote of the ANR units in Luftwaffe terms, and it is not uncommon to see expressions like II./ital. Jagdgruppe or II./ital. JG 1 in their documents.

The Allies

These are not the subject of this book, but are nonetheless indispensable to the narrative. The sheer size of these forces requires that we start further up the organisational pyramid and generalise a little. There were various structural changes in the period in question, most notably in November 1944, but the principles hold good.

Over all was Mediterranean Allied Air Forces (MAAF), incorporating units of several nations but primarily American and British ones. MAAF controlled Mediterranean Allied Coastal Air Force (MACAF); Mediterranean Allied Strategic Air Forces (MASAF), made up of US 15th Army Air Force and 205 Group RAF with heavy bombers and their escorts; Mediterranean Allied Tactical Air Forces (MATAF), comprising US 12th Army Air Force and the RAF's Desert Air Force (DAF) and Balkan Air Force (BAF) fighters, fighter-bombers and medium bombers. There was also an Anglo-American reconnaissance organisation.

MACAF will impinge on this story only rarely, mainly via its nightfighters; MASAF fought over Italy but also ranged right across occupied Europe; MATAF's forces (with the exception of BAF) gave most of their attention to Italy – DAF's title was a hangover from its origins in North Africa and not to be taken literally after mid-1943.

American aircraft were organised into Squadrons of around 12-20 aeroplanes, and these in turn were embodied into Groups, normally consisting of three Squadrons; Groups were assembled in a Wing. French and Brazilian units followed this pattern. RAF and Dominion Squadrons were about the same size (although some had up to 30 aeroplanes); three to six Squadrons made up a Wing and around five or six Wings a Group. Few of the tactical air force operations in our story involved particularly large formations of aircraft, however, usually being based on squadrons or smaller elements within them, fighters flying in fours and eights, for example.

Readers should beware the different meanings attached to Wing and Group by the Americans and British during the Second World War.

Chapter 1

Setting the Stage

The Campaign in Italy

On 3 September 1943, four years to the day after their country went to war, British troops returned to Continental Europe for more than a raid, landing at Reggio Calabria. The campaign then ran as follows:

8 September 1943: Italy declares Armistice.
9 September 1943: Allied landings at Salerno.
October-December 1943: Gustav Line (Gaeta (LT)-Termoli (CB)) is reached.
12 January-11 February 1944: First Battle of Cassino (FR).
22 January 1944: Allied landings at Anzio (Rome).
15-17 February 1944: Second Battle of Cassino.
19 February 1944: Third Battle of Cassino.
April-May 1944: Operation Diadem: breaching of the Gustav Line and the dash for Rome.
16-19 May 1944: Fourth Battle and fall of Cassino.

As May 1944 drew to a close, Axis forces were in full retreat, desperate to avoid encirclement by the Allied armies emerging from the now-broken stalemates of the Anzio-Nettuno beach-head and the Cassino/Liri Valley battles. Fortunately for the German Tenth and Fourteenth Armies, Gen Mark Clark opted for prestige over strict military logic and diverted his Fifth Army from cutting off his opponents' retreat to capturing Rome. In the event his thunder was comprehensively stolen by the Normandy landings, two days after his troops' entry into the Italian capital on the 4th. Despite the fact that the Western Allies had been fighting on the European mainland for nine months, Overlord was (and is still) hailed as the opening of the Second Front.

Italy now lapsed irrevocably into the status of a secondary theatre of war. Despite the huge forces still fighting there, and misery, injury and death on an horrific scale, Italy was in a lower league. Undeniably the war there was dwarfed by that on the Eastern Front and, as the months passed, in Northwest Europe. That does not mean that what happened in the south was devoid of significance or historical interest. Above all, to those caught up in the fighting and its attendant horrors, soldiers and civilians alike, there was nothing 'secondary' about what was happening to them.

The air war has been a particular casualty of this historical neglect, although any campaign history will include a generalised tribute to the vast Allied efforts in tactical air support and transport interdiction. Where these accounts mention the Axis air forces at all, they are swiftly dismissed. The departure of the Luftwaffe fighters is frequently treated as the last straw insofar as matters of importance or interest are concerned. We hope to show otherwise.

The Luftwaffe

The near rout beginning in mid-late May afflicted the Luftwaffe and the Aeronautica Nazionale Repubblicana every bit as much as the land forces. Ground attack units and their escort fighters had taken dreadful losses; the ground organisation was disrupted and pulling back, wrecking its airfields wherever possible before they could be overrun (delaying their operational re-use by only a matter of days but often condemning Allied personnel to live in conditions of acute discomfort in tents and other makeshift accommodation). The German Supreme Commander South West, Generalfeldmarschall Albert Kesselring had ordered on 29 May that Rome and Central Italy were to be defended at all costs but pressure of events thwarted him.

Three airfield commands were transferred from around Rome to the Perugia-Pisa area; vehicle servicing and aircraft repair echelons made similar moves. The Viterbo Fighter Control Centre pulled its staff back to Siena; radar stations south of the line Orbetello (GR)-Pescara were withdrawn to strengthen the defences farther up the Peninsula, and plans were made to establish new airfields. Flak units in Central Italy were used to reinforce Florence and Bologna, light flak being redeployed to the defence of the bomber airfields in the North and 25. Flak Div. HQ established itself in the Verona area. During the June/July retreats both heavy and light flak deployed in an anti-armour role to counter breakthroughs into the Axis rear areas. Against aircraft the flak arm was credited with a major part in allowing a more or less orderly withdrawal by impeding the constant air attacks. Nonetheless, some 200 guns were lost between Rome and the Apennines, 90 to enemy action and the rest destroyed by their operators when there was no motor transport to move them. Before the end of June a maintenance depot was set up near Florence for the guns and their attendant vehicles, which was able to bring the greater part of the surviving materiel back into action. Even so, the first orders were issued for economy in ammunition expenditure owing to supply shortfalls.

Headquarters organisations, too, were uprooted. On 29 May Luftwaffe General Commanding in Central Italy (General der Flieger Max Ritter von Pohl) had to relocate his staff from Torre Gaia, southwest of Rome, to the city's Sacro district. On 3 June Allied armour came to within 4km, causing him to decamp to Viterbo next day as the first fighting broke out in the capital. On the 5th he was joined there by Kesselring (just driven out of Monte Soratte in some haste), who shared his HQ until the 7th, Pohl shifting to Siena and the Generalfeldmarschall heading further north. Luftflotte 2 under GFM Wolfram von Richthofen was – and would remain – at Malcesine on the shores of Lake Garda, with advanced HQs at Monte Riceo (Monselice-PD) and Tabiano (Parma). The signals and supplies HQs were at Treviso.

Pohl was able to pull out his ground echelons without excessive losses of supplies and equipment. Loss of territory dictated a major revamp of the Airfield Regional Commands, Sardinia's being returned to the Reich after the island's evacuation. As early as 4 June Pohl was advised by Kesselring of plans for a fighting withdrawal to the Gothic Line and the consequent air cover requirements, which were way beyond his means to fulfil. Pohl's response next day was that any redress for the situation would depend on his receiving strong fighter and ground attack support, even if only temporarily. A need was also seen (and was to dominate Luftwaffe Italien's thinking for the rest of the campaign) to prepare for further outflanking Allied amphibious operations as had occurred on a greater or lesser scale from Sicily onwards. One precaution was the reconnaissance coverage of the harbours of Taranto, Brindisi and Bari by Bf 109s of NAGr.12 from the Balkans, capitalising on the relative safety of the overwater approach.

Pohl's task now was to cover and support the army with his aircraft and flak and protect supply lines, railways and airfields. The flak would have a secondary role in backing up the coastal defence forces. In the northernmost part of the country 25. Flak Div. was to carry out similar duties and help defend the Adriatic coast north of the Po Estuary. Jagdfliegerführer Oberitalien (Fighter Leader, Upper Italy) was in effect an outer ring of the Defence of the Reich, harrying the heavy bombers of the 15th USAAF on their way to and from their targets. Pohl was also charged with the defence of Northern Italy itself and, should this be possible, with supporting the ground forces.

Fernaufklärungsgruppe 122
Of the flying units themselves, perhaps the one with the longest service in Italy (in one permutation or another) was Luftflotte 2's strategic reconnaissance arm, Fernaufklärungsgruppe 122. The Gruppenstab and 2. Staffel, along with Wettererkundungsstaffel 26 had moved from Smolensk to Trapani in late 1941 (1. Staffel was then already at Catania but was long gone from Italy by the start of this narrative). Central Mediterranean conditions made weather reconnaissance unnecessary, and Westa 26 went over, like the other Staffeln, to maritime reconnaissance and convoy protection. Two or three submarines were successfully attacked with 250kg Trialen bombs, the destruction of one being confirmed, a rare accomplishment for what was ostensibly an overland photo-reconnaissance unit. From August 1942 sorties were flown as far as Gibraltar, and it was a Junkers Ju 88 of FAGr.122 that first spotted the convoys of Operation Torch, the landings in North Africa. Losses, hitherto light, began to mount as attempts were made to cover the

Seen conferring in their Command Post overlooking the Anzio beach-head, the successive heads of the Luftwaffe in Italy: Generalfeldmarschall Wolfram von Richthofen (second from left) and General der Flieger Maximilian von Pohl. (IWM)

strongly defended targets on the North African littoral. By November the Ju 88A was considered inadequate for the task, and Me 210s and Ju 88Ts began to be employed, marking the start of a continuing race for survivability in the face of hardening defences, although both of these latter types proved disappointingly prone to engine failure.

In the late summer of 1942 six Heinkel He 111s under Maj. Koch of the Köthen Signals Research Establishment came to Trapani and were attached to FAGr.122 for night ASV radar trials using a captured British set (valued for its capabilities in coastal work), Rostock and Lichtenstein 'S'. These last were supplanted by the far superior FuG 200 Hohentwiel, Koch's Kommando training all of FAGr.122's observers in its use. The equipment was soon fitted into Ju 188s, because the Heinkels were found to be far too slow for comfort or peace of mind. During summer 1943 the Gruppe was driven back to Frosinone on the mainland by repeated Allied attacks on its Sicilian bases. After a sojourn in France, 1. Staffel returned there equipped with GM 1-boosted Ju 88Ts. Even these suffered severe losses, and when the first night photography-trained crews arrived in June they were beset by all manner of technical and navigational teething troubles.

The next twist to the survivability spiral came from signals and communications intelligence, based on experience gained in Norway. Horchdienst (Radio Monitoring Service) operators were installed at Frosinone, alongside the Gruppe's ground controllers, to listen in on Allied R/T traffic which might presage an attack on one of their machines. Warnings were passed in a coded sequence of letters and figures giving position, height, speed and nature of the threat (jjj = 'enemy fighter', for example). The next step was to carry special operators in the aeroplanes themselves to give on-the-spot threat assessments without risk of interference from the jamming of ground-to-air communications. Another safety precaution was not to take-off and land at the same airfield, in case MAAF intruders were awaiting the aircraft's return. Elements of both the Sicily and Salerno invasion fleets were detected by FAGr.122 before the landings.

The HQ remained at Perugia from November 1943 into 1944, and the unit, now composed of Stab FAGr.122, 1.(F)/123, 2.(F)/122 and Westa 26, was commonly known as 'Gruppe Orlowski' after the major in command. With its principal mission now to warn against possible new Allied landings, the Gruppe incurred severe losses attempting daylight cover of ports. Units based in Greece eventually took over cover of Sicily and of Italy south of Bari. North of that line the Gruppe's low-altitude maritime reconnaissance continued, although the Me 410s sought safety in straight runs to their targets at 25-28,000ft. Night flying was still comparatively rare and mostly carried out by Westa 26; Düppel began to be used to good effect against AA radars during high-altitude night photographic missions, 80cm strips being discharged over the target area. Orlowski was

2.(F)/122 flew the Messerschmitt Me 410 from Spring 1943 and a couple of their aircraft were captured by the Allies in Italy. F6+QK (W.Nr.10253), shown here, crash-landed in the bed of the River Sangro on 11 November 1943. Two more 'F6+QKs' would be lost in 1944. (IWM)

The importance of NAGr.11's tactical reconnaissance over the Italian battlefront should not be underestimated. Here a Bf 109G of this unit, pictured in early 1944, shows to advantage the comparatively rare twin droptank configuration. (Petrick)

lost flying a Ju 88 in bad weather northeast of Pescara in November 1943, intercepted radio traffic suggesting he had fallen victim to two Lockheed P-38s. He was succeeded by Hptm. Schiedel, and around this time 2./122's CO, Hptm. Lütjens, was promoted major and returned to Germany. His successor, Hptm. Weinand, led the Staffel for the rest of its existence.

Heavy bombing of Perugia on 19 January 1944 put the field out of action for five days, followed by two days' dense mist (also affecting Forlì) which combined to prevent any missions during the Anzio landings. A few days previously, two British saboteurs had placed 12 explosive charges on aircraft at Perugia during pitch darkness. However the accidental explosion of a grenade killed the man carrying it and wounded his companion, alerting the Germans who removed the devices before they could do any damage. In the event, coverage of the Anzio-Nettuno beach-head was left to tactical reconnaissance aircraft. The Gruppe's nocturnal overwater operations now faced greater opposition from nightfighters and about one aircraft a fortnight was being lost.

At Perugia difficulties began to appear in the shape of inadequately trained replacement crews, whose further instruction was made impossible by aircraft shortages and omnipresent Allied fighters. The Me 410s were less troubled, many of their crews being former flying instructors. At the beginning of May bombing and strafing compelled a move back to Bergamo, although the Messerschmitts, with their smaller radius of action stayed another month at Perugia. The transfer to Bergamo brought troubles of its own. The smaller number of available airfields simplified the Allies' task in keeping them under observation; the proximity of the Alps presented navigational difficulties; and there were now very few objectives within the Me 410's range.

Nachtschlachtgruppe 9

The only flying units directly controlled by Pohl in Central Italy by June were Nahaufklärungsgruppe 11 and Nachtschlachtgruppe 9, his other close-support forces having been pulled out of the line for re-equipment, never in fact to return. NSGr.9 had its origins on the northern sector of the Eastern Front, whence ten experienced crew of NSGr.3 were withdrawn during October 1943. They were posted to Stubendorf, a centre for night/blind flying training, to convert to the Caproni Ca.314 (their previous machines had been Arado Ar 66s). The Germans had acquired a considerable windfall of Italian types following that nation's recent surrender and planned to use some against partisans in the Alps and in Istria and Croatia. Formally constituted on 30 November, 1./NSGr.9 moved to Udine, Italy, the following month to test the Caproni's combat-worthiness, initially in daylight.

In January 1944 the unit transferred to Caselle (TO) to attack guerrillas in the southern Alpine area, only to establish the Ca.314's unsuitability for combat, particularly in improvised night operations. On the 28th a second Staffel was set up, this time with Fiat Cr.42s fitted with flame dampers and other detail changes to conform to Luftwaffe standards; these aircraft were armed with a pair of 12.7mm machine-guns and racks for four 50kg bombs. Although the Ca.314 shows up in strength returns as late as 29 February, it is doubtful that any remained operational by then. It was also in January that the Allies noticed what they termed the 'E8 Communications Unit' after the Gruppe's recognition code and the motley assortment of Italian aircraft and one Fieseler Storch they had detected on its roster, not suspecting that it was a combat outfit. During February, seven aircraft of 1. and two from 2. Staffel had been logged in signals traffic, all thought to be based at Centocelle, near Rome. There was impatience with the time being taken to bring the new unit to operational readiness and at the beginning of February the then CO was replaced by Hptm. (later Maj) Rupert Frost, who was to command it to the last.

The landings at Anzio-Nettuno led to NSGr.9's 'promotion' to front-line service. Trial Cr.42 sorties were flown over the front lines following deployment of a half-dozen aircraft to Viterbo during March. Operations were essentially confined to moonlit periods since crews were inexperienced, and the biplanes carried no radio navaids and had to make a long flight over mountainous terrain to reach their targets. Sorties were flown against high-value objectives within the Allied beach-head, often in the face of very strong defences. At the outset, however, losses were few and the Fiat was felt to have proved itself operationally. Nonetheless, the biplane's days with NSGr.9 were numbered owing to supply problems and the loss of five when P-47s strafed Rieti on 21 April. The combat status of 2. Staffel's

The first aircraft to equip the newly-created NSGr.9 was the Caproni Ca.314, used by the unit only in the first two months of 1944 for anti-guerrilla operations. The unsuitability of the aircraft for night-flying led to its abandonment. Here one of the few Ca.314s of the Luftwaffe is shown in early 1944, location unknown. (Willis)

aircraft fluctuated between 're-equipping', 'operational' and 'training' during the April-June period, and its *Kapitän*, Oblt. Rolf Martini, was killed when his Cr.42 crashed at Caselle on 22 May during a mock combat with FIAT's test pilot Valentino Cus.

The way forward appeared in the inelegant shape of the Junkers Ju 87 (D-3 and D-5 models adapted to night operations with exhaust shrouds, supplementary armour and aids such as the Peilgerät DF/homing set and FuG 25a Erstling IFF), which appeared on strength returns for 29 February. The first Ju 87s detected by the Allies in 1944 were five belonging to SG 151 and based at Centocelle and Villafranca during March in a non-operational capacity. The authors believe that these were 'cast-offs' passed on to NSGr.9, or a detachment from SG 151 assisting conversion to the new type. The use of the Ju 87 for night operations apparently met some opposition in the ground attack hierarchy (from Hans-Ulrich Rudel amongst others), but Frost sold his unit extremely well and impressed his superiors by 'skilful line shooting'.

On the night of 2/3 April, from five to ten Ju 87s operated over Anzio and Allied AA claimed three of their number, RAF Intelligence commenting, 'these aircraft are reserved for harassing operations by moonlight'. In May the same source noted '20-30 Ju 87s and most probably Cr.42s operating over the battle area at points of Allied penetration, without causing significant damage', in contrast to the German belief that worthwhile results were being achieved. The damage must surely have seemed 'significant' to anyone killed, hurt, bereaved or left homeless by bombs and strafing. Although it was rare for more than 12 aircraft to be operational in the February-July period this was offset by each machine flying multiple sorties each night.

The Ju 87 was a more capable type than its predecessors in the Gruppe, with a far greater warload, and was available in greater numbers. It benefited from a tough, wide-track landing gear (valuable for night-flying from grass strips), was well equipped with blind-flying aids and economical on fuel. It was to be NSGr.9's mainstay for the rest of the war, its armour giving good protection against light AA and its very lack of speed – combats are recorded at a mere 140mph – compared with powerful nightfighters compounding the difficulties of successful interception. Pilots were often forced to lower their flaps and undercarriages just to remain in a firing position, so high was the fighters' margin of overtaking speed. The Junkers was, nevertheless, far from invulnerable.

On the night of 7/8th April a Ju 87 was seen over the Tiber and one crashed within the beach-head on the 15/16th. At the end of the month they were deployed forward from Bologna to Tuscania for missions. In the second half of May, Ju 87 practice flights were heard in the Milan-Turin area and the unit's traffic was again intercepted (E8+AH of 1. Staffel). By June the Gruppe had pulled back first to Castiglione del Lago (PG) and then to Ravenna and Forlì, with take-off facilities also available at Florence. 2. Staffel was converting to the Ju 87 but not yet operational on the type, and the Fiats had a few more appearances to make.

Nahaufklärungsgruppe 11

Pohl's tactical reconnaissance assets consisted of NAGr.11's Bf 109s, an ever-changing mixture of G-5s, G-6s and G-8s with all the various tropical modifications, conversion sets and performance boosts. By June, 1. and 2. Staffeln and 3. (which had only been formed at Ghedi during April) had withdrawn north of Rome, and by virtue of good camouflage the Gruppe suffered no air attacks on its bases. The Bf 109s took on battlefield reconnaissance in Rotte and Schwarm strength (covering the Anzio

Oberst Günther Freiherr von Maltzahn (left), who served as Jagdfliegerführer Oberitalien until August 1944, here pictured with Major Franz Götz, Gruppekommandeur of III./JG 53. (IWM)

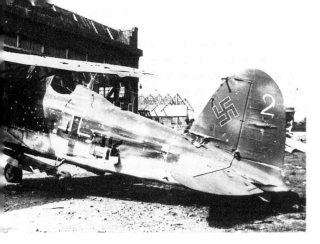

Torino, April 1944. Shown here after a heavy bombardment of the FIAT factory, two damaged Fiat Cr.42s of 2./NSGr.9. The tactical markings applied to the these aircraft indicate that they had already been delivered to the German unit which had applied a makeshift camouflage 'in the field'. Modifications from the standard Cr.42 comprised new cockpit instruments and radio equipment, exhaust flame-dampers, shortened wheel spats and the installation of two ETC 50 bomb-racks.

beaches for example, Ltn. Tornow of 1./11 being one of those to bring back photographs) and, as time went on, coastal reconnaissance. The overland missions were perforce conducted at high altitude but the maritime ones were flown low down; normal times of operation were during early daylight and late afternoon. These missions entailed a constant stream of losses to enemy fighters during 1944. The Gruppe was commanded almost to the last by Hptm. Eckerscham, but the Gruppenstab listed no aircraft of its own until 1945.

Established in Italy in late 1943, NAGr.11 can be considered – along with NSGr.9 and FAGr.122 – one of the 'core' units in this narrative and there is evidence to suggest that its aircraft sometimes doubled as fighters, either when the opportunity arose or when cornered. This would not be out of character with other NAGr. units (some of whose pilots achieved considerable victory tallies in air-to-air combat) in a Luftwaffe increasingly denied the luxury of specialisation, as commitments outran resources. Conversely, it seems that III./JG 53 and II./JG 77 gave some help with reconnaissance.

Schlachtgeschwader 4

The ground attack Gruppen had taken a severe battering throughout the Italian Campaign, the early months of 1944 being no exception. Stab, I. and II./SG 4[1] (callsign Apfel= 'Apple') had been heavily engaged over the Anzio and Cassino fronts, and their losses had led to them being pulled back from their operational base at Viterbo to Piacenza, for rest and refitting and to give a chance to train the newer pilots. During April the Allies rated their activity 'very restricted' although they returned to the fray during May, strafing in the Cassino/Gaeta area on the 3rd but moving out of the battle area again on that date. The Focke-Wulf Fw 190s were heard making practice attacks and engaging Allied fighters over Piacenza on the 11th; next day some of them were over the front lines again. From 17 May onwards there was evidence from R/T traffic that SG 4's aeroplanes were being employed as fighters although a bombing mission was aborted on the 19th, with payloads jettisoned. Twenty-four machines of I. and II. Gruppen were in the air on a mission from Northern Italy on the 21st and seven pilots were killed in combat with Spitfires. Four more casualties followed on the 25th and next day the Geschwaderkommodore, Obstlt. Georg Dörffel, was killed in action against heavy bombers near Rome.

The rear areas could hardly be called safe, and in an air raid on Piacenza on 29 May the Allies claimed the destruction of some 19 Fw 190s, although seven had (wisely) been flown as far back as Osoppo (UD) five days previously. Major Heinrich Brücker (relieved of the command of SG 4 after losing his temper and striking an insubordinate officer from another unit) later claimed that the Geschwader was absorbing 50 per cent of the Schlachtflieger School's output at this stage.

At the end of May the Geschwader went into action again, 'but with total lack of success as Jabos', and this was effectively the end of the operational line for SG 4 in Italy. Generalmajor Hitschold, General der Schlachtflieger, stated postwar that after the experience in Italy it was considered virtually impossible to operate his units in the West.

Fighters

The forces under command of Jagdfliegerführer Oberitalien, Oberst Günther Freiherr von Maltzahn, were elements of three different Geschwader, plus

During June 1944, Westa 26 was officially disbanded and 6.(F)/122 established in its place. In practice however, the unit simply changed its name and continued its reconnaissance role, even retaining its markings for some time after. On the nose and wing of this Ju 88A-6/U of Westa 26 are visible the FuG 200 (surface search) and FuG 216 (air-warning) radars. (Bundesarchiv)

Kommandeur of the last Luftwaffe fighter Gruppe to serve in Italy, Hptm. Günther Freytag of II./JG 77. (IWM)

the ANR's fighters. This was a consequence of the Luftwaffe's 'fire-brigade' approach, shuttling individual Gruppen around to meet each new crisis. On its second deployment to Italy, II./JG 51 had come in December 1943 and left for Serbia the following March; I./JG 53 had spent most of its time since December 1941 in the Mediterranean Theatre, but was withdrawn in favour of the Balkans by May 1944. In February the Fw 190s of 2./ and 3./JG 2 had come south from the Channel Coast of France to lend their weight to the hard-pressed forces on the Southern Front, the only deployment of a fighter unit so equipped in the theatre, before returning 'home' in early April. JG 2, whose 4. Staffel with Bf 109G-6s had also come to Italy, operated from Castiglione del Lago and Ponte del Diavolo (VT), losing at least nine pilots killed and four wounded between 29 February and 6 April.

With Stab/JG 53 in the process of leaving, the Luftwaffe fighters remaining in Italy by June were I./JG 4 (there since December 1943), III./JG 53, and Stab, I. and II./JG 77, under the celebrated ace Obstlt. Johannes 'Macky' Steinhoff. All were equipped with the Bf 109G-6, whose growing inferiority to contemporary Allied models is described in Stab/JG 77's KTB[2]. There was perhaps one small bright spot with the news, passed on from Berlin on 5 June, that since the end of May the G-6 was being delivered with the new improved-visibility cockpit hood (*'Erla Haube'*). Hoods for retrofitting to existing aircraft had been ordered by the Jafü and would be issued by the Pordenone Depot.

The year 1944 had been eventful for these Gruppen. As it began, JG 77 (less III. Gruppe in Romania) was on air defence duties at Caselle, often flying in conjunction with the ANR's I° Gruppo Caccia. The Anzio landings prompted II./77's move to Siena in January, joined shortly afterwards by III./53. I./4 was already in the southern zone, losing large numbers of men and machines over the front lines, as well as its Gruppenadjutant, operations officer and a number of experienced pilots in the same air raid on Perugia that so damaged FAGr.122. During January I./JG 77 made moves to Lavariano (UD) and Cascina Vaga (PV), then next month transferred to the Udine area with the Stab.

Stab and I./77 fought over Northeastern Italy and in Austrian and Yugoslavian airspace during February and March. I./JG 53 was flying defensive missions from Maniago (PN), while III./53 (CO, Maj. Franz Götz) was escorting the Schlachtflieger over Cassino and falling foul of Allied interceptors. In April Stab and I./53 moved to Bologna; II./JG 77 went south in exchange for I./JG 4, pulled back to Bergamo for rest and refit; Stab and I./JG 77 transferred to Ferrara, although the latter was officially subordinated to JG 53 until the 21st.

May had been a hard month, as the balance sheet of III./JG 53 exemplifies. With an average of 20 serviceable aeroplanes a total of 693 sorties had been achieved, in 47 missions on 28 flying days. Thirteen pilots had taken to their parachutes (six of them hurt); four Bf 109s were destroyed, seven damaged over 60 per cent (written off and good only for cannibalisation) and two more over 30 per cent. The situation and morale of the Luftwaffe fighter units at the end of the month is illustrated by the KTB of Stab JG 77:

27.05.44 Display for the Luftflotte. Macchi a good plane against fighters, Fiat G.55 a tired ship. Despite that, Macchis are running out and the G.55 will continue to be built!

30.05.44 II./Ital. Jagdgruppe has been ordered to hand over its Fiat G.55s to I./Ital. Gruppe and is to be re-equipped with Bf 109s. 4 officers, 6 Sergeants (pilots) and 20 men from the technical personnel are going to Ferrara for instruction with II./JG 77.

During the night the Jafü telephones: all Gruppen outside the Reich must immediately hand over a complete Staffel to Reich Defence. After a long argument it is finally agreed that the Gruppen will [each] give up a composite Staffel of personnel without aircraft or equipment, so that the re-establishment of a third Staffel in [each of] the Gruppen will remain possible in the future. The personnel situation of the Gruppen, especially since the measures ordered and carried out in December and January for the drafting of men into the fighting troops, is at the limit of what is responsible. If the Gruppen had worn-out planes, operational readiness would no longer be guaranteed. However, this will be reduced all the same by the brilliant employment of the fighters by the Staffs in the South.

The following were handed over:

I./JG 77 16 pilots 72 men to Fels am Wagram

Although widely known, this photo has often been wrongly captioned. This Bf 109 of II./JG 77 ('White 11') was pictured at Lagnasco (CN) in January 1944 and still carries the Geschwader's 'Ace of Hearts' insignia. Both this and the white Mediterranean Theatre fuselage band (seen on the aircraft in the background) were increasingly rare by summer 1944. (Bundesarchiv)

Air War Italy 1944-45

II./JG 77 16 pilots 73 men to Eisenstadt
III./JG 77 15 pilots 55 men to Lippspringe

The diarist might perhaps have added something about the conditions under which the German and Italian pilots were living. Reports recall the situation of American troops in Vietnam: nocturnal partisan assaults on aircraft dispersals and crew quarters, daylight holdups and shootings in town and country, on leave or on duty – even a waterborne attack on two men rowing on a lake.

Other Units

There were a great many other flying units in Italy at this time. Most were communications, training and air-sea-rescue flights, some of which will crop up later. Certain combat units would be gone from Italy before June was out or were deployed in only minimal strength. Single aircraft flew in and out from all manner of transport and liaison formations, and a detachment from IV./TG 3 was based in Italy at the end of May, but, as far as first-line Luftwaffe formations are concerned, the only one due for a longer stay was Maj. Klamke's II./TG 1, based at Gallarate (VA) with Savoia S.82s and offering a series of large and apparently irresistible targets to Allied strafers all through the summer. The transports had performed a vital service at the end of May, when their Savoias had ferried to the front anti-tank weaponry rushed in from Berlin-Tempelhof by five Ju 52s, and had helped in the moves of I./JG 2 and I./JG 53 when they left Italy.

A Focke-Wulf Fw 190F-8 of 2./SG 4 seen on a Central Italian airfield. Fighting for over a year on the Italian mainland, most of the aircraft of this ground-attack unit bore a 'desert' camouflage equally suited to the arid southern areas. (Bundesarchiv)

Aeronautica Nazionale Repubblicana

The ANR was the Air Force of the *Repubblica Sociale Italiana* (RSI), the newly-constituted fascist republic formally headed by Mussolini (weary but vengeful), in reality halfway between a puppet government and a desperate attempt to prevent the Germans exercising undisputed rule over the Italian territory they still controlled. Whereas the other parts of the RSI's armed forces were mainly employed against partisans (plaguing supply lines and wide areas of the Apennines and Alps), the ANR was the most 'professional' arm, giving useful support to the Luftwaffe, albeit on a limited scale.

Because of the military situation and a fear that captured airmen would not be treated in accordance with the Geneva Convention (let alone any mistrust on the part of the Germans of Italian loyalty), the ANR was mainly confined to the defensive. Most of its units operated over friendly territory, the only offensive arm – a group of torpedo-bombers – not needing to venture much inland although it reached out well beyond Italian waters. A medium bomber group was planned but never became operational. A transport group was sent to the Eastern Front to avoid (amongst other things) any encounter with aircraft of the Italian Co-Belligerent Air Force which had been fighting alongside the Allies (who regarded 'their' Italians in much the same way the Germans did the ANR) since October 1943.

Fighters

Squadriglia Autonoma 'Montefusco' was amongst a number of small units formed spontaneously after the Armistice but which, unlike most of the others, actually operated. This it did from the end of February 1944 from Venaria Reale (TO), flying Fiat G.55s and Macchi C.205s. After the death in combat of its CO, Cap. Bonet, on 29 March, the squadron

was officially integrated into the defence system of Northern Italy on 8 April. It was subordinated to the *Jafü* but I° Gruppo Caccia's problems led to plans for 'Montefusco's' absorption into this larger unit.

The first 'official' operational ANR unit was I° Gruppo Caccia, formed towards the end of 1943 with the Macchi C.205s then temporarily equipping II./JG 77. After a short period of operations from Lagnasco (CN), and reinforced with new C.205s now emerging from the Macchi factory, it transferred to Campoformido (UD) on 24 January 1944. It had three Squadriglie, commanded first by Magg. Borgogno and then by Magg. Visconti, charged with co-operating with German fighters in intercepting the 15th USAAF's heavy bombers en route to and from their targets in the Reich, Yugoslavia and Italy itself. From January to April many missions were undertaken and numerous losses sustained (on two occasions inflicted by the Germans themselves, owing to problems, never overcome, of identification in combat), particularly during 'Big Week' (19-25 February) and mid-late March. This, plus the mounting threat of the Allied medium and fighter-bomber forces beginning operations against targets north of the Apennines and in the Padana plains, dictated the transfer of I° Gruppo to Reggio Emilia on 24 April.

However, the Italian fighters, although intercepting P-47s and P-38s, continued to operate mainly against the heavies that during May were switched to tactical targets in Northern Italy. A high price continued to

Squadriglia 'Montefusco' at Venaria Reale (TO). Fiat G.55 'Yellow 5' in the foreground carries on its nose the new unit's insignia, Cap. Bonet's signature. This was adopted after the CO's death in combat on 29 March 1944. Sq. 'Montefusco-Bonet' (as it was known from then on) also had some C.205s, easing its incorporation into 1° Gr.C, between June and July. (Garello)

be paid in men and aircraft, the latter becoming ever harder to replace as bombardment of the country's aeronautical industry severely curtailed, if it did not

Campoformido (UD), Spring 1944. Ten. Renato Talamini of 3ª Sq., I° Gr.C. poses beside his Macchi C.205 "8–3" sporting the pilot's name behind the canopy. He went missing on 10 April while intercepting heavy bombers. I° Gr.C. was the first ANR unit to become operational, fighting alongside the German Jagdgeschwader from January 1944 and losing 35 aircraft and 28 pilots in five months' operations. (Curami)

Cascina Vaga (PV), May 1944. A Fiat G.55 of 2ª Sq., IIº Gruppo Caccia. This unit had been operational since late April, engaging in only two actions before June. By the end of May, the need to replenish the equipment of Iº Gr.C. led to the delivery of the G.55s to this unit, while IIº Gruppo was in its turn re-equipped with Messerschmitt Bf 109s.

completely stop, production. The Gruppo's strength returns show a decline from 28 serviceable aeroplanes to a mere eight between 10 April and 20 May. While a temporary solution to this problem was to come from IIº Gruppo Caccia (see below) and Sq. 'Montefusco', the morale problem among Iº Gruppo's pilots – the strong feeling of being 'used' by the Germans to protect their targets rather than Italian ones – was bound to emerge eventually.

Established at Bresso (MI) during March 1944 under Magg. Alessandrini, IIº Gruppo Caccia received its Fiat G.55s during April and took them to Cascina Vaga the following month. Although fully operational, the Gruppo had only one combat during this period. The G.55 was one of the war's best Italian fighters, but it performed best at high altitude. The kind of engagements by now taking place over Italy were mainly at medium and low level, for which the Fiat was unsuited, to say the least. This, plus the presence in IIº Gruppo's ranks of several pilots with experience (dating from the Sicilian campaign) on the Bf 109, led the Jafü to decide on its re-equipment with Messerschmitts. The G.55s would then go to replenish the exhausted Iº Gruppo.

Torpedo-Bombers

The offensive arm of the ANR was *Iº Gruppo Autonomo Aerosiluranti 'Buscaglia'*, commanded by Cap. Faggioni. The Gruppo was equipped with old three-engined Savoia Marchetti S.79s (mostly refurbished and brought up to current standards) but plans to give it Ju 88s were abandoned in the face of shortages of the torpedo variant and the delays foreseen in retraining crews. The Cant Z.1018 was ruled out for lack of suitable engines.

Although formed officially on 1 January 1944, the unit first operated on 10 March, against Allied ships moored in the Anzio Bay, coming in at 60ft with one 800kg torpedo per aircraft. A prisoner taken during that operation served with the Gruppo's 2ª Squadriglia and revealed that only his part of the unit was fully operational, based at Gorizia and using Perugia as an ALG. It had nine S.79s and crews as of 6 March and, after this mission, only another 15 torpedoes available. The other two Squadriglie were at Venegono (VA) with five or six aeroplanes and crews apiece, and there was talk (inaccurate, as it transpired) of including S.84s in their eventual equipment.

The unit was hit hard in April, almost half its aircraft being shot down by four P-47s of 57th FG USAAF during a transfer flight. Nevertheless, the Gruppo continued operating with heavy losses off Anzio-Nettuno, losing its commander on 10 April. According to radio monitoring, this raid involved two S.79s of the first Squadriglia and three of the second. Faggioni was succeeded by Cap. Marini. The main base now was Lonate Pozzolo (VA), and Perugia was still the ALG. The unit was pulled off operations in May for rest and re-equipment.

Transports

I° Gruppo Aerotrasporti 'Terracciano' – 'Tr.Gr.10 (Ital.)' to the Germans – had been operating since March 1944 with S.81s and under German command, providing transport between second-line areas of the Eastern Front. At home a second heavy transport unit, II° Gr. Aerotr. 'Trabucchi' (or 'Tr.Gr.110 (Ital.)') was officially constituted in April for the same tasks as its sister unit, but with the more capable S.82. However, the formation of 'Trabucchi' took much longer than expected, and for two months only a handful of S.82s was available to the new unit, based at Orio al Serio (BG). Additionally a ferry unit, Gruppo Trasporto Velivoli (G.T.V.), had been operating under German control since shortly after the Armistice, taking a wide variety of Italian aircraft types to concentration points in Northern Italy (usually Gorizia or Trento) then on to training schools in the Reich. From 12 May 1944 the Gruppo came under ANR control, eventually conveying over 2,000 aircraft to their new users.

Training

Only scanty basic training of new pilots was possible in Italy, owing to the paucity of training aircraft and suitable airfields. The ANR training schools were all in the Piemonte area: Scuola di volo di 1° Periodo based at Casabianca, north of Torino, Scuola di 2° Periodo at Venaria Reale (TO) and Scuola di 3° Periodo at Cervere (CN). According to an ANR report of 8 August 1944, however, only the Venaria school had achieved anything, the others being virtually at a standstill for various reasons, including strong Partisan activity in the area.

The Germans repeatedly offered the ANR the chance to send up to 1,000 pilots to train in Germany, but an initial experiment in May 1944 had such negative results that the matter was dropped until November, when I° Gruppo Caccia was sent to train and re-equip on the Bf 109. Also from November, a fighter training section was set up within 3ª Sq. of II° Gr.C., with a Bf 109G-4 and a two-seat G-12. Even the Torpedo-bomber Group had a training squadron within its ranks, but this disappeared towards the end of 1944 owing to aircraft and fuel shortages.

Morale

ANR morale was assessed by Allied Intelligence during March on the basis of admittedly very sparse information:

> It is probable . . . that the personnel consist of either the few remaining fanatical Fascist elements or . . . personnel pressed into service by threats of reprisals. These should not prove very satisfactory material for the building up of an air force, while the experiences of the IAF [Italian Air Force, i.e the *Regia Aeronautica*] during the past four years cannot have given it much faith in its own confidence.

While there is undoubtedly a measure of prejudice in this picture, the ANR's performance did exhibit (literally) fatal flaws, despite the skills and qualities of some of its outstanding members.

Notes

1. III. Gruppe was formed in France on 1 November 1943 from III./SKG 10, which, until its withdrawal from Italy, had served in a composite Schlachtgeschwader with I. and II./4..

2. Until December 1944, <u>every</u> Bf 109 fighter in Italy was a G-6, so the designation will not be repeated henceforth.

Two S.79s of 2ª Squadriglia, Gruppo 'Buscaglia' in flight over central Italy. Both are IIª Serie aircraft, but the one in the foreground carries flash dampers on the guns, a new direction finder, and a radio mast - modifications applied (together with the deletion of the gondola) to all the examples of IIIª Serie.

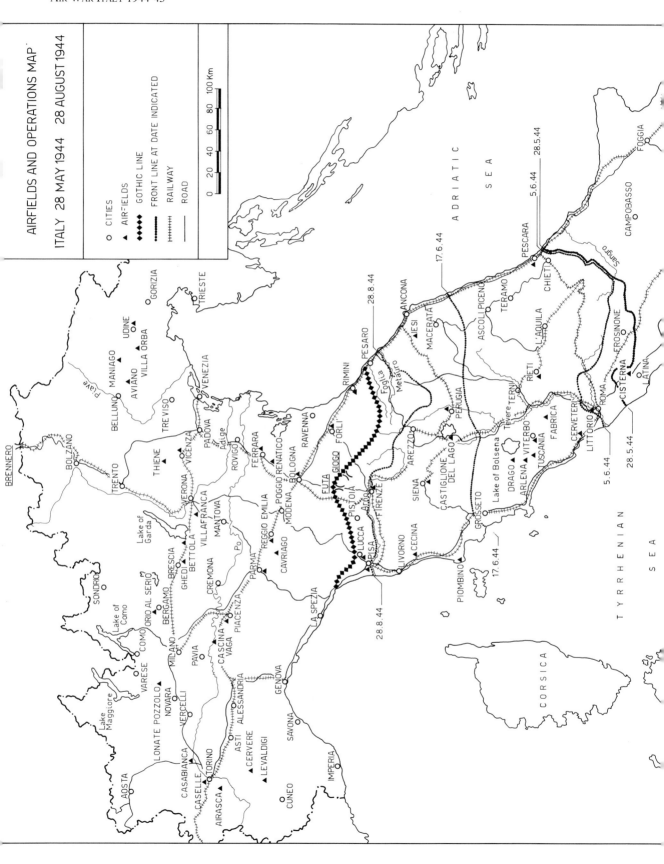

Chapter 2

June 1944

The Axis retreat, in the face of the Allied armies and a maximum effort by MAAF, was in full spate as June began. For the Germans on 1 June there was perhaps comfort in the accurate assessment of the Foreign Armies West intelligence bureau that Gen Clark would divert his forces to occupy Rome, rather than pursuing them. Even so, transport columns and communications arteries were harried continuously by both air power and partisans and though there may have seemed little immediate prospect of the German armies regrouping or consolidating, plans were soon being made to hold on the line Orbetello-Terni-north of Pescara. Even so, it was recognised that a slow withdrawal into the Appennine Position, running from Pisa to Rimini (FO) (the Gothic Line, to the Allies) might be necessary. Valmontone (Rome) fell on the 2nd and the Americans entered Rome two days later; Pescara was taken on the 10th. Other mainland towns and (just as important) airfields fell in rapid succession. Amphibious landings were made on the island of Elba on the 17th and its conquest was complete two days later.

Nevertheless, the Allied air forces could suffer reversals, both at enemy hands and self-inflicted. On the 9th strafing missions were halted temporarily owing to the high level of casualties incurred. On the same day the US 79th FG was transferred to Corsica in preparation for the planned invasion of Southern France, and fighter sweeps over French airfields began a few days later. The diversion of forces from Italy to Operation Dragoon, the August invasion of the French Riviera, remains controversial.

By the last third of the month, the Germans, having escaped the encirclement once threatened by the the two arms of the Allied advance, had pulled themselves together sufficiently to mount actions in the Lake Trasimeno area, north of Rome, and along the River Arno, aimed at gaining time for the Gothic Line fortifications to be completed. Meanwhile, small reserves were to be held ready to oppose landings on either coast. On the 23rd the following appreciation was issued:

> The enemy is resuming his attack on a broad front between the Tyrrhenian Sea and the Perugia area. Further to the east as far as the Adriatic he is following up our withdrawals. Enemy concentration areas are situated on both sides of Lake Trasimeno. The resumption of attacks to the north of Grosseto and the commencement of attacks on the Adriatic sector can be expected at any time. Temporary lulls indicate preparations.
>
> Landings must be expected in the Livorno-La Spezia and Genoa areas as well as small scale landing operations behind the left wing of the army, probably in the Rimini area.

Kesselring had to strike a balance between impeding the Allies and allowing the disorganised elements of his armies to become so heavily engaged that he lost what forces remained to him. In the event he was remarkably successful in salvaging his troops to fight again. However on the 5th he had reported to his superiors: 'In giving a responsible estimate of the general situation I must report that a real easing . . . can only be expected if immediate and strong fighter and ground attack aircraft support is provided – even if for a short time.'

It will soon become clear how far the Luftwaffe could meet such demands.

The Luftwaffe

Luftflotte 2's Operations Division planned extensively for the withdrawal and dispersal into protected locations of stores and equipment and for the surveying of new airfields in the north. Measures were to be taken for the improvement of the aircraft plotting service and, significantly for the later development of this history, an additional fighter control HQ was to be set up just north of Verona, manned by personnel displaced from Rome, Viterbo and Siena. Security was tight, so much so that staff were forbidden to hold telephone conversations in connection with the withdrawal.

While all this was going on, someone at OKL on 1 June had his mind elsewhere, issuing a statement that a resumption of Italian civil airline traffic was undesirable from the point of view of German air traffic policy!

On the 23rd Luftflotte 2 self-contradictorily undertook to 'participate in the elimination of partisans by using strong forces of aircraft not required for other duties' and to 'give direct support to the battle with the weak air forces of which they still dispose'. A series of measures was also set in train to reconstitute battered flak and other ground units for defensive and anti-partisan tasks.

Ground Attack
The remaining Gruppen of SG 4 had been withdrawn for rest and refit at Airasca and Levaldigi (CN) but provision had been made for their transfer to Ferrara and Poggio Renatico (FE) if the Allies landed on the Adriatic Coast. Large numbers of factory-coded Fw 190s were flown to the former two airfields early in the month, via Osoppo. A rearguard detachment was still at Piacenza early in June as well. The Geschwader's last combat loss in Italy was, so far as we are aware, on 31 May when Ltn. Günther Entress of 6. Staffel was killed in action against Spitfires.

Bombers
Much of the Mediterranean bomber force was by now in France from where it could also cover the Channel coast, but odd aeroplanes from several Kampfgruppen turned up in Italy during May and June. Overall control of the bombers still in Italy rested with LG 1's Kommodore, Obstlt. Helbig, himself flying as 'Master of Ceremonies' on many missions. These Gruppen (all with the Ju 88A-4) were now mainly attacking shipping and shore targets at Anzio-Nettuno or troop concentrations and transport south and west of Rome. Some attacks were also flown against partisans.

I./LG 1 was at Ghedi as well as making some use of Forlì; II./1, commanded by Hptm. von Clemm, was operating from Villafranca di Verona. Twenty-two aircraft of his Gruppe had flown there from Wiener Neustadt on 1 April, and had been flying night raids (typically of around four hours' duration) ever since, often in conjunction with elements of KG 76, staging through Villafranca for operations over Anzio and other targets remote from their own bases in the northeast. Losses in action for II./LG 1 seem to have been quite light over this period, although three Ju 88s were burned out by strafing Lightnings on 17 May; missions involved anything from one to 19 aircraft. I. and II./1 transferred to the Invasion Front on the 11th and after that all that was heard of LG 1 over Italy was traffic from two Geschwaderstab aircraft on the 16th and 22nd respectively.

The CO of KG 76 was Obstlt. Hallensleben; 5./KG 76 (*Kapitän*, Oblt. Behrens) was at Aviano (PN) and III./76 (*Kommandeur*, Hptm. Heid) at Villaorba (UD). A prisoner shot down in May said that III./76's crews were mostly inexperienced and bomber morale poor, since power was vested in 'a small clique of officers who were generally hated', alleging corruption in the award of medals etc. He also complained about the food, and referred to KG 76 ironically as 'KG Happy'. A KG 76 control station remained in Italy until mid-June, and four of its aircraft apparently transferred to Avignon on the 15th.

There were rumours that the Ju 88As would soon be replaced by the better S model. Meanwhile, because of lack of space inside the bombers, time-fused AB 36 munitions canisters had been adapted to spread clouds of chaff, and at least one aircraft had FuG 214 tail-warning radar. Aside from Allied defences, the Apennines presented navigational difficulties which had led to losses of aircraft and crews.

Nightfighters
German nightfighters were also roaming the Italian skies in early June, under the callsign 'Schwalbe' (Swallow). II./NJG 6 was part of the 7. Jagddivision, engaged in the night defence of Southern Germany, and its two deployments to Italy seem to have been a partial loan rather than a complete transfer to Luftflotte 2; on neither occasion does the entire Gruppe appear to have moved. An OKL document says that the first transfer to Lfl.2 was ordered on 30 April, with nine aircraft. According to the KTB of the Geschwaderstab, this sojourn lasted from 4-12 May

and involved eight Messerschmitt Bf 110s at Ghedi. From the Allied side the codes of ten individual Bf 110s from the Gruppenstab and 4. 5. and 6./NJG 6 were noted by Sigint.

The second spell at Ghedi began on 29 May, and was intended to last for the current moon period and involve the serviceable aircraft accompanied by key personnel. Their mission was to defend supply lines to the front. We know that at least three of the Gruppe's aeroplanes remained in the Reich, as the KTB mentions them participating in an exercise; also Hptm. Hollborn, Kapitän of 4. Staffel, appears to have stayed in Germany and 5. Staffel was temporarily in limbo as a result of establishhment cutbacks in the nightfighter arm.

On the evening of the 2nd Major Rolf Leuchs, Kommandeur of II./6, reported to the Geschwader on his force's method of operation. When darkness fell they moved down from Ghedi to their advanced base at Perugia, and from there flew freelance operations in the Rome area and along the roads between there and Florence. The aircraft withdrew again to Ghedi before daylight. No ground control was available, so all 20 sorties flown had been without success, while Uffz. Mrusek's crew had gone missing in action.

Two days later the Geschwaderkommodore, Maj Heinrich Griese, flew down to see for himself and to talk things over with Luftflotte 2. He returned that evening, agreeing that, lacking ground control, II. Gruppe's mission was doomed to failure. A conference on the 7th decided that the unit should be brought home within the next few days and receive the Ju 88G-1s about to be allocated to the Geschwader, but II./6 did not get any while in Italy.

On the 11th Hptm. Griese, II./6's Liaison Officer with Jafü Oberitalien, reported that Luftflotte 2 had issued the order for the nightfighters to return home. They left next day, and while they had eventually secured a single victory, their time in Italy was chiefly characterised by wastage of men and aircraft in combat and accidents. A memorial to their presence was a Bf 110G-4 (W.Nr.5546) found burned out under a collapsed Perugia hangar by a MAAF Field Intelligence Team later that summer.

Another 7. JD unit had been outposted to Italy at least since the arrival of a single Bf 110 at Lagnasco at the end of November 1943.[3] This was Luftbeobachterstaffel 7, whose aircraft, by now Ju 88s at Villaorba, were charged with shadowing formations of Allied heavy bombers inbound for the Reich and updating ground control on their course, speed and altitude. It appears that about half the Staffel was detached to Italy, the remainder staying at Stuttgart-Echterdingen, and that operations were primarily if not exclusively by night. The unit seems to have been an early recipient of SN2 (FuG 220) radar.

Allied night bombers reported several sightings of, or attacks by, Bf 109s and Fw 190s during the first half of June, but the authors have found no evidence from the Axis side to indicate which (if any) of their units were involved.

Night Attack
NSGr.9 was numerically strong at this stage although not at the height of its operational capability. 1. Staffel now flew the Ju 87D, while 2. was phasing out the Fiat Cr.42. Round about the 5th the two Staffeln were withdrawn from Tuscania (VT) to Brolio (AR) and another airfield in the Perugia area, with a brief hiatus in operations. They were reinforced in the course of the month by 2./NSGr.2, previously operational on the Eastern Front and latterly in training at Lida, Poland. A PoW suggested that originally it had been planned to move the entire Gruppe but that this had been called off. Such a plan would explain the reference to full-moon period operations by 'up to five' night attack Staffeln in Luftflotte 2's orders of 11 June.

On arrival in Italy 2./2 was based at Caselle, the reserve/supply base for the night attack formations, and one of the first things done there was to apply brown camouflage to the aircraft. Casabianca (TO) was slated as home for the newly-forming Gruppenstab and other subordinate formations, and preparations were entrusted to a ground detachment under Hptm. Huntjeur in liaison with T.Col. Alderighi. Operations were subsequently to be flown from fields in the Forlì-Ravenna area and occasionally by small forces from Rimini or Florence.

Tactical Reconnaissance
NAGr.11 began June at a low numerical ebb and was compelled to disband its 3. Staffel, in existence for only a few weeks, redistributing the available Bf 109s between the remaining two. By the 6th the Stab and 3. Staffel had moved back from Viterbo to Castiglione del Lago, and by the end of the month the Stab and 2. Staffel were based at Florence, and 1. Staffel at Forlì. Plans of 23 June called for NAGr.11 to fly coastal reconnaissance over the Tyrrhenian and Adriatic Seas as far as Civitavecchia and Pescara, as well as photographing enemy harbours near the front and the front itself.

Provision of tactical cover of the southernmost harbours such as Bari, Taranto and Brindisi was sought from outside Italy by the move of 1./NAGr.12 to Scutari, Albania along with escort fighters from 5./JG 51.

Long-Range Reconnaissance
The strategic recce forces were to cover Bizerta and the remaining Tyrrhenian harbours that might be used as jumping-off points for landings, and also the seas around Italy both by day and night, to spot any approaching amphibious forces. A heightened interest in the waters north and west of Corsica was noticed while over the Adriatic an intriguing pattern developed. From the 8th to the 14th two aircraft, Ju 88s or Ju 188s, took off at a precise two-hour interval and followed an identical course down the coast to Termoli and back over the sea. After that, usually only one aircraft made the nightly trip, but covered the southern part of the route twice.

The units concerned were all now grouped at Orio Al Serio (known also as Bergamo-Seriate and Bergamo-Süd) under Stab/FAGr.122; the Gruppe's CO was Major Günther Pannwitz. 1.(F)/123 was flying Ju 88Ts on day reconnaissance, averaging one or two sorties a day following a nine-day lay-off (according to MAAF Intelligence). 2.(F)/122 also flew by day with Me 410s and had a Fieseler 156 communications aircraft (F6+SK) and a Ju 88D-1 (F6+BK) sometimes flown by the Staffelkapitän, Hptm. Weinand. The Junkers seem to have been a general-purpose hack, used in May for leaflet dropping and in June for liaison, practice flights and – crewed by men of 1.(F)/123 – calibration sorties to train Würzburg radar crews. By the end of the month the +BK code had been applied to an Me 410, and Ju 88 F6+ZK figures in the log. The Messerschmitts achieved only one or two morning or evening sorties each day. On the 10th Perugia was finally abandoned as an ALG, to be supplanted by Piacenza.

Westa 26 was formally ordered disbanded on 15 June, to be replaced by 6.(F)/122. At the same time a new Westa 26 was established on the Eastern Front. In fact, it seems that the old one was simply renamed 6.(F)/122 after being re-equipped, in recognition that it had long been a reconnaissance rather than a weather-scouting outfit. Nor was any change in unit coding noted by Allied Intelligence: ten different aircraft bearing the unusual 5M+_ three-character codes of Westa 26 were heard, but none with the new F6+_P, and indeed aircraft were still flying with the 'old' codes in July. Whatever its name, except for the night of the 17th there was no break in operations. Three or four sorties were flown each night in the first half of the month, and two or three in the latter part. These usually included round trips to Rome or Naples and back over Eastern Corsica.

A mix of Ju 88A-4s and Ju 188D-2s was flown by 6./122, the latter aircraft being methanol-water (MW 50) boosted and having FuG 200 Hohentwiel anti-ship radar. The Ju 188 was appreciably faster than the Ju 88D, and had a more powerful defensive armament; MW 50 gave an extra 50kph at low altitude, enabling the 188 to match the speed of a pursuing Beaufighter. It was claimed postwar that losses diminished steadily as a result, but, offsetting this, the Jumo 213 engine was very prone to failure and crew quality was declining.

Maritime surveillance south and southeast of Italy was being undertaken by Maj Klette's Athens-based

---

Rome, 4 June 1944. A couple of armoured Sd.Kfz7 half-tracks equipped with 3.7cm Flak guns, parked beside the Castel S. Angelo. Although the pose is impressive, this photo was probably one of the last official ones taken by the Germans in the 'Eternal City'. In a few hours Allied troops will arrive. (Bundesarchiv)

A bomb-laden Junkers Ju 88A-4 of 1./LG 1 taxying out. All its markings are toned-down for night operations. This unit had left Italy by mid-June. (Bundesarchiv)

reconnaissance units, Westa 27, 3.(F)/33 and 2.(F)/123. Number 255 Squadron, RAF, destroyed or damaged several Ju 88s off Italy's 'heel' during June and these probably came from Greece.

Special Missions

The first Ju 188 at Bergamo arrived towards the end of May. Coded A3+TB, it was believed by MAAF to be attached to 1.(F)/123 and operating exclusively by night right through June, during which time it was joined by another Ju 188, A3+WB, 'apparently searching for Allied shipping off both the West and East coasts of Italy'. In fact they were unlikely to have been doing anything of the kind, theirs being the markings of the agent-dropping unit 2./KG 200. We now know that these aeroplanes, along with Ju 88 A3+NB, constituted Kommando Carmen, an outposted detachment of the parent Staffel with responsibility for drops over Italy, North Africa and later Southern France. This was supposed to be a highly secret unit and OKL, to which KG 200 was directly subordinated, would surely not have been pleased to know how well the enemy – while still ignorant of their purpose – was logging these flights. KG 200 seems to have shifted its aircraft between fronts according to need, for in July a Ju 188 marked A3+WB was operating from Riga, Latvia.

Day Fighters

It has been shown that the fighter pilots had not ended May in particularly good heart. As June began they vacated the more southerly bases as these had ceased to be tenable. I./JG 4 went from Fabrica di Roma to Lavariano in the northeast; III./JG 53 from Arlena (VT) to Maniago. I./JG 77 shifted from Dragolo (VT) to Bologna, while Stab, 4. and 5./77 remained at Ferrara, having come there from Bologna on 22 May. 6./JG 77 stayed at Poggio Renatico as a dispersal measure. This situation remained stable until 29 June when Stab and II./77 went to Aviano, only to be sent on to Ghedi and Bettola (BS) next day, where I. Gruppe joined them. I./4 was ordered to Maniago on 27 June with the proviso that the transfer should not compromise operational readiness.

The month's realignment of bases was more suited to strategic than to tactical defence and only occasional operations by the four Gruppen over the battle area were envisaged. Jafü Oberitalien was ordered on the 23rd to counter enemy air incursions in the following order of priority:

> Operations against the Reich; Operations by four-engined aircraft over Northern Italy; Operations in the Lucca-Florence area; Fighter sweeps over the Siena-Arezzo region.

In fact, OKL was shortly to deny him the means to carry out the first two of these objectives with any hope of worthwhile results.

The Aeronautica Nazionale Repubblicana

Torpedo-Bombers

After heavy losses in March and April – at least 19 aircraft in combat and accidents and many more experienced crews – Gruppo 'Buscaglia' had spent May trying to re-equip with new and updated S.79 versions. New crews came from the Squadriglia Complementare Aerosiluranti which, until 31 May, had the unofficial task of training centre for men assigned to the torpedo-bomber arm. After that, first- and second-stage training were handled by Sq. Scuola Aerosiluranti and Sq. Addestramento

Summer 1944. A 2./NAGr.11 pilot is warmly welcomed after completing the unit's 3500th mission. The fuselage of the Bf 109G-6(or G-8?) shows the small-sized tactical numbers characteristic of this reconnaissance Gruppe.
(Petrick)

Aerosiluranti respectively. The latter's CO was Cap. Dante Magagnoli.

Morale among the trainees was not 100 per cent, one crew which had made no operational flights since the Armistice being moved to defect. All of these men had avoided recall until decrees threatening dire punishment induced them to report again for duty. The five had therefore spent only a short time re-training at Venegono. Normally the aircraft there were supplied by the Germans with meagre fuel rations from the Desenzano (BS) dump. On the day of their escape, however, they found an aircraft due for transfer to another field and carrying 2,500 litres of petrol. 'Aided by the Italian habit of retiring during the afternoon' they were able to take-off from an almost deserted airfield.

About 100 men were re-training at Venegono, all of them pre-Armistice fliers recalled to service. Practice was carried out on a range at Desenzano, using wooden torpedoes. Thirteen S.79s were serviceable, four or five nearly ready for service and another three or four under repair. Two Re.2005 fighters were being experimentally fitted with 600kg torpedoes. Complete engine changes were done (in theory) at Vergiate, but aircraft sometimes remained u/s for months for lack of engines. Spare parts were obtained from Gallarate. Replacement aircraft were supplied by the Germans from Schongau near Munich; the chief repair and replacement base for Italian aircraft. Schongau supplied reconditioned aeroplanes, mainly collected after the Armistice.

The CO, Cap. Marini, knew all too well that, having rebuilt his group, his men now had to be motivated with some special mission, and his mind turned to his part in the Regia Aeronautica's attack on Gibraltar on 19 June 1943, with consequences set out later in this chapter.

Bombers
On 15 June the ANR officially constituted a bomber unit, Sq. Bombardamento 'E. Muti', equipped with the trimotor Cant Z.1007ter. This squadron was not to achieve operational status, succumbing in turn to political and fuel crises.

Fighters
At this point I° Gruppo Caccia already had six months of operational experience, gained at the expense of heavy losses in men and aircraft. By the end of May the SMAR had settled on two methods of replenishing the almost exhausted unit: transferring the former Sq. Autonoma Montefusco to I° Gruppo and taking over all of II° Gruppo's FIAT G.55s when the latter was equipped with Bf 109. By 31 May all of II° Gruppo's *Centauri* had been delivered to Reggio Emilia airfield, and within two days the Montefusco pilots had been flown in by an S.83 transport. The group was made up as follows:

Iº Gruppo Caccia – CO Magg. Adriano Visconti
1ª Sq. *Asso di Bastoni* ('Ace of Clubs') – CO Ten. Giuseppe Robetto
2ª Sq. *Vespa Arrabbiata* ('Angry Wasp') – CO Cap. Amedeo Guidi
3ª Sq. *Arciere* ('Archer') – CO Cap. Pio Tomaselli

The G.55s went to 1ª and 3ª Sq., which flew a mixture of aircraft, while 2ª had only the Macchi C.205. On 3 June, 1ª Sq. was dispersed to Cavriago, six miles from Reggio and meanwhile some of the Montefusco pilots divided between the other two squadrons began to train on the C.205.

The unit had not long been back on operations when politics again took a hand. Discontent had been brewing since March, when the ANR's founder, T.Col. Botto, was sacked and replaced by Gen Tessari. A crisis of confidence was worsened by the growing awareness that behind the fighting units and their dead was virtually nothing. A lot of offices and administrative units had been built up to serve the bureaucracy, but these had nothing to do with what the front line units were going through. These feelings were put directly to Tessari by Visconti and his men, but the general was unable to offer anything, apart from a choice for the pilots either to fight on or to leave their units and go home. Several took the second course and the Major himself asked for a period of rest.

Tessari's report read:

> Faith in fascism no longer animated the unit; "political doubts" masked an unspoken weariness and intolerance of German interference. When the real roots of the disease became clear I undertook radical surgery (15 pilots dismissed, 21 sent on leave and seven transferred to second-line units) in the hope of healing the unit . . .

The truth probably lay somewhere in between but the net result was the dissolution of 1ª and 2ª Sq. and the replacement of Visconti by Magg. Arrabito. The latter had nothing to command but 3ª Sq. under Cap. Marchesi and Sq. 'Bonet' under Cap. Torresi.

Like Iº Gruppo Caccia, IIº Gr. was composed of three Squadriglie:
1ª Sq. *Gigi Tre Osei* (from the nickname of the Ace, Ten. Luigi Caneppele) – CO Ten. Ugo Drago
2ª Sq. *Diavoli Rossi* ('Red Devils') – CO Cap. Mario Bellagambi
3ª Sq. *Gamba di Ferro* ('Iron Leg') – CO Ten. Giuseppe Gianelli

In contrast to the other group it had developed a small section much like a Luftwaffe staff flight. This Nucleo Comando was led by Magg. Carlo Miani and had three to four aircraft; although in being since May, it only began operations when the Messerschmitts arrived. The flight consisted of three officers who had not been assigned to command a Squadriglia, and from time to time it was joined by one or two pilots from the other parts of the group.

Ju 88T-1 4U+BH of 1.(F)/123 has completed its mission, the container of film to be developed will be taken by the dispatch-rider to the photo lab. The Ju 88T, fastest of the Ju 88 variants, served in Italy with the reconnaissance units 1.(F)/123 and Westa 26 (later 6.(F)/122). (Bundesarchiv)

June found II° Gr. out of action and being completely re-equipped. In view of the Germans' concerns about the operational capabilities of the G.55, its limited suitability for low/medium level combat and logistic problems stemming from the recent bombing of FIAT factories, the unit was ordered to turn over all of its 20-25 aircraft to its sister Gruppo, and began receiving Bf 109G-6s. These started arriving at Cascina Vaga on 29 May and over the next two days; they still wore radio callsigns and only later were any handed over by German units, mainly I./JG 4.

Major Rupert Frost, CO of NSGr.9. On 15 November 1944 he became the first Nachtschlachtflieger to receive the Knight's Cross. (Bundesarchiv)

Only four officers and six NCO pilots of 1ª Sq. (all with previous experience on Messerschmitts) and 20 ground crewmen went to Ferrara, ostensibly for instruction from II./JG 77 and to oversee delivery but also to prove their capabilities to the Germans. All of the other 109s had been delivered directly to Cascina Vaga and from 2 June onwards, the Italians had their first (or second) encounter with the German fighter.

On the 5th Luftflotte 2 allocated two Bf 109G-12 trainers to the Italian unit and these too came from JG 4. Since a two-seat trainer was lacking for the first two weeks, a string of accidents occurred. After the first take off and at least four landings, the training schedule comprised flights in pairs, aerobatics (almost useless but still part of the repertoire of a 'real' fighter pilot in Italian eyes), altitude flights, four-plane formations (to get used to the Schwarm or finger-four system), firing on fixed ground targets (even more useless than aerobatics), and mock dogfights. The duration of the course depended upon the skill of the individual, but never exceeded six hours' flying time. Operations were not joined until 22 June.

Transports
June saw the departure for Germany of Gr. 'Trabucchi', to complete its training attached to XIV. Fl.Kps.

Order of Battle

The strengths of the ANR and Luftflotte 2 units on 31 May 1944 are given below. Figures in brackets are serviceable aircraft. (**Note:** Figures for Kdo. Carmen are provisional only, and the same applies to all subsequent ones for this unit).

Unit	Number	Type
Gr. 'Buscaglia'	28(21)	S.79
I° Gr.C.	18(7)	C.205
	22(7)	G.55
II° Gr.C.	23(0)	Bf 109G-6
(not operational)	8(3)	G.55
Stab/FAGr.122	0(0)	
2.(F)/122	7(3)	Me 410A-1
	1(1)	Ju 88D-1
	1(1)	Fi 156
1.(F)/123	5(3)	Ju 88
Kdo. Carmen	2	Ju 188
	1	Ju 88
Westa 26	8(3)	Ju 88
Stab/NAGr.11	0(0)	
1./NAGr.11	4(2)	Bf 109G-6/G-8
2./NAGr.11	2(2)	Bf 109G-5/G-6
3./NAGr.11	9(4)	Bf 109G
1./NSGr.9	19(8)	Ju 87D
2./NSGr.9	18(15)	Cr.42
2./NSGr.2	18(12)	Ju 87D
Stab/LG 1	1(0)	Ju 88A-4 [on 25 May]

JUNE 1944

Unit	Aircraft Number	Type
I./LG 1	22(17)	Ju 88A-4 [on 25 May]
Stab II./LG 1	1(1)	Ju 88A-4
4./LG 1	7(5)	Ju 88A-4
5./LG 1	7(5)	Ju 88A-4
6./LG 1	6(5)	Ju 88A-4
Stab/KG 76	1(0)	Ju 88A-4 [on 25 May]
5./KG 76	8(5)	Ju 88A-4 [on 25 May]
III./KG 76	16(12)	Ju 88A-4 [on 25 May]
Stab/SG 4	3(2)	Fw 190A-6
Stab I./SG 4	6(0)	Fw 190A/F/G
1./SG 4	3(2)	Fw 190A/F/G
2./SG 4	3(1)	Fw 190A/F/G
3./SG 4	2(1)	Fw 190A/F/G
Stab II./SG 4	6(0)	Fw 190A/F-3
4./SG 4	7(3)	Fw 190A/F-3
5./SG 4	7(3)	Fw 190A/F-3
6./SG 4	7(3)	Fw 190A/F-3
4./NJG 6	4(3)	Bf 110G-4
5./NJG 6	5(4)	Bf 110G-4
6./NJG 6	4(4)	Bf 110G-4
Luftbeobachterst. 7	5(?)	Ju 88
Stab I./JG 4	4(4)	Bf 109G-6
1./JG 4	3(2)	Bf 109G-6
2./JG 4	3(2)	Bf 109G-6
3./JG 4	3(2)	Bf 109G-6
Stab JG 53	0(0)	en route to Reich
Stab III./JG 53	4(4)	Bf 109G-6
7./JG 53	5(3)	Bf 109G-6
8./JG 53	4(3)	Bf 109G-6
9./JG 53	4(3)	Bf 109G-6
Training Kommando	4(1)	Bf 109G-6 [on 2 June]
Stab JG 77	4(3)	Bf 109G-6
Stab I./JG 77	4(4)	Bf 109G-6
1./JG 77	6(2)	Bf 109G-6
2./JG 77	6(2)	Bf 109G-6
3./JG 77	5(2)	Bf 109G-6
Stab II./JG 77	4(4)	Bf 109G-6
4./JG 77	16(12)	Bf 109G-6

Unit	Aircraft Number	Type
5./JG 77	16(12)	Bf 109G-6
6./JG 77	16(11)	Bf 109G-6
II./TG 1	46(?)	S.82
IV./TG 3	9	S.82 [on 27 May]
Verb.St.300	11(9)	Fi 156
Verb.St.500	11(9)	Fi 156/Saiman/Fairchild
Verb.St.Lfl.2	18(12)	misc.
Seenotdienst Luft 6	22(13)	Cant Z.506

Notes

3. Also a PoW spoke of a 'squadron' moved to Aviano when the Allies began shuttle raids between England and North Africa.

Bf 109G-6s of I./JG 4. Photographed at Cascina Vaga, "White 7" and "Yellow 8" are two of the few aircraft of this unit delivered to ANR's IIº Gruppo Caccia during June. Worthy of mention are the peculiar "brown/green" camouflage and partial obliteration of the markings.

Out in the trees surrounding one of NSGr.9's satellite airfields, orders are received for the coming night. In the background, one of the first Ju 87Ds delivered to 1.Staffel is being serviced. The plane still retains its original camouflage. (Bundesarchiv)

CHAPTER 2

Operations

1 June 1944

The Bf 110s of II./NJG 6 had not had a good night on 31 May/1 June. The Gruppe complained that refuelling of its aircraft at Perugia had taken over two hours, and that inept directions had led three to taxi into craters. However, the airfield seems to have been stocked up with fuel as ordered. In the early hours of 1 June Bf 110s 2Z+CC, CM, FM, KM, DP and FP returned to Ghedi.

By day the air over the battlefront was quiet, partly thanks to a general transfer of fighter and ground-attack formations northwards, away from the endangered airfields of Central Italy. At least some aeroplanes were headed south however: Bf 109s 'Black 10' and 'Red 3' (unit unidentified) moved from Ghedi via Perugia to Jesi (AN) early in the morning. East of Brescia at 0941, Martin B-26s of the US 42nd BW reported a single pass by two Fw 190s but without result. If correctly identified they almost certainly came from SG 4.

Schiffels and Weber of 2.(F)/122 flew a two-hour reconnaissance in Me 410 F6+KK during the early daylight hours and four aircraft were sent out by 1.(F)/123. During the night three of Westa 26's Ju 88s were up, as well as a Kommando Carmen Ju 188 on a cloak-and-dagger operation.

The early evening saw four S.82s of 8./TG 1 and one of 4. Staffel leave Forlì for Perugia, while four hours later four Ju 88s of I./LG 1 arrived at Ghedi from Forlì. From Villafranca di Verona a single Ju 88 of II./LG 1 set off on a bombing mission at 2143 local time, returning an hour after midnight. NSGr.9 spent the night attacking Allied gun positions and columns in the area Artena-Giulianello-Cori, southeast of Rome; Fw. Gressler of 2. Staffel was injured when his Cr.42 crashed at Fabrica di Roma.

Six Bf 110s (2Z+CC, CM, AP, DP, FP and KP) deployed forward to patrol the roads southwest of Avezzano (AQ) without sighting hostile aircraft.

2 June 1944

In the early hours the Bf 110s flew back from Perugia to Ghedi. After one early morning mission the bulk of 2.(F)/122's effort was devoted to several half-hour training flights from Bergamo by the Staffel's Ju 88, while in the afternoon a new Me 410 was delivered from Germany. One daylight sortie was put up by 1.(F)/123, and an estimated four were flown by NAGr.11. The day fighter Gruppen were tied up in changes of base and III./JG 53 had two Bf 109s damaged and II./JG 77 another, all owing to accidents.

Retreat and regrouping made great demands on the available transport aircraft, and machines from TG 1, TG 2 and TG 3 were among those active. A rarer visitor was S.82 P6+MK of II° Gruppo Aerotrasporti 'Trabucchi', operating between an airfield in the northwest and Bergamo during the afternoon. Another singular arrival was 3Z+BA, a Ju 88 of Stab KG 77 which flew into Ghedi from La Jasse, France, early in the morning. Then in the afternoon, two Ju 88s of KG 3 were overheard coming into Aviano from Riem. All these movements demonstrate that there was (to use an RAF expression) 'a flap on'.

Ultra disclosed that 14 Ju 87s had left Vicenza around 1635 for 'an airfield in the Milan/ Turin/Genoa area' (almost certainly Caselle or Casabianca), arriving at 1800. At first they were only identified by numbers ranging between 'White 1' and 'White 19' but a subsequent decrypt revealed that they carried codes between D3+AK and D3+SK. This was 2./NSGr.2, newly drafted in from the Eastern Front and not destined to be rated fully operational in Italy until July. These Ju 87s were followed at 1700 by three more with factory markings.

Nine Bf 110s flew down to Perugia from Ghedi, starting at about 1830, and all had arrived by 2004. Apparently as part of the general withdrawal the nightfighters were trying to cover, four Ju 88s of 2. and 3./LG 1 left Forlì for Ghedi at 2130.

Through the night, Westa 26 dispatched three sorties and NSGr.9 bombed in the Artena-Giulianello area, 'with good effect' according to the Germans. At 2330 one of these raiders was picked up north of the Anzio flak area by Fighter Control 'Gonat.' The controller called in a patrolling Beaufighter Mk. VIF, flown by Sqn Ldr J.R. Bailey and Flt Sgt N. Wint of 600 Sqn. After making contact at 2½ miles they had to close in with wheels and flaps down to avoid overshooting. They visually identified their target as a Ju 87 flying at a little over 4,000ft and their first burst, with 30° deflection, struck its cockpit. The Stuka was missed by the second burst but dived into the ground, exploded and burned north of Albano Laziale (Rome). The entire action had lasted just ten minutes.

3 June 1944

Continuing their patrol, just minutes after midnight Bailey and Wint got AI and visual contact on another Ju 87. They were about to make a beam attack when it saw them, turned into the Beaufighter, jettisoned its bomb and escaped.

Given another vector in the Rome area at 0025, they acquired a target flying at just over 5,000ft, gradually losing height and taking normal evasive action. At first the radar echoes from the hills below made the blip difficult to follow. From 1,000yd the contact was identified as a Bf 110 with underwing long-range tanks. Exploiting their opponent's blind spot, the Beaufighter crew closed in astern and below to 150yd, opened fire and set the Messerschmitt's starboard wing and engine ablaze. The German aeroplane held level while two of its crew took to their parachutes, then turned over and fell to explode and burn on the ground. It was a Bf 110G-4 (W.Nr.720039) of 6./NJG 6, and the crewman who did not get out was the radio operator, Uffz. Heinz Schulz.The two survivors' names are not recorded. Bailey and Wint landed back at Marcianise (CE) at 0200, their 3½hr patrol having achieved more than both of II./NJG 6's spells in Italy combined.

Also from 600 Sqn, Australian pilot Fg Off D.W. Rees and his radar operator Fg Off D.C. Bartlett had been on patrol since 2305. Their first contact had been with a friendly Baltimore, but at 0015 and south of Rome 'Project' put them on to another aircraft which they acquired at 4½ miles. It was losing height and changing course, and they lost it when it entered the Anzio AA zone; when picked up again the target was heading north and weaving. A 15min 'chase' ensued, with the Beaufighter closing at an indicated 110-120mph and having to lower wheels and flaps. Finally the pursued aircraft was identified as a Cr.42. The nightfighter closed in from down moon and dead astern to 150ft, fired a short burst and blew the biplane up in a mass of flames. The burning pieces were seen to fall into Lake Vico but, despite this annihilation, there is no report of a pilot casualty from 2./NSGr.9.

Out to sea off Anzio 20min later the Beaufighter was given another vector. This bogey was going south and climbing. It entered the AA zone from landward, and the nightfighter wisely desisted from pursuing once the guns opened up and contact was not regained.

From 0119 local time, 19 Ju 88 bombers took off from Villafranca, the last not returning until just over four hours later. At 0636 a Bf 109, 'Yellow 11', set off from Castiglione del Lago to Viterbo: this may well have been W.Nr.710062, a tropicalised G-8 reconnaissance model from 3./NAGr.11 which the Allies found at the latter airfield on 25 June. 3./11 also reported a Bf 109 missing in action on the 3rd.

At 0520, 12 of Gruppo 'Buscaglia's' S.79s, each armed with a single torpedo, took off from Lonate Pozzolo and landed in Istres, Southern France, just over two hours later. So secret was their mission that most of the crews did not yet know the target. While they waited in suspense, the fighter pilots of II° Gr.C. had started conversion training on the Bf 109, with discouraging results: both Ten. Antonio Camaioni (1ª Sq.) and Cap. Mario Bellagambi (CO of 2ª Sq. and a future ace) wrecked Messerschmitts in landing accidents.

2.(F)/122 was shuffling its Me 410s between Perugia and Bergamo. The Staffel's only operational flying was logged by Ltn. Dietrich Stämmler, who took F6+HK up twice that morning, spending about four hours in the air with less than 90min break between sorties. 1.(F)/123 sent out two Ju 88s, the second leaving Bergamo during the afternoon to cover the Tyrrhenian and the approaches to Corsica.

At 1630 GMT it was 30 miles west of Grosseto and 40min later sighted four vessels, including patrol boats and landing craft, off Corsica's southern tip. Completing its mission, it crossed the coast west of Pisa and was down again at Bergamo by 1945.

By 1300, the first elements of III./JG 53 had reported arriving at their new base in Maniago and, like the other fighter Gruppen, spent the day relocating rather than fighting. SG 4 was likewise moving its Fw 190s to the northwest of the country, away from the battle area. In the early evening a Do 217, F3+DH of Kesselring's liaison Staffel, landed at Foligno (PG) from München-Riem.

The night of 3/4 June saw German bombers attacking in the Labico and Valmontone (Rome) areas and Nachtschlacht aircraft harassing traffic columns on the Via Casilina between the latter town and Colonna (Rome). A Ju 88A-4 (W.Nr.140527) of II./LG 1 went missing on a practice flight from Villafranca, its four crew being posted as dead or missing. Westa 26 put up at least three Ju 88 sorties after dark, one of them covering the northern Tyrrhenian from Ghedi. 1.(F)/123 also sent out a Ju 88 and KG 200 a Ju 188 which was about its nefarious business from 1840 to 2006 GMT.

Again that evening, II./NJG 6 moved up to nine of its Bf 110s forward to Perugia and was later heard active around Rome in response to Allied bombing. At 2300 a report was monitored that an Allied aircraft had been shot down by a nightfighter. The victorious pilot was Fw. Helmut Bunje, who claimed a Vickers Wellington, probably the one from 330 Wing posted missing on a raid against a bridge across the Tiber, south of Rome. Bunje's was the only success by the Gruppe during its 1944 sojourns in Italy; he was later commissioned as a Leutnant but was killed on 4 August, with a score of 12.

4 June 1944

As the Wellington raids continued after midnight there were reports of a vivid explosion in the target area and, an hour or so later, air-to-air firing 20 miles east of Lake Bracciano. It is possible that one or other incident marked the demise of another NJG 6 nightfighter, with W.Nr. 720189 failing to return. Its crew, all posted as dead or missing, were Hptm. Alfons Habermayr (pilot), Uffz. Johannes Schreiterer (wireless operator), both of 6. Staffel, and Oblt. Kraftmut Deubner. The latter appears not to have been regular aircrew but a member of the Gruppe staff company, with the post of Nightfighter Operations Controller.

Better news for II./NJG 6 came in Major Leuchs' morning report to Geschwader HQ. Uffz. Alfred Mrusek of 6. St. had returned to his unit. Mrusek reported that he had been shot down but did not know the whereabouts of his two crewmen. No date or circumstances of the incident are given and there is no record of crew casualties before the loss on the night of 2/3 June, by which time Mrusek's failure to return had already been notified to HQ.

In the small hours 17 Ju 88s flew a mission from Villafranca against troops at Valmontone and Labico, all but one returning after four hours. A III./KG 76 aircraft sent an SOS at 0015 GMT and was called by both Avignon and Verona without response while another aeroplane was called by Verona from 0302 to 0323 but was not heard to answer. This second incident may relate to the loss of a Ju 88A-4 (W.Nr.801326, F1+ET) with crew from 4./76, probably the aircraft claimed by the Beaufighter of Flt Sgt Cole and Sgt Odd of 600 Sqn at 0355, 2-3 miles northwest of Frosinone (although the German report differs on timing). Uffz. Adam Frey (observer) was killed and radioman Uffz. Michael Glas was severely injured when he baled out. Gunner Uffz. Gerhard Christians of 5./76 died and was buried in Ravenna, having taken part in the same mission aboard W.Nr.883941, F1+MN.

At 0418 another eight Junkers set off from Villafranca, all coming back about 100min later, suggesting either an aborted operation or a short range one. If the latter was the case, these may have been the bombers Luftflotte 2 sent against a guerrilla camp.

2.(F)/122 had a new Me 410 delivered from Riem and again redeployed some aeroplanes. The day's two operations were flown morning and evening from Piacenza by F6+FK, with a different crew each time. From 3./NAGr.11 Uffz. Müller was posted missing after his Bf 109G-6 (W.Nr.162529, Yellow 4) was destroyed in the Anzio area.

Twelve Spitfires of 243 Sqn succeeded in shielding the bombers they were escorting from 26 Bf 109s near Pistoia, but Sgt Spencer was missing after the combat and another pilot crashed at base but emerged unhurt. The Messerschmitts may have come from II./JG 77, which reported combat damage to one aircraft.

While American troops entered the Italian capital, this was a significant day for the ANR, too. At 1045 I° Gr.C. flew its first mission since re-equipping, 11 C.205s and 14 G.55s patrolling uneventfully over the La Spezia-Genoa area until midday. The unit's S.Ten. Mazzei was killed in a training accident which destroyed his Macchi. In Istres that morning the crews of Gruppo 'Buscaglia' were at last told their target – the British naval base at Gibraltar – and began pre-flight checks on their torpedoes, engines and instruments, for this was to be a night flight. At 2134 ten S.79s began to take off, severely burdened with extra fuel. One aborted with a broken throttle handle, but its crew rapidly rejoined the action in one of the two backup aircraft. Unfortunately, this was a 'marked' mission and this second Savoia also developed trouble, compelling Ten. Merani's crew to land at Perpignan, severely damaging their undercarriage.

The remaining nine S.79s followed a route that brought them from Cabo Não to Cabo de Palos, then from Cabo de Gata up to north of Punta de Almiña, Morocco, and then straight north to Gibraltar. Cap. Bertuzzi's plane was first to attack, at 0220. The bombers, flying in darkness at less than 180ft over the waves, and at intervals of less than two minutes, pounced unexpectedly on the Bay to drop their torpedoes.

After the first explosions all Gibraltar was blacked-out apart from the runway, from which Beaufighters began to come up. Only Cap. Marini, last to drop, was chased by a nightfighter, but he managed to evade. However it was after the attack that the biggest problems occurred. Of the nine S.79s, three experienced fuel tank trouble and had to land in Spain while of the rest – flying on the two outer engines and with the central one shut off to save fuel – four reached Istres safely and two had to put down at Perpignan.

Although German observers in Algeciras reported that the attack had badly damaged four merchant ships totalling 30,000 tons and also hit two others, the British noted that the Italians had raided the base 'without achieving anything'. They believed that up to 12 Savoias had been involved and three had been destroyed (perhaps a reference to those interned in Spain) and that mines may have been laid. There had been no damage to shipping (the harbour was strewn with torpedo nets for just such an eventuality), but the seaward side of a detached mole had been damaged. The port was closed but re-opened the following afternoon. Material damage was greatly outweighed by the propaganda value of the attack, and the proof it provided to their German allies and to the members of I° Gr. Aerosiluranti themselves that they were still alive and kicking, with an important role to play in the Mediterranean war.

5 June 1944

Seven Bf 110s had deployed to Perugia on the evening of the 4th, but their night's operations were without result as Allied bombers tried to block roads in the Terni area, and at 0330 local time 2Z+DC, +CM, +DM, +EM and +KM arrived back at Ghedi. At the same time over Gracciano (SI), the crew of a 6./NJG 6 Bf 110G-4 (W.Nr.720132) became disorientated and were forced to abandon their aircraft. Two men parachuted successfully but the pilot, Ofw. Treynogga was killed. Treynogga had

Cascina Vaga, June 1944. Two of the 19 Bf 109s delivered between 29 and 31 May to re-equip II° Gruppo Caccia. The aircraft shown here (RQ+SY and NF+FN) were among a group of four arriving on 29 May directly from Erding. They were assigned to 1ª Squadriglia, as shown by the number crudely painted inside the cross.

A few weeks later, fully emblazoned with ANR markings, Bf 109G-6s of 2ª Sq. prepare to take-off from the small field of Cascina Vaga. Training is nearly complete and on 22 June IIº Gruppo will resume operational status.

found fame of a sort in March, when he had inadvertently landed in Switzerland and been interned for five weeks.

At 1300 all three Squadriglie of Iº Gr.C. took off to intercept bombers reported in the Bologna area. These proved to be nine B-25s of 321st BG bombing the railway bridge at Polesella (RO) and they claimed (mistakenly, as so often) that they had been attacked by four Bf 109s, shooting one of them down and suffering slight damage to one bomber. In fact no Italian aeroplane was lost, while Iº Gruppo's pilots made a correct claim of damage to a single B-25. The fighters were back on the ground at Reggio Emilia and Cavriago by 1430, but five minutes later the former base was strafed by P-38s of 14th FG. Italian sources record three G.55s destroyed and another damaged, their German allies made it two *C.205s* written off and 30 per cent damage to a third.

In their Kommodore's absence – he had gone by He 111 that morning to report to General Galland – II./JG 77 found themselves in action at about the same time as the Italians, countering six waves of B-24s that dropped fragmentation bombs on the Gruppe's airfield at Ferrara. Two Bf 109s were damaged and Uffz. Berndt of 5. Staffel was injured in crashlanding his Bf 109 (W.Nr.163167, Black 8) at Ferrara after combat with the Liberators. An Allied claim of five Messerschmitts destroyed and as many damaged in action against heavy bombers seems somewhat optimistic. At 1430 a Bf 109 was destroyed and four seriously damaged when Poggio Renatico (where 6./JG 77 was based) was strafed by 25 Lightnings.

Large numbers of Fw 190s were also in the air, mostly new ones bearing factory markings and going to Airasca and Levaldigi, but some survivors of SG4's recent operations were also on the move – 'Green 1', 'White 2', 'Black 2' and 'Black 9' pulling back from Viterbo to Piacenza early in the morning.

In the early evening an offshore reconnaissance mission to Orbetello and the mouth of the Tiber was broken off owing to the Allied fighter defences. From Westa 26 a Ju 88A-4 (W.Nr.301546, 5M+H) went missing on maritime reconnaissance in the Elba area and the four members of Ltn. Hansen's crew remain unaccounted for. Unusually, both of Kdo. Carmen's Ju 188s were out during the night, single sorties being the norm. At Foligno, Do 217 F3+CH came in from Riem during the early evening.

In the course of the day, the eight serviceable survivors of the Gibraltar raid had reassembled at Istres (where they were photographed by an Allied aircraft), preparatory to returning to Italy.

After dark the night harassment units attacked transport columns and artillery positions at Grottaferrata, Frascati and the Via Casilina. At least one Ju 87, 1./NSGr.9's E8+RH, had been brought forward to Bologna from the northwestern reserve bases in the afternoon, presumably to participate in these attacks.

6 June 1944

Allied bombers were trying to cause road blocks in the Viterbo area, leaving the stalled Axis traffic prey to follow-on attacks; II./NJG 6 was doing what it could to stop them. At 0113 Wellington 'L' of 142 Sqn., on its bombing run, spotted two Me 110s below and about 400yd away. One of the fighters turned in and was taken under fire by the Wellington's rear gunner, causing it to break away. The second Messerschmitt came in to 300 yards dead astern but was lost to sight after becoming the target of two short bursts.

At 0510, Oblt. v.d. Daele and Uffz. Blaschek left Perugia on 2.(F)/122's 3,000th mission (or at least *a* 3,000th mission – two such are recorded in the Staffel's KTB!), returning just over two hours later. Their Me 410, F6+QK, apparently suffered some kind of accidental or technical mishap sufficient to end its operational career, but it will reappear in rather odd circumstances.

Early in the morning the eight S.79s still flyable took off from Istres, landing at Venegono at 0700 (where they were 'caught in the act' by MAAF Sigint) and then flying on to Lonate, arriving there at 0930. During the day an uneventful patrol was flown by I° Gr.C. and 6./JG 77's Gefr. Zein was injured and his Bf 109 (W.Nr.163156, white 3) destroyed in an emergency landing at Bergamo. A Bf 109 was claimed damaged near Trieste by the USAAF's 309th FS.

At 1800 a Ju 52, F5+PH, was setting out for Florence, carrying out communication/ liaison duties on Luftflotte 2's behalf. During the night harassing attacks concentrated on roads northwest of Rome. Three Ju 88s left Villafranca on a mission at 2140, all returning safely an hour after midnight.

7 June 1944

At 0040 seven Ju 88s left Villafranca on another four-hour mission, probably harassing roads north and west of Rome. At 0229 Wellingtons reported three bursts of air-to-air firing near Orvieto and two Bf 109 sightings, but no claim or loss resulted. At about 0600 four Ju 88s of 4./KG 76 (F1+AM, +CM, +IM and +TM) landed at Aviano from Ancona and that morning the Geschwader queried the whereabouts of F1+ET, missing since the 4th.

At Orio al Serio (Bergamo) that morning an official ceremony marked the departure for Germany of the 500 men comprising II° Gruppo Aerotrasporti 'Trabucchi'. They were bound for Goslar, where 48 S.82s were already waiting for them to complete their training and become operational.

Again little was attempted and less achieved by the day fighters: I° Gr.C. flew a patrol without contact and III./JG 53 had a Bf 109 destroyed by ground fire in 'friendly' airspace. Following the Normandy landings Obstlt. Steinhoff ended consultations with G.d.J. prematurely and returned to Italy.

During the day and succeeding night, the usual quota of reconnaissance sorties was flown, one of these apparently by 4U+BH of 1.(F)/123, which moved forward from Bergamo to Perugia early in the evening. Bombers again attacked roads west of Rome, but the weather hampered observation of the results, aside from the outbreak of two fires. North of the capital, six Bf 110s were patrolling the roads used by German troops and a raiding Wellington crew had the disquieting experience of seeing an unidentified aircraft with a white belly (suggestive of pale grey Luftwaffe nightfighter camouflage) pass right over them on a reciprocal course. All that II./NJG 6 could record for this night's operations was that one Bf 110 damaged its undercarriage on landing.

8 June 1944

Around 0100 RAF bombers again reported opposition from single-engined fighters: Wellington 'H' of 142 Sqn saw air-to-air firing near Orvieto, and 'Q' claimed hits on a Bf 109 with a white nose light south of Lake Bolsena. The rear-gunner saw a flash from the enemy aircraft, which dived away on the starboard quarter as the Wellington evaded to port. Over Trasimeno, a 231 Wing aircraft saw an Fw 190, again with a nose light and manoeuvring as if to attack, but managed to evade it.

Just before 0500 GMT, Me 410 F6+KK (crewed by Dietse and Bendorf) landed back at Perugia, having completed 2.(F)/122's *second* recorded '3,000th mission', then flew on to Bergamo a couple of hours later. At 1735 eight Spitfires of 451 Sqn took off on a last light reconnaissance, encountering a Ju 88 near Pistoia. Wg Cdr E.J. Morris and Flt Lt R. Sutton attacked and shot it down, other members of the formation seeing it crash in flames and explode. 1.(F)/123, which sent out five aircraft that day, had lost Ju 88T-1 W.Nr.430913, 4U+GH, along with Obfhr. Scherpf and his three fellow crewmen, all killed. German sources put the crash southeast of Chiusi (SI), quite some way from Pistoia.

At 1830 2./122 dispatched F6+HK (Schmidt and Grahl) from Perugia on a 70min sortie, while on night missions proper were four Westa 26 aeroplanes and a Kdo. Carmen Ju 188. During the day NSGr.9 brought three Cr.42s and a pair of Ju 87s to Bologna; after dark Bf 110s patrolled in the Viterbo-Rieti area but made no contacts.

9 June 1944

At 0222 a Ju 88T of 1.(F)/123 took off from Perugia and flew down to North Africa to photograph Bizerta and Ferryville, returning to Istres after eight hours aloft. At 0250 two more Ju 88s had left Perugia, this time for Bergamo – 1.(F)/123's 4U+BH and Carmen's A3+NB; at 0730 F1+AA of Stab KG 76 landed at Villafranca from Linz-Hörsching. Late in the afternoon a rare Ju 86 (DR+IK) was active over Northern Italy.

I./JG 4, III./JG 53 (both from Maniago) and II./JG 77 scrambled against escorted B-24s returning from the Reich and, although 20 victories were claimed overall, II./77 in particular suffered heavy losses in men and machines. From 4. Staffel Fw. Kurt Neubert (W.Nr.163587, White 6) baled out after combat with Spitfires, only to be shot up and killed on his parachute over Portogruaro (VE); Fw. Rudolf Flindt (W.Nr.163758, White 9) and Uffz. Richard Kurz (W.Nr.163510, White 10) baled out wounded at Udine. Uffz. Rudolf Holz (W.Nr.163153, Black 3) of 5. Staffel was wounded and took to his 'chute over Tramonti (UD); 6. Staffel's Ltn. Franz Nägele (W.Nr.441129, Yellow 3) died taking on the bombers over Monte Aleso (UD) and Uffz. Walter Dieckhoff (W.Nr.163133) was wounded and baled out at Maniago.

Uffz. Siegfried Kier of 1./JG 4 (W.Nr. 162680, White 5) also parachuted with injuries, at Lavariano. From 7./JG 53, Uffz. Horst Köhler's Bf 109 (W.Nr.161150, white 10) took hits in the cockpit while attacking the bombers over Treviso and he was wounded; 8./53 found that Uffz. Wolf Reihlen (W.Nr.163154, Black 5) was missing after combat with P-38s near Udine. According to Ultra, I./JG 77 also took part, scrambling 12 Bf 109s after the heavy bombers and another four to look for stragglers. They claimed one P-47 shot up but reported two pilots baled out and two missing.

Ltn. Herrmann. of 7./53 and Ofw. Polak and Uffz. Scheer of 8. claimed B-24s (the latter's 11th kill); Stab/77 made contact with a box of 20 Liberators at 6,000m over Venice at 1100, and Obstlt. Steinhoff shot one down. The Americans lost three bombers in Italian airspace, but no neat tally with the German claims is possible, for I° Gr.C. now intervened. Five C.205s and eight G.55s took off at 1030 to intercept and claimed to have shot down two bombers (by Ten. Robetto and S.M. Chiussi of 1ª Sq.) and damaged another, for no loss of their own.

The escorts claimed 10-0-2 Bf 109s, and an hour or so after these combats 1st/Lt. Richard J Geyman of 94th FS shot down a Cant Z.506B of Seenotdienst 6 between Brioni Island and Pola (today Brijuni and Pula, Croatia).

Another hour later, eight Spitfires of 451 Sqn, led by their CO, encountered seven Bf 109s south of Florence. Three were claimed shot down (by Flt Lt Robert, Flt Lt Sutton and Fg Off James), another was damaged (by Sqn Ldr Kirkham) and the rest turned tail. 1./JG 77 was the German formation involved and it reported Ofhr. Josef Czibulski (W.Nr.163513, Black 5) killed and Ltn. Hans Tomschegg (W.Nr.162449, White 11) missing.

About ten Bf 110s patrolled the Viterbo area without any sightings, although a 415th NFS Beaufighter contacted one in the Anzio area, only to lose it soon after. All that II./NJG 6 had to show for the day's efforts was two aircraft 25 per cent damaged in crash landings at Perugia: Fw. Patta's crew was unhurt, as was Ltn. Mahr's, but pilot error was blamed for his accident.

Leaving its Trieste target, another 231 Wing Wellington was followed for 10min by an unidentified aircraft with a rounded tail and a white

---

Inside a sandbagged blast-pen at Reggio Emilia, a Macchi C.205 of 3ª Sq., I° Gruppo Caccia awaits the next scramble. After the 'crisis' of mid-June, this Squadriglia and Sq. Montefusco were for several weeks the only operational sections of the Gruppo.

light on its starboard wing; evasive action was taken and the e/a was eventually lost. Given the description and location it could perhaps have been a Ju 88 of L.Beo.St.7.

Sixteen Ju 88s left Villafranca at 2207, all returning four hours later; the bombers had struck targets off Nettuno in a heavy raid developing from midnight, hitting six ships. Attack aircraft went after supply traffic on the coast road south of Viterbo, obtaining many hits and, in what was probably a training accident, 2./NSGr.9 had a Ju 87D-3 (W.Nr.100090) crash at Caselle, killing Uffz. Karl Defele.

An Italian pilot's girlfriend poses as an 'airwoman' under the nose of a Macchi of 2ª Sq.

10 June 1944

III./JG 53 scrambled 14 Bf 109s against Liberators and made contact (but seems not to have scored) and an uneventful patrol was flown by Iº Gr.C. At around 0830 II./JG 77's aircraft landed at Poggio Renatico, Ferrara and Lavariano after engaging heavy bombers without loss.

Between 1030 and 1100 Ferrara airfield was bombed by 140 B-24s. Three Bf 109s were destroyed and 11 so badly damaged that they had to be returned to the factories; four ground crewmen were wounded and 5./77's workshops burned out. Unexploded bombs littered the landing ground, and II./77 had to be withdrawn to Poggio Renatico until they were dealt with.

Bad weather over the Apennines on the night of the 10/11th forced the cancellation both of nightfighter operations and a planned mission by Gr. 'Buscaglia' to Nettuno Bay. It seems that reconnaissance missions were flown (flash bombs falling over Bari) and Carmen sent out two Ju 188 sorties. Fifteen of II./TG 1's Savoias landed at Ghedi at 2210, charged with transferring personnel and equipment of the bomber force to Belgium for anti-invasion duties, but they too were then grounded by the weather.

11 June 1944

Five II./NJG 6 Bf 110s were active between Ghedi and Perugia from 0117 and one flew from Bologna to Ghedi. At 0445 two Bf 109s of 1./NAGr.11 were due to start from Jesi on a recce of the Rimini/Ortona (CH) area; an hour later 2.(F)/122's F6+KK (Neumann and Meister) set off from Perugia on a mission, only to be 95 per cent damaged in a crash landing at Forlì at 0845. Both men were brought back to Bergamo that evening in Ju 88 F6+BK. Meister did not fly again until 19 August and his pilot not until 13 November, when the two crewed up again.

Ltn. Platte (W.Nr.760226, Yellow 4) of 6./JG 77 was posted missing after combat with B-24s at 0740, southwest of Russi (RA), and 14 fighters of III./JG 53 also took on these bombers and their P-38 escort. A Bf 109 claimed by 251 Wing Spitfires near Pistoia was in I./JG 77's area of operations, but no other evidence of its identity has been found.

During the day 15 Ju 88s of I./LG 1 left Ghedi for Belgium, and 21 of II. Gruppe left Villafranca for northern France. Nevertheless, that night 30 bombers mounted a strong final attack on shipping off Anzio. The bombers' transfer was aided by II./TG 1, whose aeroplanes (in the face of bad weather and the Allied air threat) arrived by circuitous means in Chièvres.

12 June 1944

Four Savoias of 8./TG 1, among them Helmut Schwarz's 1Z+KS, had been ordered on the 10th to transport 'a fighter Gruppe' to Brussels-Melsbroek.[4] They flew to Aviano at low level in the comparative safety of evening twilight. Loading problems delayed the planned dawn departure until 1620 on the 11th. Staging through Gallarate, they got away late in the afternoon, only to be turned back by the weather. They then transferred to Airasca in the hope of a night flight over the Alps once conditions improved, finally leaving at 0250 on the 12th and flying low up the Rhône to Lyon by moonlight. They were then diverted to Bonn-Hangelar, then to St Trond, and got to Melsbroek early on the 13th. In less than an hour they were on the return trip and, after diversions to Rhein-Main and Riem, were back at Gallarate that evening.

At 1041 on the 12th a Lufthansa Ju 52, D-ASPI, left Venice for Riem. Six Bf 110s of II./NJG 6 transferred home to Germany but their take off orders came 'far too late' and they only arrived during the afternoon, some with unserviceable radios.

That afternoon 276 Wing's radio monitors intercepted a report that an Me 410 would be up at 0445 next day to fly the route Piacenza-Corsica-Central Tyrrhenian-Corsica-Bergamo. This was an opportunity the RAF was not going to miss.

13 June 1944

At 0448, just three minutes later than expected, Ofw. Jackstadt and Uffz.(?) Stauch of 2.(F)/122 took off in F6+FK, and all seems to have gone well until 0708, when they were crossing the coast at low level near La Spezia. There they were jumped by Spitfires of 451 Sqn flown by Fg Offs Jones and Mercer. F6+FK returned shot up and crashed in flames; neither crewman flew again for ten days.

At 0911 two Stab/JG 77 Bf 109s scrambled against heavy bombers returning from the Reich, but Obstlt. Steinhoff's droptank was not feeding and so no contact was made. I° Gr.C. scrambled at 1055 with II./JG 77 and I./JG 4, to intercept bombers in the Venice-Udine area. The Italians had dogfights with the P-51 escort and S.M. Luigi Di Cecco's C.205 fell to the 15th AF's second-ranking ace, Maj Herschel H. Green of the 317th FS, 325th FG ('The Checkertail Clan'), 20 miles northeast of Venice. The Italian pilot put his burning Macchi down in a cornfield and escaped safely, while the rest of his unit landed at Aviano at noon, later returning to Reggio Emilia.

Ogfr. Przykling (W.Nr.162990, yellow 3) of 3./JG 4 was killed in combat near Udine and his aircraft may have been the Bf 109 shot down west of the city by 2/Lt Tatman, also of 317th FS. Uffz. Pläschke of 7./JG 53 and Uffz. Scheer of 8. Staffel each claimed, within the space of five minutes, a B-24 shot down (the latter's twelfth victory); Ltn. Böhm of III./53's Stab claimed a P-47. II./JG 77 reported one aeroplane lost in combat and III./53 two missing but no details are available of the circumstances and there are no other Allied claims.

NAGr.11 transferred from Castiglione del Lago to Florence and its 2. Staffel wrote one aircraft off in an accident. In the early evening a Luftverkehrsgruppe Ju 52, A7+HK, landed in Osoppo from the Aviano/Piacenza area, and it may have been this aircraft that was later found burnt out on Cazaux airfield in France. This unit's activities had been noted since 27 May, with 14 Ju 52s mainly operating between Munich and Villafranca.

Nine Ju 87s and Cr.42s attacked assembly areas and gun positions in the Viterbo/Montefiascone/Orbetello area with bombs and guns during the night of the 13/14th and, as on the previous night, a Carmen Ju 188 flew a mission. There was also a plan for Ju 88s to fly a (reconnaissance?) operation from Italy and land in Southern France that night. A single aircraft of Stab/NJG 6 flying between Ghedi and Vicenza was the last heard from that unit in Italy. In all, Luftflotte 2 achieved 114 sorties.

14 June 1944

Spitfires of 251 Wing, escorting 36 Mitchells of 310th BG north of Pistoia, encountered 12 Bf 109s and Wg Cdr Morris shot down one of them. The German formation was probably from II./JG 77 which reported an aircraft lost in action but no injury to a pilot.

1./NAGr.11 had a Bf 109 damaged by enemy action while on a sortie, and Flt Lt G.R. Gould DFC gained 241 Sqn's first aerial victories when that evening he single-handedly shot down two Bf 109s over the Adriatic as they headed for the Yugoslav coast. These probably came from NAGr.12 in the Balkans. German bombers attacked guerrilla-held zones northwest of Varese, and 2.(F)/122 sent up a photographic flight, apparently over Axis-held territory, as well as a mission over Allied lines.

Westa 26 sent a Ju 88A-4 (W.Nr.301154, 5M+F) on a night reconnaissance to cover the sea around Elba, the Italian west coast and the eastern exit of the San Bonifacio Strait. Oblt. Harbauer and his three crew were charged in particular with observing Allied minesweeping activity off Livorno, but none of them returned and their fate remains unknown.

15 June 1944

I° Gr.C. was now assigned to patrol the Livorno-Pisa area, a region receiving particular attention from DAF's fighters in view of the forthcoming Elba landings. Led by Wg Cdr A.D.J. Lovell, eight of 243 Sqn's Spitfires fought '30 Macchis' (actually 20 mixed C.205s and Fiats) at 14,000ft over the Apennines south of Piacenza. Victories were claimed by Lovell (the G.55, MM.91087 of 3ª Sq.'s S.Ten Morettin, who baled out but died of his wounds) and W/O Daveson (1ª Sq.'s. S.Ten. Sajeva, who crash landed his G.55). Lt Burls and Flt Lt Burke each claimed an e/a damaged (which the authors cannot confirm, unless it was the Bf 109 2./NAGr.11 reported missing), but none of the Spitfires was hit.

That night Kdo. Carmen sent out its last (detected) mission for a fortnight.

16 June 1944

The day saw a total of 83 fighter sorties. I° Gr.C. scrambled twice, with no result beyond the loss of M.llo Forlani's G.55 (1ª Sq.). Its engine overheated and caught fire, forcing him to bale out. Four Stab/JG 77 Bf 109s transferred to Lavariano, and at 1048 took part in a scramble against heavy bombers. An hour later they were in action against a box of 20 B-17s, 45 Lightnings and 15 Mustangs near Zagreb. This escort proved too strong, and there were no victories or losses, but Uffz. Walter Holz (W.Nr.162039, red 10) of 2./77 was killed scrambling from Bologna.

A Gr. 'Buscaglia' S.79 suffered engine failure just after take-off, tried to land, got caught in a strong crosswind and was severely damaged when its undercarriage collapsed. A further mishap came with a report that a Bf 109 had shot up friendly shipping.

Ju 188 A3+TB of Carmen left Istres at 1430 and was down at Bergamo at 1600, and Stab/LG 1's Ju 88 L1+AA arrived at Ghedi at 1935 from Brussels-Melsbroek.

17-18 June 1944

On the 16th, He 111 VD+OW, with Hptm. Weinand aboard, made a 15min flight to help train Würzburg radar crews. On the 17th six such trips were flown by Me 410 F6+LK and one by Ju 88 F6+BK, as well as an operation by Me 410 F6+CK. Next day, Gruppenkommandeur Pannwitz and Staffelkapitän Weinand were up twice in Fi 156 F6+SK, on the first occasion for an hour, on the second a mere five minutes. Bad weather put paid to any Axis operations on the night of the 17/18th.

19 June 1944

The troubles of the reconnaissance Staffeln rarely came singly and losses tended, for whatever reason, to cluster on certain days. On the 19th the capture of Elba was completed, so the island was something of a magnet for both sides' aircraft.

The 347th FS, 350th FG, claimed credit for a number of enemy aircraft turning back when confronted by its patrols during the month. On this day two P-47s of its Blue section, flown by Lts. Schareck and King, were at 17,000ft heading for Cap Corse, at around 0515.[5] Their controller advised them of a hostile coming south at 10,000ft and vectored them to the small island of Capraia (LI), with orders to proceed at low level. After a couple more vectors it was reported that the bandit was now heading back northeast, so the Americans orbited the west tip of Elba, sighting an Me 410 on the deck. This was F6+EK of 2.(F)/122, crewed by Oblt. v.d. Daele and Uffz. Blaschek and operating out of Piacenza, where they had deployed three days before.

It was now 0522 and the Americans dropped their belly tanks, shortly afterwards taking fire at 1,000yd from the Messerschmitt's left barbette. Passing over Elba they also came in for intense but inaccurate AA fire. Schareck closed in and with three bursts managed to start the German aeroplane's right engine smoking before it crossed the coast at Follonica (GR). Schareck's electrics died on him and King took the lead in a 305mph chase that continued until northeast of Arezzo and the exhaustion of his ammunition. He scored several hits on the enemy's tail and wing, and was the object of seven short defensive bursts in return. The Americans headed for home at 0545, avoiding flak from Punta Ala (GR) on the way; the 410 landed at Bergamo, badly shot up but with its crew safe.

On dusk patrol in his P-39 over a convoy near Pianosa (LI), Lt Elbert R. Carpenter of 347th FS, 350th FG was shot down and killed by what was thought to be an Fw 190 which immediately disappeared into the dark clouds.

On patrol to Elba, six Spitfires of 242 Sqn encountered a pair of Bf 109s from 2./NAGr.11, northeast of Piombino at 2015. In the ensuing action both were shot down by W/O Doherty and, coming down well within their own territory, it seems that their pilots were unscathed. 2./122's misfortunes returned when, on an evening mission, F6+CK had to belly-land after a mere 12min in the air. There is no report that the crew were hurt, but the aircraft did not fly again until almost a month later. Westa 26 was luckier, achieving three night sorties without loss.

20-21 June 1944

On the 20th 2./122 put up two recces, one of them from Piacenza, and Pannwitz and Weinand flew there from Bergamo mid-afternoon in Fi 156 F6+SK, returning early in the evening. Among eight aircraft sent against partisans at Gattinara (VC) was Ju 87 D3+DK of 2./NSGr.2, crewed by Ofw. Toni Fink and Fw. Johannes Nawroth but bad weather turned them back shortly after leaving Caselle. As on the previous day, a pair of Gr. 'Trabucchi' S.82s was active between northern airfields. Eleven of NAGr.11's Bf 109s left Jesi, nine for Forlì and the others for Florence.

Next morning Stab/JG 77 put up a Schwarm of Bf 109s on freelance patrol in the Florence area without contacts or losses but an aircraft of I. Gruppe was lost on an operational sortie. 2./NAGr.11 reported Ofw. Stölting missing after his Bf 109G-6 (W.Nr.410568, White 2) was shot down by fighters 10km north of Pisa.

The conversion of II° Gr.C. to the Bf 109 was almost complete, but had not been trouble-free. Early in the month Serg. Luigi Marin had hit a petrol bowser on his take-off run and was lucky to escape the ensuing fire and explosion. On the 14th S.Ten. Giuseppe Di Santo (3ª Sq.) had to land with only one undercarriage leg extended, badly damaging his aircraft. Now, on the 21st, the Messerschmitts of Ten. Luigi Pollo (1ª Sq.) and M.llo Elvio Saccani (2ª) collided while manoeuvring to land: the aircraft were 60 per cent and 70 per cent damaged respectively and Saccani was killed. Also that day three P-47s (probably French) strafed the airfield at Cervere (CN), the base of Gruppo Complementare Caccia, destroying several Cr.42s and the Fiat Br.20 used by this unit as a transport.

22-23 June 1944

I° Gr.C. was back in action at noon along with JG 77 and II° Gr.C. (on its first operation with the Bf 109), taking on 400 B-24s and 60 P-38s in the Bologna-Ferrara area. Four Lightnings were sighted by 2ª Sq.'s C.205s while climbing to reach the Italians. Despite Cap. Guidi's order to wait, Serg. Petrignani, with M.llo Fibbia close behind, dived and got on the tail of Lt Tolmie (of the 97th FS, 82nd FG). At first his tracers fell between the P-38's tail booms, but he tightened his turn and was beginning to score hits when he saw another American sitting on his tail. A sharp split-S followed by a vertical dive got Petrignani out of trouble just as Fibbia was announcing over the R/T that the first P-38 had exploded. I° Gr. claimed two of the escort shot down and two probables, but in fact only Tolmie was missing.

II° Gr.C. sent up 11 Gustavs from Cascina Vaga but achieved nothing, the general opinion being that flying discipline had been poor. S.Ten Di Santo confided to his diary: 'Yesterday our pilots made one of the worst combats possible, we can't go on like this . . .'

Orio al Serio (BG), 8 June 1944. Me 410 F6+KK flown by Hptm. Dietse and Fw. Bendorf is welcomed back to base after completing 2.(F)/122's 3,000th mission. Note how only one spinner carries the Staffel's red band. (Petrick)

Hptm. Weinand, Staffelkapitän of 2.(F)/122, who was to lead the unit up to the end of the war, speaking here with one of his men. (Petrick)

Three of Stab/JG 77's Bf 109s had deployed to Villafranca and scrambled at 1320, sighting about 100 bombers at 7,000m over Ferrara. Being 2,000m lower down, they could not intervene and the rest of the Geschwader was driven off by Lightnings. Bombs fell on the city of Ferrara and the Poggio Renatico airfield perimeter; II./JG77 incurred accidental damage to one aeroplane during this action. MAAF reported that south of Ferrara its aircraft had met '25 Bf 109s, C.202s, Fw 190s and Re.2001s.'

A scramble by I° Gr.C. on the 23rd did not lead to contact.

24 June 1944

Luftflotte 2 put up a total of 53 fighters during the day. At 0950, three Bf 109s of Stab./JG 77 took-off from Poggio Renatico airfield, joining 20+ Messerschmitts of II./77 for a freelance mission along the east coast from Ancona to Ravenna. Off Pesaro at 1050 they intercepted three P-51s of the 31st FG that had been dispatched to search for a rescue launch in enemy waters. The ensuing dogfight lasted only four minutes, and ended when Fhj.Uffz. Fährmann shot down one P-51, its pilot baling out before it crashed into the sea. The other Mustangs managed to shake off their pursuers, later finding and escorting the launch as planned. The Germans, fearing the arrival of more enemy fighters, gave up the chase and headed for their airfields, landing at 1100.

At Cascina Vaga, ten Messerschmitts of II° Gr.C. scrambled from the grass surface (three of 1a Sq., four of 2ª and three of 3ª), but W.Nr.163849, flown by S.Ten. Gino Gamberini of 3ª Sq., failed to reach take-off speed and, veering off course, turned over. Gamberini was unhurt but trapped in the cockpit and during attempts to raise the aeroplane with a lorry-mounted crane petrol fumes ignited, immediately engulfing the aircraft in flames and immolating the pilot. On investigation it emerged that the airplane had been sabotaged by an aircraftman who claimed (postwar) to have been a partisan. He had stuffed rags into the oil cooler and supercharger intakes, preventing the engine achieving full revs. This was only one of dozens of incidents of sabotage experienced by the ANR (though few had such tragic consequences), showing that there was a real civil war going on in Italy in 1944-45.

The other nine Italians, unaware of the tragedy, were directed by the Jafü towards the Gulf of Genoa, where enemy aeroplanes had been reported. At 1755 they intercepted 11 P-47s of Groupe de Chasse II/5 'Lafayette' bombing the railway bridge south of Ovada (AL). In the ensuing mêlée the Italians claimed two enemy aircraft shot down, by Ten. Drago and S.M. Cavagliano, but they apparently confused the P-47s' spins and the darker exhaust gases of their P&W R-2800 engines with certain victories.

In reality, the 'Lafayette' aeroplanes were unharmed apart from some damage to the aircraft of Sc. Lesieur and, when the Italians suddenly disappeared again into the clouds, they headed back to Corsica. II° Gruppo returned to Cascina Vaga at 1830, intending to celebrate what they thought were their first victories with their new machines, but news of Gamberini's death stifled any enthusiasm. On the French side, the inconclusive result of the combat was attributed to insufficient dogfight training, and gunnery practice with towed targets was proposed.

25 June 1944

The Luftwaffe put up 39 fighter sorties on freelance patrol over Rimini and convoy escort near Trieste. Escorting bombers to Rimini, the Spitfires of Fg Off Johnstone and Plt Off English of 241 Sqn were lost, and while the former was rescued by a Walrus amphibian, the latter was posted as missing. English said something incomprehensible over his R/T, but on looking round Johnstone saw an aircraft behind him which he at first took for his comrade's. As he noticed that it had a white spinner (and therefore was not a Spitfire), gunfire struck his aircraft and he had to jump. It was surmised that English had been shot down by the same Messerschmitt.

MAAF papers also contain the following entry: '1045: 4 Me 109s attacked H.S.L. [High Speed Launch, for air-sea rescue] escort 5 miles N.E. PESARO.'

At 0740 four Stab/JG 77 Bf 109s deployed to Maniago but the heavy bombers they were to attack flew away to the east so no action ensued. The Germans returned to base and that afternoon flew an uneventful patrol.

The ANR suffered two more accidents: S.Ten. Luziani of II° Gr.C. (W.Nr.163279, black 2) was killed when his engine cut and he tried to jettison his canopy, only to be struck by the armoured headrest; Serg. Taen and 1° Aviere De Biagi of G.T.V. died when their two-seat liaison machine crashed on a ferry flight to Gorizia. That night 3ª Sq.'s quarters in Reggio Emilia were attacked by partisans with grenades and automatic weapons; no one was hurt but nor were the assailants caught.

26 June 1944

Of 95 Lfl.2 sorties, 83 were by fighters. Stab and I./JG 77 shifting four and 14 aircraft respectively to Maniago to meet heavies returning from the Reich. They met around 40 Liberators and 50 Lightnings at 3-4,000 m northeast of Zagreb at 1035. Their attacks were seriously hindered by high-level escorts and: 'It was again demonstrated to Jafü and the [Luft]Flotte that for the effective engagement of heavy bomber formations it is urgently necessary for us to employ our own top cover Gruppen in Italian airspace . . .'

Nevertheless, Ofw. Klein (Stab/77) and Oblt. Deicke (6. Staffel's Kapitän) each destroyed a Liberator, the latter for his 15th victory. Three of the Stab/77 Gustavs landed at Ljubljana, one at Gorizia, and in the course of the afternoon 12 of I./77's aeroplanes arrived back in Bologna from Maniago.

That afternoon, over the Apennines southeast of Parma, 12 Spitfires of 238 Sqn led by Flt Lt Small set on: '11 mixed Bf 109s and C.202s [which were] quite oblivious of the presence of trouble until our Spits started shooting'.

Fg Off Hansen and Plt Off Nice each claimed a 109, and two other e/a were damaged. In fact they had bounced four Fiats and three Macchis of I° Gr.C. and shot down only a single C.205, Serg. Gianni Arrigoni's '3-2'. Arrigoni crashed and was killed at Monte S. Pietro (BO). The authors cannot elucidate the day's other reported clash, when the 79th FG claimed 0-1-3 Bf 109s from six Bf 109s and six Fw 190s encountered over Imola.

'White 16', an S.79 of Sq. Complementare Addestramento Siluranti, took off from Venegono at 1450, intending to desert. Pilot S.M. Antonio Lombardo and his four colleagues flew at 35m for five minutes so that nobody could note their heading, then climbed to 4,500m, ignoring the prescribed corridors, and crossed the coast northwest of La Spezia without being fired upon. After that they flew on the deck, the W/T Operator, S.M. Angelo Parisi, sending an SOS and adding 'S.M.79 escaped from Germans, making for Catania'. Reaching Sardinia and thinking their fuel too low, they gave up their idea of reaching Sicily. Contacting Cagliari/Elmas, Parisi asked for a bearing which (after hurried consultations) was given. Information about wind speed and direction was withheld, however, and the pilot, unable to see the windsock, landed with the wind on his tail, slightly damaging the undercarriage.

27 June 1944

There was considerable activity on northern airfields involving the transfer of Caproni types, apparently with the Reich as their eventual destination. A rare Do 17Z (KD+KG) and two He 111s were active between Bolzano and Lonate in the afternoon.

Two operations were flown by I./JG 77: 11 planes patrolling Forlì and Rimini, then eight providing protection for a sea rescue mission and again a patrol over Rimini, an area also covered by four Bf 109s from Stab/77 without incident. II./77 was less fortunate. One of its aircraft was shot down into the sea at 1110, but the pilot was rescued by a fisherman.

Also 2./NAGr.11 reported a Bf 109 destroyed in an accident.

II° Gr.C. finally made the transfer to Lavariano, due to take place the day before to join in the heavy bomber interception but prevented by bad weather. In the event there was no call on the 12 Gustavs and they returned to Cascina Vaga. At Reggio Emilia 12 Spitfires of 238 Sqn. caught I° Gr.C. taking off and Lt House claimed destruction of three Bf 109s. In reality two G.55s were destroyed and one damaged, with no pilots hurt.

At about the same time in the early evening as Ju 88 4U+AH was leaving a southerly airfield (perhaps Ravenna or Rimini) for Bergamo, 5M+P, 5M+R and 5M+X were making the same trip in the opposite direction, landing at 1835.

28 June 1944

At 0820 an He 111 (VJ+SY) left Lonate for Bad Voeslau, and the day saw many other transport and transfer activities including the departure of Ju 88 5K+GK from Ghedi for Le Culot at 0450 (these airfields had both recently been used by I./LG 1, and the presence of an aeroplane in the markings of 2./KG 3 is something of a mystery).

Eighty-six freelance fighter sorties were mounted in the Forlì-Rimini-Ancona area. At 1330, southwest of Rimini, a Schwarm from Stab/JG 77 spotted four Spitfires at 1,000m altitude and 1km away. The Messerschmitts could not catch the DAF aircraft, but Hptm. Werner Gutowski, Geschwader Adjutant, had his aircraft hit in the tail by friendly flak. 145 Sqn chased two Bf 109s, again near Rimini, and '12 Fw 190s' pursued Kittyhawks of 239 Wing in the battle area with no loss on either side.

During the morning, four Ju 87s in factory markings arrived in Bergamo from Erding, carrying on to Caselle next day. Early that evening 22 Stukas bearing operational codes deployed to forward bases from Caselle: 12 of 1./NSGr.9 to (probably) Ravenna and ten of 2./9 to Forlì.

29 June 1944

The 29th saw the start of another transfer of fighter units to more northerly airfields and the atmosphere was tense, as Stab/JG 77's KTB describes: 'For three days the bridges over the Reno right and left of the Geschwader accommodation have been attacked by fighter-bombers. Bologna is on continuous alert'.

At 0836 four Bf 109s of the Stab flew from Poggio to Aviano. I. and II./77 were leaving for the same destination and, around 0900, 12 Spitfires of 451 Sqn spotted the customary 'Bf 109s and Fw 190s' taking off from Calderara Di Reno (BO). Once the enemy was airborne the Spitfires attacked and Fg Off Bray and Flt Sgt Vintner each shot down one, while Fg Off Sidney got a probable. Fw. Heinrich Wolters of 2./JG 77 (W.Nr.162998, Red 11) died over Poggio and from 1. Staffel Ltn. Richard Heller (W.Nr.163201, White 9) was killed at Ferrara. In return the flak brought down a Spitfire.

Poggio was later strafed by the 79th FG, costing II./JG 77 two more 109s and a Ju W.34.[6] At Bolzano G.T.V. suffered another loss when S.Ten. Machi crashed during a ferry flight.

Around midday, three Spitfire Mk.VIIIs from 92 Sqn and three Seafire LF Mk.IICs of 807 Sqn (Fleet Air Arm) were escorting 12 Baltimores of 21 Sq. (SAAF) to Cesena (FO) marshalling yards, only to meet '25 to 30 Me 109s and FW 190s who seemed to fill the sky.' In fact they were up against ten II° Gr.C. Bf 109s (operating out of Maniago), plus some from JG 77.

Cap. Bellagambi claimed one of the bombers, but Lt van Niekerk was able to bring his aeroplane, hit in the port engine, back to crash-land at Tortoreto (TE). As for the fighter action, lasting roughly half an hour, from the target to south of Ancona:

> In the dice that ensued Lt Boy (SAAF) managed to get in a telling burst from 400 yards and claims an FW 190 damaged for it spun down to deck level before managing to pull out . . . High lights . . . occurred when F/L L Smith shook off 4 Me 109s that had fastened onto his tail by a series of steep turns at full bore, when Lt V Boy and his No.2 – Sub/Lt Robinson – were jumped by 11 Me 109s but managed to extricate themselves somehow and when F/L B Gardner was pursued and gradually overhauled as he flew full out at deck level. Fortunately three of them broke off just north of Ancona but one 'persistent B – -' as Ben put it came on, closing to 500 yards. Here Ben broke into him and after an exchange of fire the 109 made off North . . .

The Axis had no casualties in this clash,[7] but near Bologna two II° Gr.C. Gustavs ran into a dozen P-47s of the 64th FS, 57th FG. After a chase up and down the area's valleys: 'Lt Mannon saw his tracers striking the fuselage of one enemy aircraft that was blue-grey in colour with Italian markings and number 6 on the side and green smoke emitting from it . . .'

Although Mannon made no claim, M.llo Bolzoni (3ª Sq.), his Bf 109 afire, crashed to his death

minutes later (eyewitnesses said his aircraft exploded in mid-air seconds before crashing).

In mid afternoon a Kette of Bf 109s was scrambled by Stab/JG 77 to look for an 'English flying boat' reported on the water 20km north of Ravenna. Finding nothing[8], they reverted to a freelance patrol which proved uneventful. During the evening the Geschwader learned that it would be moving on to the airfields round Ghedi (BS) next day.

That evening Ju 88 5M+R came back to Bergamo (probably from Ravenna) and this may be connected with a round trip (Bergamo-Ravenna and back) made by 2.(F)/122's Ju 88, F6+ZK, with two men from that Staffel plus two of Westa 26 aboard. At 1930 Do 217 F3+CH of Verbindungsstaffel Ob.SW arrived in Florence from Munich.

Orders had been issued for night attack missions, the first to be launched at 1945, attacking southwest of Lake Trasimeno and south of Perugia at 2030. The second would leave at 2200 and attack the same areas 45min later, approaches and departures for both strikes following a direct course. Targets had been identified by 334. Inf. Div. in the Barbi (SI) area but at 1900 Kogen Mittelitalien signalled that these could not be attacked since the moonlight was not yet bright enough. Nonetheless, 20 to 25 sorties were put in against the Orvieto (TR)-Chiusi (SI) road and artillery batteries south of the latter town.

30 June 1944

At first light, advance parties from the various elements of JG 77 set off to make Bettola ready for the fighters due to move in that evening. II./JG 77 established itself on the main field and I. on the runway to the east. After an uneventful patrol over Bologna four aircraft of the Stab put down at the new base.

II./NJG 6 operated in Italy in June 1944, patrolling by night in the area around Rome to cover roads used in the German retreat but apparently scoring only one confirmed victory. This aircraft belonged to the unit but was lost three months earlier when it landed by mistake at Dübendorf, Switzerland. Bf 110G-4/B2, W.Nr.5547, 2Z+OP, was flown by Ofw. Treynogga of 6. Staffel who was interned for five weeks before being repatriated, to be killed in Italy on 5 June 1944 when his Bf 110G-4, W.Nr.720132, crashed at Gracciano (SI). (Creek)

Three I./JG 4 pilots were reported missing after combats about 50km southeast of Zagreb: Gefr. Rohlfs of 1. Staffel (W.Nr.26066, White 7) and from 3./4 Fw. Horn (W.Nr.163579, Yellow 8) and Fw. Schäfer (W.Nr.162760, Red 3). These losses do not obviously tie in with 12th USAAF claims over Hungary, nor an action between P-47s and 12 Bf 109s over Bologna at 0915, in which two of the latter were claimed destroyed for two Thunderbolts damaged. Over Lucca P-47s had an inconclusive encounter with 'four Fw 190s.'

At 1545, ten of II° Gr.C.'s Bf 109s took off on patrol and intercepted eight Spitfires from 232 Sqn near Bologna, attacking the first section but being forced on to the defensive by the second. Most of the Messerschmitts climbed away but two (both from 3ª Sq.) dived for the clouds, followed by W/Os Green and Tutill. The former hit the aeroplane of Serg. Stella, who force-landed in a dry river bed near the village of Budrio (BO), only to collide with a horse and cart, wounding himself and killing the animal and driver. Tutill saw one of his cannon shells explode aft of the other 109's cockpit before it dived away. In fact Ten. Mancini's aeroplane was so badly damaged that he, too, had to crash-land (safely this time) before he could reach Cascina Vaga.

M.llo Galetti's (3ª Sq.) claim of a Spitfire shot down is refuted by RAF records – all returned safely.

A curiosity of this action is the British report that '... one e/a appeared to have no markings on fuselage except a green and pink diamond', obviously a hazy vision of the Italian flag.

To add to the ANR's misfortunes, S.Ten. Marinucci of I° Gr.C. was also hurt in a training accident, and his G.55 destroyed.

During the evening, Spitfires of 237 Sqn unsuccessfully chased a Ju 88 and later a Westa 26 Ju 88T-1 (W.Nr.430910, 5M+D) went missing on a night reconnaissance to Ancona and the Tremiti Islands. This aeroplane may have fallen in what was rated at the time an inconclusive exchange of fire between an American Beaufighter VI and a Ju 88, ten miles southwest of Pianosa.

Capt William E. Larsen and 2/Lt. Joe F. Draper of the 417th NFS had taken off at 2120 for a freelance patrol with 'Bandbox' and were vectored on to a bandit 50 miles north. Descending to 200ft they got their first AI contact, at 2 to 3 miles, at 2323.

> Our own altitude was 200 feet and [the] bandit was below us. We followed him on a southerly course ... The moon was bright and at the range of about a mile and at altitude of 100 feet, I hit his 'prop-wash'. I still could not get a visual, even though he was going down the moonpath.
>
> At a range of 1500 feet, altitude 50-75 feet, I obtained a visual. I recognised the bandit instantaneously as a Ju 88 by the bulbuous nose and long fuselage aft of the wings ... As I was closing in, he turned east into the dark part of the sky and ... I took a quite long (3-4 seconds) burst with a 1 ring deflection. I did not observe any strikes and I lost my visual as soon as he was out of the moonpath. Upon his turning into the dark ... I was left in the moonpath & received return fire from him. All I could see at this time was red tracer from the muzzles of two guns ... None of the bullets hit my aircraft.'

The pursuit continued north/northeast for about ten minutes without obtaining another visual, then the German began to climb, reaching about 500ft according to Draper's AI. Larsen stayed at 100ft, planning to attack close-in from below, but:

> 'As soon as he reached 500ft, he "peeled-off" and disappeared off our tube into the ground scatter off the coast of Italy. We lost him, as did all ground stations ...'.

Three night harassment aircraft attacked traffic columns in the Buonconvento (SI)-Ombrone Bend area.

Notes

4. Bombers seem more likely, possibly KG 76.
5. Times are taken from American sources and are difficult to reconcile with German ones; nonetheless it is clear that both accounts describe the same combat.
6. Stab/NAGr.11 also reported a Ju W.34 destroyed by strafers on the 29th.
7. KTB of Stab/JG 77: 'Combat with 8 Spitfires east of RIMINI over sea ... at 4000m, without success or loss.'
8. However, Uffz. Scheer of 8./JG 53 was credited with a Catalina, his 13th victory, during June.

On a forward airfield a Ju 87D-5 of 1./NSGr.9 is serviced for the coming night's mission. The wave-mirror pattern of light brown (sand) over the standard camouflage was adopted by NSGr.9 following the arrival of its first Ju 87s. (Petrick)

Chapter 3

July 1944

The Ground War

Having registered dramatic progress in Italy, Allied forces began to be depleted in preparation for the planned invasion of Southern France, necessitating major redeployment and a halt in the advance, allowing the Germans to stand on the Pisa-Rimini line. Kesselring launched a major anti-partisan effort, ordering a savage programme of hostage taking and counter-terror from which he thoughtfully exempted Italian Fascist Party members. By the end of the month 337 'enemy' were dead and 1,438 prisoners had been taken[9]; 182 German captives had been set free.

Preparations for the landings also saw the move of MATAF HQ to Corsica and a reduction in the tactical air strength available for Italy. Even so, some major centres were gained, including Siena, Cecina (LI), Ancona and Arezzo, some of whose names will recur as a focus for aerial activity.

The Luftwaffe

Luftflotte 2's HQ was now at Salsomaggiore (PR) and Komm.Gen. Mittelitalien at Bagno a Ripoli (FI).

Fuel

On the 5th Luftflotte 2 prohibited with immediate effect all passenger, courier and transport flights within its sphere, even if they had war importance; II./TG 1's aircraft were to be flown only in exceptional circumstances. Next day a message from Göring was relayed, notifying 'deep inroads' into aviation fuel supplies.

Long-Range Reconnaissance

The organisation of these units took another step nearer rationalisation when 1.(F)/123 was withdrawn from Italy (to be disbanded during August) and 4.(F)/122 was brought in from Königsberg, East Prussia, in its place, having been preparing some weeks for the move. The newcomers were equipped with GM 1-boosted Ju 188s fitted with cameras. After a period at the start of the month when 2./122's Hptm. Weinand stood in for him, Major Pannwitz resumed command of the Gruppe's three Staffeln in Italy, all now based at Bergamo.

During late July and into early August (apparently with some inkling of what was in prospect in Southern France) attempts were made to obtain cover of the Sardinian harbours, including no fewer than 14 failed missions to La Maddalena (SS), defeated by fighter defences and mechanical troubles. These sorties demonstrated that daylight flying, even in boosted Ju 188s, was not feasible, and Pannwitz was among those killed. His place was taken by Obstlt. Ernst Domnick, who came from a staff posting and had limited operational experience. He started out with a speech to his new command on future aircraft production policy. The only offensive air weapons to be built from now on would be flying bombs; all other plants would concentrate on jet fighters; the Me 410 would go out of production and the experimental Me 510 would not be mass-produced. The Me 410 did cease to be built in September, and the strength of 2.(F)/122 dwindled along with the supply of these aircraft.

A new tack was tried in the Gruppe's electronic war during the summer when Luftflotte 2 ordered one of the FuG 200-equipped aeroplanes into action with a captured British IFF set on board. In bright moonlight near Elba the Junkers was approached by a Beaufighter which came within 100m before dipping its wings and flying away – to the great relief of the German crew, one imagines. During a second such operation, five nights later, the IFF carrier was shot down 20km northwest of Corsica and the ruse was abandoned. What FAGr.122 did not know was that MAAF Sigint now had 'fullest details of routes to be followed at least one hour before [reconnaissance] flights commence.'

Tactical Reconnaissance
At Florence, Stab and 2./NAGr.11 were the most southerly-based elements of the Luftwaffe in Italy. Along with 1./11 at Forlì they were positioned to give tactical coverage of the whole battle area and both coasts, although the Gruppe was still below strength, even after contraction to two Staffeln. By the end of July, Stab and 2./11 had moved to Poggio Renatico. The Gruppe's aircraft operating in pairs down the Adriatic Coast had numerous encounters with the Spitfire Mk.VIIIs of 241 Sqn during July, usually – but not always – coming off worst.

Night Attack
As the month began, 1./NSGr.9 was operating out of Ravenna and 2./NSGr.2 from Rimini, having newly moved into the line, while 2./9 was still at Caselle (well away from the front but in the heart of 'bandit country'), completing conversion to the Ju 87 but soon to be back in action. On the 3rd the Army was informed that during the moonlight period Ju 87s would be flying from the Forlì-Ravenna-Rimini area to attack Macerata, with Loreto (AN) as their alternative target. Officially, Stab/NSGr.9 was established on the 12th and 2./2 was renamed as 3./NSGr.9 at the same time. In practice the former measure had been in the works since the end of June, and there was a delay of two or three weeks before the latter took effect to the extent of painting new code letters on the aircraft.

This reorganisation did not go ahead entirely without trouble. On the 20th the Kommandant of Koflug 18/XI had to go to Caselle to follow up accusations by Maj. Frost that he was not getting proper support from Oblt. Heinert, the airfield Kommandant. Heinert was able to refute these allegations and after a further discussion with Frost the matter was closed. Unfortunately for Heinert, next afternoon his car broke down on the Caselle-San Maurizio road. He and his Italian interpreter were trying to push it when a Lancia stopped a short distance away. Four partisans emerged and ordered them and the Italian driver to put their hands up, but the Oblt. went for his pistol and was shot. Attacks such as this were a constant hazard in the Turin area.

A shot down prisoner told interrogators that the Gruppe did not operate on moonless nights but that multiple sorties were being flown at full moon. The aircraft were fitted with the FuG 101 radio altimeter and FuG 7A communications set, but radio silence was observed for fear of eavesdroppers. He said the Gruppe consisted of three Staffeln of nine aircraft each and that all were shortly due for transfer to Casabianca.

A few days later another crew gave more information. 1./NSGr.9 had, they said, 12 aircraft and crews. Replacement aeroplanes were brought by ferry pilots from München-Riem, crews came from the Replacement Training Unit at Stubendorf and both men and machines were in good supply. The aircraft were Ju 87D-3s and -5s with a cruising speed of about 240-250kph bombed up, and 280 kph without bombs. Losses were 'fairly severe' and 1./9 had lost six machines in the recent full moon period. The captured crew had made eight sorties in all, among them an attack on targets of opportunity in the area of Lake Trasimeno.

Operations were supposedly limited to a period seven days either side of the full moon, each crew making its own way to the target and attacking individually; tactical briefings were often given by the Ia, Major Frank Neubert. Bomb loads were frequently just one AB 500 cluster unit and had never gone above 1,000kg; bombs were dropped from 1,000m and flares had never been used. It was strictly forbidden to bring bombs back. A small airfield ten minutes' flying time west of Ravenna was given as an alternative landing ground if home base was unavailable.

Some of NSGr.9's men responded to Göring's call for volunteers to serve in the Reich Defence units, but at a conference between Gen.d.S. Hitschold and Luftwaffe Chief of Staff Koller it was noted that, as of 6 July, the Gruppe was 14 crews short of establishment. With 11 volunteer pilots due to depart for Germany as they spoke, a deficiency of 25 would result and this was insupportable if operational readiness was to be maintained. Since all 11 had special night-attack training, Lfl. 2 was strongly opposed their posting. Major Frost's lobbying of his superiors succeeded, and he told the men concerned that they should count themselves lucky, since a fighter pilot in Germany would have a short life expectancy. For NSGr.9's casualty rate that summer to seem preferable, the plight of the fighter arm must indeed have been grim.

The morale of NSGr.9 was reckoned very low by the interrogators, 'largely owing to the understandable desire of one and all to avoid any unpleasantness so near to the end . . .' A senior member of the Staffel, a Hauptmann, was said to confine his operational activity to switching the airfield lighting on and off. The Gruppe had never been seen 'at least by its own members, as anything else but an emergency solution to the problem of giving assistance to the German Army'. For their part, the Allies conceded that:

> The creation of this night harassing attack force was, although an emergency measure, not without a certain nuisance value when weather permitted, and acted favourably on the German morale at a time when all hope of audible and visible air support was nearing zero point.

As for what German troops themselves thought . . .

On the 23rd 278. Inf.Div. had urgently requested air support, and on the 29th XIV. Pz.Kps. had nominated five targets around Montopoli in Val d'Arno (PI) for attention, including artillery positions. Two days later Komm. Gen. Mittelitalien was obviously nettled by complaints that these last missions had not been flown, yet aircraft had been operating nightly in the Pontedera (PI) area, about 10km to the west. He replied that these sorties had been precluded in the last few days by the weather and that anyway target areas were decided according to navigational possibilities and the state of their defences. In operations since the 26th one quarter of the available aircraft and crews had already been lost[10]. Accordingly he was not mounting operations against single targets but had resorted to road patrols on a broad front to disperse the opposition.

There were, however, more positive exchanges with the ground troops, and in late July the Flivo of 15. PG Div. passed on information obtained from local civilians about the location of British XV Corps' HQ, with the suggestion that it would make a suitable target for the Gruppe.

Fighters

Early in July the Allies rather belatedly decided that, with the disappearance of callsign Altvater ('Patriarch'), III./JG 53 had left Italy. JG 77, newly pulled back to Ghedi and Bettola, found that in spite of a visit two weeks earlier by Steinhoff to spell out requirements, nothing had been done to construct the necessary blast pens for their Bf 109s. There were only six inadequately camouflaged boxes, of the wrong type and fit only to be pulled down right away. Operations were now to be flown under the control of Jafü Oberitalien, involving both Gruppen of JG 77 and II° Gr.C. using the Sirmione promontory on Lake Garda as assembly point. Despite the Geschwader's respect for the professional qualities of the Italian pilots, operations were still hamstrung by inadequate radio communications – a problem dating back at least to the battles over Sicily a year before and clearly still unsolved.

As early as 4 July the High Command had decided that a fighter Gruppe must be withdrawn from Italy and that it ought to be I./JG 4. It was to leave its aircraft behind and be re-equipped in the Reich. On the 10th an order was issued that both the JG 77 Gruppen and I./4 must hold 100 men in readiness to hand over 'for the establishment of new divisions'. Given that Stab, I. and II./77 were already 320 short of their establishment for technical personnel, this order would, in practice, entail disbandments. A conference of Kommandeure was convened on the 11th, and next day the order was rescinded, but the fighters were not yet out of the woods.

On the 7th Maltzahn had told Oberst Handrick of the High Command that his fighters were too few to tackle heavy bomber formations going to and from the Reich, and there was discussion about whether numbers were the main reason or whether bases were too far from the bombers' routes. On the 17th an emissary from Gen.d.J. Galland, Hptm. Schmoller, arrived in Milan to acquaint himself with the state of the Jagdgruppen in the Southern Theatre of Operations, including operational capabilities, manning and the need to equip a high altitude Gruppe for top-cover work. He flew back to Berlin on the 20th, and three days later an order came that I./JG 4 and I./JG 77 were to be transferred to Germany to be re-equipped, their existing aircraft being passed to II./JG 77 and II° Gr.C. Newer pilots in training with I./4 would also be sent on to II./77.

This meant that Stab/JG 77 was superfluous in Italy – a single German Gruppe could be commanded directly by the Jafü – and Steinhoff flew up to Berlin to confer on what it was to do next. It turned out that they were to go to Fels am Wagram in Austria, where Steinhoff would lead formations in defence of the Reich. On the 28th the Oberstleutnant was awarded the Oakleaves and Swords to his Knight's Cross.

Meanwhile, Maltzahn ordered that II./77 was not to go into action again until the inexperienced pilots were trained and even then it would no longer take

Maj. Günther Pannwitz (left) commanded FAGr.122 until his death in action on 21 July 1944; beside him is Oblt. Brinkmann, Kapitän of the Gruppe's 6. Staffel. (IWM)

on the heavy bombers. Instead it was to fly 'the most cautious freelance patrols possible'. What was more, it would not at present be possible to provide Bf 109s with the improved-performance DB 605 AS engine.

On the 25th, the date intended to mark the start of the withdrawal of I./4 and I./77 from operations, one pilot of the former unit defected to the Allies. He took with him documents confirming the presence of three fighter Gruppen in Northern Italy and revealing their callsigns; he also told of the plans for their movement away from Italy and for the use of men and aeroplanes to reinforce II./JG 77. All aircraft of JG 4 were, he said, armed with an MG 151/20 cannon and two MG 131 machine-guns, except two, one of which belonged to the Kommodore. These had one 3cm MK 108 with 60 shells. He claimed that some aircraft of JG 77 were equipped with three MK 108s, one firing through the propeller boss and one under each wing.

The difficulties caused by the German retreat are reflected in the story of this man's attempt to join his unit, beginning on 26 June, when he and 12 others were posted from 1./JGr. West (Ergänzungsgruppe) in Stargard to JG 53. The Geschwaderstab of this unit was supposed to be in Tricesimo (UD), but when the group arrived there on 29 June, they found that it had moved to Germany two days earlier.

The 13 novices were sent after them to Lippspringe, only to find that the Stab had moved again, this time to Baranovici (USSR). A signal was sent there asking for instructions for the new arrivals and orders came to post them to JG 77. On 7 July they were sent back to Italy with orders to report to JG 77 in Maniago. Arriving in Udine, they were told that Stab/JG 77 was now in Poggio Renatico. Once there, they learned that the whole Geschwader had moved to Bettola. The defector and some of his comrades finally caught up with their new unit on the 15th, and the others arrived singly or in pairs 2 to 4 days later; they had had to hitch-hike because continuous Allied bombing had disrupted transport.

In Bettola Steinhoff told them they would be assigned to I./JG 4 in Maniago, operating under JG 77's control. It turned out that only 1. and 3./JG 4 were operational; 2. Staffel had disbanded as they had no aircraft or pilots left and their ground echelons therefore serviced the remaining Staffeln. The new arrivals were divided between the two active Staffeln, each of which had seven Bf 109G-6s and one G-12 trainer. Most of the pilots were inexperienced newcomers without operational training. The PoW and his group spent ten days there, during which time only one operation was flown. Nine of the Gruppe took part, but did not meet the enemy.

On the 25th orders came from Maltzahn for JG 4 to move to Germany for reorganisation, and the new intake was to transfer to JG 77, joining one of the two Gruppen in Ghedi.

The ANR

Fighters

After a bad experience on 1 July, I° Gr.C., which had by now absorbed the disbanded Sq. Autonoma 'Montefusco-Bonet' into its ranks, left the increasingly unsafe base of Reggio Emilia the following day for Vicenza. The next few days were used to settle the unit in and to organise its services on the new airfield as well as training the new pilots received after the mid-June 'crisis' and giving the older ones more experience on the G.55. On one of these flights on 6 July, S.Ten. Cacciola was killed in a crash near Dolo (VE). On the 12th a group of pilots was detached to Thiene airfield, seven miles north of Vicenza, as a precaution in view of the limited dispersal facilities available at the main base.

The Gruppo was not to return to action until the 20th, when four more losses were sustained, and did not fly again in the two days after that. CO Magg. Arrabito having been killed on the 20th, command was given provisionally to Cap. Marchesi (3ª Sq.) pending the return of Magg. Visconti from his extended leave. Although not intensively engaged during July, I° Gruppo lost nine aircraft and six pilots in its five combats (as well as one man and his aircraft in training), a bad month by any standards.

By contrast, II° Gr.C. had one of its most active months, thanks to the Allied launch of Operations Mallory and Mallory Major, aimed at destroying all the bridges across the Po. After a combat on the 1st, the Gruppo transferred next day from Cascina Vaga to Villafranca di Verona (VR) and reported to the Jafü 'that the state of technical readiness of the Gruppe was not in any way up to present operational demands'.

Operations were nevertheless rejoined on the 5th and after this there was barely a day when sorties were not flown, although not all brought enemy contact. During this period the Gruppo began to employ the 'Occhio di Lince' (Lynx Eye) section of four aircraft as top cover for its main formation.

In the middle of the month Ten. Gianelli was relieved as CO of 3ª Sq. and replaced by Ten. Luccardi of 2ª Sq. The reasons for this are unclear, but misunderstandings between the former commander and pilots of his own and other Squadriglie may have been a factor. In the latter part of the month several Bf 109s were drawn from the delivery and maintenance centre at Vizzola Ticino (VA), whose slow but steady deliveries raised the unit's strength from 13(7) Bf 109s on the 20th to 26(17) on the 31st, despite five combat losses over the same period. In all during July the Gruppo had seen 15 combats, nine pilots killed in action and two baled out as well as a pilot and his aircraft lost in an accident.

Torpedo-Bombers

Gruppo Buscaglia was every bit as busy as the fighters. With around 20 aircraft ready for operations it was prepared to take on enemy vessels, not only in Italian waters but much further afield, off Greece and North Africa. After an Adriatic sally the unit sent aeroplanes to Greece and the survivors were back in Italy by the 14th. The Gruppo then spent a few days on the ground at Lonate Pozzolo, recuperating and preparing for a second tour of duty in the Eastern Mediterranean. Overall strength fell off both due to combat losses and to strafing of their base. Five S.79s were destroyed in this way on the 29th for example.

The Bf 109G-6, W.Nr.160756, in which Uffz. René Darbois defected on 25 July 1944. Although we are unable to see if the 'Yellow 4' (covered by a tarpaulin) was partly obliterated like the other markings, reports on this aircraft attest to the green and brown camouflage adopted in Italy by I./JG 4. This aircraft is now in the National Air and Space Museum, Washington DC.

Order of Battle

ANR unit strengths in early July were as follows:

Unit	Aircraft	
	Number	**Type**
Gr. Buscaglia	28(20)	S.79 [10 July]
Iº Gr.C.	32(10)	C.205 & G.55 [2 July]
IIº Gr.C.	26(16)	Bf 109G-6/G-12 [2 July]
Sq.Aut. Bomb.to	14(0)	Cant Z.1007 [10 July]

Luftflotte 2 units on 30 June had:

Unit	Aircraft	
	Number	**Type**
Stab/FAGr.122	0(0)	
2.(F)/122	3(3)	Me 410A-3/B-3
	1(1)	Ju 88D-1
	1(1)	Fi 156
4.(F)/122	8(?)	Ju 188D-2 [not yet in Italy]
6.(F)/122	4(2)	Ju 188D-2
	2(1)	Ju 88A-4
1.(F)/123	5(4)	Ju 88/Ju 188
Kdo. Carmen	2/3	Ju 88/Ju 188
Stab/NAGr.11	0(0)	
1./NAGr.11	5(?)	Bf 109G-6/U3
	4(?)	Bf 109G-8/U3
2./NAGr.11	1(?)	Bf 109G-5/ U2/R2
	6(?)	Bf 109G-6 & G-6/U3
	1(?)	Bf 109G-8/R5
1./NSGr.9	22(14)	Ju 87D
2./NSGr.9	22(11)	Ju 87D
2./NSGr.2	14(2)	Ju 87D
L. Beo. St. 7	3(3)	Ju 88 [on 10 July]
I./JG 4	14(5)	Bf 109G-6 [on 2 July]
Stab JG 77	6(6)	Bf 109G-6
I./JG 77	23(10)	Bf 109G-6
II./JG 77	34(21)	Bf 109G-6
II./TG 1	46(36)	S.82
Jafü Oberitalien	1(?)	Bf 109G-6

Notes

9. Civilians suffered heavily too; in the village of Marzabotto (BO), for instance, 1836 people were slaughtered by the SS.
10. A postwar British source suggests that some of these casualties were made good by drafting in replacements from the Balkans.

Two S.79s of Gr. 'Buscaglia' at Lonate Pozzolo. 'B1-09' in the foreground carries the definitive camouflage for night operations consisting of dark green overall, grey numbers and obscured markings. The S.79 behind (an older IIª Serie version) still retains earlier styles of camouflage and markings.

Chapter 3

Operations

1 July 1944

From 0815, I. and II./SG 4 began to leave Italy, 32 Fw 190s quitting Levaldigi and 34 Airasca, en route for München-Riem. A few stragglers followed on next day.

That Reggio Emilia was a risky airfield was amply demonstrated at 1115, when six C.205s and five G.55s of I° Gr.C. that had just scrambled were attacked eight miles to the south by 11 P-47s of the 66th FS, 57th FG. As Lt. Richard L. Johnson recounts:

> I said, "Jackpot Squadron break right" [and] we did except for Jansen's left side flight of four . . . We were instantly at it. The enemy aircraft reacted like a covey of frightened birds. A sort of disorganised mêlée followed. I shot one almost instantly [and] with no hesitation hit two more . . .

The P-47s first went for the four Macchis on top-cover patrol and shot down two, killing S.M. Boscaro (2ª Sq.). S.Ten. Pezzi managed, although wounded, to crash land his machine with 80 per cent damage. The next Italian aeroplane to go down was the G.55 of 3ª Sq.'s CO, Cap. Torresi, killing him on his first day in command. From the same unit, M.llo Spazzoli baled out wounded. The last to fall was the C.205 of Ten. Beretta who parachuted safely.

The Italians claimed two enemy aircraft shot down but the Americans suffered just one Cat. 1 damage and two Cat. 2. 66th FS's claims showed similar optimism: six destroyed (two by Lt. Cleveland, the others by Lts. Bettinger, Johnson, Davis and Rahn) and two damaged (both by Johnson). Even these dubious figures illustrate the Italians' problems holding their own in a dogfight. The Americans identified their opponents as 'clipped-wing Bf 109s' but Johnson had been keenly interested in aircraft since childhood and '. . . I knew they were no 109s, I said G.55s. No one except for myself and one other . . . had ever even heard of them.'

Twelve II° Gr.C. Bf 109s scrambled late in the morning to patrol as far south as Bologna, intercepting 11 P-47s of the 85th FG that were bombing a railway bridge. Four of the Messerschmitts dived on the USAAF aircraft and the Italians claimed one victory and the Americans two damaged. In fact no P-47 was lost, but Cap. Mancini's Bf 109G-6/R6 '<I' crashed, killing him at 1155 near Minerbio, southeast of Bologna. North of that city Fw. Lang of 2./77 was wounded while flying a liaison Saiman 202 (MM.52204, Red 1). I./JG 77 reported an aircraft missing and this may have been the Bf 109 claimed by 57th FG.

Night sorties totalled 33. All but five were attacks on road traffic and artillery positions west and southeast of Lake Trasimeno including the Tiber Valley from Bastia to Piccione. 2./NSGr.2 deployed D3+AK, +DK, +EK and +QK from Caselle to Rimini during the evening and 2./9 had a Ju 87D-3 (W.Nr.1244) crash at Forlì, Ogefr. Büttner and Uffz. Pendel being killed. On a photo mission to Naples a 1.(F)/123 Ju 88T-1 (W.Nr.430050, 4U+MH; callsign GM+CI) came down at 2330 at San Martino (Lugo-RA) and burned out. The pilot, Ofw. Strehl, and his three comrades all died.

2 July 1944

I° Gr.C. made its overdue change of base, 11 C.205s and eight G.55s transferring from Reggio Emilia to

Vicenza during the afternoon. Seven more Macchis made the trip next morning, and the wisdom of this move was shown that afternoon, when a strafing attack on Reggio accounted for just one Saiman liaison aircraft. II° Gr.C. also transferred, 20 of its aircraft leaving Cascina Vaga from 1420 onward, heading for Villafranca. One of the Bf 109s on this flight was the first G-12 trainer conversion (W.Nr.19319, CJ+MG), dating from 1942.

Thirty-eight fighters (presumably German) flew a freelance patrol south of Bologna, leading to an inconclusive encounter with 601 Sqn in the Faenza area, and an anti-Partisan mission was undertaken by two He 111s and five Fi 156s. At 2020 the Spitfires of Plt Off White and Flt Lt Michie (241 Sqn) scrambled from Fermo and met a Rotte of yellow-spinnered Bf 109s on the deck off Ancona, 14 minutes later.

> Michie was first on the scene, White's engine having given trouble, and turned to attack but the starboard German got on his tail and began firing with zero deflection. After two full turns the 109 rolled out and flew toward Ancona, fired on by Michie at long range but escaping into the haze. White had by now arrived and chased the other Messerschmitt which had not stayed to assist its companion and obtained hits on its tail as it went flat out, doing violent evasive action and trailing black smoke. He broke off the chase when his ammunition ran out.

II./TG 1 entered the reconnaissance business when Oblt. Lankenau took S.82 1Z+HN out looking for partisans round Vergiate (VA). After low-flying aircraft had been fired on, the unit had installed two underwing 20mm cannon on one of their transports, outside the propeller arcs, intending revenge on the guerrillas, but this initiative produced no action.

A Ju 88A-4 (W.Nr. 550435, 5M+G) of 6.(F)/122 was lost on night reconnaissance to Ancona and the Tremiti Islands, Ltn. Werner Scheibel and his three crew being posted missing. They were probably shot down by Sqn Ldr Patten and Sgt. Blundell's Beaufighter (255 Sqn). The night of 2/3 July saw 25 attack sorties against traffic around Cecina and west of Lake Trasimeno.

3 July 1944

Twenty-seven JG 77 aeroplanes set off on patrol but Ofw. Klein (Stab/77) aborted with engine trouble. At 1125, between Bologna and Ferrara, they found Mitchells escorted by Spitfires from 237 and 238 Sqns Sqn Ldr Archie Wilson of 238 logged: 'Fighter sweep and area cover to B-25 bombing Ferrara. 20+ 109s up high but they wouldn't play & beat it. [Fg Off] Dinks Moubray of 237 bounced a sucker (Me 109) and shot it down'.

Or as JG 77's KTB put it:

> Contact in [map square] SC. 20 medium bombers at 6,000m with 20 Spitfires as escort at 6-9,000m. Combat with escort. Within two minutes the Spitfires had made a full turn from 6,000-9,000m [and got] behind our own planes. Provision of AS engines is becoming ever more urgent.

Moubray's victim was probably a Bf 109 of 2./JG 77 (W.Nr.162294, Red 4), whose pilot, Ltn. Kolb, baled out wounded near Legnago (VR).

Reportedly, two Fw 190s attacked Allied units at Pontelagoscuro (FE) and after dark 32 Ju 87 sorties were sent against logistics in the Loreto-Macerata area. 1./NSGr.9's E8+VH caught fire during start-up at 2150; the flames could not be extinguished and its bombload exploded an hour later, destroying the aeroplane. At almost the same time a Ju 87 was shot down northeast of Lake Trasimeno by the Beaufighter of W/O Ewing and Flt Sgt Chenery (600 Sqn). At 0030 this crew claimed another destroyed plus one damaged. The lost aircraft were Ju 87D-5s from 2./NSGr.9: W.Nr.141010 (Uffz. Kapahnke and Gefr. Happe killed) and 140994 (Uffz. Jägers killed).

4-5 July 1944

At 0235 a night fighter of the 417th NFS exchanged shots with a Ju 88 about three miles southeast of Gorgona Island (LI) but without result. Eight freelance fighter sorties were flown in the Ravenna area. Later, two Ju 87s deployed from Caselle to Rimini; 2./NSGr.9's Junkers E8+BK, +HK and +OK moved up to Forlì and 3./9 bombed Loreto.

2.(F)/122's last Ju 88 (F6+ZK) was flown to Riem early on the 5th. From midday four Bf 109s of Stab/JG 77 flew a freelance patrol south of Bologna and across to the Adriatic, clashing with 'eight Thunderbolts' in the vicinity of Forlì. No success was claimed, but DAF recorded that four e/a from a 32-strong group had attacked and damaged a Kittyhawk between Forlì and Cesenatico (FO). The coincidence of numbers and location suggests this was the same incident.

Also at noon a joint mission was flown, involving I. and II./JG 77 from Ghedi and 16 aircraft of II° Gr.C. from Villafranca, using Sirmione on Lake Garda as their RV. Action apparently resulted, as 5./77's Uffz. Schemel (Bf 109 W.Nr.162560) is listed as wounded in combat and parachuting south of Pieve (BS). Lacking radio communication, the German and Italian units could not reassemble.

Six hours later, eight II° Gr. aeroplanes intercepted B-25s of 340th BG bombing a bridge at Ostiglia (MN), the Americans claiming that the fighters 'engaged aggressively by firing rockets'. The Italians' attacks led two of the bombers to crash-land at their base while the B-25 gunners claimed one Bf 109 probably destroyed. The Spitfires of 232 Sqn on an area sweep to cover the bombers, intervened after a few minutes against what they saw as 'Me-109s and Fw-190s'. A dogfight ensued in the Modena area, W/O McCann claiming damage to a Bf 109 'with Italian Fascist markings on the wing' while W/O Armstrong and Flt Sgt Rimes shared in the shooting down of an 'Fw 190' in German markings. II° Gr.C. lost Ten. Palermi (2ª Sq.) and M.llo Secchi (3ª Sq.) killed.

War Correspondent Wilhelm Zimmermann describes some of NSGr.9's 70 sorties to Loreto and Porto Recanati (MC):

> ... where numerous enemy HQs have ensconced themselves immediately behind the front ... the road running by the town ... is used by the enemy as a supply route to the front ... Uffz. Waissnor wants to attack the town from the east so the [moon]light ... will reveal all the details of the countryside below him. Then suddenly he ducks beneath a cloud layer. "What a silhouette my "Marie Heinrich" [E8+MH] must make on that" he thinks. That would be something for the nightfighters. Quickly he turns away to approach from the south-west. Enemy AA nearly had him, its lines of tracer pass right and left of the machine like red pearls. Through the [ventral] window he recognises the streets and houses of the town ... As he sees a rewarding target ... he throttles back ... waits a few moments more until it comes into his sight and pulls into a dive. The AA fires like mad. Waissnor doesn't let that bother him. As the plane pulls out he sees his bombs have hit. Dark red flames are climbing from the rapidly spreading inferno.
>
> Uffz. Schwobe in "Anton Heinrich" goes in again after the bombs have dropped ... after an AA emplacement that has been putting up a dense curtain of fire round the town. As he dives on it, cannons firing, it goes silent: the gunners prefer to take cover! ... He pulls out over the sea, again coming under fire. It must be from torpedo boats whose wakes show as dark streaks in the water ... He fires recognition flares but the boats don't cease fire – it's the enemy! ... [He] dives on [them] and fires until out of ammunition ...
>
> Landing at base, Schwobe meets Fw. Pieper. This 38 year-old ... was just a hair's breadth from not coming back. As he dived ... on his target ... AA fastened on to him [scoring] several hits on the fuselage [of] his "Caesar Heinrich." Although ... his cockpit glazing was sprayed with oil, [he] brought his Ju 87 safely home.
>
> ... the serviceable aircraft are loaded up again and once more are off against the enemy. Fw. Stuber ... dives his "Heinrich Heinrich" on a column of vehicles ... fires and explosions show he has obtained good hits. [Then] he sees a huge fireball ... disappear behind the hill the town stands on. Has a comrade been shot down? The flames that shoot up after impact settle the matter ... Oblt. Begemann and his gunner have sealed their mission with death."

The engine of his Ju 87D-5 (W.Nr.140999, E8+OH) had been hit but in fact Rolf Begemann parachuted into captivity. His gunner, Uffz. Hermann Lehr, also jumped but his fate is unknown.

6 July 1944

On the evening of the 5th, eight of Gr. 'Buscaglia's' S.79s (B2-02, -03, -05, -08, -09, -10, -11 and -12) had taken off from Lonate, coming down at Treviso at 2050, B2-11 being damaged during landing. At 0010, minus B2-02 and -03 which had engine trouble, the five serviceable aircraft set off on a route parallel to the Dalmatian coast before turning towards their target, Bari.

The first Savoia ran in at 0245, but its torpedo failed to drop and it only succeeded in alerting the AA defences. The guns damaged the second attacker (B2-10) and forced it to break away, and it ditched off Ancona at 0420. Two others reported success: Ten. Ruggeri (B2-12) claimed a ship sunk and Ten. Perina (B2-09) a destroyer hit, the loss of an 8,000-ton merchantman and damage to another.

Thirty-one fighter sorties were sent up, and if the day was inconclusive for the ANR (a clash south of Bologna between a four-strong patrol from II° Gr.C. and Allied aircraft brought no result) this was not so for the Luftwaffe. At about 0930 JG 77 scrambled against 60 B-17s in the Verona/Vicenza area,

Vicenza, July 1944. At dispersal in one of the cornfields round the base, this C.205 of 2ª Sq., I° Gr.C. shows variations to markings that had appeared by summer. Not only is the white fuselage band missing but the absence of the "Angry Wasp" nose insignia is unusual.

proceeding without their Kommodore who had landed with droptank problems. His wingman, Gottfried Fährmann, followed him 45min later.

At 1050 the Boeings were sighted at 7,000m. During the run-in two Bf 109s of II./77 collided[11] and the Germans got the impression they were under attack. The Messerschmitts went into a hard dive, fragmenting their formation, but there were Mustangs beneath the bombers.

Ofw. Günter Klein (W.Nr.162395, <A) and Uffz. Hansch, both of Stab/77, were attacked by five escorts southwest of Verona, the fight drawing them down from 3,000m to the deck. Although Hansch shot down one of the P-51s, both German aeroplanes were hit and their pilots had to bale out. Hansch was unhurt, but Klein became caught up on his 109's tail and was killed. Wounded in action was 2./77's Fhj.Fw. Herbert Abendroth (W.Nr.161111, Red 7) who parachuted west of Verona.

Cr.42s E8+WK, +DK, +RK, +OK and +FK (probably no longer operational) landed at Ghedi around noon from Caselle while six Fw 190s left Bergamo for Riem about the same time. After dark, 44 attack sorties were mounted against Allied traffic near Loreto and 255 Sqn's Beaufighters claimed 4-0-1 Ju 87s round Ancona. German records give the same total but with 1-0-1 attributed to AA fire. The victors were Fg Off Bretherton and Fg Off Johnson (three: all seen to crash); Sqn Ldr McLaren and Fg Off Tozer (one: crashed in the sea, two parachutes seen); and Flt Sgt Griffiths and Flt Sgt Kimberley (one: diving headlong but not seen to crash).

This last aircraft was probably that of Ofw. Wilhem Böwing, as his gunner for that mission, Johannes Nawroth relates:

. . . an ammunition depot had been hit and it was an intoxicating sight. . . the way everything kept exploding. . . and then it happened: an English nightfighter opened fire . . . the pilot said the controls were hit and he could no longer hold the Ju. We dived, then. . . recovered and then another dive. Suddenly the Ju was flying straight and by this time we were at 300m. at most. As the pilot kept telling me to jump, I did so from low level. I struck my hip on the stabiliser, turned myself round and pulled the ripcord and . . . I was soon on the ground. However the pilot had been able to fly the Ju 87 back to Rimini . . . In the early morning I was transported to a casualty clearing station, then to hospital in Forlì and after that by hospital ship from Cesenatico (FO) to Venice and from there to Merano (BZ).

Known NSGr.9 casualties were both listed as shot down by Beaufighters: 2. Staffel lost the D-3 of Uffze. Erich Ackermann and Hermann Kasper (W.Nr.100355) and that of Ltn. Fritz Itzstein and Gefr. Wilhelm Rumholz (W.Nr.100382, E8+NK). The latter were both wounded and apparently bellylanded their aircraft at Falconara, where it was later found by the Allies.

7 July 1944

A Ju 88 was shot down by a Beaufighter of 600 Sqn, 15 miles northwest of Elba, with wreckage seen in the sea. This may have been a 6.(F)/122 aircraft (W.Nr.301500, 5M+R) that disappeared, having set out on the 6th for a reconnaissance of the west coast down to Naples and taking in eastern Corsica. Ofw.

Emil Braitsch and three others aboard were posted missing.

At 0320, a 417th NFS aircraft met a bandit at 50-100ft over the sea and flying through the moonpath. There was a 220mph chase with intense fire from the German, who escaped. A Bf 109 damaged by fighters was reported by 2./NAGr.11, and this may have been in the encounter between a pair of 109s and A-36s of the 86th FBG over Ferrara airfield, the Americans claiming a Messerschmitt destroyed.

In all, 70 fighters were sent up. At 1010, on freelance patrol from south of Bologna to the east coast, three Bf 109s of Stab/JG 77 attacked a Lightning 25km west of Rimini at 8,500m but it outclimbed them. II° Gr.C. lost Serg. Saletti, shot down and killed when 13 Bf 109s attacked 'Bostons' escorted by P-47s, but could claim no compensatory success.

Amongst 19 Ju 87s operating (some flew double sorties) were five of 2./NSGr.2 deployed to Florence, and in the course of prolonged bombing at Umbertide (PG) 56 casualties were suffered by Allied troops. Another target was traffic on the Monteriggioni-Siena road. A Ju 87D-5 of 1./NSGr.9 (W.Nr.141029, E8+HH) was shot down by a 255 Sqn Beaufighter (Fg Off Reynolds and Plt Off Wingham) 15km south of Ancona. Uffz. Erwin Mokrus and Gefr. Hans Wagner were posted missing, and a second aircraft reportedly failed to return.

8 July 1944

Reynolds and Wingham scored again in the same area, shooting down Ju 87D-3 W.Nr.1266 of 2./NSGr.9, with the deaths of Ogefre. Fritz von Bork and Ulrich Tröster. At 0217, north of Lake Trasimeno, Fg Offs Jefferey and Brewer of 600 Sqn claimed destruction of a Ju 87 which may have been a D-5 of 2./9 (W.Nr.141722), shot down with radio operator Uffz. Artur Ballok wounded. At 0210 a 417th NFS Beau chased a hostile to Livorno harbour but its shots brought no result.

The success of Cap. Marini's unit at Bari led the torpedo Group's command to deploy aircraft to Greece to attack Allied convoys in the Aegean. At 0545 on the 7th ten (two each from 1ª and 2ª Sq. and six from 3ª) set off, initially, for Belgrade. B2-02 and B3-09 aborted and put down at Villafranca but the others reached their destination. At 0700 on the 8th the eight S.79s left Yugoslavia, arriving at Salonika at 0850. Two were damaged landing in a strong crosswind, but were repaired, and at 1800 seven Savoias flew the last leg of their journey to Eleusis, B1-02 having had starter motor trouble.

Thirty Bf 109s of JG 77 deployed to Tulln/Vienna, scrambled from there and landed in Erding – three countries in one morning. Inexperience among groundcrews delayed take off, an encounter with P-38s forced premature jettisoning of droptanks and contact was not made with the heavy bombers. There were no losses, however. At 0942, II° Gr.C. sent off nine Gustavs from Villafranca on what proved an uneventful two-hour sortie. At Savigliano (CN) Hptm. Hans-Horst Graf of 4./SG 4 was killed on a ferry flight in Fw 190F-8, W.Nr.930850.

That evening, west of Piombino, Spitfires chased – but could not catch – an 'Me 210', in all probability Me 410 F6+IK of 2.(F)/122, in which Schiffels and Weber flew the Staffel's only mission of the day. At last light 244 and 7 SAAF Wings' Spitfires were dispatched in the hope of catching 'Stukas' being moved from their dispersals at Rimini, Ravenna and Forlì. 1 Sqn (SAAF) made two runs over Forlì, and saw nothing, but in shooting up Rimini 244 Wing claimed an aircraft destroyed, its type unascertainable in the gathering darkness. This did not prevent 17 Ju 87s operating in the same areas as the night before.

9 July 1944

Early in the morning 24 of JG 77's Bf 109s deployed to Tulln but the American bombers went to the Balkans, not the Reich, so the Messerschmitts soon returned to their Italian airfields. There were many landings away from base in deteriorating weather, and two I./77 machines were damaged. Uffz. Ernst Goosmann of 5. Staffel (W.Nr.161189, Black 3) crashed at Zell-am-See, Austria, and died next day of his injuries.

Late in the afternoon Gr. 'Buscaglia' got reports of a large convoy heading towards Sicily, and it was estimated that by midnight an attack would be possible.

10 July 1944

At 0005 seven S.79s (B1-00 and -02; B2-03; B3-03, -04, -05 and -11) rose from Eleusis and MAAF Sigint reported: '... 4 S.79s on radar 40/50 miles N. Cyrene, but they didn't find what they were looking for. From 0218 to 0231 heard them homing on Athens.' In fact, while B1-00, B1-02 and B3-11 dropped their torpedoes unsuccessfully against other shipping, Ten. Morselli (B3-03) did find the convoy but a defective release precluded a hit.

At 1625, 11 Bf 109s scrambled on II° Gr.C.'s second mission of the day, meeting 36 B-26s of 320th BG and 12 Spitfires of 154 Sqn south of Modena 50min later. The bombers had just raided the bridge at Marzabotto (BO), and their escorts were able to ward off the '15+ Bf 109s and Fw 190s'. One flight engaged the Italians, Flt Lt Boyle and Fg Off Cooper claiming damage to two and one respectively. ANR claims of damage to two 'Bostons' and two Spitfires were somehow transformed into 1ª Sq.'s Ten Valenzano and S.M. Cavagliano each being credited with a fighter shot down. In reality 154 Sqn suffered no losses.

At 1530 orders were given for night attacks from Ravenna, Rimini and Forlì against several targets, but only eight sorties ensued. Three Ju 87s of 1./NSGr.9 took off from Ravenna around 2200 to attack motor transport near Siena; their alternate target was M/T on the Ancona-Loreto coast road. They made a refuelling stop at Forlì and each aircraft was loaded with one AB 500 and two AB 250 cluster bomb units. At midnight, joined by two aeroplanes from 2. Staffel, they left Forlì, planning to attack at one minute intervals.

The Ju 87D-5 of Obfhr. Klaus Wolff-Rothermel and Gefr. Hans Lankes (E8+GH, W.Nr.141025) failed to find the primary target and so made for Loreto. Their compass became u/s and, unable to locate their secondary objective, the pilot jettisoned his bombs into the sea. He then set course for home, inland and parallel to the coast. At 0230 and around 25 miles north of Ancona E8+GH was attacked by a Beaufighter which damaged its engine, causing the two Germans to bale out and fall into Allied captivity. The fighter was probably that of McLaren and Tozer (255 Sqn), who shot down a Ju 87 near Ancona, watching it explode and burn on the ground.

11 July 1944

At 0142 Sqn Ldr Jim Bailey and Flt Sgt Wint of 600 Sqn claimed a Ju 87 northwest of Lake Trasimeno, but there are no details from the German side.

At 0930 nine II° Gr.C. Bf 109s took off from Villafranca, while from Ghedi a patrol of six I./JG 77 Messerschmitts also scrambled. The Italians were led by Magg. Miani, and one section by Cap. Mario Bellagambi. Meanwhile, a formation of French B-26 Marauders of 31^e Escadre de Bombardement (six from GB I/19 'Gascogne' and the rest from GB II/20 'Bretagne') escorted by 12 Spitfires of 238 Sqn RAF, was heading for a fuel depot in Piacenza.

At 1105, during the bomb-run, the Spitfire escort noticed: '... enemy aircraft flying in pairs but in two distinct gaggles on South Easterly course 10-15 miles away at 20-21,000ft, identified as Me-109s'...

The Italian and German fighters manoeuvred to a position astern of the bombers and Flt Lt Small, escort leader, ordered his Blue Section (on top cover) to jettison their fuel tanks and attack the first group of bandits. Two JG 77 Messerschmitts broke away and climbed, closely followed up to 7,500m by Blue Two (Lt. van Rensburg) who fired short bursts, observing something drop off near the port wing root of the rear aircraft. The Bf 109 (W.Nr.163189, <) flown by Uffz. Richard Kurtz of 4./77, continued climbing for a few seconds then went into a spin, disappearing into the layer of clouds below, its wounded pilot finally managing to recover from the dive and crash land near Isola Dovarese (CR). This was the second time the unfortunate Kurtz had been wounded in just over a month.

The second climbing Messerschmitt, flown by Fw. Albert Ullrich (6./77), was attacked by Blue One (Fg Off Simmonds) who fired two short bursts, hitting the Bf 109, Fg Off Johnson observing moments later an aircraft spinning down in flames and a parachute open above it. The German pilot reached ground safely in the Mantua area. The other Blue Section Spitfires, followed by those of Red section, attacked the rest of the enemy formation when all but two of the Bf 109s pulled out, disappearing in pairs.

The two Bf 109s that had slipped through the escort were those of Cap. Bellagambi and his wingman, Serg. Talin, attacking the last 'Bretagne' flight. The guns of the two 'Diavoli Rossi' aeroplanes were aimed at Marauders '37' and '34' respectively and their fire was accurate.

Bellagambi's cannon shells were lethal, not only hitting the starboard engine of '37' but also killing co-pilot Adjt. Despinoy, whose body blocked the passage to the nose section. S.Lt. Atger, the bombardier, found himself trapped in the nose compartment, while the pilot, Lt. Cornet, unable to do anything, kept on flying the dying bomber, ordering the rest of his crew to bale out. Only four jumped from the burning Marauder however.

Serg. Talin hit the rudder of Col. Hentges' B-26 '34' while the Spitfires tried, after their initial surprise, to pursue the Italians: Red One, Red Three (Plt Off Forrest) and Green Three (W/O Taylor) fired several bursts without result. Thirteen of the 16 Marauders bombed the target, and after a wide turn headed home, closely followed by the regrouped escort.

One of the very rare photos showing G.55s of I° Gruppo Caccia. Coming both from Sq. 'Montefusco-Bonet' and II° Gr.C., these aircraft were incorporated into 1ª and 3ª Sq. as a stop-gap, pending a planned re-equipment with the Bf 109 that in fact materialized only six months later.

The Italian and German Messerschmitts left the area, protected by the clouds, and the four I./JG 77 Gustavs landed at Ghedi. The nine from II° Gr.C. were over Villafranca at 1120, touching down one after another and heading for their camouflaged revetements, scattered over the surrounding fields. In the French formation '34' was forced to slow down, losing contact with the others but escorted well into friendly airspace by the Spitfires. The British fighters landed on the Ste Catherine strip at 1205, the Marauder's rudder lasted long enough for it to reach Villacidro and land safely.

12 July 1944

Responding to a report of a convoy near the African coast, five S.79s (B1-00, B3-02, B3-03, B3-04 and B3-05) took off at 0025, but adverse weather in the target area meant that the convoy was not located and only Magg. Marini (B1-00) torpedoed a cargo vessel, claiming it probably sunk. On the return route and short of fuel, Cap. Chinca (B3-04) and Ten. Monaco (B3-02) had to ditch, both crews being rescued by a German seaplane a few hours later.

In view of these losses, the six surviving Sparvieri left for Belgrade by way of Salonika, in nightmarish weather. Four flew on but two turned back for Salonika, not getting back to Lonate until 1700 on the 14th, the others having reached home at 0950 the previous day.

The 340th BG's B-25s (36-strong), after attempting to raid a target in Ferrara, were intercepted in the Comacchio (FE) area by ten II° Gr.C. fighters with others from JG 77 (and perhaps JG 4: 59 were up altogether). Before battle was joined, Ten. Fissore of 1ª Sq. was seen to dive in his undamaged aeroplane into the Adriatic. It was believed his oxygen had failed. The Italians claimed two 'Bostons' shot down, though their HQ communiqué spoke only of three damaged. In fact the Americans lost none but I./JG 77 had a Bf 109 damaged in combat and Fw. Ullrich (W.Nr.441320) of 6./77 was wounded.

That afternoon four of II° Gruppo's Bf 109s made a single pass on some French P-47s and M.llo Desideri (3ª Sq.) was mistakenly credited with a victory. Uffz. Ewald Schummer of 5./JG 77 achieved something more solid by forcing down an intact B-24. Hit by flak on an 8th AF mission to Munich, it was making for Allied-occupied Italy with a dead crewman aboard. II./JG 77 was assembling over Ghedi for an operation when Schummer spotted the Liberator, whose pilot, recognising his hopeless position, was persuaded to land. The bomber was parked in one of the big blast pens of Ghedi's southeastern dispersal area, but MAAF soon knew its whereabouts.

13 July 1944

Five II° Gr.C. Messerschmitts and 22 from JG 77, took off at 0935 to intercept the customary raiding formation of B-26s and P-47s. The ANR pilots claimed damage to four of the 86th FS, 79th FG, escorts. The latter claimed to have shot down an Fw 190, more probably a Bf 109 of Stab/77.

On the 8th Ltn. Dragou Ratkovicic and his NCO air-gunner (both of 1./Kroat. KG 1) had taken off from Zagreb to exchange their Do 17 for a more serviceable one belonging to 7. Staffel in Sarajevo. There they met four other airmen and all judged it the right time to decamp to the Allies. Since the new aeroplane was not ready and the weather unfavourable they had to wait five days to make their escape. At 1400 on the 13th the six took off for Bari in Do 17Z '0309' and belly-landed in a field near Alberobello (BA), handing themselves over to Yugoslav naval authorities.

Fw. Albert of 6./JG 77 poses beside the cockpit of his 'Yellow 6' in a lull between two scrambles. Although of poor quality, this photo is interesting both because it is one of the few available of JG 77 in Italy in 1944 and because it shows the name 'Betty' painted on the side panel.
(via Roba)

14 July 1944

There was a major – and confused – fighter action between Reggio Emilia and Modena. Twenty-five Bf 109s of JG 77, plus 12 of II° Gr.C., scrambled against 15th AF B-24s but after take-off were vectored instead against a formation of twin-engined aircraft. The B-25s of 340th BG were en route to a bridge at Corbola (RO) when JG 77 hit them, and as the Stab's KTB tells it:

> 1035: At 4000m in RB3-SB9 contact with around 48 Mitchells and Spitfire escort. Two Mitchells were shot up effectively by Oblt. Steinhoff and Uffz. Hansch. Because Fhj.Fw. Fährmann was badly hit during the attack and had to bale out, the probable crash of the two Mitchells could not be observed. Fw. Fährmann came back unhurt. The Kommodore's Bf 109 likewise had such severe hits that it had to be sent to the factory.

Apart from these casualties Oblt. Kurt Hammel, 1./JG 77's Kapitän, was shot down and wounded by Spitfires at Carpi (MO), his Bf 109 (W.Nr.163175, White 8) being 25 per cent damaged.

As the Mitchells completed their bomb-run, II° Gr.C. joined in and Ten. Drago (1ª Sq.) and Serg. Talin (2ª) claimed one each, though none was in fact lost. However, four Spitfires of 232 Sqn, diverted from another escort mission, caught the Italians east of Parma at about the same time as a section of 325th FG P-51s arrived on the scene (the latter from escorting the B-24s that originally provoked the German scramble). The Italians had barely escaped the Spitfires (W/O McCann claiming a 109 damaged) when they came into the Americans' sights. Major Caple damaged one Gustav and Maj. Green shot down Serg. Santuccio's (2ª Sq.) 20 miles southwest of Ferrara, killing the pilot.

This saturation of an area with simultaneous raids made it almost impossible for the limited Axis fighter strength to resist effectively, allowing the Allies to carry through a mission to destroy the B-24 forced-landed at Ghedi two days earlier. Thirteen P-38s of the 82nd FG, escorted by others from the 14th FG, arrived at 1830, dive-bombing the B-24's revetment: 6¼ tons of 500lb frag clusters were dropped, four hits were scored inside the pen and the Liberator was left burning. A P-38 of the 95th FS was hit in one engine by flak and had to crash-land near Fornovo di Taro (PR). An Italian boy who, with other children, managed to get to the wrecked bomber next day, reported: '. . . the plane lay with one wing on the ground, completely holed all over'.

15-17 July 1944

Late on the 15th JG 77 deployed 24 aircraft to Tulln but the expected heavy-bomber incursion did not materialise and the fighters were back in Italy the same morning. II° Gr.C. flew three days of patrols without enemy contact, although medium bombers were sighted on the 16th but fuel was too low to allow an engagement. During this mission Ten. Mancini (3ª Sq.) tried to bale out following engine failure, became tangled on his Gustav's tail and died when it crashed near Montanara (MN).

Several aircraft gathered at Piacenza on the evening of the 16th: six Fw 190s from Bologna and five from Rimini (all presumably 'stragglers' from SG 4), and six Ju 87s including E8+SH and E8+AB. 4.(F)/122 sent F6+EM to Tirana in the afternoon.

On the 17th Stab/JG 77 flew morning and evening patrols, to Parma-Bologna and Alessandria respectively. Uffz. Hansch returned early with the endemic problem of inadequate feed from his droptank.

Fhj.Uffz. Rüth of 3./JG 4 was killed when his Bf 109 (W.Nr.163351, Yellow 9) crashed at Provesano (PN) during a practice flight. Three ANR men died when an S.79 of Squadriglia Scuola Aerosiluranti crashed. During mid-afternoon tactical reconnaissance aircraft were detected returning after a mission in the Livorno area; soon after five Cr.42s landed at Vicenza, probably from Ghedi and perhaps on their way to Yugoslavia. From 1900 onwards, six Ju 87s landed at Ravenna from Piacenza and later 15 NSGr.9 aircraft dropped bombs on Bardi (PR) and nearby Varsi in support of Operation Wallenstein II. Both villages were well behind German lines, and this was an anti-partisan mission.

18 July 1944

B-24s were heading for Munich that morning, and 46 aircraft of JG 77's two Gruppen were sent against them, along with seven of II° Gr.C.'s Gustavs. They met the bombers over Pordenone, but were unable to inflict any damage, and the plan was to land at Maniago and attack again on the return flight. Obstlt. Steinhoff and his Staff Flight had deployed there, ready to lead this second attempt, but only the Italians could land, the Germans being driven away by enemy fighters. Consequently there was little to show for the day's effort, just a Bf 109 of I./JG 77 damaged in combat.

19 July 1944

Fifteen miles northwest of Ancona at 15,000ft, Blue and Black Sections of 241 Sqn, on an early morning patrol, gave chase to a pair of Bf 109Gs diving away northwest. Arriving separately on the scene, there was initial confusion as the Spitfires attempted to gain attacking positions on one another before going after the Germans. Flt Lt Turkington's fire knocked a large piece off one Messerschmitt's port wing, and with more bursts set it on fire as it started to climb inland just south of Senigallia (AN). The 109's pilot (almost certainly from NAGr.11) parachuted over friendly territory and the Spitfires were subjected to intense flak.

A German-Italian morning mission against medium bombers was uneventful, as the two groups of fighters missed their RV. At 1815 seven II° Gr.C. aircraft tried again, taking on 'Bostons' in the Parma area. The ANR initially claimed three bombers damaged and '. . . each trailing black smoke'. At unit level these claims were converted into confirmed victories for 1ª Sq.'s M.llo Cavagnino, Serg. Mazzi and Serg. Marin. The Spitfire escort from 154 Sqn was little better, claiming destruction of a Bf 109 and an Fw 190, II° Gr.'s losses amounting to one Bf 109 damaged and making an emergency landing at Reggio Emilia airfield.

At about the same time, the 85th FS was in action between Parma and Reggio,[12] claiming two Fw 190s damaged, and Maj. Ewing of the 86th FS claimed a Bf 109 near Valeggio (MN). These actions may relate to two I./JG 77 Bf 109s reportedly destroyed in combat when German fighters sought to engage heavies bound for the Reich.

Flt Lt Ormerod's Spitfire Mk.IX was among four 72 Sqn aircraft patrolling that evening at high-level between Livorno and northern Corsica. He sighted an Me 410 and chased it for over 100 miles before getting in a position to damage it 20 miles north-northwest of the island. The Messerschmitt would seem to have been Galle and Gerstner's F6+FK of 2.(F)/122. It crash-landed at Piacenza, ending its career with the Staffel, although both men were flying again after nine days.

20 July 1944

The day's fighter sorties totalled 40 and, in a rare understatement, II° Gr.C. claimed 1-0-4 B-24s from a formation attacked by four of its Messerschmitts between Udine and Aviano at 0955. The kill was variously assigned to Ten. Drago and Serg. Mazzi, but in reality the 485th BG had lost two aircraft in this action.

On its first operation 1° Gr.C. scrambled at 1305 from Vicenza and Thiene with ten C.205s and 12 G.55s, intercepting a formation of B-24s in the Udine area. These were escorted by P-51s of the 308th FS (31st FG) and P-38s of the 48th FS (14th FG), each unit covering a different height band, whose intervention wrecked the Italians' attack. Two C.205s and two G.55s were lost, Magg. Arrabito (Gruppo CO) was killed, as was S.M. Sgubbi of 2ª Sq.; Ten Biron (3ª Sq.) baled out of his G.55 (MM.91101) near Ponte Di Piave (TV) and Ten. Beretta's C.205 (MM.92271) crash-landed near Villaorba.

The Americans claimed 3-0-2, crediting the kills to Maj Dorris and Lt Goebel (308th FS) and Lt Brezas (48th FS). All of the claims were for Bf 109s except for Dorris, somewhat nearer the mark with his 'C.202'. The Italians thought they had got a P-38 'probable', plus damage to two more and to three of the bombers.

2./NAGr.11's Oblt. Kasbar had to bale out of his Bf 109G-8/R5 (W.Nr.200452, White 3) over Castellarano (RE) after a reported combat. 2nd/Lt Hearne and Fg Off Inglis of the 417th NFS shot down an unidentified type 10 miles east of Montecristo Island (LI) between 2310-2325, probably a Ju 88A-4 of 6.(F)/122 (W.Nr.301547, F6+EP) in which Uffz. Konrad Metz and his three fellows went missing.

21 July 1944

At 0830 Luftflotte 2 enquired of Fl. Div.2 whether a FAGr.122 aircraft with the Gruppenkommandeur aboard had landed in Southern France. The aeroplane in question was a Ju 188D-2 of 4.(F)/122 (W.Nr.290183, F6+HM), missing from a mission to photograph La Maddalena, Sardinia. Piloted by Oblt. Fritz Müller, it was also carrying Major Pannwitz, perhaps seeing for himself the difficulty of covering this tough target.

It appears that the Ju 188 was shot down by 92 Sqn. The Spitfires of Sqn Ldr Cox and Lt Manne were on early patrol over Gorgona Island at 20,000ft when they saw what they took to be a Ju 88 7,000ft above them. Attacking from below they set its engines on fire and it crashed near Cervarezza (RE). None of those aboard escaped and four of the five are still missing.

At 0740, 14 Bf 109s of II° Gr.C. scrambled from Villafranca and an hour later were in action against 20 B-24s at 22,000ft over Pola and 19 German fighters may also have been involved. Ten. Drago made a stern attack on the next-to-last Liberator in the right hand group and it fell out of formation on fire, eventually crashing into the sea. Another was claimed by Ten. Valenzano, but only one loss was reported by the Americans, from the 455th BG. The Messerschmitts trickled back home over a three hour period, so some must have made interim landings. Villafranca's KTB says they were minus three of their number, but the authors can only confirm the loss of S.M. Luigi Feliciani of 2ª Sq., killed in action.

Flt Lt R.W. Turkington and Lt R.V. Lyon (SAAF) of 241 Sqn, flying respectively as Black One and Black Two, took off from Fermo on a last light patrol in Spitfire Mk.VIIIs. They were briefly delayed when Lyon was forced back by engine trouble, but he was soon aloft again in a spare aircraft. Two hostiles were plotted 38 miles northwest of Ancona at 17,000ft and, after a succession of vectors, Lyon saw them at 2048 when they were two miles west of the town. From there on there were effectively two engagements. The Bf 109s (as they proved to be) split up and the RAF pilots each followed one, Turkington hampered by a drop tank that would not drop and an intermittently defective radio.

Lyon attacked first, climbing between the two Germans, both of whom were emitting a lot of black smoke. He took the right-hand one, its companion having jinked away violently to port, fired from dead astern at 250yd but saw no strikes. He followed his opponent's radical evasive turn and fired again, at 70° deflection. The Messerschmitt immediately burst into flames and Lyon began looking for the other, but was assured by his leader that he was already after it. The South African pilot then watched his victim fall, the port wing and other pieces coming off in the process, and crash within Allied lines southwest of Ancona. The pilot did not get out and the aircraft continued to burn on the ground.

Turkington pursued the second Bf 109, which had headed north in a dive. He caught up as it crossed Senigallia harbour 'on the deck', and knocked pieces off it with two short bursts. A third started a big trail of glycol from the starboard radiator and left that wing root burning. Overflying the bridge on the River Cesano, the Messerschmitt was burning badly and its pilot jettisoned his hood and began to climb. A long burst from the Spitfire struck the German's cockpit area, leaving Perspex shards in Turkington's spinner. At this, all of the Bf 109's guns began firing blue-green tracer, its speed dropped rapidly and Turkington had to break off to avoid a collision. It was last seen going down in flames, but some 'pretty bad' flak from the town curtailed the RAF pilot's curiosity and he headed home.

The destroyed German aircraft were Bf 109G-6s of 1./NAGr.11 and by grim coincidence their tactical numbers were identical to their opponents' callsigns: 'Black 1' (W.Nr.163609, Oblt. Meyer) and 'Black 2' (W.Nr.163617, Uffz. Möbius). The Rotte was reported overdue at 2030 and both men were posted missing.

22-23 July 1944

Bad weather on the 22nd precluded fighter operations, and the ANR withdrew several Bf 109s to the Vizzola Ticino maintenance depot.

On the 23rd Cap. Marchesi led six Macchis and 12 Fiats on a late afternoon patrol in the Ostiglia-Piacenza area, meeting no Allied aircraft, and a patrol by II° Gr. was as uneventful. Another FAGr.122 'shuttle' was apparently underway, for a Ju 88 reconnaissance sortie from Bergamo landed in

Southern France. Another Ju 88 evaded the 111th TRS near Cremona.

24 July 1944

In the morning, MAAF bombers struck the FIAT Railway Works in Turin and the SPA Bodywork Factory, killing 28 people and wounding 136. Forty-four fighters were sent against medium bombers over the western Po plain. Seven Macchis and seven Fiats of I° Gr.C. patrolled from 0800-0900 GMT in the Piacenza area without contact. II° Gr.C. at Villafranca put up 12 Bf 109s in the Cremona area at the same time, missing their rendezvous with JG 77 and landing an hour later. Meanwhile JG 77's Kommodore flew by Lufthansa to Berlin to confer with G.d.J. Galland about his Geschwaderstab's future employment.

Around midday NSGr.9 flew an unusual mission after audacious partisans stole a lorry from Caselle's airfield garage, driving off over the perimeter track and southern runway. A Ju 87 was sent off to find the thieves, but without success.

Over on the east coast at 2040 two Spitfire Mk.VIIIs of 241 Sqn were patrolling over Senigallia at 21,000ft when Hurler control vectored them on to two bogeys 35 miles to the northwest. Shortly afterwards they sighted a pair of Bf 109s a little below them and heading south. Half-rolling on to the Germans' tails, they agreed that Black One, Fg Off J.E. Walton, should tackle the second bandit, and Black Two the first.

As Walton closed in his target jettisoned his droptank and half-rolled to starboard, going into in a moderate dive. Dead astern, Walton fired from 400yd, observing hits on the 109's fuselage and tail until warned that the other 109 was behind him, itself followed closely by Black Two. Walton broke off to avoid his pursuer's fire, then tried to get on its tail.

During the manoeuvre he lost both visual and R/T contact (a plug had come adrift), and next observed the other three aeroplanes milling around below him and going down. He was unable to intervene before the first bandit shot Black Two into the sea.

Walton gave chase towards Pesaro but the gathering darkness made it his first duty to find out if his wingman had survived. He disengaged but found no trace of the other pilot. Circumstantial evidence points to the Bf 109s being from NAGr.11 although there is no record of damage to one of its aeroplanes on the 24th.

2.(F)/122's Ofw. Jackstadt flew a late-evening sortie in F6+BK but the relative timings apparently preclude his from being the Me 410 that ran into 92 Sqn's dusk patrol. The two Spitfires chased this aircraft from north of Corsica to a few miles off Nice and saw black smoke coming from its engines. This incident was to have a confusing sequel, when, on 12 August, a Field Intelligence Team filed a report on the wreck of an Me 410 which they said had crashed on Cecina North Airfield after being shot down on 24 July.

The aircraft, thought 'probably' to have been on reconnaissance from Southern France, had been on fire in the air and was completely burnt out. Nonetheless it was identified as W.Nr.170090, F6+QK. However, 2.(F)/122 lost no aircraft this day and had not had an F6+QK in the air since 6 June and that machine, although apparently suffering some technical damage, had returned safely to Perugia, so how this one came to be where it was is not known.

Otherwise 6.(F)/122 lost a Ju 88 in a non-operational accident and one of Lfl.2's reconnaissance Ju 188s landed in Tirana.

CJ+MG was the first dual-control trainer conversion of the Bf 109. An ULTRA decrypt revealed that in July 1944 it was serving with II° Gruppo Caccia. (Creek)

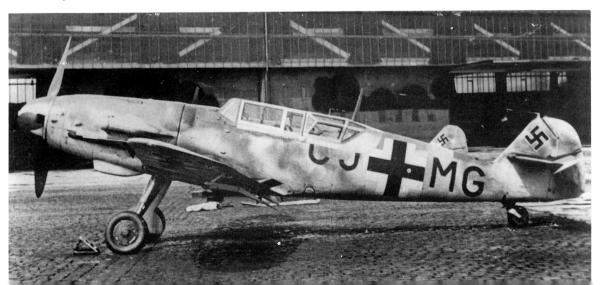

Defecting from the Croat Legion, this Do 17Z (W.Nr.2899, Z8+AH) came down in Southern Italy on 30 July 1944.
(via Crow)

25 July 1944

In a busy day for transfer flights an Fw 190 (Black 3, GS+BX) left Levaldigi for Osoppo while G.T.V. ferried 21 Saiman 202s from various places to Bolzano, nine continuing over the Alps to Baltringen, Bavaria.

In the Mantua-Modena area I° Gr.C. sent up eight C.205s and eight G.55s at 1015. In combat with a group of P-47 bomber escorts they claimed one shot down (by Ten. Zuccarini of 3ª Sq.), another probable (by S.M. Morabito of 2ª) and five damaged. This action has not been correlated with any Allied reports. Twenty-three Bf 109s were transferred to Austria, among them 13 of II° Gr.C. which left Villafranca at 0820 to arrive at Tulln/Vienna at 1010. Forty minutes later they went into action against B-24s. No success resulted, but Ten. Pignatti di Morano was killed by the P-38 escorts.

At 1535 eight Bf 109s of 1./JG 4 and a like number from 3., led by Staffelführer Meyer, were airborne from Maniago on a transfer to Ghedi, there to be absorbed into JG 77. All carried droptanks and two were G-12 trainers. The pilots, fresh from flying schools and replacement units, had just received operational training with I./JG 4.

Uffz. René Darbois, flying 'Yellow 4' (W.Nr.160756), was a native of Metz in Lorraine and considered himself a Frenchman. He had long ago resolved to desert to the Allies and now saw his chance. Since absolute radio silence had been ordered, he flew alongside his leader, indicating that he felt ill and could not continue. A quick check on a map and the officer pointed towards Treviso airfield, directly below.

Darbois peeled off, but his wingman followed. He waved him back to the formation and once out of sight changed course and height frequently (hoping to confuse German radar) and switched off his FuG 25 IFF after passing Venice. Aiming for the airfields around Rome, he flew south over the Adriatic, coming inland north of Pescara.

After encountering bad weather over the Apennines he gained the Volturno River valley and sought a landing ground, choosing Santa Maria Capua Vetere (CE). Darbois circled the field with wheels and flaps down and wagging wings, indicating a desire to land. The tower gave a green light and he made a perfect landing to the surprise and excitement of 72nd Liaison Squadron.

The Luftwaffe posted Darbois missing, listing his aircraft (why is not clear) as W.Nr.160653, White 4[13]. The Bf 109 was taken to America, and during the 1970s was restored (in new colours and markings) for exhibition at the National Air and Space Museum, Washington DC. Darbois subsequently flew under the alias "Guyot" with the Free French GC I/3, based in Corsica, and commanded a helicopter unit in the Indo-China war.

26 July 1944

An attempted reconnaissance of La Maddalena by FAGr.122 was again broken off in the face of Allied fighter defences.

In all, 31 Axis fighters flew freelance patrols in the Parma-Mantua-Modena area. I° Gr.C. contributed eight C.205s and seven G.55s which (and again no Allied corroboration has been found) intercepted 12 bombers and ten P-47s, claiming slight damage to nine of the former and one of the latter. II° Gr.C. returned to Italy after an overnight stay in Tulln and scrambled 11 Messerschmitts that afternoon against a dozen P-47s of the 86th FS (79th FG) bombing a bridge northwest of Brescia. The opposing formations apparently met south of Piacenza, the Americans reporting an attack by 11 'blue-nosed' Bf 109s and both sides' ensuing claims were wildly exaggerated.

The Italians credited themselves with three P-47s shot down (by Cap. Miani, Ten. Drago and S.M. Ancillotti), the Americans with six Bf 109s (one each for Lts Hilgard and Steiner, two each for Lts Head and Hancock), four of whose pilots were seen to bale out. Actual losses from the 86th FS were nil; II° Gr.'s were confined to Ancillotti's aircraft (2ª Sq.) – he parachuted safely.

A Caproni Ca.148 took off from Gallarate for a test-flight, strayed off course and landed at Locarno, Switzerland. The aircraft (SP+CM) had been converted by the Luftwaffe to carry paratroops; it probably belonged to Parachute Army High Command like the pair lost in strafing five days later. The observer was returned, but the pilot chose internment.

Sixteen night attack sorties were mounted around Ancona, but AA fire was very heavy and results could not be observed. Uffz. Richard Schwobe and Gefr. Günter Schlichting of 1./NSGr.9 (Ju 87D-5 W.Nr.141738, E8+FH) went missing there.

Also that night aircraft of 3./NSGr.9 left Cavriago (RE) to bomb Livorno where the AA defences were augmented by the guns of ships in harbour. Ofw. Otto Gieger and his gunner, Ogefr. Karl Gabauer (Ju 87D-3, W.Nr.1369) were approaching base in fog when they hit a power line and were killed. Fw. Hans-Joachim Deutsch and Ogefr. Erwin Kaufmann (in D3+CK) had to make an emergency landing on the way home after taking hits from a nightfighter and the latter was badly hurt. Fw. Otto Brinkmann and Ogefr. Franz Till also made an emergency landing.

27 July 1944

Fg Offs Monard and Hawkes of 241 Sqn were on dawn patrol when vectored on to a bogey approaching Ancona from the northwest at 19,000ft. Off Rimini they saw a sequence of Very lights and then a pair of Bf 109s that they chased across the Po, by now at deck level and harassed by moderate but inaccurate flak. Monard hit the first Messerschmitt in the port wing and it immediately dropped its tank. It opened its throttle and, pouring black smoke, tried to outclimb him but he hit it in the tail with cannon fire as it reached 1,500ft and it went into a dive. The pilot jettisoned his hood, rolled the plane on its back and baled out, the aircraft crashing near Loreto.

Hawkes closed in to hit his opponent in the port wing and beneath the engine. Something fell off the belly of the Messerschmitt and it began to gush white smoke, climbed to 300ft then turned sharply down, hitting the ground and blowing up near Adria (RO). The German had taken hardly any evasive action throughout the combat. 2./NAGr.11 reported the loss of two aircraft but both pilots appear to have escaped injury; 241's ORB remarked that: '. . . this was a particularly good show . . . the first time that either of [our] pilots had ever seen an enemy aircraft. In fact F/O Hawkes has only done 7 operational hours.'

Ten. Zuccarini led 13 of I° Gr.C.'s aircraft aloft but again the patrol was uneventful and it is not clear which unit contributed the day's ten other Lfl.2 fighter sorties. Sq. Aut. Bombardamento 'Muti' was carrying out training flights and S.Ten. Amore died at Ghedi when his Cant Z.1007 was destroyed in an accident.

That evening, 241's dusk patrol came off worst when Flt Lt Turkington and a new South African pilot, Lt. Goodman, were bounced by another pair of 109s. Although the assailants were spotted in good time, Goodman took little evasive action and, despite repeated urging from his more experienced leader to tighten his turn, was hit all along the fuselage. Turkington saw a parachute open off Fano, but was engaged by the two Germans, one of whom appeared particularly capable and continued the combat for 10min after his wingman had broken off.

An Me 410 sighted by four Spitfires during the evening at 27,000ft and 15-20 miles north-northwest

As a Flight Lieutenant with 241 Sqn., R.W. Turkington, DFC and Bar (centre) had a run of successes against the Bf 109s of NAGr.11 in July 1944. He was promoted to Squadron Leader and went on to command 601 Sqn. (IWM)

of Cap Corse may have been F6+DK, flown by v.d.Daele and Seegert of 2.(F)/122.

Off Rimini, Fg Offs Reynolds and Wingham of 255 Sqn, shot a Ju 87D-5 (W.Nr.140755) of 1./NSGr.9 into the sea where it burned fiercely. The pilot, Uffz. Werner Waissnor (a 'founder member' of NSGr.9), was killed and Gefr. Hermann Koch wounded. 2./9 lost a D-1 (W.Nr.2008) west of Modena, both Ogefr. Franz Spörr and Flg. Gustav Leumann being injured. The cause of this loss is not known. Over in the west, the same Staffel had a Ju 87D-3 (W.Nr.110459) shot down by AA fire south of Pontedera (PI), Uffz. Kurt Urban being wounded and his radio operator Uffz. Gottfried Lässig going missing.

28 July 1944

In the early evening Me 410 F6+DK (Galle and Gerstner) flew from Bergamo to Istres in preparation for a mission next day, and from 1732-1751 aircraft of NAGr.11 were heard operating south of the front line.

At 1400 orders had been issued for the night's harassing operations around Arezzo and LXXV., I. FJ and LXXVI. Korps were all asked to mark their front lines from 1945-2230 by firing coloured light signals or lighting fires. At 2245, after an unfortunate brush with what proved to be a friendly Baltimore, Flt Sgts Waitman and Goff of 600 Sqn claimed a Ju 87 shot down, six miles southwest of Colle di Val d'Elsa (SI).

29 July 1944

Flt Lt Turkington had just arrived at Falconara with aircraft of 241 Sqn when he was told that a plot was coming up on the board and asked would he like to intercept? Wearing just shorts and shirt, Turkington and Flt Lt Harland took off, sighting two Bf 109s at 16,000ft, silhouetted against cloud. Harland, 'flying a somewhat tired aircraft', was left behind, and Turkington could not jettison his droptank but still managed to catch the Messerschmitts. He hit the port one around the cockpit and fuselage with cannon fire and Harland saw it diving vertically toward the sea northeast of Pesaro 'with little chance of pulling out' (it was claimed as a probable); the other 109 was hit, started emitting white smoke and dived away steeply. The Spitfire's starboard cannon jammed, but Turkington continued with his remaining guns and the German went into the sea about 20 miles northeast of Rimini aerodrome.

1./NAGr.11 reported the loss of a Bf 109G-6/U3 (W.Nr.162050, Black 6), shot down by fighters 30km east of Rimini with Ltn. Metz missing. The day's claims brought Turkington's score with 241 to four destroyed and one probable, all in July. A week later he was a Squadron Leader (subsequently becoming 601's CO) and his recent successes won him a bar to his DFC.

At 0937 GMT, Galle and Gerstner's Me 410 landed at Bergamo after a 2¼hr mission from Istres. Fifty minutes earlier Carmen's Ju 188 A3+TB had returned to Bergamo from Riem; at 1220 Luftverkehrsgruppe Ju 52 A7+GL left Airasca for Lyon. About 15 attack sorties were launched against road traffic in the Bucine/Arezzo area that night. Flt Lts Thompson and Beaumont of 600 Sqn, vectored by Syrup control, pursued a Ju 87 through 'considerable evasive action' before shooting it down in flames near Sarsina (FO) at 2343.

30 July 1944

In the morning 1./NSGr.9's Ju 87 E8+CH deployed from Caselle to Ravenna, followed early that evening by an Fw 58 (E8+CB) of the Gruppenstab. Ltn. Albeiu Vouk and four others, all defectors from 1./Kroat. Lw. Legion, crash-landed their Do 17Z-5 (W.Nr.2899, Z8+AH; callsign PF+EN) in southern Italy during the day.

The Croatians' unit had been supposed to move with its aircraft to Eichwalde and they were first to take off. The five had decided on escape some time previously, and intended landing near Bari. The pilot flew a few miles toward Germany then altered course to westward, finally crash-landing near Cerignola (FG).

I° Gr.C. put up 18 aeroplanes at 0955 to intercept, in the Novi Ligure-Piacenza area, 17 B-25s of 17th BG escorted by 12 Spitfires of 232 Sqn. In a fleeting action Ten. Beretta claimed a Spitfire shot down, but actually caused only cannon-shell damage to its tail unit. S.M. Morabito was hit by W/O McCann, who reported: 'Behind the Me-109s, 6 G.55s attacked and in one head-on pass I fired and saw strikes on the engine of one of them, followed by black smoke as it dived away . . .' McCann only claimed the Fiat as damaged but it never recovered and crashed near Sampierdarena (GE), killing its pilot.

Nineteen aircraft of II° Gr.C. hit the same Allied formation, the action developing in the Piacenza-La Spezia area from about 1030, the Allies understandably seeing the two attacks as one. II° Gr. lodged no claims, but lost two aircraft; M.llo

Desideri was killed in a crash near Torriglia (GE) and Serg. Mazzi's aeroplane fell near Bobbio (PC). The pilot had baled out safely, but was captured by the partisans controlling the area. The Spitfires claimed just one Bf 109 shot down (Fg Off True) and a G.55 damaged (W/O McCann) in this phase of the combat.

At 1930 two Ju 188s (F6+AM and IM) of 4.(F)/122 landed at St Martin-de-Crau, France, (1.(F)/33's base) with a view to covering Bizerta early next day. Neither was fully serviceable on arrival and though the resident unit set to work it seemed unlikely that the mission could proceed as planned. By 2200 it was reported that one aircraft would be ready to go at 0315 but the operation was called off.

Information from the German side is lacking for both nightfighter victory claims that night. Fg Off Bretherton and Flt Lt Cunningham (255 Sqn) chased a low-flying Ju 88 into the sea 25 miles northwest of Ancona, modestly claiming a 'probable' and Flt Sgt Cole and Sgt Odd (600 Sqn) claimed a Ju 87 southeast of Florence.

31 July 1944

An S.82 (W.Nr.61 829) from II./TG 1 crashed at Vicenza at 1600, during a ferry flight, killing Gefr. Rohlfing of 5. St. Three more of the unit's aircraft were destroyed in strafing at Gallarate that morning. The same attack had accounted for two Ca.148s and a Ca.133 decoy. Slight damage was done to two of II° Gr.C.'s Bf 109s and one belonging to the Caproni Company, while the flak brought down one of the attacking Thunderbolts and damaged another. Six Reggiane 2002s that left for Lyon, France, were probably destined for counter-insurgency duties with Geschwader Bongart.

Despite losing four S.79s and its sole Cant Z.1018 when Lonate was strafed on the 29th, Gr. 'Buscaglia' was ready on the 30th to return to action in the Eastern Mediterranean. Six of 2ª Sq.'s aircraft took off, again in dreadful weather, heading for Belgrade-Semlin. In the event, conditions were so bad that they put down at Villafranca (where Ten. Neri's B2-04 crashed on landing), and were followed next morning by another eight aircraft. Two then continued their journey to Belgrade, but Ten. Pandolfo's B1-00 was caught by the Balkan Air Force at 0700 on the 31st and shot down south of Otočac, Croatia.

The intentions of the night's harassing effort were to attack targets in the area Pontedera (PI)-Casciana Terme (PI)-Certaldo (FI)-Bucine (AR)-Arezzo. Ground troops were to be prepared to mark the front lines from 1945-2230, whenever German aircraft fired white Very lights. During August an Allied Intelligence team looked over the remains of a Ju 87 near Cicogna (AR) on the north bank of the Arno, thought to have been shot down on the night of 31 July/1 August; one man's parachute had failed, while the other was unaccounted for.

Notes

11. Fw. Sliwa of 5. Staffel (flying W.Nr.162695, Black 4) was killed at Villafontana (VR) when his parachute failed. Uffz Hoffmann of Stab II./77 (W.Nr.161065) was injured and baled out at Bovolone (VR).
12. According to their map reference, but the location is described as 'Ostiglia area', further north.
13. Ultra reports, apparently of aircraft landing from this transfer at Maniago, mention neither a White nor a Yellow 4, so perhaps neither arrived.

Villafranca, July 1944. S.M. Pacini of 3ª Sq., II° Gr.C. poses in front of his 'White 2'. The Bf 109 shows the 'fasci' under the wing but lacks the 'Gamba di Ferro' badge on the nose.

On 20 August 1944, two pilots of 5./JG 77 apparently lost their bearings during a ferry flight and force-landed in Switzerland. Here, both 'Yellow 12' (Fw. Tanck) and 'Yellow 3' (Flg. Nehrenheim) are shown as they appeared to the first rescuers. (Bundesamt für Militärflugplätze)

Chapter 4

August 1944

The Ground War

The Allies occupied the southern part of Florence on the 4th and declared the campaign in Central Italy over, although it took another week completely to liberate the city. The post-Diadem pursuit was over and the Allied Armies had suffered 34,000 casualties during it. There was now no real hope of breaking through the Gothic Line and on to the Emilian Plain before the end of summer but plans were set in train for attacks against the Line's centre and eastern end which seemed to offer the most promising avenues of advance. Kesselring's losses in the phase just ended had been 63,000 and he too feared the removal of divisions to France, despite having to face the prospect of a renewed Allied onslaught of his own, at a time and place he could only guess at.

The Luftwaffe

Dragoon hit the French beaches on 15 August, rapidly overwhelming the German defenders and their minimal air support. II./JG 77 was rushed in from Italy to reinforce the fighters *in situ* but was pulled out within days. The South of France was obviously untenable and emergency measures were set in motion, accompanied by a flurry of signals and whistle-stop tours of Northern Italy by Kesselring and Richthofen. On the 18th Fl.Div. 2 and its subordinated units, KG 26, III./KG 100, 1.(F)/33, 2./NAGr.13 and II./JG 77, were placed under Luftflotte 2, along with torpedo and guided weapon servicing echelons. The badly-weakened bomber units were to rest and restore their serviceability.

A confusing sequence of orders began to be issued concerning where the bombers should go. Stab, I. and II./KG 26 were to go to München-Riem and Memmingen, Bavaria. Then Kaufbeuren was mentioned, along with preparations at Cameri (NO), Lonate and Gallarate to receive advance detachments from the Geschwader. Certainly work was under way at Cameri from the 20th in expectation of II./KG 26 and Majors Aller and Martin of Lfl.2 were there on the 30th to discuss the move; III./KG 100 was destined for Villafranca. Meanwhile, at noon on the 21st, von Richthofen was making new dispositions of his own. NAGr.11 was redeployed and II./TG 1's transfer reaffirmed.

On the 22nd, orders went out for all aircraft and crews of 1.(F)/33[14] to move to Bergamo-Seriate at once, and the ground echelon to Landsberg. Next day the German Nineteenth Army was told in response to its complaints at lack of reconnaissance cover that 1./33 and 2./13 were down to one operational aircraft apiece.

The Luftwaffe also elected to compound its difficulties by trying to disband the ANR, but that story is for the next chapter.

Fuel

On 10 August OKL issued an instruction which would have a decisive effect on the conduct of the air war on every front, although its worst effects would be delayed for a short while yet. The renewal, this time in earnest, of Allied heavy bomber raids on the oil industry in German-controlled Europe now compelled economies even in operational flying. Flights by four-engined aeroplanes needed special permission, reconnaissance was limited to what was essential and combat missions had to have good prospects of success.

In Italy this stricture was supplemented eight days later by a directive that all aircraft tanks be drained immediately. FAGr.122, NAGr.11 and NSGr.9. were exempted from this, but the Italian first-line units were not. II./TG 1 had been ordered out to Niedermendig, Germany, on the 10th – its S.82s had already begun to leave – and sufficient petrol was to be provided to get them as far as Munich. As it transpired, they did not return to operations after leaving Italy.

Minehunters

On 21 July Luftflotte 2 had asked Komm.Gen. Griechenland (Greece) if a Schwarm of mine-seeking aircraft (probably Ju 52s) could be got ready in the coming days for a short spell of operations in the Adriatic. This apparently went ahead, for it was signalled that the detachment in Gorizia on 10 August for a special task would be rejoining other elements of the the Minensuchgruppe in eight to ten days.

Long-range Reconnaissance

On the 7th Feldluftgau XXV instructed its subordinate units to support FAGr.122's serviceability, to ensure that the small number of aircraft available could provide the necessary reconnaissance cover. This was, 'important for the entire conduct of operations by the armed forces in Italy and necessary in view of present Allied air activity and German losses'.

2.(F)/122 flew about 85 sorties during the month amid a mass of transfer flights, mostly back and forth between Bergamo and Ghedi and also involving 4. and 6. Staffeln. The upshot of all this was that 2. again took up residence in Ghedi, the move happening on the 8th and 9th (spurred by an air raid on Bergamo on the latter date). This return to their old base, destined to last about six months, was dictated partly by the need to disperse assets over a number of fields, and partly by the restricted number of targets that the Me 410 could reach from the more northerly aerodrome.

Ghedi was not without its own problems, the whole Po Valley being almost constantly patrolled by Allied fighter bombers, which sometimes caught an Me 410 returning home at low altitude over the Alpine foothills and efforts were made to redirect incoming aeroplanes to 'clear' airfields. A new measure during August was the creation of five ground observer stations, Brigitte 1-5, passing warnings of hostile aircraft to German reconnaissance aircraft. The ground echelons could only move their mobile workshops around the airfield during early morning or late evening. Despite the forward basing, cover of the front lines was now rarely achieved, however badly it was needed by friendly troops, and overwater work became more common. It appears that an Me 410 was loaned to Fl.Div. 2 in France, for on the 17th Luftflotte 2 called for its immediate return.

An Me 410 pilot taken prisoner during the month said that all of 2. Staffel's aircraft were fitted with GM 1 boosting, but that only two had the FuG 101 radio altimeter. Of the Staffel's ten crews most were young and inexperienced; faint hopes were entertained that they might in future get Me 262s, details of which had been learned from former Staffel members recalled to Germany. As his interrogators put it, 'P/W was filled with praise of the Me 262. Unfortunately his knowledge was not commensurate with his enthusiasm.' He had also heard of experiments with fitting a jet engine to the Me 410, giving a 150kph boost to its maximum speed.

4. and 6. Staffeln had their permanent base at Bergamo for almost all the rest of the war, although individual aircraft would often fly particular missions out of another airfield. Also, a detachment under Ltn. Vaibora was installed at Villafranca from 17 August, apparently for dispersal, and remained there five weeks. Ju 188s +DH, +KH and +SH of 1./122 arrived in Ghedi on the 27th and may have been the three D-2s that 4. Staffel received 'from other units'.

Coincidental with Dragoon, the Allies noticed a major change of emphasis in FAGr.122's missions from the Adriatic to the Ligurian Sea, but daylight photographic attempts were continually frustrated by the defences. The night photographic Ju 188s were far more successful, especially since Allied harbours tended to be brightly lit and easily found. These aircraft, operating without ground control, covered Naples, the Riviera ports and those in Corsica, and Adriatic harbours right down to Bari and Taranto (staging through Udine for the last-named targets). The Ju 188 was disturbingly prone to engine failure at height and to electrical malfunctions owing to poor materials and low standards of workmanship (neither surprising nor undeserved given Germany's heavy reliance on forced and brutalised labour).

As the German units were squeezed into a gradually diminishing area, their navigation problems worsened. The five main radio beacons were so close together that homing became very difficult, not being helped by MATAF's habit of shooting them up. In part compensation, the main ground control at Canazei (TN) kept FAGr.122 informed of the whereabouts of Allied beacons, their frequencies and recognition signals. The German crews could then exploit these 'hostile' facilities by way of their own direction finders. Only skilled operators could listen in to warnings broadcast on the Gruppe's tactical wavelength, since the traffic was brief and heavily jammed.

Tactical Reconnaissance
NAGr.11 began August at Poggio (Stab and 2./11) and Forlì (1. Staffel). On the 17th its Kommandeur visited Piacenza to prepare for the basing there of 'up to 30' of his aircraft within about 12 days, although in the event only the Stab and 2. Staffel made the move. Meanwhile, 1./11 was ordered to Bologna on the 21st and some elements of the Gruppe were probably in Caselle some three days after that.

On the 22nd 2./NAGr.13 had been ordered there from France to recover its strength and NAGr.11 was to provide it with logistical support. The situation in France meant that coverage of Army Liguria's zone, the Franco-Italian border and the roads west of it, was urgently needed for fear that the Allies might decide to get into Italy by the back door. It seems that the intention was to use Rotten of NAGr.11's Bf 109s from Caselle, and perhaps also 2./NAGr.13 when it had recuperated.

Fighters
I./JG 77 was moved by train to Oldenburg, Germany, on 31 July and 1 August. On the latter date two trains carried I./JG 4 to Kassel-Rothwesten. On the 15th II./77 was transferred to France, only to return to Ghedi on the 20th with 25 aircraft (a strength more than doubled by the month's end). Also on the 20th, Stab/JG 77 transferred to Bergamo. The needs of Reich Defence and the collapsing Western Front were clearly bearing ever more heavily on Luftflotte 2's meagre resources, but August represented something of a low point for the Reich's armed forces in general before the rebuilding and regrouping of the autumn.

KG 200
A Czech who deserted to the Allies had served with KG 200 at Finsterwalde in August and September 1944. He said that two captured B-17s were based there and had flown two nocturnal missions to Greece to infiltrate saboteurs. On each occasion, so returning crewmen had told him, a stop-over was made in Italy to pick up the group of agents that was to be dropped.

Night Attack
The bulk of NSGr.9's operations seem to have been clustered in the first four nights of the month (the lead-up to full moon) and the last five. One signal spoke of operations resuming as soon as Fl.Div.2's ground echelons (from France) were ready in Italy. Strength was down quite sharply from the high numbers, never again approached, of mid-late July. According to a PoW, the transformation of 2./NSGr.2 into 3./NSGr.9 took place on 3 August, although the necessary order had been issued some time earlier. With the change the Staffel's Ju 87s gradually lost their 'D3+' codings and were re-marked with NSGr.9's 'E8+'; operations were flown from Cavriago and Palata (BO). 1. Staffel

NSGr.9 groundcrew servicing a newly-arrived Ju 87 D-5 (notice the lack of wave-mirror camouflage). The close-up shows to advantage the MG 151/20 cannon with its anti-flash muzzle and the bulbous extension added to the exhaust flame-dampers. (Bundesarchiv)

was at Ravenna and 2. at Vigatto (PR) during August.

A shot-down pilot described 3./9's situation and tactics. Since the beginning of June, six aircraft had been lost, only two of them in action. Reserves of men and material were adequate and readily available, and the late-August strength of the Staffel was ten crews and aircraft. All the latter were Ju 87D-3s except for one D-5, marked E8+AL, flown by the Staffelkapitän. No particular target was given for the night – only an area where targets of opportunity should be attacked. Bombs were released from between 1,000 and 2,000m and ground strafing was carried out from as low as 100m. Attacks were invariably by moonlight, using dead reckoning navigation because lakes and rivers showed up well. On approaching home base the pilot identified himself by switching on his downward recognition lights. If he could not find his own base, he would try for 2. Staffel's at Vigatto. The approach of a nightfighter was generally heralded by a loud crackling in the intercom, and standard evasive action was a sharp turn followed by a steep dive.

According to the prisoner, commanders were Major Frost (Gruppenkommandeur and Kapitän of 1. Staffel); Oblt. Scheven (Kapitän of 2. Staffel); Hptm. Eduard Reither (Kapitän of 3. Staffel).

Mistel

The Mistel (composite aircraft) unit KG 101, lately in action against the Normandy invasion fleets, signalled its intention to use Italian airfields for landing if called upon to operate off the coast of Southern France, but no such missions took place.

The ANR

Fighters

I° Gr.C. only operated during the first few days of the month. Thereafter the Gruppo was not called on to fly and its members began to wonder what was afoot, suspicions being heightened when their supposed allies drained the petrol from their aircraft. II° Gruppo started August resting after its exertions the previous month, although a few patrols were flown, plus training flights and gunnery exercises. A group of new pilots arrived from an experimental preliminary training course held in Liegnitz, Germany, from May to June. Among them were S.M. Baldi and Sergenti Benzi, Archidiacono and Tampieri, who will figure again in this story.

The enemy was encountered on the 8th, for the first time in ten days. For neither the first nor the last time a relatively strong ANR force had an entirely inconclusive engagement. However, even in the midst of such episodes and much darker days in the ANR's history there were highlights of gallantry and flying skill.

On 11 August an order was issued by SMAR for the creation of a new Fighter Group: this specified that the former Gruppo Complementare Caccia based at Cervere (CN) would be renamed III° Gruppo Caccia, transferring to Vicenza. I° Gr.C. would go to Ponte S. Pietro (BG), leaving to the new unit 24 pilots and 81 personnel together with its aircraft, since re-equipment with the Bf 109 was intended.

Of all these orders only the transfer of the newly-constituted III° Gr.C. was effected, together with the few of its old Macchi C.202s that survived an Allied fighter-bomber attack on Cervere. Since the Bf 109s promised by the Germans for I° Gr.C. failed to materialise, the unit remained at Vicenza, sharing the

Savoia S.82s of II./TG 1. This heavy transport Gruppe spent much of summer 1944 ferrying elements of other Luftwaffe units out of Italy before it too was withdrawn in August and disbanded soon after. (Bundesarchiv)

Obstlt. Johannes Steinhoff (right), Kommodore of JG 77, was among the most active officers during 'Operation Phoenix' trying repeatedly but unsuccessfully to convince the Italian fighter commanders to accede to the German plan for the ANR's dissolution. With him is Hptm. Theodor Lindemann, Kommandeur of I./JG 77, whose Gruppe was based in Italy until the end of July 1944, when it and I./JG 4 left for Germany. (Prien)

field with their new comrades while the personnel of one Squadriglia were posted to Thiene, awaiting orders and aircraft that would, as they soon realised, never arrive.

In many ways this air force was a microcosm of events in a divided country and amongst a tired, hopeless population of an artificial state fighting a lost war. And this was before the Germans launched their dubious intrigue of late August.

Torpedo-Bombers

Allied intelligence on Gruppo 'Buscaglia' was detailed: '[it] has three *Squadriglie* from which 17 aircraft have been identified (two of the 1ª Sq., eight of the 2ª and seven of the 3ª)'. Radio traffic allowed MAAF to follow the unit's August deployment to Greece, its actions there and some of its aircraft's return home. This tour of operations had been a stiff test of the capacities of the Gruppo's men and aeroplanes and was near enough the swan-song of the ANR's torpedo arm. The crews were rested, and work begun to get the S.79s back on line, serviceability having sunk as low as six out of 14. Although expecting a lay-off, the Gruppo had no idea of how long it would turn out to be once politics took a hand.

Transports

With the Eastern Front collapsing, I° Gr. Aerotr. 'Terracciano' was withdrawn to Bautzen, where on 21 August came the OKL order for it and II° Gr. Aerotr. 'Trabucchi' to disband. The latter had never attained operational status and was still in Goslar. The end of August and September saw a struggle by the COs of the Italian transport groups to avoid mass transportation of their men for employment by the Germans as 'workers' in Holland.

Back in Italy, Gruppo Trasporti Velivoli had changed COs from Cap. De Camillis to Magg. Zigiotti in July then, during August was reduced to a nucleus of no more than 20 pilots. The remainder were posted to other units, including III° Gr. Aerotr., due to be commanded by De Camillis. The events of August scotched plans for that unit, while G.T.V. was simply disbanded.

Order of Battle

On 31 July Axis units' strengths were:

Unit	Location	Aircraft Number	Type
Gr. Buscaglia	Lonate	21(16)	S.79
I° Gr.C.	Vicenza	13(7)	C.205
		18(9)	G.55
II° Gr.C.	Villafranca	26(17)	Bf 109G-6/G-12
It. KGr.	Lonate	14(0)	Cant 1007 (forming)
Stab/FAGr.122	Bergamo	0(0)	
2.(F)/122	Bergamo	6(5)	Me 410A-3/B-3
4.(F)/122	Bergamo	6(4)	Ju 188D-2
		4(3)	Ju 88T-1
6.(F)/122	Bergamo	3 ⎫	Ju 88A-4
		2 ⎬ 3	Ju 88D-1
		2 ⎭	Ju 188D-1
		2 (1)	Ju 188D-2
Kdo. Carmen	Bergamo	2/3	Ju 88/Ju 188
Stab/NAGr.11	Poggio	0(0)	
1./NAGr.11	Forlì	4(2)	Bf 109G-6/G-8
2./NAGr.11	Poggio	7(4)	Bf 109G-5/G-6/G-8
Einsatzstab/NSGr.9	Caselle	0?	
1./NSGr.9	Ravenna	13(7)	Ju 87D
2./NSGr.9	Rimini	11(8)	Ju 87D
3./NSGr.9 (*2./NSGr.2*)	Rimini	10(8)	Ju 87D-3/D-5
Jafü Oberitalien	Villafranca(?)	1(1)	Bf 109G-6
L.Beo.St.7	Villaorba	?	Ju 88
I./JG4	in transit	–	
Stab JG77	Bettola	6(3)	Bf 109G-6
I./JG77	in transit	–	
II./JG77	Ghedi	42(31)	Bf 109G-6
Verb.St.300	?	7(7)	Fi 156
Verb.St.500	?	6(6)	Fi 156/Saiman/Fairchild

Notes

14. Equipped with a mix of Ju 88s, Ju 188s and Me 410s.

CHAPTER 4

Operations

1 August 1944

2.(F)/122's first sortie was perhaps the last operational flight by Staffelkapitän, Hptm. Weinand, who was out for just under two hours in F6+EK with Müller as his observer.

At 0950 I° Gr.C. sent six C.205s and nine G.55s to intercept bombers and escorts in the Mantua-Verona area. The ANR pilots claimed a Boston plus damage to a P-47, but lost the G.55 of Serg. Balduzzo, who baled out safely. Just after midday, strafing at Villafranca finished off the Gr. 'Buscaglia' S.79 damaged on 30 July, the flak claiming a P-47 in return. Late that afternoon Albenga (SV) was shot up and five Cant 1007s were destroyed; nine more under construction were damaged as were five Piaggio P.108s in a hangar.

Twenty-one Nachtschlacht sorties were mounted, attacking Allied transport. Three reconnaissance aircraft were out and returning from Anzio, a Ju 88T-1 of 6.(F)/122 (W.Nr.430759, F6+OM) crashed at Vercelli, killing Uffz. Klemm.

2 August 1944

6.(F)/122 reported two more Ju 88s and their eight crew missing during the night of 1/2 August: a D-1 (W.Nr.430145, F6+CP) flown by Uffz. Rudolf Beck and an A-4 (W.Nr.300219, F6+NP) piloted by Uffz. Franz Wentzlaff. There are two Allied claims of Junkers shot down: one into the sea off Algiers at 0140 by a 256 Sqn Mosquito XIII, the other by a Beaufighter of 255 Sqn, 15 miles east of Ancona and a couple of hours later.

276 Wing recorded: '04.00-05.00hrs. – 9 S.79s from Villafranca to Vienna area. Due to leave Vienna at 0300 hrs/3rd for Jugoslavia, probably Nish. (AHQ, E. Med were keenly interested).' In fact their intermediate destination was Semlin airfield (Belgrade), where they landed safely, leaving at 0300 the following day for Eleusis, Greece. After receiving information from German reconnaissance of 30 merchant ships and four escorts north of Cyrenaica, a mission was planned for the 4th, with eight S.79s.

At 0430 three Cr.42s left the Turin area for Trento, and it was probably the same aircraft that flew from there to Osoppo next day. Forty-five minutes later Galle and Gerstner of 2./122 took off on a mission from the unusual starting point of Bologna (where they had arrived the evening before), returning afterwards to Bergamo.

At 0820 Magg. Visconti led four Macchis and seven Fiats of I° Gr.C. on a patrol in the Mantua-Piacenza area. They met not the enemy, but heavy (friendly) flak around Verona, possibly as a result of poor liaison between fighter controllers and the guns. Serg. Cimatti of 2ª Sq. died when his G.55 was hit and crashed near Lonigo (VI). By contrast, II° Gruppo patrolled for 95min between Bologna and Parma without incident.

Missions by 24 P-47s of the 85th FS, 79th FG, against Gallarate and Bergamo led to claims of 33 Axis aircraft (Ju 88s, S.79s, Me 410s) destroyed or damaged on the former airfield and four on the latter, where flak killed Lt. Vincent Millican.

At 1530 a Ju 188 of FAGr.122 set off to photograph Bizerta but was back an hour later because its air-warning radar had broken down. The task was rescheduled for 0300 on the 3rd and obtained coverage of the Tunisian coast from the Gulf of Tunis to Cap de Fer although Bizerta itself was obscured by cloud.

On the night of the 2nd/3rd, 20 Ju 87s strafed roads in the Marina di Pisa-Arezzo area. A 600 Sqn Beaufighter (Flt Lt Thompson and Fg Off Beaumont) claimed one destroyed at 2240 and another damaged northeast of Florence, and W.Nr.2614 with Uffz. Heinrich Laufenberg and Fw. Werner Hensel aboard was posted missing by 3./NSGr.9, though Hensel later made his way back to the unit.

A 4.(F)/122 Ju 88 reported lost on operations (but not attributed to enemy action) may tie in with an aircraft shot down at 2317 off Cape Corse, which was called by its control for 1½hrs afterwards. A 417th NFS Beaufighter (Lts William R Williamson and Dan B. Cordell) made the kill on the basis of no fewer than 17 bearings and six fixes from 276 Wing's No.1 Field Unit at Tomino, Corsica. There was heavy return fire from the German dorsal gunner and the Beau was struck on its nosecone by debris, but the Junkers crashed into the water about 27 miles off the Cape.

3 August 1944

Plt Off Crooks and Sgt Charles of 600 Sqn brought down another Ju 87 at 0300, probably a D-3 (W.Nr.1120, E8+PK) flown by Ofw. Hans Wolfsen and Gefr. Hans Wilk of 3./9, both posted missing. At 0317 a Kdo. Carmen Ju 188 (A3+WB) reached Bergamo from Tirana; at 0900 a Ju 88 of 6./KG 77 was reported overdue, presumed lost, from a reconnaissance from France into Italian waters west of Sardinia. Ultra suggested that I./JG 4 operated from Udine, but it seems unlikely that this was any more than activity associated with their transfer.

That night 1./NSGr.9 lost two Ju 87D-5s in rapid succession near Arezzo, both to 600 Sqn. Plt Offs Jefferson and Spencer – in the face of fire from its dorsal guns – accounted for one at 2235 southwest of the town; Fg Off McDonald and Sgt. Towell got another near Città di Castello (PG) nine minutes later. Uffz. Herbert Fietz and Fw. Karl Rasinski (W.Nr.131613, E8+DH) and Uffz. Helmut Krüger and Ogfr. Günter Tschirch (W.Nr.131150, E8+BB) were posted missing.

4 August 1944

Fg Off Bretherton and Flt Lt Cunningham of 225 Sqn, patrolling since 2355 on the 3rd, shot down a Ju 88, seeing one parachute open before it crashed and burned. 6.(F)/122 logged an aircraft missing, but there are no reports on the loss of any crew.

Off North Africa only three of Gr. 'Buscaglia's' torpedo-bombers found and attacked the convoy they were seeking, claiming one 7,000 ton ship sunk and two damaged. These claims are partially confirmed in Allied reports: SS *Samsylarna,* her engine room flooded, was successfully beached off Benghazi and later refloated.

Three S.79s were heard homing on Athens early on the 5th after the strike. Five Savoias landed safely back at Eleusis; a sixth ditched near Argos owing to fuel shortage, its crew being rescued by the Germans; the seventh landed in Crete for the same reason but the eighth crashed off the island, M.llo Jasinski and his crew being posted missing.

The log books of several I° Gr.C. pilots record a scramble at 1020 in the Verona-Brescia area and a combat with P-38s in which one was shot down by S.M. Di Cecco (2ª Sq.); we have however found no record of any American loss that day.

In the early afternoon a couple of P-47s of the 346th FS, 350th FG, on a training flight in the Piombino area, were surprised to spot a Fiat G.55 with ANR markings flying low along the coast. The Americans approached it, noticing two men gesticulating from the cockpit as the undercarriage was lowered. The G.55 was duly escorted to land at Piombino airfield at 1530. Its pilot, wearing an immaculate flying suit, was M.llo Serafino Agostini, a FIAT test pilot. His passenger, in civilian dress and with a suitcase containing documents, was Ten. Francesco Gentile, an Allied agent parachuted behind German lines two months before in Piedmont, to collect information with the help of local partisans.

The coming of the G.55 (the first to fall intact into Allied hands) had been announced on 31 July in a radio message from Gentile, alerting the Allies to expect it between 2-6 August in Bastia, Corsica. On the afternoon of the 4th M.llo Agostini prepared to test G.55 MM.91150 from FIAT's Mirafiori (TO) airfield; the hour and the heat made for lax security. (The Federale of Turin later wrote to Mussolini that Signor Nardi, the Director of FIAT Aeronautica was known to have aided and abetted the "theft" of the G.55.) Taxying slowly, its canopy open, the G.55 passed the airfield boundary as Gentile swiftly emerged from some concealing bushes and climbed into the cockpit of the Centauro, taking the seat while Agostini sat on his lap. Before anyone noticed anything, the G.55 was taking off. It did not make for Corsica but held course for Rome, but the encounter with the P-47s dictated a landing at Piombino. Agostini and Gentile were brought to Rome that evening and the G.55 was flown there on 15 August.

Despite the full moon, bad weather over Central Italy that night led to the cancellation of operations by NSGr.9.

5-6 August 1944

Northwest of Ancona an enemy aircraft was alleged to have fired 'three rockets or shells' at a Beaufighter; from 4.(F)/122 a Ju 88D-1 (W.Nr.430796, F6+HM) suffered engine failure 10km east of Ravenna and Ltn. Mader and his three crew were lost.

Bad weather again cancelled attack missions intended for the night of 6/7 August but eight reconnaissance sorties were scheduled for the morning, to cover both coasts.

7 August 1944

At 0203 GMT an aircraft 'of Westa 26 or 4.(F)/122' sent out a distress signal and was called by its ground station for another three hours without response. That night seven S.79s set out again from Eleusis, this time to intercept a convoy of 27 ships and four light escorts west of Malta, but the weather was prohibitive and they failed to find it. Wishing to avoid their previous mission's fuel problems, they returned to base, homing on Athens from 0218-0231 on the 8th.

8 August 1944

W/O James and Sgt. McGibbon of 255 Sqn were patrolling over the Adriatic when, despite sustaining hits from its ventral guns, they shot down a Ju 188F-1 of 6.(F)/122 (W.Nr.280229, F6+FP). It fell at 0410 on agricultural land at Borella (FO), and the farmer dumped the scattered remains into a pit. The fragments were picked over in January 1945 by a Field Intelligence Unit, which established the aeroplane's W.Nr. and the fact that it had carried FuG 200 ASV and FuG 216R warning radars. All four of Uffz. Günther Rissmann's crew died.

After an uneventful patrol by 19 Bf 109s the day before, II° Gr.C. was back up with 16 aircraft and intercepted Marauders of 3 SAAF Wing, escorted by Spitfires from 241 Sqn, north of Ravenna at 0950. Despite the Italians' numerical advantage there was only skirmishing without a shot fired. 241 Squadron's ORB commented: 'It is a sorry reflection of the state of the Luftwaffe that 20 plus of their aircraft cannot succeed in damaging even a single aircraft when only six Spitfires are escorting 12 Marauders'.

To make matters worse, a 4.(F)/122 Ju 188D-2 (W.Nr.290172, F6+EM) was destroyed by 'friendly' flak near Venice and all five of Fw. Gerhard Freytag's crew killed. An operational instruction flight in the Bologna area by 26 German fighters for the benefit of new pilots went off without incident, and NSGr.9 put up 17 sorties against road traffic between Marina di Pisa and Arezzo.

9 August 1944

A Ju 88A-4 (W.Nr.550209, F6+DP) of 6./122 took off from Bergamo at 0100 to look for Allied shipping in the Adriatic. Two hours later and headed south, it was attacked by a 255 Sqn Beaufighter (Bretherton and Cunningham again). The Germans got in some accurate return fire 'and [a] dogfight ensued' but a two-second burst from the fighter set the Junkers' starboard engine afire. It came down into the sea 40 miles northwest of Ancona at 0305 and three of the crew were later rescued by an RAF Walrus, but radio operator Ogfr. Walter Haas was missing, presumed dead.

Bergamo-Seriate airfield was heavily bombed at 0945 by B-26s of the 42nd BW. They left 50 craters in the concrete runway and fragmentation bombs carpeted the south dispersal area, 'starting numerous fires, destroying eight aircraft and damaging others. There was a direct hit on one Ju 88 which exploded . . . 3 e/a took off just before bombing. One e/a crashed 10 miles from the airfield.' A PoW claimed, and Ultra confirmed, that all of 6.(F)/122's FuG 200-equipped aircraft were destroyed. Fl.Div. 2 was asked to provide cover that night, and in the meantime a radar-equipped aeroplane was to be ferried to Ghedi immediately.

II./JG 77 had a Bf 109 accidentally damaged on operations and 1./NAGr.11 lost another in similar circumstances. From Cameri four ancient Fiat Cr.20 biplanes were dispatched to the Reich in the wake of the six (rather more valuable) Fw 190s ferried out the previous day. Twenty-two German fighters patrolled southeast of Ravenna without contact.

That morning four Saiman 202s of G.T.V. left Bolzano for Baltringen but once across the Alps they ran into Mustangs of 364th FG, 8th USAAF near Schongau. Three of the Italians escaped at tree-top height but M.llo Giuseppe Zorn was shot down and killed by 1st/Lts John Gawienowski and Frank T. Kosloski of 384th FS.

Owing to losses sustained and the difficulty of operating against targets at the extremities of the S.79's range, it was decided to bring Gr. 'Buscaglia' back to Italy. The Group wanted to borrow a Luftwaffe Ju 52 to help transport their equipment and personnel home, but this was refused on the grounds of petrol shortage, so 12 ground crew and much equipment had to be left behind at Eleusis. There were several other instances of the Luftwaffe's unhelpfulness, of which their refusal to provide transport to and from dispersal areas is typical. During the afternoon the six remaining serviceable aircraft flew to Semlin.

A Ju 188 of 6.(F)/122 at Bergamo/Orio al Serio. Just visible under the nose are the aerials of the FuG 200 Hohentwiel radar. These aircraft were maintained and serviced well away from the runway, their camouflage removed only at dusk, when they were prepared for the routine recce missions. (Bundesarchiv)

10 August 1944

2.(F)/122 continued its move from Bergamo to Ghedi during the morning, F6+KK carrying out a 90min mission on the way. What seems to have been a new F6+DK spent the day moving from Neuruppin to Munich to Bergamo and, lastly, to the Staffel's new home. At 1046 in Villafranca, 20 Bf 109s of II° Gr.C. scrambled amidst showers against Allied formations reported south of Milan, returning without contact or loss around 1½hr later.

This was to be the last Italian operation for over two months; I° Gr.C. had not flown for several days already. From 10 August the Germans busied themselves siphoning the petrol from all the ANR aircraft and storing it in drums nearby, ostensibly because it was required for other tasks. The Italians were sceptical. S.M. Di Cecco wrote in his log book, '10 August 1944: The Germans have spoiled everything. Enough of war! Let's go back home!' But a more convincing explanation was not to be offered for many days yet. The Luftwaffe, meanwhile, kept on flying.

An Me 410 (W.Nr.170087, F6+IK) crewed by Ltn. Dietrich Stämmler and Uffz. Arthur Karsch left Ghedi (where it had arrived just over 12hr earlier) at 1900 and headed out for a reconnaissance mission over the Tyrrhenian. Thirty minutes later, F6+GK (v.d. Daele and Blaschek) lifted off on what was to be an uneventful 90min flight. At the same time, in Falconara, 241 Sqn's Fg Off Monard and Plt Off White (both in Spitfire Mk.VIIIs) went to cockpit readiness.

At 1940 the Spitfires were scrambled. Monard's radio reception faded, and he was forced to hand the lead over to White. The bogey was eventually sighted at about 3 miles' range and they turned to port to cut him off, closing in to 300yd astern. The bogey was now clearly identified as an Me 410, and it opened tracer fire on Monard from extreme range with its port barbette gun but took no evasive action (at 500ft and 320mph over water there was limited margin for manoeuvre). White started firing and closed in to 150yd and observed strikes on the Messerschmitt's port engine, which began to belch white smoke. As the Me 410 turned slightly to port, Monard attacked, hitting the port wing, fuselage and starboard engine with cannon shells and blowing off fragments. Both engines were now on fire, return fire had ceased and the Messerschmitt went into a slight climb just before the pilot appeared to lose control and his aircraft dived steeply into the sea, leaving a fierce fire burning on the water. There were no parachutes and both Germans are listed as missing.

Meanwhile, near Foggia, a Do 17Z (carrying a Croat shield and the number '0107') had force-landed in a field after an opportunistic defection. Pilot Ofw. Sulijman Kulenovic and gunner Ofw. Zvonko Schweiger were members of 3./Kroat. KG 1. They had been under arrest, suspected of partisan sympathies, but had been taken to Forcngai airfield to explain some defect in their Dornier to the ground crew. Around midday an air raid alert sounded and they were ordered to fly their machine out, along with two others. Arriving at Koprivnica, they talked their officer into letting them go to Italy and landed at 1715 after an uneventful flight.

At 2155 a Ju 88 (F6+NP) set out on a reconnaissance that was to last just over six hours and at 2022 a Gr. 'Buscaglia' S.79 was heard homing on Villafranca di Verona, but bad weather forced attack missions to be cancelled.

11-12 August 1944

Gr. 'Buscaglia's' crews rested at Semlin for two days, then five S.79s (the sixth having reached Italy the day before) took off at 0200 on the 11th for Lonate Pozzolo. Poor liaison with the local flak again led to tragedy. Some of the ANR aircraft were shot at by the Germans and Ten. Morselli's S.79 was hit, crashing near the airfield. Only the pilot survived.

This dispersed the formation, and the four S.79s reached Italy separately. Allied monitors noted that at least two of the aircraft that had taken part in the abortive mission of the 8th were involved, plus one from 3ª Sq. and another from 2ª. Two were heard homing on Verona's D/F station in the early hours, but the second had apparently lost its bearings, as it was plotted 25 miles northeast of Genoa at 0310 GMT and 25 miles southeast of Piacenza half an hour later, finally landing there to refuel. It was perhaps this aircraft that was the subject of 'a vain request for news . . . the following day'.

On landing, the S.79 was duly tanked-up with 8m³ of B4 and sent on its way. This apparently straightforward action led to a flurry of questions from Koflug 2/VI as to why fuel had been provided. It transpired that Koflug had failed to notify Piacenza that Italian torpedo aircraft returning from operations should not be refuelled. S.79s B2-05, B2-08 and B3-09 landed at Lonate from Semlin at about 0430.

Overnight it was inferred from radio traffic that a Ju 188 had encountered an Allied nightfighter, as it was called without response, but there is no reported claim or loss. Fl.Div.2 flew a radar reconnaissance from 2050, filling-in for Lfl.2's still unserviceable aeroplanes. Two Ju 188s went out that night on a 'special task' and NSGr.9 put up 19 sorties on a broad front between Marina di Pisa and Senigallia. On the 12th four S.82s of II./TG 1 left Gallarate for Riem and at 1936 Lfl.2 reported the take off of two more 'borrowed' Fl.Div.2 Hohentwiel aircraft.

13 August 1944

Fhr. Richard Hesse and Uffz. Helmut Seegert's Me 410 (W.Nr.170150, F6+GK) started from Ghedi at 1928 on a photo-reconnaissance of the waters east and north of Corsica. F6+KK (Bayer and Lensing) had left a few minutes earlier to cover the sea between La Spezia and the French Riviera. The Staffel had put up two early morning missions as well.

After leaving Ghedi, F6+GK began climbing and crossed the coast near La Spezia at a height of 10,000m on a southerly course. Two Spitfires took Hesse completely by surprise – the first indication of their approach was an outbreak of fire in the

---

On 4 August 1944, this Fiat G.55 defected to the Allies, landing at Piombino. It was flown by FIAT company test pilot M.llo Agostini and carried a passenger - an Italian officer working as an Allied agent. It was examined in detail by Allied Intelligence and taken to England on 17 March 1945, where it remained on charge at RAE Tangmere until scrapped in the late '50s. (Alexander)

Messerschmitt's port engine. One fighter flew a little behind and below the other, so that when Hesse tried to evade the higher one by diving he ran straight into the fire of the second and received another burst in the same engine. The fire got out of control, the cockpit filling with smoke, so he ordered his observer to bale out before he himself left. Although Hesse (later rescued by a Catalina) saw Seegert parachuting, the latter was never found.

That night, 35km southeast of Bergamo, a Kdo. Carmen Ju 188A-2 (W.Nr. 170492) crashed owing to an engine fire, killing Ofw. Kornhoff, Ltn. Klingohr (Carmen's commander) and three crew. The aircraft had been on an operational sortie. Ju 88 F6+NP of 4./122 completed a night mission from Ghedi without mishap, but 1./NAGr.11 lost a Bf 109 in an operational accident.

14-21 August 1944

Most of the 14th saw only reconnaissance and transfers on the Axis side, but at 2330 the crew of a 600 Sqn Beaufighter claimed to have damaged an He 177, by now a decided rarity, near Pescara. The 15th began inauspiciously for 2.(F)/122 when one of its Me 410B-3s (W.Nr.190124, F6+DK) crashed and burned 20km northwest of Mantua. Ltn. Fischer was killed, but his observer, Uffz. Kemna, was unhurt on this occasion. At 2126 F6+FK (Borrmann and Stauch) was 15 per cent damaged in an accident at Treviso.

On the 15th at 0800, 28 Bf 109s of II./JG 77 transferred to France[15] to bolster the new invasion front, the men and equipment being conveyed by nine II./TG 1 Savoias. They were back in Ghedi inside six days, leaving several aircraft shot up and burned out on Caritat landing ground.

Hptm. Weinand took F6+CK from Ghedi to Bettola on the evening of the 16th, damaging it in the process. At 1700 a P-38 belly-landed at Milan-Linate owing to fuel shortage, its pilot being taken prisoner. Kesselring had a busy couple of days, arriving at Villafranca from Parma in a Fi 156 at 0620 on the 16th and leaving for Riem aboard an He 111 20min later. Next evening he landed at Piacenza in a Ju 188 (F3+AH) and flew on in a Storch; the Junkers was refuelled and returned to Germany early on the 18th.

On the 18th 1./NAGr.11 lost a Bf 109 in an accident and the following day Uffz. Oettel of 5./JG 77 was killed when his Bf 109 (W.Nr.163210, Black 3) crashed south of Pavia. The same Staffel lost another two aeroplanes on the 20th when Fw. Tanck (W.Nr.165719, Yellow 12) and Flg. Nehrenheim (W.Nr.163956, Yellow 3) lost their bearings on a ferry flight and landed at Beundenfeld near Berne, Switzerland, at 0800. Both aircraft were damaged on landing and their pilots remained interned until 14 November.

During the 18th and 19th II./TG 1's Savoias left Bettola and Gallarate for Riem. The next day, two of its Ju 52s (W.Nr.7213, GA+VA and W.Nr.130723, 8T+BV) crashed and burned at Courmayeur (AO) on the slopes of Mont Blanc, killing their eight aircrew. They had been en route between Gallarate and Orange and the losses were attributed to probable enemy action, although accident now seems more likely. Between midday and early evening about a dozen Bf 109s, almost certainly from II./JG 77, flew from Airasca to Ghedi I and Gefr. Gerhard Ebert of 7. Staffel (W.Nr.165719, <) was shot down and killed over Levaldigi (CN).

On the 21st Luftflotte 2 issued orders that, with immediate effect, only aircraft of NAGr.11, NSGr.9 and FAGr.122 should be fuelled by aerodromes under Koflug 2/VI. In other words, nothing was to be done for the ANR. The only other item of note for the day was accidental damage to two 1./NAGr.11 Bf 109s.

22-24 August 1944

On the 22nd a 256 Sqn Mosquito XIII on an intruder mission in the Ghedi area claimed a hit on the port engine of a Ju 88. Two Bf 109s, 'lightning flash' and 'White 8' flew from Airasca to Ghedi early in the morning of the 23rd. Me 410 F6+DK apparently ended its career with 2./122 when Dirich and Scheuer crashed it in Padua that evening. The pilot was flying again within three days, however. 92 Sqn saw Bf 109s over La Spezia early next morning but was more successful in the same location 12hr later when Flt Lt Montgomerie and Fg Off Taylor were on dusk patrol. The latter claimed one probable from a pair of Bf 109s, but the German (from 1./NAGr.11) was only damaged.

Notes

15. A few others followed next day.

*Messerschmitt Bf 109G-6/R5/R3 – W.Nr 162057 of 2./NAGr.11 –
Castiglione del Lago (PG), June 1944*

*Messerschmitt Bf 109G-6/R6/R3 of Nucleo Comando, IIº Gr.C.
Flown by Cap. Mancini – Cascina Vaga (PV), June 1944*

Fiat G.55 of 1ª Sq., Iº Gr.C. – Reggio Emilia, July 1944 – (Reconstruction)

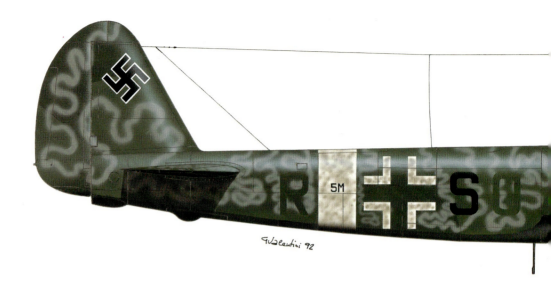

*Messerschmitt Bf 110G-4/R3/B2 – W.Nr. 720189 of 6./JNG 6.
Flown by Hptm. Habermayr – Perugia, June 1944 –
(Reconstruction)*
Radar layout: combined FuG 220 SN-2b
antenna array on the nose with FuG 212 in the middle.

*Junkers Ju 88A-6/U of Westa 26 –
Orio al Serio (BG), June 1944*
Radar layout: one FuG 200 antenna mast mounted on the nose with the remaining antennae mounted on each wing leading edge just outboard of the engine nacelles; FuG 216 VR radar antenna is visible under starboard wing.

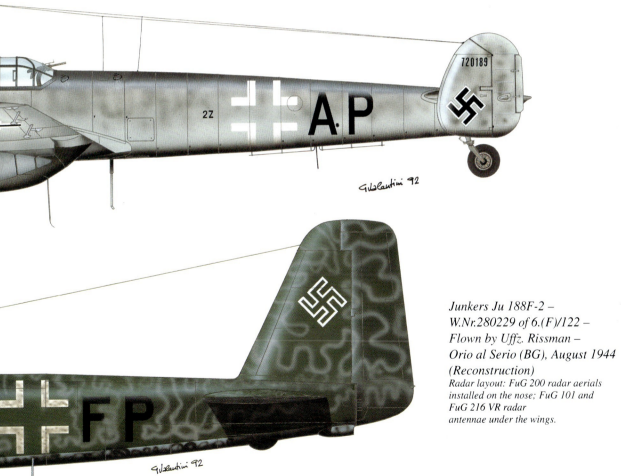

*Junkers Ju 188F-2 –
W.Nr.280229 of 6.(F)/122 –
Flown by Uffz. Rissman –
Orio al Serio (BG), August 1944
(Reconstruction)*
Radar layout: FuG 200 radar aerials installed on the nose; FuG 101 and FuG 216 VR radar antennae under the wings.

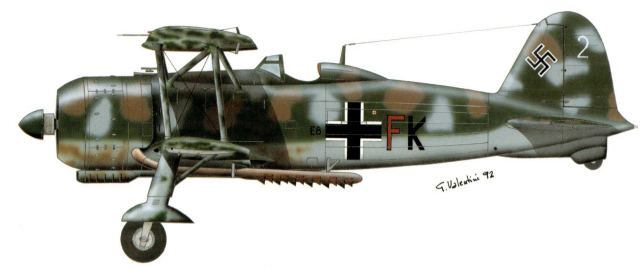
Fiat Cr.42 of 2./NSGr.9 – Caselle (TO), May 1944

Messerschmitt Bf 109G-6/R3 of 8./JG53 – Maniago (PN), June 1944

Focke-Wulf Fw 190F-8 of 1./SG 4 – Piacenza, June 1944

Chapter 5

Operation Phoenix

The diary of S.Ten Di Santo, II° Gr.C.:
25 August 1944: Muster at 0800. Everybody has to go to the airfield. The roll is then called at the Villa Sicurtà. The Germans want to disband the Italian Air Force. The Germans have surrounded the village. What a beautiful situation! In the evening everything seems quieter but the German sentries are still there. The worst thing is the possibility of being taken to Germany...

The origins of the operation that nearly brought about the ANR's dissolution probably went back a couple of months before August 1944. There were two main considerations prompting the Germans towards the disbandment idea, one military, the other political.

The former began to take shape in June, after the Gustav Line's fall, the loss of Rome and the Allied armies' onrush towards the Apennines and the Northern Plains. Given the possibility of failing to stop the advance on the Gothic Line, and thus having an enemy breakthrough into the Po Valley, preparations were being made for the speedy evacuation of the territory South of the Po and West of the Ticino in case the situation deteriorated further. This entailed further withdrawals of the whole ground organisation and stores, and the rendering unserviceable of the airfields that lay in the threatened area (e.g. Reggio Emilia and Cascina Vaga). The transfer of the Italian fighters to Vicenza and Villafranca in July was only one of the moves foreseen in case of a further enemy advance, the last of which would probably have to be ANR units' disbandment, incorporating their aircraft (and possibly their personnel) into the Luftwaffe to avoid a second '8 September 1943', leaving dozens of aircraft in Allied hands.

Although by August this threat seemed to have diminished, the political attitude of the Germans towards the ANR was increasingly hostile. Also, nervousness had begun to spread through German HQs and top brass after the failed 20 July Plot against Hitler. The Germans never entirely trusted the Italians, even though an effective Italian air force could have eased some of the Luftwaffe's burdens and boosted the RSI Government's status and morale.

The main problem was that the Germans had never seen the point of the RSI Air Ministry, full of bureaucrats hindering the fighting units, rather than supporting them. When on 25 July Mussolini decided to split the offices of ANR's Under-Secretary and Chief of Staff, installing in the former Col. Manlio Molfese and leaving only the latter to Gen. Arrigo Tessari (who had assumed T.Col. Ernesto Botto's responsibilities in March), the German response was formally to reject the new Under-Secretary. When Tessari, too, was dismissed by Mussolini just before 25 August, the Germans had had enough and decided to intervene '. . . as the Duce had replaced ANR's Chief of Staff too many times without asking anyone's permission . . .', and also to avoid the ANR 'being stifled by excessive bureaucracy . . .'.

That Tessari's replacement just served as an excuse was demonstrated by the fact that the Germans had already siphoned the fuel from all Italian aircraft on the main airfields. Everything was ready for the launch of 'Operation Phoenix', planned by Lfl. 2 to disband the ANR and establish an 'Italian Air Force Legion' under German commanders. A plan of action had been drawn up on the 21st, including numbers and locations of ANR personnel.

The operation involved both Italian and German officers, although some of the latter refused to take part. The most important to withhold his co-operation (owing to his good comradeship with many ANR Commanders) was the Jafü, Maltzahn, who was consequently posted away from Italy on the 23rd. Carried out with Richthofen's blessing, the operation also involved the direct participation of JG 77's Obstlt. Steinhoff, Obstlt. Dietrich (Liaison Officer to the Italian Fighter Command), Oberst Gravath and Oberst Beherend (Liaison Officers to I° and III° Gruppi Caccia respectively) and several other German officers. On the Italian side, those most involved were: Gen. Tessari, T.Col. Falconi (CO of the Gruppo Complementare Caccia) and Col. Fagnani (Air Ministry). As S.Ten. Di Santo's diary (above) shows, this was a dramatic experience for all the Italians involved.

On the afternoon of 24 August Villafranca's KTB reported the landing of five Stab/JG 77 Bf 109s from Bettola. This was no routine flight – one of the pilots was Steinhoff himself, who had organised a meeting in Custoza (VR) that evening. This was to involve the Italian Fighter Command, the COs of I° and II° Gr.C. and T.Col. Foschini (CO of the ANR Fighter Units). Oberst Beherend presented to the Italian officers a proclamation to be read to their units the following day. Great was the Italians' surprise and embarrassment, trying to explain to the Germans the ill-feeling that such a document would surely provoke among their men. Foschini gained permission to telephone the Air Ministry in Bellagio (CO), but only managed to speak with Fagnani, who, apparently without knowing its exact content, ordered him to read the proclamation to all personnel. However, the Germans also claimed to have reached an agreement with T.Col. Falconi.

Meanwhile, Luftwaffe troops had surrounded the villages of Valeggio sul Mincio (the quarters of II° Gr.C.), Monticello Conte Otto (VI) (quarters of I° and III° Gr.C.); Lonate Pozzolo, Castano Primo (MI) and Venegono (the bases and quarters of the torpedo-bomber units) and all the main ANR airfields as well as the Area Commands (Turin, Milan and Udine, for example), commandeering all telephone lines.

On the morning of the 25th German officers and armed troops arrived at all the Italian units with orders to read the proclamation to them:

Airmen of Italy, Soldiers of the Signals and Ground Echelons!
Your fight is threatened with suffocation by bureaucracy and excessive administration. The Luftwaffe High Command has therefore decided, in agreement with the Italian Government to abandon its previous methods of co-operation with the Italian Air Force.
It is up to you to choose either voluntarily to join the newly-founded Italian Air Legion and, alongside your German comrades, to fight on unconditionally in the German Wehrmacht under German leadership and to fly until the common victory for the New Order in Europe and the rebirth of a new Italy and thereby to become the nucleus of an eventual great Italian Air Force or
to enlist in the Air Defence Divisions that are to be established in what has hitherto been the Italian Air Force.
Field Marshal Freiherr von Richthofen summons you to the fight for freedom and honour and to your Homeland's defence.
The fallen heroes of your people in this war are watching you. Let not their sacrifice have been in vain.
Enlist as volunteer warriors in the new Italian Legion.

They were then to proceed immediately to separate those who agreed to join the 'Legion' from the dissenters. After the reading there was much bewilderment among the Italians. What was going on? Why this sudden change? Why do away with the Italian uniform and flag? Who had issued such orders and, above all, did the Duce know what was going on? As usual with the Germans, only vague answers were forthcoming, and in most cases none.

On the morning of the 25th, in Valeggio, Steinhoff again met Foschini and Alessandrini at II° Gr.C.'s command post, speaking directly to the unit's pilots. After praising their performance in combat, he said that, owing to conflicts with the Italian Air Ministry, the German High Command had decided to disband the ANR and set up an Italian Legion under their direct command, adding that '. . . the collapse of the Italian Army and Navy' would soon follow.

The response of Alessandrini and his men to this ultimatum was a curt refusal, no one enlisting in the Legion. The same happened at Vicenza (I° Gr.C.) and Lonate Pozzolo (Gr. 'Buscaglia'). At the latter airfield precisely seven of the 854 men joined the 'Legion'. Only a part of the newly constituted III° Gr.C. decided at first to accept, under German pressure. The unit was still split between Cervere, Vicenza and Thiene and hoped, in its commander's absence, to gain time to find out what was happening.

The Germans naturally tried to exploit surprise, and succeeded with some of the training and second-line units and rear echelons. An optimistic German situation report at 2300 on Day One speaks of a 25 per cent volunteering rate in Venegono and almost 100 per cent in Lonate, with figures of 40 per cent, 80 per cent and 100 per cent elsewhere. The main problems were over the protocol of who should mount guard and what uniforms and badges should be worn in the new set-up. They had, however, underestimated the determination and *esprit de corps* of the fighting units. Although repeatedly threatened with deportation to Germany if they did not join the 'Legion', almost none of the 2,300 in the first-line units succumbed. Their resistance not only stopped the operation in its tracks, but led III° Gruppo Caccia's personnel to retract their provisional acceptance and present their own conditions: to join an Italian Legion '. . . fighting in Italy, in Italian uniform, under the Italian flag and never swearing an oath to Hitler'.

The Allies learned of all this from an ANR officer who defected in October:

> In Milan, while the premises of the principal Italian units were surrounded by SS troops, a German Liaison Major called together all the Italian officers at their Headquarters and announced [the dissolution of the ANR], giving as a reason that [it] was more of a hindrance than a help . . . The Italians had a choice of three courses, to form part of an Italian 'Air Legion' (with flying duties), to enter a Flak organization, or a concentration camp. Those who accepted either of the first two would swear an oath to Hitler, wear German uniform and be ready to go to Germany.

Anyone signing up would be considered a German soldier 'and as such enjoy all his rights' (the idea of a Wehrmacht soldier having many rights, let alone enjoying them, is a little difficult to grasp). This informant suggested that the ANR's Commander telephoned his government and secured 48hr for his men to reach a decision, during which time they were confined to quarters.

The Italians who had co-operated with the plan and now recognised its failure adopted varying tactics. Falconi flatly refused to recognise the RSI Government, considering himself a member of the Italian Legion under German command; Tessari on the 29th addressed a memorandum to Mussolini, trying pathetically to pass it all off as a misunderstanding and saying that he was not even aware that the Germans had acted without prior agreement from the Duce and his government. Meanwhile, things began to settle down on both sides, many German officers showing some perplexity and lowered morale with the dawning realisation that Operation Phoenix had failed.

When Mussolini and his government finally found out what was happening (this was no earlier than 27-28 August; that afternoon the Duce met the Vice Chief of Staff, T.Col. Cadringher, Magg. Marini and Cap. Bertuzzi of Gr. 'Buscaglia' and Ten.Col. Morino of Comando Aerotrasporti), their immediate reaction, including protests to Hitler, slowly (if only partially) restored the situation. The Germans nonetheless decided to seize all the aircraft and usable material they could. Between 30-31 August JG 77 pilots transferred 16 Bf 109s of 'the former II./ital. JGr.' from Villafranca to Ghedi. They forbade any flying by the Italians, leaving the two Gruppi Caccia and Gr. 'Buscaglia' grounded.

There is no escaping Phoenix's short-sightedness, an operation achieving a degree of moral, political and operational damage the Allies could never have hoped for. The Germans' nett gain had been repossession of a few Bf 109s and the lasting allegiance of a mere handful of men, but at what a price! Two badly needed fighter and one torpedo-bomber groups out of action and many lower ranks going home (200 deserted from the Tele-communications Regiment's Casale Monferrato (AL) barracks) until the situation had settled – in many cases this meant indefinitely. Last but not least, the events engendered among Italian pilots a distrust of the Germans even stronger than the latter felt for them. The time required to heal these wounds was in short supply; all of September was to be wasted pending official German permission for the ANR to be re-equipped and renew operations.

A NAGr.11 Bf 109, 'sheltered' by a bombed-out building. Note the white wingtips and tailband, as well as the truncated underwing cross. (Bundesarchiv)

The crew of a Ju 188D-2 of 6.(F)/122 pose in front of their aircraft after flying the unit's 3,000th mission. The aircraft's undersides are blackened for night camouflage and its FuG 200 aerials are mounted slightly differently from the plane on page 86. (Bundesarchiv)

Chapter 5

Operations

25 August 1944

The war in Italy did not pause, despite Phoenix. Human tragedies continued on small and large scales. In the small hours Ogfr. Emil Carstens, Awol since the previous day from Cameri airfield, was cycling back from a visit to a female cook working at Lonate Pozzolo. He never got back to barracks. Three days later his corpse, shot through the head, was pulled out of the Villorese Canal at Palazzolo, Milan. An investigation concluded that he had been ambushed by partisans near the Ticino Bridge; his rifle and bicycle were never found.

On defensive patrol between 0200 and 0525, a Beaufighter of 255 Sqn, crewed by Flt Sgts Dinham-Peren and Fawkner Corbett, claimed the probable destruction of a Ju 88 or 188 in the Ravenna area. DAF records include a pencilled 'no traces' while German sources say only that a Ju 88 broke off a mission to Naples in the face of fighter opposition. At dawn over La Spezia an attempted reconnaissance by a Rotte of Bf 109s from 2./NAGr.11 was intercepted by the Spitfires of Fg Off Taylor and Flt Lt Montgomerie of 92 Sqn. Montgomerie's shooting down of one of the Messerschmitts is attested to by Luftwaffe records. In the late afternoon a pair of NAGr.12's Bf 109s carried out a 95min low-level mission covering Pescara and the promontory of Gargano.

2.(F)/122 put up two early-morning and two evening sorties. At 1735, Ju 188s F6+LP and +HP took off in quick succession for Bergamo, ending their three-day stopover at Ghedi.

In the wider world, Finland began peace talks with the Soviet Union, General de Gaulle entered Paris to receive the German garrison's surrender and Romania declared war on Germany. One side-effect of the Romanian *volte face* showed up in Italy that evening: a Bf 109G-6 (W.Nr.166133), flown by the ace, Captain Constantin Cantacuzino and liberally bedecked with American markings, landed at Foggia. From the radio compartment in the rear fuselage emerged Lt Col. James A. Gunn, USAAF, shot down over Romania and now bearing diplomatic messages from King Michael to the Allied High Command. An American pilot wrecked the Bf 109 while test-flying it next day.

In Italy at 2300, the Allies launched an offensive against the Gothic Line that was to make good progress for nine days before worsening weather and sharp German resistance wore it down.

26-27 August 1944

A 1./NAGr.11 Bf 109 is listed destroyed by fighters on the 27th, but there is no corresponding claim. The same Gruppe's 2. Staffel lost an aeroplane to accidental causes on an operation.

The night of the 27/28th saw the first NSGr.9 activity for that moon period. About 20 Ju 87s operated against road traffic around Florence and one was claimed at 2231 by Thompson and Beaumont of 600 Sqn near Arezzo, while another may have fallen to AA fire. On the east coast, 3./NSGr.9 bombed Fano and Pesaro.

28 August 1944

At 17,000ft east of La Spezia two Spitfires of 92 Sqn met four Bf 109s, one of which made a head-on pass at Plt Off Hackett. Turning to starboard, his wingman, W/O Newman, dived after it, while the other Germans 'beat a hasty retreat'. Closing in, Newman fired five short bursts, scoring hits and 'causing such alarm and despondency inside the cockpit that the pilot baled out just before the aircraft crashed in flames'. The Bf 109 was from 2./NAGr.11 and its destruction was confirmed by Ultra. At Villafranca a medium-bomber raid burnt out a Bf 109G-12 and damaged 12 other ex-ANR Messerschmitts.

The sleek form of a Ju 88T-1 taxying towards a less streamlined Italian steamroller, probably used for smoothing taxi-tracks and runways. By September three examples of this version, together with six of the more advanced T-3, were still operating in Italy with 4.(F)/122. (IWM)

At about 2120, six aircraft of 3./NSGr.9 took off from Cavriago to bomb bridges and attack motor transport near Arezzo. They were to go in singly, and each carried one AB 250 and four AB 70 bombs. In one of these aeroplanes (Ju 87D-3 W.Nr.100396, E8+KL) were Fw. Otto Brinkmann and Uffz. Franz Scherzer, their call sign for this operation being Adler (Eagle). Southeast of Florence, about an hour into their flight, they were suddenly attacked by a Beaufighter of 600 Sqn (that of Plt Off Judd and Fg Off Brewer, who had chalked up another victory an hour earlier), which scored strikes in the starboard wing tanks, setting them alight. The bomb load was jettisoned, but the fire grew worse and Brinkmann gave the order to bale out. After landing, Brinkmann made contact with the Italian police who first shot him through the arm but then gave him (so he thought) directions to the German lines. In fact they had sent him to British troops and captivity. Scherzer was posted missing.

At 2345 northeast of Florence, Wg Cdr Styles and Fg Off Wilmer (again of 600 Sqn) also shot down a Ju 87. Although three kills were therefore claimed that night, the authors know of only two German losses, the second being a Ju 87D-5 (W.Nr. 141039) of 1./9. Its pilot, Uffz. Günther Voss was posted missing. Ofw. Toni Fink was hurt when D3+GL was shot up by a nightfighter after bombing Pesaro but he and gunner Ogefr. Egon Zantow got back safely to Palata.

29-30 August 1944

Number 92 Sqn continued its run of success by damaging one of a pair of Bf 109s. At 1300 it was again signalled that Nachtschlacht aeroplanes would be up from the Parma-Reggio-Ferrara area that night, focusing mainly on the eastern sector of the front. Operating south and west of Pesaro, Judd and Brewer now achieved the impressive feat of shooting down three Ju 87s in the space of an hour, starting at 2110. Uffz. Hans Vossen's crew of four went missing in Ju 188D-2, W.Nr.150227 (F6+MM) during the night of the 29th.

The next afternoon, pilots from II./JG 77 were busy ferrying eleven Bf 109s 'of the former Italian Fighter Group' from Villafranca to Ghedi, apparently destroying one and damaging another. At 2200, Ju 188 F6+LP set out on a mission from Ghedi after a day that had seen three Me 410 sorties and two rapidly aborted attempts.

31 August 1944

Capt E.R. Dixon (SAAF) of 241 Sqn. was flying a first light patrol inland along the River Po at about 30ft when his wingman, Plt Off D.F. White spotted an unidentified aircraft about three miles away at a similar altitude, heading west. The two Spitfire Mk.VIIIs turned and closed in, identifying the bogey as a Ju 87 with 'the usual dark mottled camouflage'. White was best placed, and fired from dead astern but without apparent result as the German tried to evade with 40° turns but without shooting back. Dixon then made a quarter attack, obtaining strikes on the port side of the Junkers' engine cowling. The enemy aircraft immediately began to smoke and crashed in a field, bursting into flames on impact. Dixon overflew the wreck, but could see no survivors amid the dust and smoke. Their squadron's ORB speculates that the Ju 87 might have been on a ferry flight, and hoped 'that a high ranking officer of the Luftwaffe was flying it'. German records confirm the

aeroplane's loss but say nothing of personnel casualties.

Ghedi had quite a busy day, starting just before 0500 GMT when two Ju 188s, F6+BP and F6+LP, arrived from Bergamo. Subsequently, JG 77 ferried in another five ex-ANR Bf 109s from Villafranca. Late in the afternoon 2.(F)/122 sent off two Me 410 sorties, the first aircraft (F6+CK with Ofhr. Walter Grigoleit and Uffz. Wolfgang Habicht) returning to base after only 26min then taking off again a few minutes later. Both aircraft were back on the ground by 1840. At 1942 Ju 188 F6+FP left on a mission and presumably landed back at its home base of Bergamo, while 3./NSGr.9 was out 'road-hunting' south of the River Metauro.

ABOVE:
Real 'workhorse' of the Luftwaffe, the Fi 156 Storch was used in Italy for liaison duties with both first-line units and operational commands. F5+DP shown here belonged to the Operational Staff of Luftflotte 2 and, together with several other aircraft (Ju 52s and He 111s, for example) carried out liaison and transport duties. (Bundesarchiv)

BELOW:
One of the most feared threats to an Allied pilot – Flak. Linked by a close communication network to the Jafü, the radar stations could alert the AA units to incoming aircraft. Here, an Italian Artiglieria Contraerea (Ar.Co.) unit equipped with 90/53 guns in the country near Verona. (Pagliano)

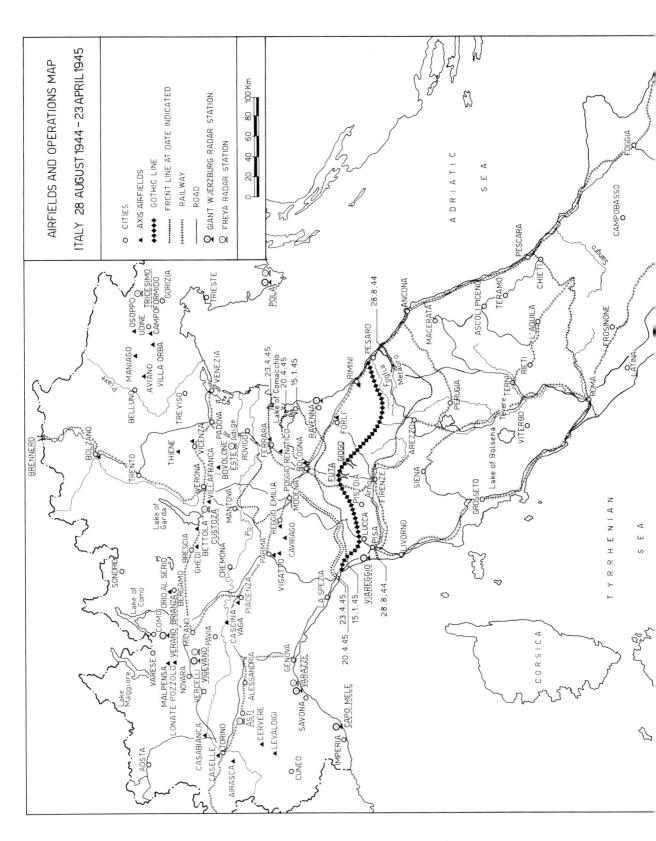

Chapter 6

September 1944

Reorganisation – A Field Marshal Departs

In September the last Luftwaffe fighter units, Stab and II./JG 77, quit Italy. In due course the newly-reforming ANR would be expected to bear the airborne defence burden almost entirely alone. Organisationally, it was appreciated that the remaining Luftwaffe resources in Italy were now too small to warrant command by the full panoply of a Field Marshal and an Air Fleet. Accordingly, Richthofen and his staff were withdrawn to Vienna and the reorganisation he had first suggested in June took place. The Mittelitalien Command's staff was combined with that of the administrative/supply organisation Feldluftgaukommando XXVIII, all being presided over by Pohl, as Kommandierender General der Deutschen Luftwaffe in Italien, and a staff of 600. He controlled the flying units, flak and ground organisation, and was responsible for servicing the ANR. The command was formally inaugurated by OKL on 6 September and moved into the former Lfl.2 HQ at Malcesine, Lake Garda, on the 15th.

Richthofen flew out of Villafranca at 0645 on the 1st, in an He 111 bound for Eschborn, Germany, and 276 Wing duly monitored the flight, but without identifying the passenger. It must be doubted whether his departure was universally regretted. A defecting Italian General, well acquainted with Kesselring and Richthofen both officially and privately, claimed that relations between the Field Marshals were strained and that each had engaged in political manoeuvres to do down the other; also, Richthofen had accused his brother officer of turning his back on the Luftwaffe. The Italian described Richthofen as 'a man with neither manners nor scruples, who dabbles in Nazi politics and . . . is quite incapable of making a firm decision'. On assuming his command, he had dismissed experienced staff in favour of his own acolytes and informed his Italian Chief Liaison Officer that he had no use for Italy or Italians.

In October 1944 Richthofen was invalided out of the service after an operation on a brain tumour, and died shortly after the war.

Prospects
The situation for the first half of the month, as reported by a staff officer makes gloomy reading:
> Hostile air activity continues to demonstrate the enemy's absolute air supremacy in the Italian Theatre.
>
> The expected reinforcements did not arrive. With the few reconnaissance aircraft repeated attempts were made to gain the necessary insight into enemy movements, especially those at sea. Some night ground attack aircraft still at our disposal brought appreciable relief to the fighting troops on several occasions.

The 'expected reinforcements' were presumably those units withdrawn from Southern France, none of which in the event carried on the fight from bases in Italy, despite the preparations made.

Pohl seems to have been determined to make the most of any assets to hand, aside from lobbying energetically for more to be transferred to him. By 28 September the framework had been agreed for reactivating the ANR, including plans for its expansion as resources permitted.

The Luftwaffe

The flying units in Italy were at just about their lowest numerical ebb. Later other factors would result in less operational capability being realised from an ostensibly more powerful force. The order of battle on 31 August was:

Unit	Aircraft	
	Number	Type
Stab/FAGr.122	0	
2.(F)/122	5	Me 410A-3/B-3
4.(F)/122	6	Ju 188D-2
	3	Ju 88T-1
	6	Ju 88T-3
6.(F)/122	7	Ju 188D-2
	1	Ju 188F-1
Kdo. Carmen	2/3	Ju 188D/F
Stab/NAGr.11	0(0)	
1./NAGr.11	1	Bf 109G-6
	11	Bf 109G-8
2./NAGr.11	5	Bf 109G-5/U2/R2
	3	Bf 109G-6
	5	Bf 109G-8/R5
Stab/NSGr.9	1(1)	Ju 87D-5
1./NSGr.9	7(4)	Ju 87D-5
2./NSGr.9	12(10)	Ju 87D-3/D-5
3./NSGr.9	11(9)	Ju 87D-3/D-5
Jafü Oberitalien	1	Bf 109G-12
Stab JG 77	2	Bf 109G-6
	5	Bf 109G-6/U4
II./JG 77	38	Bf 109G-6
	14	Bf 109G-6/U4
	2	Bf 109G-12
L.Beo.St.7	6(3)	Ju 88 [on 3 September]
Verb.St.300	8(7)	Fi 156
Verb.St.500	6(6)	Fi 156/Saiman/Fairchild

Whether we should add to the above a 'dirty-grey B-26', seen on several occasions by MATAF crews and allegedly enemy-operated, is debatable.

Logistics

The fuel supply situation was getting serious, although the full impact would not bear on Italy just yet. From the end of August manpower was progressively combed out in favour of the ground forces, although similar measures had been carried through before to some extent. 'Surplus' airfields continued to be put out of commission while facilities were improved at some of the remainder.

Night Attack

On 5 September Stab and 1./NSGr.9 were at Ferrara, opposite the Eighth Army; 2. and 3. were at Cavriago and Vigatto respectively, facing the Fifth Army. The next day an advance party was in Bovolone, preparing the way for 1. Staffel's arrival a week later. Immediately after that 2./9 transferred to Ghedi, and on the 16th aircraft from 3. began flying in to Villafranca from Cavriago II, followed five days later by others from Aviano and Piacenza. Early the same day, five Ju 87s arrived in Ghedi and six at Vicenza.

Operations were sporadic, interspersed with numerous training flights, and on the 12th it was announced that missions would not resume until the New Moon period. A table of organisation, apparently from September or October, lists NSGr.9's commanders as follows:

Gruppenkommandeur	Major Frost
Ia	Major Rohn
Adjutant	[handing over]
1. Staffel	Hptm. Hegenbarth
2. Staffel	Obltn. Kuchenbuch
3. Staffel	Hptm. Reither

Tactical Reconnaissance

1./NAGr.11 started the month at Bologna and 2. at Piacenza, both apparently still positioned to provide coverage of the front lines with their comparatively short-range aeroplanes. Allied estimates credited the Gruppe with ten sorties a day in the early part of the month. Fuel was provided at Villafranca on the 13th for elements of NAGr.11, an advance party arrived next day and a contingent of 2. Staffel aircraft flew in from Piacenza two days after that. They did not remain long, moving on the 25th to Udine, where the Gruppe was to see out the war. Among the aircraft making that transfer was a single Fw 190, a type not on NAGr.11's recorded strength at the time, but possibly a precursor of an associated unit which came officially into being in October.

Long-Range Reconnaissance

The strategic units were in Ghedi and Bergamo and were requested on a number of occasions during the month to provide photo cover in association with planned operations by special naval raiding forces against Ancona and other targets. (A request on the 17th for fighter cover to be laid on as well seems a

An interesting close-up of a Ju 87D of 2./NSGr.9. In May 1945 this aircraft (E8+GK, W.Nr.2600) was found by Allied troops, abandoned on Bovolone airfield. Although the night assault variants of the Ju 87 are nowadays identified as the D-7 and D-8, wartime German documents speak only of the D-3 and D-5 in service with the Nachtschlachtgruppen. (Petrick)

little optimistic). A milestone of a kind was passed in the course of September when, according to a PoW, 4.(F) and 6.(F)/122 flew their 3,000th mission.

The month also saw a continual flurry of non-operational flights by the three resident Staffeln of FAGr.122, shifting aircraft back and forth between Ghedi, Bergamo and occasionally Bettola. Amongst these movements are logged one Ju 188 of 1.(F)/122 and two more carrying the 'H' code letter of that Staffel but attributed to 6./122, suggesting perhaps that the former was surrendering aircraft to bolster the latter. Also notable is the number of 2./122's missions aborted within minutes, apparently owing to the appearance of Allied fighters.

By the beginning of the month the Ju 88 had finally passed out of service with 6. Staffel (a couple in their 'old' markings soldiering on with 4.), leaving only 188s from then on. These were a mixture of BMW 801-engined F-models and Jumo 213-powered Ds which not only required different spares but different grades of fuel. Higher-performance aircraft might have been good news, but an alarming statistic for the month is the loss rate of Ju 188Ds to accidental causes; three from 4./122 and seven from 6., according to one source. Although known incidents involving death or injury are somewhat fewer, the situation can scarcely have helped aircrews' confidence in their equipment. Engine failure seems to have been a prime cause of these losses, but, even so, all but one of the BMW versions had been sent away to other units or to overhaul by the end of the month. Similarly, 4./122 transferred its BMW 801-engined Ju 88T-1s to other units during September, leaving it with only T-3 (Jumo 213) models.

Fighters and Nightfighters

As September began, the detachment of Luftbeobachterstaffel 7 was spending its last few days at Villaorba; Stab and II./JG 77 were at Villafranca and Ghedi respectively – also soon to be gone but yet to suffer their last casualties in Italy.

A Controller Without Fighters

Although the General had no operational fighters as yet, he did gain a new Jafü Oberitalien during September. Maltzahn was succeeded by the former JG 27 pilot, Oberst Eduard Neumann[16]. He inherited an Operational HQ on Castle Hill near Verona with sub-HQs at Udine and Milan, a usable radar system and a plan (codenamed with complete transparency 'Threatening Danger South') to draft in approximately four fighter Gruppen if there was an emergency (one wonders just how bad things would have had to get). Neumann's reflections on what he found in Italy are of some interest:

In contrast to the Air Ministry, the purpose of which was not immediately apparent, the General Staff of the ANR, with its economical establishment, its sense of duty and its spartan outlook made an excellent impression. The Chief of the General Staff, T.Col. Baylon, an exceptionally good type, was the moving spirit behind the operational sections of the Air Force. He and his Quartermaster-General, T.Col. Bonzano, were known to me from Africa days, when they were both Commanders of Gruppi, and I well remember their keenness on operations. Our former good relations now stood us in good stead.

Whereas there was no pronounced political trend among the officials at the Air Ministry, the General Staff and the flying personnel were not to be regarded as fascists. Baylon was, in fact, suspected of being an 'A-fascist', a euphemism applied to anti-fascists when reports had to be submitted to Mussolini . . .

Factors which determined [thinking ANR members'] continued adherence to the German cause were a desire to avoid going down in history for a second time as a people who could not keep faith, and the fear that Italy without firm leadership would be driven to anarchy. The bulk of the rank and file, who had formed no political opinions of their own, clung to leaders who were known . . .

Neumann also had perceptive comments to make on the operational qualities of the Italian airmen, but these are better discussed in the context of their actual performance on returning to action. The Allies had meanwhile concluded that 'it is probable that measures of control taken to prevent acts of disloyalty have so restricted the activity of the Fascist IRAF that it has little operational value'.

The ANR in Limbo

This was probably one of the longest months endured by the Italian pilots. Nothing happened, they had neither aircraft nor reason to hang around, so they spent time on marching, physical exercise, football matches, parties and dinners – everything but flying. On the 10th even the German liaison detachment assigned to II° Gruppo was transferred from Valeggio to a new, unknown posting.

This lull led some pilots to go home on indefinite leave, but the strength of ANR units saw a relatively small drop, despite what had happened in the previous month and the still uncertain situation. Those who remained, however, formed an even more solid group and their determination to continue fighting if the Germans gave them the chance was that much greater. This was recognised by the new Jafü and the reactivation of the Italian fighters was one of the first problems he had to face.

While talks went on about reviving the ANR, it became clear that most of its smaller units would have to go and that the new set-up would concentrate on the fighters, with a secondary role for the torpedo-bombers. Between 11 and 30 September the following units (some only existing on paper) were disbanded:

Gr. Complementare Caccia

Comando Aerosiluranti { Comando Sq. Scuola / Comando Sq. Addestramento

Gr. Complementare Aerotrasporti
Sq. Bombardamento 'E. Muti'.

These measures broke the stalemate keeping the two transport groups' personnel in Germany. By the end of October the almost 1,000 men of these units had returned to Italy where some were to be employed as infantry under the misleading designation 'anti-paratroop units'.

After much discussion, on the 27th a telegram went from 'Robinson' (OKL's codename) to the Luftwaffe's Quartermaster-General, detailing the '. . . conditional approval of OKL and agreement of Duce and Under Secretary of Italian Air Ministry for the operationally usable parts of the ANR . . .'. The message led to an 'Agreement for the Re-establishment of Italian Flying Units of the Italian Republican Air Force', signed on 30 September:

1.) Planned establishment – 1 fighter Gruppe, 1 torpedo-bomber Gruppe with ground echelon, 1 signals detachment. Further units as personnel and materiel permit.

2.) Leadership – **A)** German Gruppenkommandeure and Staffelkapitäne with Italian deputies, except in the Torpedo Staffel where there will be a German Special Duties Officer. **B)** German Kommandeur can partly delegate command to Italian Deputy. **C)** Later on, if training and operations as well as military leadership and maintenance of military interests are firmly established to German standards, leadership by Italian Kommandeure, Staffelkapitäne and other unit commanders is planned.

3.) Military formalities – **A)** the units referred to at '1' are Italian formations although subordinated to German Commands in every respect. **B**) Italian uniform, ranks and insignia. **C**) Italian Flag and oath of allegiance. **D**) German national markings on aircraft with Italian ones adjacent. **E**) Acceptance and selection of personnel via German/Italian induction centres. **F**) Appointment and promotion of officers only with the agreement of GOC Luftwaffe in Italy, with the advice of the Italian Air Ministry.

From the following day the ANR rose from the ashes and went back to war, rather like a Phoenix.

IIº Gruppo Caccia
Preference was given to IIº Gr.C. both because its pilots had flown Bf 109s until only a month before, and because this unit was less troublesome than Iº Gr.C., whose recent history had seen several morale crises and disciplinary problems (it is worth remembering that one of their pilots, S.Ten. Alberto Graziani, had even deserted to Corsica in his C.205, on 28 May 1944).

Iº Gruppo Caccia: September/November 1944
At the beginning of September the pilots led by Magg. Visconti were transferred to Albino near Bergamo. Although no aircraft are known to have been with the unit at that time, some of them apparently survived the Germans' revenge, if a reported encounter with C.205s (*see* 23 September) is to be believed. What is more, a German strength report of 10 October mysteriously lists 10 (7) aircraft with the officially disbanded Iº Gruppo, but it is certain that these aircraft were not flown operationally.

During the long rest period, and since the Germans allowed the ANR to reconstitute only the one fighter unit, morale was unavoidably low and prospects uncertain. Several pilots and other personnel left the unit, but most chose to stay and see what would happen. That there was a will to preserve the Gruppo is shown by an SMAR document stating that from 1 October the name of the unit was changed to Iº Gruppo Caccia 'Asso di Bastoni' (Ace of Clubs) with its Squadriglie as follows:
1ª Sq. 'A. Brighi'
2ª Sq. 'M. Marinone'
3ª Sq. 'G. Bonet'.

An interesting episode could be further proof that the unit still had some aircraft. On 15 October Magg. Visconti was contacted by an emissary of the Regia Aeronautica now fighting alongside the Allies in Southern Italy (commonly known as the Italian Co-belligerent Air Force). He was told that the Allies had prepared two airfields to receive aircraft of Iº Gr.C., should he choose to defect. Visconti declined the offer, provided the Germans did not try to dissolve his command a second time.

After several meetings with the German authorities and strenuous efforts by Visconti to get authorisation for re-equipment and a return to operations, OKL finally approved the provision of Iº Gr.C. with Bf 109s. Training, however, was to take place in Germany as the Italian theatre could no longer be considered safe. In early November Iº Gruppo's men took the train for Germany and, after a troubled journey through the snow and a brief stop at Memmingen, arrived at their new base of Holzkirchen.

On the night of 4/5 September 1944, 600 Sqn.'s Sqn Ldr Burke and his Navigator Flt Lt Whaley shot down a Ju 87 of NSGr.9 whose explosion engulfed their Beaufighter Mk.VI in burning debris, with the results shown. (IWM)

There, training began almost immediately, as on the 6th a few pilots flew with Luftwaffe instructors in a Bf 109G-12, but it soon became clear to the Germans that some of the Italians had to start from scratch, graduating from the Klemm Kl 35 to the Bf 108 and then on to the Bf 109G-12. Moreover, the only G-12 was soon damaged and things slowed down pending the arrival of another from Italy, since the Germans would not allot one of 'their' trainers to the Italians. This, added to the heavy snow and the continuous passage of Allied bomber formations over the airfield, meant that November was almost completely wasted.

Personnel of 2./NAGr.11 cheer the pilot of 'White 6' after the unit's 4,000th mission. This photo shows both the unit insignia on the board (it was rarely applied to the aircraft) and the small size of the tactical numbers on the fuselage. (Bundesarchiv)

The Ground War

September saw the Allies closing up to the Gothic Line as the Germans hurried to occupy its defences. Under air cover which at times achieved record levels – 804 tactical sorties on the 18th, for instance – the Allied armies breached the eastern sections of the Line during the first days of the month, while on the central sector the assault was delayed until the defenders and their reserves were (so it was hoped) preoccupied with the situation on the Adriatic coast. The Fifth Army opened its offensive on the 10th and fought its way up Highway 65, through the Futa and Il Giogo passes. Even then no decisive breakthrough could be achieved, the Germans withdrawing (as ever) to the next set of prepared positions, aided – as their opponents were impeded – by rain and mud. The mountain fighting ground slowly and miserably on through the coming months. Bologna was to remain just outside the Allies' grasp almost until the last.

The expulsion of the Wehrmacht from the greater part of France permitted the strengthening of air support in Italy, and MATAF HQ returned to the country on the 25th, four days after the capture of Rimini by the Eighth Army.

Notes

16. According to Neumann's postwar recollection, his service as Jafü Rumänien (Fighter Leader Romania) lasted from January 1944 to the end of August 1944.

Chapter 6

Operations

1-2 September 1944

On the 1st 2.(F)/122 put up a couple of evening missions and Ju 188 F6+LP sortied from Ghedi at 2055, apparently returning to Bergamo after completing its task. The next day, two Spitfires of 87 Sqn met a Bf 109 at 8,000ft which attacked one of the Spits head-on, but the other got on the German's tail and drove him off. At Cameri a Ju 88 arrived, carrying an advance party of II./KG 26 under Oblt. Altmann, but otherwise the 2nd inaugurated the long string of accidents that would characterise September for the Luftwaffe. Gefr. Close of 5./JG 77 (Bf 109G-6 W.Nr.412585, Black 11) was shot down and killed by a German aircraft over Cervia (RA), while Ju 188D-2 F6+BP from 6.(F)/122, crashed north of Cremona, killing two of its crew and wounding another.

3 September 1944

For the British the war was now five years old, and Sqn Ldr Neville Duke of 601 Sqn was able to mark the occasion with his 27th and 28th victories. Shortly after dawn, three Bf 109s from 1./NAGr.11 'paid for their folly by running into Spitfires from 244 Wing'. The Germans were crossing the coast near Cesenatico and bound for home when set on by Duke and Fg Off Hamar:

> Cloud position was ideal for evasion but the Hun took little advantage of it. This was much to their detriment as opening fire from 800 yards the CO got strikes on one from which the pilot soon baled out. Fire quickly burst from the second he attacked and there was another quick bale out. The third at which F/O Hamar got in a burst scurried away, diving for the deck.

Low on fuel, Hamar broke off and the surviving Messerschmitt 'was last seen making for home at nought feet'. Both of the shot down pilots, Ofw. Holstein (Bf 109G-8/R5 W.Nr.200685, Black 3) and Uffz. Möller (W.Nr.200023, Black 1), were wounded.

2.(F)/122 put up two early morning and three evening sorties. On the last of these Ofhr. Walter Grigoleit and Uffz. Wolfgang Habicht were killed when their Me 410B-3 (W.Nr.190159 F6+KK) crashed on take off at Ghedi.

At 1830 at Sarajevo/Rajlovac airfield, Yugoslavia, Fähnriche Ivan Mihalovich and Nonrad Kovacevic ordered ground personnel to prepare a Bücker 181 (marked '7415' and carrying the Croat shield) and a few moments later took off. At 1,200m over Metkovic they were fired on by light flak; crossing the Italian coast they tried to head for Bari but lost their way, sighting the Manfredonia peninsula in failing light. They made a good landing in a field at Amendola by moonlight, and spent several hours trying unsuccessfully to interest Allied personnel in taking them prisoner. Towards midnight an Italian policeman guided them to a military police post, where they were taken in. They had come to Italy intending to join the 'RAF Legion' they had heard about on the radio, and where they believed they would be taught to fly modern fighter aircraft. 3./NSGr.9 again bombed Pesaro that night.

4-5 September 1944

On the night of 3/4 September eight Ju 87s attacked Eighth Army positions on 5th Div's front and were set about by patrolling aircraft of 600 Sqn. From

103

0008 onwards four Junkers were claimed destroyed and another damaged southwest of Rimini. Judd and Brewer, repeating their success of a few nights ago, got the first two inside 12min, at 0400, Flt Sgts Cole and Odd shot down another and, 8min after that, Sqn Ldr Burke and Flt Lt Whaley destroyed one, sustaining damage when it exploded and they flew through the burning wreckage, and damaged another. One of the Junkers seemed to attempt a forced landing but sadly it hit an obstacle and caught fire. Four NSGr.9 crews recorded casualties from Beaufighters on the 4th: from 2. Staffel Gefr. Erwin Schertel was killed and his pilot, Uffz. Kurt Urban, died of his wounds three weeks later in hospital; from 3./9 Ofw. Wilhelm Böwing and Ogefr. Josef Jantos failed to return as did Ogefr. Rolf Möhrke and Fw. Oskar Hug, while Ogefr. Paul Sonnenberg, severely wounded, was taken prisoner.

The following night brought a virtual repeat performance in the same region. Fg Offs Rees and Bartlett claimed victims at 2305 and 2315; and Flt Lt Davidson and Plt Off Trelford shot down a third at 0234. For good measure a crew of 255 Sqn damaged a Ju 88 southeast of Falconara, despite accurate return fire.

Attacking airfields around Udine on the 5th, 260 Sqn destroyed two Bf 109s of 2./NAGr.11 and damaged another. Probably also from NAGr.11, 'the story of the lone wolf of the Luftwaffe took a step further out of the legend stage . . .' when 601 Sqn. met a Bf 109 heading northwest at 10,000ft over Cesena. Sqn Ldr Daniels and Sgt Watford chased it to Ferrara and the officer attacked but the German evaded, '. . . ample proof that they were dealing with no sprog'.

Nine B-25s of the 321st BG were bombing the railway bridge at Polesella (RO) when they were attacked by four Messerschmitts. While one of the their own aeroplanes was damaged, the Americans claimed a Bf 109 shot down and Fhj.Ofw. Volke of 6./JG 77 (W.Nr.441456) was killed at Mirandola (MO), about 32 miles from the target area. Gefr. Burgstaller of 7./JG77[17] (W.Nr.163612, white 7) crashed 5km east of Villafranca, his death was also attributed to air combat. These were probably the last Jagdflieger to die in Italy.

6-28 September 1944

The 6th seems to have passed off uneventfully, although 2. and 6.(F)/122 were active. On the 7th, General der Flieger Mahncke visited Villafranca to inspect its camouflage measures, and substantial amounts of B4 fuel were delivered from Rovereto (TN) next day. On the 8th, the crew of Ltn. Herbert Spousta's Ju 188D-2 (W.Nr.150242, F6+GP) died in a crash at Rovato (BS), while another (W.Nr.290184, F6+JM) went down 5km south-southwest of Bergamo, with Fw. Rudolf Obentheuer and two of his crew injured.

On the 9th at 0925 four Bf 109s and two Fi 156s of Stab JG 77 transferred from Villafranca to Wien-Aspern, led by Obstlt. Steinhoff. That evening, Flt Lt Hearn DFC, leading six aeroplanes of 112 Sqn, spotted a 'Ju 88' on the deck over northeastern Italy. He gave chase in his Mustang III and, with one gun firing, hit the bandit's starboard engine, which gave off black smoke. The stricken aircraft kept turning to port and crash-landed on an aerodrome in a cloud of dust. Hearn's victim was in fact an Me 410, F6+EK (Ofw. Jackstadt and Uffz. Schütze), which made its emergency landing at Treviso at 1830. The aircraft was done for, but the crew were flying again after a week. Elsewhere, nine Bf 109s were claimed damaged on the ground by Spitbombers.

3./NSGr.9 attacked the Pesaro-Cattolica (FO) sector on the nights of the 9th, 10th and 11th. On the 12th, 14 Ju 87s bombed Allied artillery positions, after which operations were suspended for lack of moonlight.

Two pairs of Bf 109s from NAGr.11 flew dawn patrols on the 16th, over the Adriatic and Ligurian respectively, the latter mission being broken off in the face of Allied fighters.

The next day, 1 Sqn SAAF claimed an Me 410 destroyed. The squadron was about to set course for base after an operation when the German was spotted flying straight and level at 2,000ft, just north of Bologna. Capt Brebner attacked, but his windscreen became covered in 'Gerry oil'; Lts Wallace and Ross followed-up and set the 410's port engine alight, whereupon; 'The pilot threw in and landed on his belly . . . with the aircraft burning fiercely. Nobody was seen to leave the aircraft.' At 0732 F6+CK (Klinka and Misch) made its emergency landing near Lugo. The crew survived and were back on ops after a mere four days, not so their shot up aircraft.

During the day, seven Bf 109s (probably from JG 77 or 'repossessed' ANR machines) left Ghedi for Riem. A MATAF sighting of four Fw 190s is hard to account for, and so is an unmarked Storch southeast of Pistoia.

At 0315 on the 11th Thompson and Beaumont of 600 Sqn claimed another Ju 87, 10 miles southwest of Rimini. On the 12th, after ten days at Cameri,

Oblt. Altmann's Ju 88 set out for Neubiberg at 0730, the arrival of II./KG 26 'no longer to be expected'. Over Udine two P-38s of 82nd FG saw two Bf 109s (almost definitely from NAGr.11, given the date and location) eastbound at 1220; they manoeuvred as if to get on the Lightnings' tails, but then broke off. That night, all four of Ltn. Gottfried Heene's crew were injured when their Ju 188D-2 (W.Nr.150235, F6+LP) came to grief. Over the next few days the Germans busied themselves with repositioning NSGr.9 and NAGr.11, although long-range reconnaissance efforts were kept up and a milestone passed on the 14th when II./JG 77 left for Riesa-Canitz, Dresden. No more Jagdgruppen would be seen in Italy.

On the night of the 14/15th partisans inflicted heavy damage on a Saiman 202 of Lfl.2 parked on the edge of Caselle airfield. At 1115 on the 17th, troops of the British 56th Division reported an attack by two aircraft, perhaps connected with the reported destruction of a 1./NAGr.11 Bf 109 by AA fire. The next day, 1./11 had two cases of accidental damage to its aeroplanes, while Schiffels and Meister of 2./(F)/122 were twice forced to abort an early morning reconnaissance in F6+IK. Near Rimini at 1300, B-25s saw 'three probable Me 109s, painted black'. Black German aircraft were reported so often over Italy that it is tempting to think they were more than mistaken observation.

On the 19th 2./11 had a Bf 109 damaged, again in an accident, and Kommando Carmen lost Oblt. Dümcke and Uffz. Bomke killed, as well as Ofw. Gladeck severely injured when their Ju 188D-2 (W.Nr.160062, A3+RD) crashed 2½km west of Bergamo. They had been on a night practice flight, lost orientation on their landing approach and hit a high-tension cable; the Junkers was destroyed in the ensuing crash and fire. 2.(F)/122 put up three sorties plus one aborted within 10min; 4./122 returned Ju 88 BC+PK to Riem and Ju 188 +CP of 6. Staffel started on a mission from Ghedi at 2042.

The 20th saw little but an op by Schiffels and Meister of 2./122, in F6+IK. At 2350 the following night a Ju 188D-2 of 6./122 (W.Nr.150239, F6+LP) crashed owing to engine failure, killing its crew. Two Bf 109 Rotten were heard flying tactical reconnaissance over the east coast at 1705 on the 22nd, while the Me 410s achieved three missions and as many false starts. The next day, 6./122 lost yet another Ju 188D-2 (W.Nr.150043, F6+EP) in a crash 7km southeast of Bergamo that again took the lives of the entire crew. No fewer than five Ju 188s of 4. Staffel visited Ghedi that day, while 3./NSGr.9 was forced to abandon twilight training flights because of enemy incursions into the Mantua region. There was an odd encounter (odd because no Italian units were functioning) on the 23rd, when Allied aircraft sighted a small number of Macchi C.205s and 1st Lt Voll of 308th FS claimed one shot down over Belluno at 1300. At 2046, Ju 188D-2 W.Nr.150043 crashed 7km southeast of Bergamo, the deaths of Uffz. Helmut Kirchner's four-strong crew closing a dismal month for 6.(F)/122.

A Ju 87D-5 of NSGr.9 on one of the bases on the Padana Plain. Under its belly is a strange cylinder, most probably a general-purpose container minus its nose cap.
(Bundesarchiv)

The last of the KG 100 detachment left Villafranca for Giebelstadt in an He 111 on the 24th, and 244 Wing Spitfires chased a bandit from Rimini to Venice without catching it. That evening four Ju 87s from 3./NSGr.9 were on training flights between Verona and Bovolone. On the night of the 25/26th, six Ju 87s attacked artillery and searchlights in the Adriatic sector, but seven from 3./NSGr.9 that left Villafranca at 1920 were forced by bad weather to abandon their mission, landing within the hour.

3./NSGr.9 spent an hour flying training sorties in co-operation with Würzburg radars on the 27th, but at 1650 the next day one of its aeroplanes crashed and burned northwest of Verona, killing Ofw. Toni Fink and Ogfr. Egon Zantow.

29 September 1944

Apart from sending men in pursuit of a group of partisans who had ambushed a train, the German detachment at Cameri also dispatched 11 Fw 190s from the Weserflug-CANSA factory on the first stage of their journey to Germany. One of those that set off during the afternoon did not get far. It was shot down near Fontanella (BG) by a P-47 of the 346th FS flown by Maj Andrew R. Schindler and exploded, its pilot parachuting safely.

2.(F)/122 sent F6+RK out twice, with a different crew each time. The early morning mission apparently passed off normally, but that in the evening was aborted after only 8min and then resumed five minutes after that. Also from Ghedi, Ju 188 F6+DP made the short hop back to Bergamo after a two-day deployment.

30 September 1944

At 1730 Cameri's last two Fw 190s took off. Ten Ju 87s attacked their former base at Rimini by bright moonlight, while 19 sorties achieved hits on artillery and traffic convoys in the same area. Seven machines from Villafranca took part, returning without loss around 2115, after almost 2hr aloft. Between San Felice sul Panaro and Finale Emilia (MO) a 1./9 Ju 87D-5 (W.Nr.131440) was wrecked in a crash that injured Fhj.Fw. Gerstenberger and Ogfr. Lotsch.

Notes

17. Formerly 4./77: renamed 7./77 in July as part of a reorganisation in which each Gruppe would later expand from three to four Staffeln.

One of the Bf 109s delivered to re-equip IIº Gruppo Caccia after the enforced hiatus of August-September. 'White 6' of 3ª Sq. shows the new application of the ANR markings on the fuselage alongside the German ones and the system, peculiar to this Squadriglia, of repeating the individual number on the nose.

Chapter 7

October 1944

The numbers of operational aircraft available to Pohl increased considerably. Most significant in the long term was the reactivation of the ANR – not in the guise of an 'Italian Legion' – and the return to operations of II° Gruppo Caccia on the 19th. KG 200's Sonderverband Einhorn flew its Fw 190F-8s into Villafranca on the same day, and another Fw 190 unit would appear on the Italian scene, Seenotteilstaffel 20 (Land).

MAAF was severely troubled by the weather during the month, and the Axis probably likewise.

Fuel

The effects of the Anglo-American strategic bombers' systematic targeting of the Axis oil industry were quick and catastrophic. The British Air Ministry estimated that in September a large Luftflotte was consuming 200/300 tons (274/411m^3)[18] daily, compared with 500 tons (548m^3) in earlier years, and by October desperate measures were in hand.

As usual, Italy was not the priority, and Pohl was required to surrender most of his stocks. Of 3,600m^3 held at the beginning of the month, 2,066 were dispatched to Germany. Deliveries came to just 116m^3, and the reconnaissance aircraft consumed 300 (a third down on normal), while the Italian fighters got just 35m^3, about enough to fill the internal tanks of 80-90 Bf 109s.

Economies were rigorously enforced, and every effort was made to exploit local resources of oil, methane and other gases as petrol substitutes. However, none was usable in aircraft, and the Allies harried these sources of supply too. In future, fighters and night attack units would be allocated about 200m^3 each month, and reconnaissance units 300m^3, though even these pathetic amounts would fall. The KG 200 detachments requisitioned their petrol separately from OKL; not that this conferred immunity from shortages.

Men and Material

Other supplies became tight during the autumn too, thanks to transport and production problems accumulating within the Reich, the understandable treatment of Italy as something of a sideshow and the interdiction of lines of communication. Wherever possible, Italian industry was used to compensate for shortfalls, and workshops and depots were moved back to the northern part of the Po Plain or into the Alps.

More and more manpower was being taken for the Army. At the end of August Luftflotte 2 had had about 100,000 men, 11,000 of them Italians. By the end of October 24,000 Germans were gone, and it was decreed that German units could include up to 40 per cent Italian personnel. Although most of the natives carried out their duties faithfully, desertion presented a significant problem. It must be said, however, that the Germans, on whose testimony this assessment is based, seldom spoke generously of their comrades in arms.

The Luftwaffe

Seenotteilstaffel 20 (Land) – and NAGr.11

Translatable as 'Sea Rescue Part-Squadron 20 (Landplanes)' and abbreviated to Seenotstaffel 20, this unit first appears on the 20 October Order of Battle as a new one in process of formation.

During autumn 1944, Seenot units were being cut back and, when Luftflotte 2 withdrew, Italy no longer had a regular flying-boat or seaplane rescue Staffel. Instead, a search unit was established, commanded by Oblt. Langer and flying Fw 190s, to assist the rescue boats. These aeroplanes were also employed to watch for any Allied amphibious threat to the Venice area and in fact Fw 190s were most often reported by day in situations suggesting their use for overwater/coastal reconnaissance or as fighters. Certainly the Allies did not recognise their existence separate from NAGr.11, with whom they were co-located at Udine (the whole Gruppe was there by 15 October, and would stay until the end of the war).

Aircraft delivery records suggest that no Fw 190 fighter models were sent to Italy but, whatever their origins, four A-8s were on SNSt.20's strength by the 31st.

Unicorns and Self-Sacrifice

Established in February 1944, *Sonderverband Einhorn* (Special Force 'Unicorn')[19] was to have been a suicide squadron, in the hope that 'self-sacrifice' could redress Germany's numerical inferiority. Its founder, Oblt. Lange, thought that the greatest material effect would come from attacking Allied invasion fleets with manned glide-bombs. Despite this weapon's non-existence, the Staffel was constituted with 120 volunteers. The impossibility of developing a suicide weapon within a reasonable timescale rapidly became clear, and an April conference suggested attacking ships with an Fw 190 carrying a 2,500kg bomb.

Most of the volunteers had glider experience and at first only rudimentary Fw 190 training was envisaged, but it became obvious that more would be needed to give them any chance of reaching a target. Practicalities then dictated a 1,100kg bomb, which Lange felt promised too little destruction in exchange for a man's life.

Unpreparedness and waning political enthusiasm precluded operations against the Normandy landings. By swearing to die only in a manned bomb the self-sacrificers were unintentionally outliving thousands of their more conventional Luftwaffe colleagues and most agreed to sign a new declaration covering any aircraft. Lange's intransigence was judged a disruptive influence and on 23 August he, Oblt. Schuntermann and six others – collectively termed Sonderstaffel Einhorn – were visited in Ansbach by KG 200's Ia.

Six days later it was reported that Einhorn would train only for ground attack with 'the heaviest load', striking targets at twilight, within 'the small radius of action (150km)', although other sources suggest that attacks on ships were still contemplated. Its aircraft were used against the Nijmegen road bridge during the Arnhem battles, then on 5 October it was: '. . . due to transfer to Upper Italy . . . with 14 Fw 190s (ground attack aircraft with the heaviest bombs). Planned operational bases: Villafranca and Udine.'

The 'Special Staffel' was to leave Achmer next day, its 'flying apparatus' being consigned to Holzkirchen railway station, Bavaria.

The Sonderverband's 'special aircraft' arrived at Villafranca on 19 October under Schuntermann, now a Hauptmann. Lingering thoughts of daylight anti-shipping missions were promptly abandoned for lack of escort fighters. The pilots therefore decamped to Ghedi for ten days of night-flying on the Ju 87. Sources variously describe this as conversion to the Ju 87 or even combat missions, but it is more likely to have been training and local orientation.

NSGr.9

Pohl's Ic, Hptm. Erich Seebode, reported that NSGr.9 had flown 108 sorties without loss, although Allied nightfighters made a number of claims.

On the 9th the Littorio Division urgently requested the bombing of five villages around Pavia, all well within Axis-held Northwest Italy but notorious partisan country. It does not look as though NSGr.9 complied. Instead, two days later, Malcesine announced that nightly operations were to be flown from Verona against roads on the central sector (i.e. around Bologna) despite the unfavourable moon phase. The Gruppe appears to have been inactive on 24 nights, mainly because of bad weather, and another urgent request for support on the night of the 20/21st went unfulfilled.

At the beginning of the month all elements bar 3./9 (in Aviano) were listed at Bovolone. Nevertheless, Ju 87s were still operating from Villafranca on the 3rd, and nine days later Bettola's 'immediate evacuation' led 2./9 to transfer to Ghedi around a week later. 3./9 probably moved to Aviano from Villafranca soon after the aforementioned mission, but was operating from (if not based at) the latter field again by the month's end.

Long-Range Reconnaissance

A Pole who spent two months, ending on 18 October, on guard duty at Ghedi relayed rumours of an impending transfer to the Reich around the time he was posted. He reported seven Me 410s based at the field and '. . . believed that the unit was 2(F)/122, but was certain that the a/c had the figures F6+-K painted on them. He was also certain that it was a long range reconnaissance unit.' The Me 410s were moved daily from a large semicircle of concrete shelters. Weather permitting, two aircraft took off each day between 0600-0700 and another two between 1600-1700. Also, in favourable weather, Ju 88s (usually a pair) came from Bergamo either in the early morning or early evening. Different aircraft arrived each time, refuelled and took off on their missions before 2200, returning subsequently to Bergamo.

A former 4.(F)/122 ordnance sergeant said that the Staffel generally mustered about six available flying crews and three to seven operational aircraft, all on night reconnaissance and carrying the F6+ code, Hptm. Hirdes was Staffelkapitän. He stated that 6. Staffel had moved to Ghedi during October (probably only a partial or temporary detachment in fact).

Two prisoners originally from 6.(F)/122's ground echelons described life at Bergamo-Seriate from August to October. When they were posted to the infantry on 20 October there were rumours that the Staffel was to withdraw to Graz in Austria and that an advance party had gone ahead. They claimed (inaccurately) that 6. Staffel was nocturnal and 4. diurnal. There were around 20 operational aeroplanes plus three or four of the Stab (all Ju 188s), and eight or nine regularly flew night missions. Aircraft in revetments were covered with netting and branches, and any left outside were similarly camouflaged. Fifteen dummy aeroplanes in the dispersals were never moved around owing to shortage of personnel for the job. Aircraft required for the night's operations were brought from dispersal just after dusk and parked near the operations hut to await take off; 6. Staffel was active from early evening until dawn. For aircraft returning from night missions, the southern edge of the runway was illuminated with alternate red and white lights until the machines had touched down.

One asserted that the aeroplanes bore the letters AM+ followed by letter combinations such as CU, RT, LK etc., and denied ever seeing FAGr.122's usual markings. On the left side of their noses the Junkers bore a crest with a yellow owl on a white background, the badge that 6./122 inherited from Westa 26. Each Staffel had about six flying crews, and Oblt. Brinkmann (RK) captained 6. Staffel.

Detailed descriptions were given of flak defences, buried fuel tanks, pipelines and ammunition dumps. Maintenance was done in the open air, the mobile workshop consisting of three vans. There were about 30 ground crew in 6. Staffel. Air and ground crews were billeted in Redona (BG). 4. Staffel lived in the Villa Santa Maria, the ground crew of 6. in a school, and the aircrew in the Villa Santa Francesca. The photo lab was in a large yellow building, the 'Mussolini Heim'.

Geschwader That Never Were?
Two Geschwader were ordered disbanded in Italy at the end of October: KG 35 and JG 17. They were probably set up to embody Italian volunteers into the Luftwaffe after 'Phoenix' but never amounted to more than a few personnel and a liaison aeroplane or two. KG 35 did 'operate' in October, three of its men returning wounded to Villaorba after an anti-partisan sweep on the 19th.

Order of Battle

On 30 September the strengths of the operational Luftwaffe flying units in Italy were:

Unit	Aircraft	
	Number	Type
Stab/FAGr.122	0	
2.(F)/122	6	Me 410A-3/B-3
4.(F)/122	4	Ju 188D-2
	5	Ju 88T-3
6.(F)/122	4	Ju 188D-2
	1	Ju 188F-1
Kdo. Carmen	2/3	Ju 188D/F
Stab/NAGr.11	0	
1./NAGr.11	1	Bf 109G-6
	10	Bf 109G-8
2./NAGr.11	4	Bf 109G-5/U2/R2
	1	Bf 109G-6
	8	Bf 109G-8/R5
Stab/NSGr.9	1	Ju 87D-5
1./NSGr.9	10	Ju 87D-5
2./NSGr.9	9	Ju 87D-3
	3	Ju 87D-5
3./NSGr.9	8	Ju 87D-3
	3	Ju 87D-5
Jafü Oberitalien	1	Bf 109G-6

The ANR

II° Gruppo Caccia
Following OKL's directives during late September, II° Gr.C. was chosen as the first ANR unit to re-form.

It would be the sole fighter defence of Mussolini's 'Republic' for months to come.

From the first week of October the Bf 109s assigned to II° Gr.C. were ready at Vicenza[20] and Thiene. They were old aircraft, in most cases probably the same ones seized by II./JG 77 in August and left in Italy when that outfit returned home and was re-equipped with the new G-14 and G-14/AS models. According to various official and personal documents, the first collection of Bf 109s by the Italian pilots was on the 7th and within a week all of the aircraft were taken to Villafranca.

On the 11th one of these transfer flights almost ended in tragedy when six 109s being flown in from Thiene by 2ª Sq. pilots were met by a furious barrage from Villafranca's German flak (the KTB tactfully refers only to 'strong flak defence' against American fighter-bombers!) Miraculously no aircraft were hit, and they orbited at a safe distance until the mistake was realised and a safe landing became possible. This was but one instance of the perennial lack of German-Italian co-ordination, never completely overcome and the cause of some avoidable losses in the coming months.

Training to refresh some of the old pilots and break in 2ª and 3ª Sq.'s new ones began on the 17th in a Bf 109G-12 flown by M.llo Galetti, while all of 1ª Sq. transferred to Ghedi next day. Twenty-four hours later II° Gr.C. was back in action. The authors have no earlier figures, but on 20 October the Gruppo had 25 Bf 109s (15 serviceable).

I° Gruppo Aerosiluranti
After two months' negotiations it was finally agreed that the Group should carry on its activities. On the 12th Magg. Marini addressed his men, telling them what had been decided and announcing that the unit was changing its title from 'Buscaglia' to 'Faggioni'. This came about because, during August, the newspapers had announced Buscaglia's death while flying for the Co-belligerent Air Force near Naples. Until then he had been listed missing, presumed dead, after a mission on 12 November 1942. This failure to perish in the cause of Fascism made him somewhat less of an inspirational figure and the tactical markings of the Gruppo's S.79s were henceforth prefixed 'F' instead of 'B'.

From the 12th, maintenance and repair recommenced on the aircraft and some went to the factory at Vergiate for overhaul. Meanwhile, Marini had several conferences with the Italian and German staffs, and gradually his faith in the latter's goodwill towards him and his unit diminished. On the 28th several of his S.79s were strafed, but the best 14 were kept and operations planned to start the following week.

The Land Campaign

A prolonged stalemate in the ground fighting began, though a great many people were still being killed. The advance up the Serchio Valley was postponed at the beginning of the month; the dropping of 1,661 tons of bombs by MATAF and MASAF on the 12th still left the Fifth Army nine tantalising miles short of Bologna, where it would remain for another six months. The Eighth Army continued up the east coast from one river line to the next, taking Cesena on the 21st and continuing to the River Ronco. The offensive was called off on the 27th, and bad weather on the last day of the month brought both air and ground operations to a standstill.

Notes

18. German documents mostly use the cubic metre or m³ to measure fuel stocks – it equates to 1,000 litres or 227 Imp gall; otherwise they use metric tonnes (about 1.37m³).
19. Also referred to as a Staffel, Schlachtstaffel, Sonderstaffel or Sonderkommando and which ended up, officially at least, as plain 13./KG 200.
20. Where 40 parachutes were delivered for the Italians on the 6th.

A rare shot of a Fw 190 of Seenotstaffel 20 taxying at Campoformido. The unit, established in October, ostensibly for "search and rescue" work, operated in practice alongside NAGr.11 which shared the same base.

CHAPTER 7

Operations

1-12 October 1944

To open the month, NAGr.11 sent out an hour-long mission at 0633 and another from 1555, each involving a pair of Bf 109s. The long-range reconnaissance units put up seven sorties. North of Modena an F-5 claimed to have been attacked by an Fw 190. Bad weather cancelled planned operations by Villafranca's Ju 87s on the 1st but on the 2nd: 'The Hun was active in a small way, dropping flares and butterfly bombs in the Rimini area. No damage or casualties [were] reported.'

The Americans could achieve more than this, and next morning eight P-47s of 64th FS wrought havoc in Ghedi's dispersals. That evening it was announced that bomb craters had closed the field to all aircraft. NSGr.9 dropped 60 tons of bombs on the night of the 3/4th. Deutsch and Nawroth of 3./9 (flying D3+CL) destroyed a road juction in the pass below Monte Oggioli with a direct hit and went on to strafe traffic columns. After 13 minutes on the ground they went back to attack the Florence-Firenzuola road. Their third and fourth sorties that night were to start a big fire in Firenzuola itself and to hit the pass road again.

The reconnaissance effort for the day included Me 410s over the Ligurian both morning and afternoon and a look at Marseille at 1031. A Ju 188 covered the Franco-Italian border and there were five NAGr.11 sorties.

During the morning of the 4th, six Bf 109s were overheard in transit from Gallarate to Vicenza – an indication of the ANR's revival. Twenty-three Ju 87s flew a total of 86 sorties on the central and eastern sectors of the battle front that night, focusing mainly on Firenzuola (FI). Over Cesena at 2020, a Ju 87 was claimed by Wg Cdr Styles DFC and Fg Off Wilmer DFM of 600 Sqn. At 2030 weather conditions forced the cancellation of planned dusk-dawn operations from Verona against road traffic.

The following day opened with two tactical reconnaissance sorties from 0513-0613 on the route Venice–Po–Rimini–Pola, but at 1230 orders were again issued cancelling night attacks on account of the weather, the same happening for the next two nights. Even so, on the 8th Ogefr. Heinz Schönauer and Uffz. Siegfried Hellmann of 1./NSGr.9 were killed when their Ju 87 crashed at Roverbella (MN) during a non-operational flight. Also, Stab/NAGr.11 had an Fi 156 destroyed in an accident

On the 11th, the total reconnaissance effort was seven long- and four short-range aircraft giving day and night coverage of both Ligurian and Adriatic. Borrmann and Stauch of 2.(F)/122 (Me 410 F6+MK) had to break off a photo mission to Ancona because of bad weather, but sighted ships 40 miles east of San Benedetto del Tronto (AP) at 1655. They had attempted missions three times during the day with different aircraft, in each case aborting within 15min, only getting away on their fourth try. II° Gr. C. had their *contretemps* with Villafranca's defences (see above), and transport columns south of Bologna were attacked that night.

On the next afternoon the 64th FS shot up Bergamo-Seriate, claiming damage and destruction to several Me 410s, Ju 88s and a Do 217. Lt Dorval was hit by flak and crashed in flames on the southeast dispersal area, and Lt Adams was missing when the Americans re-formed. One of the Ju 188s out that night was flying down the middle of the Adriatic when at 2120 it obtained contacts on its FuG

111

200 off the Po estuary, duly announcing the fact not only to its own controllers but (unwittingly) to MAAF Sigint.

13 October 1944

An incident on the 13th had its origins 11 days earlier in (of all places) Karachi, India[21], when 2nd/Lt Martin J. Monti, USAAF, was posted Awol. He was of Italian descent and had visited that country pre-war. He had, so he said later, became tired of sitting around in a Replacement Battalion and had hitched rides on transport aircraft to 'join his buddies' in Italy. Arriving in Foggia, he approached the CO of the 82nd FG, a unit where he had friends and requested a transfer but was turned down. Returning to Naples, he saw an F-5E (a recently-delivered reconnaissance model, No.44-23725) at Pomigliano, base of the 354th Air Service Squadron, and succumbed to a desire 'to see what the front line looked like'. He evidently talked his way past several US and British personnel, getting a clearance certificate to test the Lockheed's engine; he also acquired a parachute. Monti took off at 1229 and was not heard of again until 13 May 1945, in Milan. He met up with American troops, claiming to be an escaped PoW from the 82nd FG, shot down on his first mission, and was – at first – debriefed as such, only to be arrested a few days later.

A version of what had happened in the interim emerged at his Court Martial that August: the charges were desertion and wrongful misappropriation of a P-38 aircraft 'of the value of more than $50'. In his defence he testified that he had been hit by flak, lost one engine and baled out near Milan. Held prisoner in Italy and Germany for about four months, he escaped with the intention of heading into Switzerland, but ended up by April in Milan, awaiting American troops. A string of prosecution witnesses testified that the P-38 had not been officially released, and a former comrade of Monti's told how he had opined that the peoples of Italy, Germany and the USA had been misled into war by propaganda. Monti talked of getting to Italy, flying towards Switzerland and parachuting into internment after giving suitable 'distress signals.' This witness concluded: 'In my opinion [he] was merely trying to get out of fighting. I do not believe that he would sell out to the Germans, but he was so queer and strange that he might well do this.'

The court found Monti guilty of being absent without leave (in substitution for the charge of desertion) and of stealing the P-38. He was sentenced to dismissal from the Service and to 15 years' confinement. Harsh as this sentence was, it might have been more so had this court heard evidence[22] of what really happened over Milan that Friday the 13th:

> Air situation, 13 October
> 1500 hrs: *landing* of a Lightning on Milan-Linate Airfield. Pilot (American) taken prisoner. *Aircraft undamaged* (unarmed reconnaissance model with built-in camera).

(The report is from Luftwaffe Airfield Regional Command 18/XI, Cardano al Campo (VA), the italics the authors').

The F-5E was brought to Villafranca a few days later where it was photographed by Ten. Brini of 2ª Sq. and Flight Mechanic 1° Aviere Galli. It had already been sprayed yellow on its undersides and had German national markings applied. On 25 October, escorted by a Schwarm from II° Gr.C., it took off for Germany; the Bf 109s broke off over the Alps and the flight was recorded in S.Ten. Ezio Dell'Acqua's log (3ª Sq.). The Lockheed was incorporated into the so-called 'Beute-Zirkus Rosarius', as T9+MK. This unit was equipped with captured aircraft for testing and demonstration flights for the benefit of Luftwaffe operational squadrons. US troops recaptured 44-23725 at Schwangau, Germany, in May 1945.

14 October 1944

During the late afternoon 72 Sqn Spitfires encountered what they thought was an Me 410 near Bergamo-Seriate aerodrome, and six pilots shared in its destruction. Their recognition was faulty, for they had shot down a Ju 188D-2 (W.Nr.150500, F6+AP) of 6.(F)/122. Only one crew member seems to have survived, Oblt. Bodo Freisenhausen, Ofw. Josef Franken and Ogfr. Friedrich Regitz being killed.

Another 6./122 machine, F6+GP (next off the assembly line after Freisenhausen's aeroplane and destined to be the Staffel's next casualty) flew from Bergamo to Ghedi in the morning, returning later on. Two new Me 410s were delivered to 2./122 from Riem, and F6+NK flew an afternoon mission.

15-31 October 1944

The night of the 15/16th brought three suspect radar contacts. Beaufighters scrambled and chased the last of these for 20min in low cloud before it evaded them. One of these bogeys dropped four flash bombs over Falconara and '. . . evidently got away with

On 13 October this brand-new Lockheed F-5E was delivered intact to the Axis forces at Linate airfield (MI) by a deserting USAAF pilot. Here, the aircraft already repainted with Luftwaffe markings and painted yellow on its undersides, is shown at Villafranca, first camouflaged with tree branches and then just before being flown to Germany. (Gori+Lucchini)

some interesting pictures'. NSGr.9's operations were cancelled yet again, but the 17th brought an unusual (if inconclusive) encounter around midday, between MACAF Beaufighters and three pairs of Bf 109s over the Gulf of Venice. None of the authors' ANR sources mentions the incident, so it is suspected that NAGr.11 was involved – it was on their patch.

At 1635 on the 18th a NAGr.11 aeroplane reported running into AA fire, and that night Budapest called an S.79 of Gr. 'Faggioni' around 2200 – the authors have no idea what it was up to. Nevertheless, the ANR was stirring, and next afternoon II° Gr.C. went back into action.

Fourteen Bf 109s of 2ª and 3ª Sq. took off from Villafranca and eight of 1ª from Ghedi, to intercept a group of 30 Marauders out to bomb a Mantua railway bridge. They belonged to the 319th and 320th BGs and were sighted first by 1ª and 2ª Sq., who curved to attack the 320th's formation and then broke off to intercept the less numerous 319th. The combat report of S.M. Baldi (flying 'Black 5') has the sighting taking place at 1402 over Goito, with a head-on attack four minutes later. Despite a claim of one B-26 shot down, no victories were gained during this first pass, but 2ª Sq.'s attack a few minutes later scored heavily.

A flight of B-26s was cut in half by Cap. Bellagambi's men as they pressed their attacks to within 50ft of the bombers' tails. Bellagambi himself took on '93' of the 440th BS and scored many hits, continuing his attack for almost 30secs. The bomber, piloted by 1st/Lt Roberts and with both engines on fire, fell out of the second flight, the whole crew baling out seconds before it blew up over the target.

The second B-26 shot down ('97') was attacked by S.M. Fornaci, Sanson and Ancillotti in repeated passes which set fire to its bomb bay and forced the pilot, 1st/Lt O'Bryant, to pull out of formation and jettison his bombload before all aboard abandoned ship. With one engine on fire and the other smoking badly it crashed south of the target.

The third to fall was '88', and USAAF reports point to this victory being scored by Serg. Talin. His 'Yellow 4' closed right in, hitting and setting alight the starboard engine, but its own motor was hit in turn. While 1st/Lt Treadwell began the jettison procedure, Talin's smoking Messerschmitt kept firing, making the Marauder's other engine smoke. When the bomber started spinning, its pilot lowered the undercarriage, but only two parachutes were seen before it crashed about 15 miles west of Mantua.

The rest of the 319th's formation was scattered, but it sustained no more losses, although its members' astonishment was manifest in shouts of 'Italian fighters!' over the radio. This was the first enemy attack the unit had experienced in eight months and the absence of waist and nose guns (immediately reinstalled after this combat) did not help, although the bombers claimed a score of 2-4-1.

The Italians claimed seven bombers shot down by 2ª Sq. (for whom the heat of battle can be invoked as an extenuating circumstance) and four by the other Squadriglie (which took almost no part in the action). The Villafranca KTB reports that '. . . a further 5 bombers were shot down in the area Vicenza-Padua', but no mention of any such combat appears in Italian or Allied documents.[23]

The only II° Gr.C. loss was Serg. Talin who managed to nurse his damaged Gustav to within 2km of the airfield before it exploded in mid-air, killing him and leaving only a mass of metal scattered burning in the fields. Nevertheless, the Italian Group's achievements on its 'first' mission were rewarded with a personal message of congratulation from Kesselring.

A Ju 188D-2 of 6.(F)/122 (W.Nr.150501, F6+GP) left Bergamo at 1721; from 1748 to 2001 control warned of night fighters but at 2115 there was no news of it and next day the Luftwaffe searched the Adriatic for the missing aircraft. It had been caught by a 417th NFS Beaufighter (Lts Hyram J. Allen and William E. Grinnell) at 1930, 10 to 15 miles southwest of Cremona. Their fire hit the Junkers' rear fuselage and it spiralled steeply to port. Losing the German in clouds, the Americans claimed only a 'probable', but Ofw. Kurt Rautenburg and three comrades were posted missing. Three other FAGr.122 aeroplanes had been out that night, and the last of them broke off its patrol at 2253 with engine trouble.

On the 20th target data was requested for Nachtschlacht operations resuming next evening. Reconnaissance sorties totalled six long- and nine short-range (the latter unusually by groups of three rather than two aircraft). There was photo cover of Toulon, Marseille and the Côte d'Azur; 2./122 got two sorties away but had *four* further attempts aborted. Allied bombers struck Milan that day, the Germans estimating that 2,000 people were killed, including 200 children in a school in the city's Gorla district.

On 21 October at 0700 a German aeroplane photographed Jesi airfield and a combat took place over the mountains around Lake Garda between seven Spitfires of 72 (Basutoland) Sqn, on an armed reconnaissance and II° Gr.C. The Italians were alerted belatedly, and 11 Bf 109s of Nucleo Comando (one), 2ª (seven) and 3ª Sq. (three) took off

Parked inside a shelter in Villafranca, Cap. Spigaglia's Bf 109G-6 shows the Luftwaffe insignia (a single blue chevron in this case) adopted by Nucleo Comando, II° Gr.C. This was one of the earlier G-6 versions mixing the d/f loop and the tall radio mast. (Pagliano)

from Villafranca at 1050, while eight from 1ª Sq. were up 5min later from Ghedi. The RAF fighters were intercepted over the Lake's southern corner, the combat mainly involving 2ª Sq. Although one Spitfire was claimed shot down by S.M. Sanson, 72 Sqn suffered no losses, itself claiming a Bf 109 shot down by Fg Off Hendry, two damaged by Flt Lt Galitzine and Lt Jackson, plus another probably damaged by Sgt Bell. The DAF claims were close to the truth. Cap. Bellagambi's aeroplane was so damaged that he had to crash-land, while Sanson's Gustav, with half of its rudder and a whole elevator shot off, managed to evade its pursuers, reach Villafranca and land safely.

A 4./KG 200 Ju 188 (A3+MD) arrived at Vicenza from Erding in the afternoon. At 1330 orders were given for Ju 87s from Villafranca to strafe Allied road traffic in front of the 'Central Alpine sector' from dusk to 1900, but the weather supervened. From the 21st cancellations became almost daily routine for NSGr.9 until the last night of the month, although some aircraft clearly did manage to get into the air from one or other of its bases in the intervening period.

On the 22nd Uffz. Thomsen of 1./NAGr.11 went missing in the Rovigno area (now Rovinj, Croatia). He was flying an MW 30-boosted Bf 109G-8/R5 (W.Nr.202059, Black 12). That night six to ten German aircraft operated between Ferrara and Rimini, dropping bombs to the west of the latter town. From 23 to 25 October bad weather prevented ANR operations, but not the delivery of new aircraft by 3ª Sq.'s pilots. On the 25th there was a fruitless scramble. New pilots were arriving and the end of the month was spent training them on a Bf 109 G-12 and an old G-4, though rain continued almost daily.

On the morning of the 26th an aircraft of Stab/NSGr.9 (E8+WB) left Vicenza for Innsbruck. There was a sudden upsurge of activity at Villafranca on the 27th with 38 training/practice flights and 23 more the next night.

Fighter missions were flown on 30 and 31 October, but if the former was uneventful the latter had dire consequences from both the tactical and moral points of view. Two P-47s of the 346th FS (1st/Lts Tomlinson and Dailey) were flying a sweep over the Po valley and had strafed a truck and a staff car near Lonato (BS) when they confonted 27 Bf 109s scrambled from Ghedi and Villafranca at 1315.

This is how Tomlinson described it:

... I looked up and saw this large number of Me-109s overhead. They appeared to be about 8,000ft [and] to peel off one at a time and dive down at us firing their cannons. These were the first enemy fighters I had ever seen. We were down so low that all I could do was to try to pick up enough speed and then pull up and shoot head-on into the diving Me-109s.

Lt Dailey and I became separated and it was just a matter of survival for us. The Me-109s put five 20mm explosive shells into my P-47 while firing head-on. I saw two Me-109s that had crashed from the smoke and explosions on the ground. Needless to say I was terrified and when I ran out of ammo I headed South towards Pisa.

I got as low as I could at tree-top level and used water injection to gain as much speed as I could ...

The Diary of the 346th FS finishes the story:

By the time they turned for home, the enemy had lost 3 Mes definitely, 2 others probably destroyed and 1 damaged ... During the dogfight, Lt Tomlinson's aircraft was hit ... in the tail section, shooting away his elevator trim tabs and his tail-wheel, causing his hydraulic system to go out.

IIº Gr.C. lost two dead: Ten. Biasi (2ª Sq.) and Ten. Canavese (3ª Sq.), both crashed near Desenzano. The former was shot down while manoeuvring very low[24] and the latter, betrayed by inexperience (it was his first combat), pulled up right in front of one of the P-47s, offering the easiest of kills. The Italians claimed two P-47s shot down, by Ten. Filippi (2ª Sq.) and M.llo Covre (3ª Sq.). From their inability to shoot down two Thunderbolts despite a 13:1 superiority it was obvious that they lacked the requisite leadership and tactical skills.

After dark 15 to 20 of NSGr.9's aeroplanes attacked forward positions south of Bologna, strafing a radar station in the Florence area at 2015.

Notes

21. In 1944; now in Pakistan.
22. Monti, who apparently had a history of association with far-right causes, was later tried and convicted on more serious charges, however.
23. Another formation of the 320th BG was attacked by enemy fighters while bombing a bridge at Calcinato (BS) on the same day. It is possible that the second batch of claims stems from this (inconclusive) combat or even from flak units.
24. Writing to the man's parents, Cap. Bellagambi suggested that he may have hit the ground with a wingtip.

ABOVE:
A group of 2ª Sq. pilots poses near the shelter containing Bf 109G-6 'Yellow 0'. (L. to R.) S.M. Ancillotti, Ten. Biasi, the Sq.'s Medical Officer, Ten. Filippi and S.Ten. Brini.

BELOW:
'White 6' of 2./NAGr.11 taxies at Campoformido. The Gruppe's recce missions were flown to the last, albeit at a reduced rate. (Petrick)

Chapter 8

November 1944

Fuel

At 953m³ of B4 and 160m³ of C3, stocks were about a third of what they had been at the start of October, and they would halve again by December. Reconnaissance sorties accounted for 334m³ of the petrol used.

At a conference on the 8th the Luftwaffe's Quartermaster General reviewed the seriousness of the overall situation. Only two months' supplies were on hand, despite strict curbs; no B4 (for Bf 109s, Ju 87s and inline-engined Ju 88s and 188s) could be allocated to Italy before 1 January, but 100m³ of C3 for reconnaissance (by BMW 801-engined Junkers and the Fw 190, as well as some later Bf 109 models) could be supplied by 1 December. In the event deliveries to Italy seem to have been rather better than anticipated.

The lack of petrol also meant that for 'Threatening Danger South' (an Allied landing in the Gulfs of Venice or Genoa) only three Gruppen of JG 27 could be counted on as reinforcements. That unit's high-altitude Gruppe and SG 10 would not be able to operate.

The Luftwaffe

Traffic between station Geier ('Vulture') in the Udine area and aeroplanes with the callsigns Larve ('Larva') 2,3 and 5, plus frequent sightings around Udine of Bf 109s and Fw 190s, led MAAF to suspect that a small German fighter unit was still there. The passing of plots on Allied formations was judged inconsistent with reconnaissance activity, although with hindsight these would be as valuable in *avoiding* the enemy as for interception.

MATAF bombers made some colourful reports, which are hard to explain except as hectic mistaken observation: a Bf 109 'brown gray with spotted yellow circles'; others 'dark gray green with white stripes on fuselage from cockpit back and black crosses with white outline on wings'; alleged G.55s and C.202s 'speckled brown and gray, light undersurfaces and German insignia'; Fw 190s in black with German markings; mixed Messerschmitts and Focke-Wulfs 'painted black with red spinners and silver bellies'. The only day fighters which the authors know to have been in Italy in November, however, were Bf 109s in standard Luftwaffe camouflage with Italian national markings alongside the German Balkenkreuz.

Night Attack – Figaro and Egon
Einhorn's first operation took place, without loss, and Maj Seebode (recently-promoted) found it 'specially noteworthy that this Staffel has been converted to night operations in quick time'. NSGr.9 flew 166 sorties, braving poor visibility and strong AA and fighter defences. Its missions were directed against the Eighth Army around Rimini/Forlì and the Fifth Army's attempted advance along Highway 65, the Florence-Bologna road through the Northern Apennine passes. Good results were reported, including large fires; the strafing of individual vehicles and M/T columns had caused considerable damage, and AA and artillery positions had been silenced. MAAF noted that German troops marked out their own lines with flares to guide the bombers, but 'very little damage and few casualties [were] caused to our ground forces'.

During November some initially mysterious radio traffic began to issue from station Figaro, in the Padua area, passing plots 'on some type of flying machine' to other ground stations. MAAF speculated at first that these were experimental guidance for a remotely-piloted aircraft, on the basis of excerpts such as 'Machine is carrying out orders very well... we are now guiding it back'. On the 16th the traffic showed that the aircraft was directed against some kind of target, and on the 28th the release of bombs was reported.

The correlation between Figaro signals and dusk attacks by Fw 190s led them to conclude that this was the Egon blind-bombing system, guiding Einhorn's aeroplanes to their targets. This was accomplished by two Freya radars interrogating the aircraft's FuG 25 IFF transponder and triangulating on its position, the controller using these plots to pass instructions to the pilot. Luftflotte 2 had been asking for this aid since April 1944 and NSGr.9 had reportedly made Egon test flights about the end of August. During November the Luftwaffe Signals Branch discussed radar jamming support for NSGr.9 but decided it would not be feasible with the available equipment, aircraft and fuel.

On the 3rd it was decided to shift 1./9 from Bovolone to Villafranca as soon as the airfield situation permitted (although reportedly some operations were still flown from there at the month's end); 3./9 was moved back from Aviano to Villafranca on the 9th.

Reconnaissance
Sorties totalled 122, a typical pattern being two by day and three at night. Overwater coverage was unaltered while NAGr.11 was only active on a limited scale. Several battle reconnaissances were mounted over areas of the most intense fighting, as well as scouting of partisan territory and special photographic sorties over friendly areas. Aside from aborted attempts, 2.(F)/122 achieved 28 daylight missions. Seenotstaffel 20 attained its peak strength of ten Fw 190s, all serviceable on the 10th.

Flak
Luftwaffe flak claimed 92 Allied aircraft (including 22. Flakbrigade's 1,000th victory), Navy and Army gunners another 24. Eleven MAAF aeroplanes crashed without apparent Axis intervention, almost as many as were credited to fighters.

The ANR
II° Gruppo Caccia
New deliveries were such that, by the 2nd, II° Gruppo Caccia boasted its highest number of aircraft since June. Among them, later in the month, were some G-14s, as recorded in S.M. Baldi's log (1ª Sq.).

Meanwhile, bad weather started hampering operations, daily postponing the Group's transfer to Aviano, rumours of which had already spread throughout the unit. Nevertheless, on the 4th all the aircraft of the three Squadriglie flew to Aviano. This move was only provisional; a proper transfer followed some days later.

Air-raids on the 18th halved the unit's aircraft strength, and two days later the pilots were back at Villafranca, taking delivery of new aeroplanes from the Germans in the last ten days of the month. These machines, along with others repaired at Aviano, soon returned the Gruppo to combat readiness. On the 27th 3ª Sq. flew to Aviano (some of 1ª's men making the same journey, both by road and air) and 2ª went to Osoppo (UD) the next day.

The Germans felt that the Italians had proved themselves in action and accorded them a mention in Wehrmacht dispatches for a score (in five days of enemy contact) of four heavy bombers, six medium bombers and four fighters, for three losses of their own.

I° Gruppo Aerosiluranti
By the middle of November the Group had about ten serviceable S.79s, and Magg. Marini informed HQ that he was again ready for operations. By now Ghedi had been prepared as an alternate base for the unit and the ten aircraft transferred there on the 20th.

Between 25 and 30 November a convoy of three merchant ships was reported leaving Ajaccio, probably bound for Toulon. Marini asked the Germans to keep it under observation but later in the evening, when the attack should have commenced, he found that this request had not been fulfilled. He had a stormy personal meeting with General von Pohl, whom he told openly that he did not wish to continue operations unless an Me 410 was assigned to his unit, under his control, for reconnaissance purposes.

RIGHT:
Following his claim in the combat of 5 November, S.M. Pacini watches an aircraftsman painting the silhouette of a Marauder on the tail of his 'White 1' at Villafranca. This 3ª Sq. pilot will be killed in action only a few days later, on 10 November 1944.

Order of Battle

Strengths and locations on 2 November were as follows:

Unit	Location	Aircraft	Commander (at 13.11.44)
Gr. 'Faggioni'	Lonate	14(?)	Magg. Marini
I° Gr.C.	in transit	0(0)	Magg. Visconti
II° Gr.C. (less 1ª)	Villafranca	42(27)	Magg. Alessandrini
1ª Sq.C.	Ghedi		Ten. Drago
Stab/FAGr.122	Bergamo	0(0)	Obstlt. Domnick
2.(F)/122	Ghedi	8(6)	Hptm. Weinand
4.(F)/122	Bergamo	8(8)	Hptm. Hirdes
6.(F)/122	Bergamo	4(4)	Oblt. Brinkmann
Kdo. Carmen	Bergamo	2/3?	Ltn. Thurnhuber
Stab/NAGr.11	Udine	0(0)	Hptm. Eckerscham
1./NAGr.11	Udine	12(7)	Hptm. Weidman
2./NAGr.11	Udine	13(8)	Oblt. Holzapfel[25]
Seenotstaffel 20	Udine	4(4)[26]	Oblt. Langer
St. Einhorn	Villafranca	14(7)	Hptm. Schuntermann
Einsatzstab/NSGr.9	Bovolone	3(2)	Major Frost
1./NSGr.9	Bovolone	12(6)	Hptm. Kuhle
2./NSGr.9	Ghedi	11(8)	Major Rohn[27]
3./NSGr.9	Aviano	10(8)	Hptm. Reither[28]

Marini was severely reprimanded for insubordination and finally, in exasperation, went off and flew his own reconnaissance in an S.79. He covered the Straits of Bonifacio but bad weather drove him back without sighting the convoy. On the 26th orders went out for the unit to be ready for operations off Ancona in the imminent full-moon period.

MAAF – Interdiction and Counter-air

MATAF was given as its principal future objectives enemy lines of communication, especially the isolation of Italy from the Reich. Support for ground operations was to be drastically cut. Operation Blockade and the air Battle of the Brenner Pass officially began on the 4th, the same day that bombers claimed the destruction of a Luftwaffe HQ in Milan. MATAF made its first penetrations of Austrian airspace on the 11th, while 15th AF abandoned transport interdiction in favour of the strategic offensive against Germany's oil supplies.

The other major effort by MAAF was an attempt to put down the renascent menace of German and Italian air power in Italy. On the 11th it was noted for example that 'the Italian Fascist Air Force now appears to be an effective operational command'. Strategic and tactical bombers joined in trying to deliver an absolutely crushing blow to the Axis bases, and fighter-bombers extended the campaign over 12 days. The Germans issued an appreciation the day after the heavy raids:

> From the planning of these attacks it could be deduced that the continuous transfers of the II./Italian Fighter Gruppe had not escaped Allied notice. To avoid failures [they] attacked almost all the airfields concerned simultaneously. Doubtless the Allies found the activity of the Italian fighters disagreeable. As Allied four-engined operations are flown without fighter cover, Axis fighter potential had to be eliminated in one blow.

MAAF believed that it had 'put paid to any effective activity by the Fascist flyers for the rest of the year and further limited the small GAF effort'.

Notes

25. Apparently succeeded by Hptm. Köbring – date uncertain.
26. Figure for 31 October.
27. It was around this time that Rohn was posted to command NSGr.2 in Western Germany. He was accidentally shot and killed by a Hitler Youth patrol in March 1945.
28. Reither later moved to a staff posting with *Gen.d.S.*

A Ju 87D-5 of NSGr.9 taxies back to its dispersal with the aid of two groundcrewmen seated on the wings. As was common in this unit, the aircraft's individual letter is repeated on the wheel spats and the underwing crosses have been completely painted over. (Bundesarchiv)

Fiat G.55 – MM.91150 – Flown by M.llo Agostini – Piombino (LI), August 1944

Messerschmitt Bf 109G-6/R3 of 1ª Sq., IIº Gr.C. – Flown by S. M. Cavagliano – Aviano (PN), November 1944

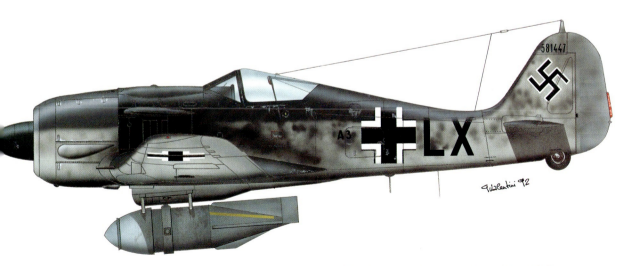
Focke-Wulf Fw 190F-8 – W.Nr.581447 of Sonderverband Einhorn – Villafranca, December 1944 – (Reconstruction)

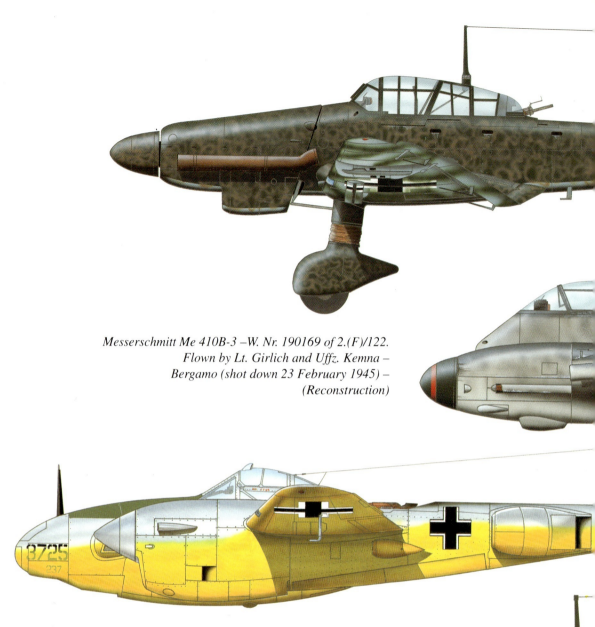

Messerschmitt Me 410B-3 – W. Nr. 190169 of 2.(F)/122. Flown by Lt. Girlich and Uffz. Kemna – Bergamo (shot down 23 February 1945) – (Reconstruction)

Savoia Marchetti S.79 III – 2ª Sq., Iº Gr. Aerosil. "Faggioni" – Lonate Pozzolo (VA), October 1944.

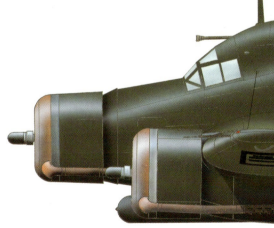

Junkers Ju 87D-5 – W.Nr. 2600 of 2./NSGr.9 – Cavriago (RE), September 1944

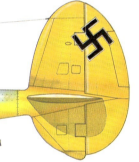

Lockheed F-5E – Ser. No. 44-23725 – Flown by Lt. Monti – Villafranca (VR), October 1944

Messerschmitt Bf 109G-6/R3 of 3./JG4 – Maniago (PN), July 1944

Macchi C.205 of 2ª Sq., I° Gr.C. – Vicenza, July 1944

Messerschmitt Bf 109G-6/R3 – W.Nr. 163956 of 5./JG 77 – Flown by Flg. Nehrenheim – Beundenfeld (Switzerland), August 1944

CHAPTER 8

Operations

1-4 November 1944

The first three days saw little, if any, Axis flying, although at 2045 on the 3rd German aircraft reportedly strafed II Corps positions south of Bologna. 2./122 made up for lost time on the 4th, dispatching six sorties.

All of IIº Gr.C.'s aircraft (17 from Villafranca, 10 from Ghedi) took off at 1000, landing at Aviano 45min later. The Italians had little more than an hour to settle in before warning came of bombers returning from German and Austrian targets. Only six Bf 109s (drawn equally from 1ª and 2ª Sq.) scrambled, led by Cap. Bellagambi and intercepting seven B-24s at 1230. The bombers belonged to the 484th BG and the Italians shot down two but claimed three. Cap. Bellagambi got a B-24J that had become separated from the main formation, shooting it down into the sea 10km south of the River Piave's mouth. The second was downed in the same area by Ten. Rosas. The third was claimed by Ten. Valenzano (1ª Sq.), but was corrected to a 'probable' in the official communiqué.

One Bf 109 was hit and badly damaged by the Americans' defensive fire, leading M.llo Cavagnino (1ª Sq.) to make an emergency landing on a small, flat strip of ground. The aircraft came down safely but its canopy refused to open. Through the sliding side-panel Cavagnino called for help from a few farmworkers keeping well back from the smoking aeroplane. At last two came to the rescue and forced the hood open; the pilot jumped out and ran, dragging them to safety. Seconds later the Bf 109 exploded. The other five Messerschmitts landed at Aviano at 1310.

During the afternoon a KG 200 Ju 188, A3+RD (a successor to its 'namesake' lost in September) was active between Riem and Bergamo. Fifteen to twenty Ju 87s struck forward positions near Bologna, 11 of them having left Villafranca shortly after 2000. A 1./NSGr.9 Ju 87D-5 (W.Nr.130669, E8+FH) crashed 14km south of the latter airfield. Its crew, Ofw. Karl Zander and Uffz. Heinz Eickhoff, perished from accidental causes, and not under a nightfighter's guns as first thought.

5 November 1944

Ju 188 F6+AM was in the air between 0700-0800 and two tactical reconnaissance sorties covered Venice, the Po Estuary, Rimini and Pola. At 1100 Allied mediums were reported in the Lake Garda area; B-26s of the 320th BG on their way to bomb the railway at Rovereto (TN). Twenty-three Bf 109s scrambled, interception following about half an hour later.

Five Italian pilots were each unofficially credited with a bomber. Only three were actually shot down; two in the combat and one which crashed later. The first was a 441st BS aircraft, '01' piloted by 2nd/Lt Truman C. Cole, shot up just before reaching the target. Lacking evidence to the contrary, this kill should be credited 'confirmed' to S.M. Pacini (3ª Sq.), as reported by the communiqué from ANR HQ.

The second was '86', flown by 1st/Lt James R. Longsdon. This kill belongs both to Cap. Bellagambi and S.M. Cavagliano, who claimed it separately but whose accounts coincide completely on the way the bomber crashed; '. . . dropping a leg, pulling up its nose and spinning down into the mountains east of Lake Garda . . .'. This description also matches the USAAF Missing Air Crew Report, confirming that the B-26 was attacked independently by the two Italians and credited separately to both.

More often than previously thought, II° Gruppo's pilots (mainly those of 1ª and 3ª Sq.) used to paint girlfriends' names on their aircraft. An example is supplied by Bf 109G-6 'Black 12' of S.M. Cavagliano, here based at Aviano. The name 'Linin' was followed on the other side by the wording 'L'è bon!' (It's nice!). It's interesting to note that the Italian flag has yet to be applied behind the cockpit, where faint white lines mark the area to be painted.

The third victory is even more difficult to attribute, since B-26 '84' piloted by 1st/Lt Charles Kamanski, although badly hit and emitting smoke, completed its bomb run and had almost reached Corsica before the engines failed, forcing the crew to bale out. All were later picked up by the Air-Sea Rescue Service. This bomber was most probably that attacked by S.M. Baldi and Ten. Camaioni and credited to both as shot down but in reality seen only 'to leave trailing black smoke . . .'.

The bombers' gunners scored too, not only compelling S.M. Ancillotti to crash-land his Bf 109 (W.Nr.162467) near Pescantina Veronese (VR), but also wounding Ten. Camaioni and forcing him to make a one-wheel landing at Villafranca, soon followed by the Gustav of S.Ten. Rosas (2ª Sq.) with similar problems. This is a rare incident in which identical accounts survive from Germans, Italians and Allies. The last heard one pilot's R/T warning, 'Arrivo senza gambe!'[29]. Sixteen Bf 109s landed at Villafranca, the others at Thiene at noon; the following day all of 1ª Sq. flew to Ghedi.

At 1220 GMT a Ju 88T-3 of 4.(F)/122 (W.Nr.330220, F6+HM) left Bergamo on a daylight photographic mission to the Brenner Pass area, piloted by Oblt. Heinz Hoeb. It was later the subject of 'anxious enquiries by Bergamo'; at 1440 there was still no news of it. It had been chased by aircraft of the 5th FS and shot down near Innichen, right on the Austrian border, killing all four aboard. To compound FAGr.122's misfortune, a 6. Staffel Ju 188D-2 (W.Nr.150264) crashed at Bergamo, killing one crewman and injuring three. F6+HP operated from Bergamo that evening but it is not clear if it was the victim. NSGr.9 operated in the same general area as the night before, seven of 3. Staffel's Ju 87s leaving Villafranca at 1705. About 32 tons of bombs had been dropped over the two nights. Operations then ceased until the 9th.

6-9 November 1944

A wildly misleading report (compiled in London) refers to 'at least 21 Me 410s' over the Ligurian on the 6th. In reality 2./122 put up three sorties from amongst its six serviceable aeroplanes, then did not fly again until the 10th. Around mid afternoon an 'Italian Tac R' was purportedly active over the Po Valley.

On 7 November Ten. Drago of II° Gr.C. was promoted to Capitano, while M.llo Galetti 'celebrated' his promotion to Sottotenente with an accident following an uneventful scramble by 12 Messerschmitts. After his Bf 109's engine caught fire Galetti got rid of smoke in the cockpit by jettisoning the canopy and then crash-landed successfully. Bf 109 'Yellow 9' (ex-II./JG 77) was flown from Cameri to Villafranca where it was passed to II° Gr.C.

'Late [in the] afternoon [of the 8th] some six Ju 87s and Fw 190s operated in the Forlì-Ravenna area. Two . . . were destroyed . . .', one by AA fire, the other by a Beaufighter, according to a contemporary report. Allied sources refer to strafing and bombing at Firenzuola the next night as well. A Ju 188D-2 (W.Nr.150525, F6+HP) of 6.(F)/122 crashed at Bergamo on the 8th, injuring Fhj.Fw. Schuster and Ofw. Scheithauer.

10 November 1944

IIº Gruppo Caccia was in combat against Marauders again, this time two formations of the 320th BG. Twenty-two Gustavs scrambled from 1215-1220, intercepting the bombers 20min later on their return route, in the Lake Garda area. The Italians claimed two B-26s shot down by S.M. Baldi and Camerani (1ª Sq.), plus three probables.

The Americans described things somewhat differently. They were attacked 'unaggressively' over Desenzano by a 25/30-strong formation consisting mainly of Bf 109s but also including (so they said) G.55s, C.202s and Fw 190s, and a more determined attack developed as the bombers were coming back over Cremona. The first pass came in from 11 o'clock, by groups of eight, four and two fighters in line abreast, some of which then swung around to make rear or beam attacks. They desisted while the bombers were engaged by flak but then took up where they left off. It was the flak which the Americans credited with damaging 15 of their aircraft, while another 16 Marauders of the same Group, bombing rail sidings at Peri (VR), suffered one B-26 damaged in an attack by 18 fighters. The bombers claimed the destruction of an Fw 190 and a Bf 109, plus five of the latter damaged. In fact 21 fighters made it back to their bases at 1315, and the only part of this claim that the authors can confirm is combat damage to S.M. Baldi's Bf 109. The Italians' sole loss was to another cause.

Eight P-47s of 64th FS happened to be in the area and, as reported by 57th FG's diary:

> . . . at approximately 1300hrs., 25 twin-engined bombers were seen flying SW at about 12,000'. An Me-109 was spotted above them at 14,000'. It dived on the bombers then turned off and came directly at our formation which was at 7,000'.
> . . . our a/c cornered the Me-109 which bore German markings, and five pilots claimed equal parts of the Me-109 destroyed. Pieces flew off the fuselage, and the aircraft, smoking, dived into a hedge and exploded . . .

The unfortunate pilot was S.M. Pacini, who had probably become separated from the others and followed the bombers, hoping for a kill. S.Ten. Di Santo's diary says: 'Pacini hasn't come back. Poor guy! Another one, why? He has been betrayed by the quest for glory.' It may have been Pacini's Messerschmitt that was seen by 17th BG – a single Bf 109 below their formation. Two and a half hours later a strafing attack by twelve Mustangs and P-47s on Villafranca burned out the Bf 109G-12 that Di Santo was meant to fly to Germany[30] and damaged two more Messerschmitts.

NSGr.9 attacked troops in the mountain passes along Highway 65 that night, heralded by red and purple smoke shells from the Fourteenth Army's artillery marking their targets. Six or so Ju 87s climbed from a low approach over the River Savena, firing white flares to warn off the friendly flak that engaged them from Pianoro (defying orders not to fire on single-engined aircraft by night) before splitting into twos and threes, at heights ranging from 65 to 100m. They dropped phosphorus and fragmentation bombs and at least one 500kg weapon.

11 November 1944

Shortly after midday 18 B-25s of the 310th BG claimed to have been followed from Cremona to Lake Garda by 15-20 Bf 109s and Fw 190s bearing the striking paintwork referred to above, but no attacks resulted. Seven Ju 87s left Villafranca on a mission late in the afternoon and at 0545 next morning the same number went out again, these dusk-to-dawn attacks departing from the usual moonlight-only tactics.

12 November 1944

German tactical reconnaissance activity 'was the greatest so far recorded this month'. At 0655 one saw Allied aeroplanes; that afternoon another was warned of MAAF fighters but avoided them; at 1326 reconnaissance aeroplanes were over the Bologna/Ferrara area. At 1459, south of Imola a group of German aircraft ran into Allied fighters and after the engagement one of the former reported having a damaged fuel tank. He flew a northerly, homeward course and apparently landed in the Padua area.

The whole of IIº Gr.C. was now ready to transfer properly to Aviano (the move on the 4th was just a try-out). One aim was to get the unit further away from Allied fighter-bombers. At 0820 eight Bf 109s of 1ª Sq. took off from Ghedi and were over Villafranca a few minutes later. There, ten Gustavs from the rest of IIº Gruppo were about to take off and join them. Up to then they had been unaware that four P-47s of the 346th FS that were also approaching the base. Here (in 1st/Lt Tomlinson's words) is what happened:

> We had been up in the Brenner Pass strafing at dawn and were heading back. Capt. Michel was a rather fearless individual and he led me right thru the Villafranca airfield at tree-top level.

To my surprise (and probably to the Me-109 pilots'...) I was flying head on down the runway with the Me-109s just taking off. Their wheels were just being retracted...

The Italians' reaction is well described by S.M. Ancillotti:

... due to the early morning hour, a thick mist hung over the airfield and visibility was just adequate. The first section ready to take off was made up of Cap. Bellagambi, Ten. Ambrosino and me. No sooner had we lifted our undercarriages from the ground than we saw at the airfield's perimeter Thunderbolts coming head-on! Thanks to Bellagambi's prompt reaction we managed to avoid their attack, tightening our formation and climbing almost vertically at full throttle to turn the tables and attack the enemy fighters from above.

In the meantime Max (Ten. Longhini) was taxying behind us, at the head of the second section of three and having reached take-off speed, he had already lifted his tail. He vaguely noticed a certain confusion of aircraft at the end of the field but at first he thought that we had started doing aerobatics.

Then he saw our three Messerschmitts emerge from the milky haze at full throttle and he realised that the approaching planes were Thunderbolts. He lost no time and fired at them while retracting his undercarriage, scoring hits.

The other aircraft taking off didn't notice anything and the short combat was fought by our four aircraft with some of 1ª Sq. joining in the mêlée...

Two S.79s of Iº Gr. Aerosiluranti at Ghedi in November 1944. By mid-October the unit had changed its name from 'Buscaglia' to 'Faggioni' (following the news that the former airman, far from dying in action late 1942, had survived and joined the Italian Co-belligerent A.F. only to perish in a training accident; thus the unit was re-dedicated to its first CO, KIA on 10 April 1944) and changed its codes accordingly, an 'F' replacing the 'B'. (Apostolo)

Lt Tomlinson's account continues:

I only remember that we went around in some tight turns for a while and fired out all our ammo. It was very confusing with all the Me-109s trying to join up at low level.

I do remember that Capt. Michel took a 20mm shell into the cockpit that went right thru the parachute he was sitting on and came out on the floor near his feet. He had a lot of smoke in the cockpit and we were out of fuel so we headed for home.

Capt. Michel was wounded but reached Pisa safely, claiming two probables and one damaged, while the Italians were so sure they had shot him down that a victory was credited jointly to Ten. Longhini and S.Ten. Fagiano in the ANR HQ teletype.

Despite this encounter, the transfer to Aviano took place (it seems that the ten aeroplanes from Villafranca landed after combat and made the trip mid-afternoon). Over the following days the rest of the Group's aircraft arrived at this airfield whence interceptions of 15th AF bombers were thought possible.

3./NSGr.9 dispatched its second mission of the day at 1645, involving ten aircraft – probably a maximum effort.

13-15 November 1944

An early morning sortie was put up by 2.(F)/122 on the 13th, and next day F6+SK was crashed on landing from a mission at 1550, never to fly again. The observer, Ogfr. Wachtfeidl, was back up within five days but his pilot, Fhr. Sewald, did not fly for 18 days.

An hour or so later at Villafranca three Einhorn Fw 190s were making twilight practice flights when one ran into another that was parked, damaging both. Training seems to have been intense at this airfield, with 13 flights recorded and 22 the next day. IIº Gruppo's first days in Aviano were marred by the death of Nucleo Comando's S.Ten. Berti on an engine-

Three of NSGr.9's Ju 87s wait at dusk for their next mission. The D-5 in the foreground, carrying four SD 70 bombs, is interesting for the dark camouflage stripes on its undersides and its lack of cannon flash-dampers and dive-brakes. (Bundesarchiv)

test on the 15th. His Bf 109 lost power and, too low to recover, crashed a mile short of the runway.

16-17 November 1944

During the night of the 15/16th, four flash bombs exploded over Falconara. Beaufighters scrambled, one chasing a contact for 20min in low cloud, but it 'got away with some interesting pictures'. At 0725 a Ju 188 of 6.(F)/122 landed at Ghedi from Bergamo, only to return home that evening. Borrmann and Kranz of 2. Staffel flew a 50min mission in the early afternoon.

There was an unconfirmed report that, at 1000, three or four *Ju 88s* strafed Highway 65 and, as if this were not strange enough, a 'possible single-engined jet' was reported 5 miles north of Vicenza. However, the 16th was to see one of the most celebrated episodes of the Italian air war; the encounter which made the 15th Air Force's Capt John J. Voll (308th FS, 31st FG) the top-scoring American ace in the Mediterranean Theatre.

Flying his P-51D *American Beauty*, Voll had aborted an escort mission with radio and electrical malfunctions. He sighted a Ju 88 over the sea and pursued it to about 10 miles southeast of Aviano, where he shot it down. Thus engaged, at around 1115, he was attacked from above by '7 Fw 190s and 5 Me 109s'. Turning on them – all the more remarkably for a lone flier in a defective aircraft – he claimed the destruction of two Focke-Wulfs and a Bf 109, an Fw 190 and an Me 109 probably destroyed, and two Messerschmitts damaged. These kills took Voll's score to 21 (three ahead of his nearest rival), but his CO reported that the pilot was violently sick on alighting from his P-51 at home base, so he may not have felt like celebrating at first. Unfortunately none of our sources has enabled us to identify losses among the Italian-based Axis units corresponding to Voll's claims.

Combats definitely took place between the 15th AF and the ANR, but not until somewhat later. At noon Cap. Drago led eight Bf 109s of 1ª Sq. off from Aviano. They noticed scattered groups of B-17s with P-51 escorts returning from a raid into Germany, and half an hour after take-off, at 24,000ft, they intercepted a Fortress escorted by P-51s of the 332nd FG, becoming entangled with the latter. Both Drago and Ten. Renato Mingozzi claimed P-51s shot down, and S.M. Guido Minardi claimed a B-17.[31] This encounter lasted some 10min and led right down to the deck.

As this battle was abating, 2ª Sq. sent up eight aeroplanes, headed by Cap. Bellagambi. At 1310 they ran into a group of escorted B-17s near the mouth of the River Livenza. Ten. Filippi, S.M. Mazzanti and Ten. Longhini each claimed a B-17, the last-named being shot down and killed by P-51s only minutes after his victory. Other B-17s were damaged as the ANR aircraft continued their attacks out over the Adriatic before turning back to land. Two of the Messerschmitts were set upon by P-51s of the 307th FS, 31st FG, and pursued to low level; 1st/Lt Bobby A. Bush shot down Ten. Vinicio Ambrosino, but the other Italian evaded the Americans. Claims were also made by Capt Luke J. Weathers Jr at 1330 in the Udine area (two Bf 109s destroyed) and by 2nd/Lt Junior R. Hanson (one Bf 109) near Aviano, 30min later but the authors have not matched these claims with any Axis losses.

At 1723 traffic was intercepted that a tactical reconnaissance aircraft had completed its mission on the east coast and was headed for home. At 1645 eight Ju 87s of NSGr.9 set off on an operation from Villafranca; otherwise there were two transfer flights and five training sorties from the airfield. MAAF's reconnaissance aircraft had photographed 13 Ju 87s on Villafranca's northern dispersal area during the day, and another five at Vicenza.

As mentioned above, the night ether brought radio traffic from station Figaro, guiding an aircraft towards a target. The significance of this was not grasped at first, but it was soon to bring a rude shock for the Allies.

At 1906 the next evening a Ju 188 took the air, only to be warned of fighters half an hour later. An hour after that it reported that it was aborting its mission because its FuG 200 radar had gone u/s. At 2140 it was homing and was then called by its control for an hour after that, but there is no Ju 188 reported lost for this date.

18 November 1944

During the night of 17/18 November a major assault began on the increasingly troublesome Axis airfields. 205 Group's heavies deposited 212 tons of bombs on Campoformido and Vicenza, insufficient to prevent a pair of tactical reconnaissance aircraft flying a 60min sortie from the former at 0815, south over the Adriatic as far as Pola.

The next morning 15th AF joined in, hitting the same fields, plus Villafranca and Aviano, with 952 tons of bombs. In Villafranca at around 0840 GMT Liberators were reported approaching from the southwest. At 0955, 85 B-24s carpeted the runways, landing ground and dispersals, the Germans estimating that 7-8,000 fragmentation bombs were dropped. Seven military personnel were hurt, and four local civilians killed and 12 seriously injured; a horse and seven cattle also died. Both external and internal communications were disrupted.

An Fw 190 and three Ju 87s were burnt out; five 190s had splinter damage and the same number of Ju 87s was slightly damaged. In mid-afternoon three Thunderbolts shot up the dispersals, igniting another Ju 87. It was reckoned that the landing ground would be unusable for 24hr and the Commandant, Obstlt. Sachs, called in the Todt Organisation to assist his men with repairs.

At Campoformido the runway was hit and its lighting put out of action, leaving the field unusable for night landings. Repairs in progress dictated caution in day flying. NAGr.11 reported a Fi 156 destroyed and one damaged from the Gruppenstab and four Bf 109s destroyed and six damaged, divided equally between the two Staffeln. It is also notable that SNSt.20's count of serviceable Fw 190s dropped from ten to three between 10 and 20 November.

At 1800 Fl.H.Kdtr.207/VII at Ghedi (but also responsible for Bergamo and Bettola) reported two Germans killed, five seriously and six slightly injured, and six Italians killed and an unknown number injured; about 100 Italian civilians, primarily Todt Organisation members, had been killed or severely injured. Of 15 aircraft, two remained undamaged. Despite this, 2.(F)/122's Oblt. v.d. Daele and Uffz. Blaschek took F6+AK on reconnaissance over the Ligurian that afternoon. This aircraft did not sortie again for five weeks.

Aviano suffered likewise, as described in the diary of S.M. Bonopera, an armourer with II° Gr.C.;

> This morning we sustained a tremendous bombardment. Early in the morning 17 Spitfires[32] circled low over Maniago, then they jettisoned their fuel tanks but almost immediately the alarm siren howled and coming from the sea flight after flight of B-24s headed toward our airfield, showering large and small bombs everywhere.
>
> No sooner had the alarm sounded than Capitano Bellagambi wanted to take-off but the German Command refused. Instead the order . . . was given when the American bombers were already overhead and . . . Bellagambi retorted that he wasn't going to take-off anymore.
>
> When, just before 10 o'clock, the bombardment ceased, the field looked like it had been ploughed and almost all our aircraft had been hit and damaged.

From photos, MAAF estimated that they had put paid to 50-60 enemy aircraft (their count was complicated by the presence of decoys and second-line machines). Axis sources, although incomplete and contradictory suggest the following:

Unit	Type	Destroyed	Damaged
Einhorn	Fw 190F-8	1	5
Stab/11	Fi 156	1	1
1./11	Bf 109G	2	3
2./11	Bf 109G	2	3
NSGr.9	Ju 87D	4	5
SNSt.20	Fw 190A-8	–	c.7
II° Gr.C.	Bf 109G	6	14
	Total	16	38

This numerical setback was temporary, and the units had probably been spared far worse by their elaborate dispersal and camouflage measures.

19-27 November 1944

At 0930 on the 19th NAGr.12 reported achieving 100 per cent photographic cover of Bari harbour. 2./122 was busy with transfers, operational and test flights; no aeroplanes were up on the 20th, but two missions took place the next day. The 22nd saw 'flights to the front' (not counting towards the mission tally). Operations were again mounted on the two succeeding days, but the Staffel remained grounded from the 25th-27th. On a number of occasions between the 19th and 27th Ju 188s of 6./122 would arrive at Ghedi in the morning, apparently spend the day on the ground, then return to Bergamo.

During the night of 19/20 November an A-20 of the 47th BG was attacked by four single-engined aircraft, but sustained no damage. Offensive action was not resumed until the 21st, when four or five Ju 87s and 'two Me 109s' were reported over Forlì from 1710-1730. The next day both NAGr.11 and FAGr.122 were ordered to provide photo coverage of partisan-held areas. Uffz. Kurt Schulze's Ju 188D-2 (W.Nr.150258, F6+EP) was destroyed in a crashlanding 5km south of Bergamo; he and a crewman died, one was injured. While raiding Villafranca that night an A-20 was again attacked but not damaged, another had an enemy aeroplane close to 100ft only to blink a white light.

Between S. Martino and S. Bonifacio (VR) on the 23rd, Allied fighter-bombers attacked a train carrying 350 tons of bombs for Aviano; 35 of them exploded, causing major damage in the vicinity. Early that evening about seven unidentified aircraft bombed and strafed Forlì. A Ju 87D-5 (W.Nr.141018, E8+JH) was shot down by W/O Smith and Flt Sgt Dunford of 600 Sqn, 25 miles east of Comacchio; Obfhr. Bernhard Buckow and Uffz. Artur Berkemeyer were posted missing. The same Beaufighter claimed another Junkers damaged.

Night attack operations resumed on the 27th, when 16 aircraft dropped HE and incendiary bombs over the Front.

28 November 1944

While German troops achieved local success in recapturing Monte Castellaro and Monte Belvedere, the day passed without particular incident for the Luftwaffe, although a train with 17 fuel wagons arrived in the Western Airfield District. 2.(F)/122's effort was confined to a half-hour test flight by F6+VK and a two-hour midday reconnaissance by Ofhr. Jackstadt and Uffz. Schütz in F6+ZK. Ferrying plans included the delivery of two Bf 109s to Udine and three to Osoppo.

Shortly after 1600 two Ju 87s of 1./NSGr.9 took off from Bovolone, detailed to attack targets of opportunity (artillery positions, troop/transport concentrations, bridges) in the Anglo-Polish sector. In the first of these aircraft (E8+CH) was Staffelkapitän Hptm. Kuhle, and in the second (Ju 87D-5 W.Nr.131086, E8+DH) were Fw. Kaspar Stuber and his gunner, Uffz. Alois Adami. Stuber was one of the Gruppe's original draft of pilots, having flown He 46s with NSGr.3 in Russia before

Würzburg radar emplacements in the Po Valley. The radar system in Northern Italy never attained complete coverage although the more militarily sensitive areas were included. Allied air supremacy gradually forced the abandonment of fixed stations in favour of mobile ones like that shown in the second photograph.

transferring to Italy in December 1943. He had 311 operations to his credit, 75 of them in Italy and held the German Cross in Gold, as well as being shortly due for the gold pilot's clasp. Adami had joined the Gruppe on 26 February, crewing-up with Stuber in May or June. Stuber was just back from three weeks' leave and his usual E8+BH was unserviceable.

With a 500kg fragmentation bomb under its fuselage and four 50kg incendiaries on its wing racks, E8+DH set off toward Forlì, navigating by dead reckoning and radio and visual beacons and skirting clouds. At 1630 a Beaufighter Mk.VIF (BT299, 'T') of 600 Sqn scrambled from Falconara to patrol the Forlì-Faenza area, crewed by Sqn Ldr Archer and Flt Lt Barrington. At 1705 'Syrup' vectored them on to a possible bandit at 12,000ft and three minutes later Barrington had AI contact on two aircraft at 3½ miles. It took another five minutes to get a visual; the bogeys were staggered, with one 500ft above and 300yd to starboard of the other. Archer closed on the former, identifying it as a Ju 87. He reported; 'At this moment both aircraft seemed to sight us. The port aircraft dived away to port, the other one that we were following dived steeply for cloud cover below.'

Stuber recalled that the Germans were flying just above a cloud bank when Adami spotted the nightfighter emerging from the clouds behind them. It closed swiftly and opened fire with cannon and machine-guns. Archer saw numerous strikes on the Ju 87's fuselage and port wing and, with no chance to take evasive action, it became unmanageable. He described how it: '. . . turned to starboard, pouring out smoke as pieces [broke] off the wings and fuselage. A large centrally placed bomb [came] away at this moment.'

Stuber, concluding that his rudder had been hit, gave the order to bale out. Coming down about 5 miles southwest of Forlì, he was promptly taken prisoner by Polish troops but Adami was killed when the Junkers spiralled steeply into the ground with bombs still on board and was totally destroyed. The whole action had lasted just three minutes.

The nightfighter was sent north at full speed after the other Ju 87. A feeble AI contact was followed up but the bogey drew away, outclimbing the Beau (a rare feat for a Stuka but child's play for an Fw 190, which it may have been). A Ju 87 was claimed brought down by AA fire but is not identified in surviving records. Closer to home, 2./NSGr.9 lost a Ju 87D-5 in a crash at Fornaci (BS) in which another 'founder member', Uffz. Franz Spörr, died.

Six hostiles were estimated to have operated round Forlì (some reportedly bombing German positions). A Fifth Army Command Post was attacked, with military and civilian casualties, and Highway 65 was strafed. The Army reported that two Fw 190s attacked Forlì at 1725. Over the airwaves an aircraft reported release of a bomb to its ground control station. At 1745 transmissions resumed, but at 2001 the aircraft under guidance was reported lost and the station soon shut down again. Overall, NSGr.9 flew 24 sorties and Einhorn five, 14 of this total being from Villafranca.

At 1800 a Kdo. Carmen Ju 188 took off from Bergamo, flew down the Adriatic and came inland just south of Senigallia. Its track then took it to Florence and it was down at base at 2027. Next day, Komm. Gen. reported to KG 200's Berlin HQ that the aircraft's task was successfully carried out at 1911 from a height of 1,700m, but that the result of the operation was not yet available. Thanks to Ultra this information was with MAAF early on the 30th.

At 2330 Lts Deakyne and Perkins in a Beaufighter Mk.VI of the 417th NFS shot down a Ju 188 southeast of Saint Tropez. This was Fw. Hans Krieg's Ju 188D-2 (W.Nr.150044, F6+DP) of 6.(F)/122, and all four crew were injured.

29-30 November 1944

At about 2015 on the 29th a bombed-up Beaufighter was hit by light flak, crashed and exploded on Bovolone airfield. Its pilot, Lt Ralph Mulholln USAAF, had set a southerly course on his aeroplane's autopilot before parachuting into captivity. Southeast of Cannes next evening another Beaufighter (from the 417th NFS) intercepted a Ju 188 at 200ft and got hits on its starboard wing. The Junkers evaded by diving and was chased as far as Genoa, dropping chaff as it went, before the nightfighter broke off.

Notes
29. Literally, 'coming in without legs!'
30. See I° Gr. Caccia – September chapter.
31. These claims are not confirmed by USAAF documents.
32. And probably P-51s also.

CHAPTER 9

December 1944

On the 8th, Desert Air Force flew 613 sorties, its record to date, dwarfing what the Axis could manage for the entire month. MAAF on the 23rd gave a succinct, quite accurate and less than usually dismissive overview of the Luftwaffe and ANR in Italy:

> The enemy air force . . . barely exceeds 150 aircraft of all types. This is an increase of about 40 per cent on the air situation at the beginning of October.[33] *Small as the force is, it contains all essential air weapons with the exception of heavy bombers*[34] whose place is taken in this theatre by a small force of Fw 190s capable of carrying very heavy calibre bombs.
>
> The offensive air force consists of 30 Ju 87s of NSG 9 based at Villafranca, Vicenza and Bovolone. Their normal role is ground strafing and harassing of our forward areas by moonlight but when the weather is good they operate in the non-moon period. These Ju 87s have recently been joined by about 10 Fw 190s operating almost entirely out of Villafranca. They have already operated at dusk and may possibly do so by night using radar control to locate their targets.
>
> The rest of the German Air Force consists of strat. and tac. reconnaissances. A mixed force of Me 410s, Ju 88s and Ju 188s of F.122 operate from Ghedi and Bergamo. Their function is to cover the coastal areas of the Ligurian and Adriatic Seas for shipping movements. Tac reconnaissance is carried out by 15 Me 109s of NAG 2 [*sic*] operating from Udine.
>
> The Italian Fascist Air Force consists of a Gruppe of 40-50 Me 109s based in the Villafranca area with alternative airfields at Udine. Their function is to keep the Brenner route open by attacking the bombers of 57 Bomb Wing whose main task is to deny the enemy the use of the Brenner and Tarvisio routes from Germany. These 109s have never come south of the River Po. 15 SM.79s have recently appeared at Lonate. They are believed to be torpedo carriers but have not yet operated. If and when they do, their targets will probably be the shipping concentrations in the harbours serving 5th and 8th Armies.

Several reported sightings of jet- or rocket-propelled aircraft were dismissed as mistaken identification on the grounds – correct as it turned out – that the Germans would spare no such aircraft for Italy for some time to come.

The Luftwaffe

'Ramming Aircraft in Italy?'
This eye-catching headline in an Allied bulletin came from a 'boastful fighter pilot' admitted to a Verona military hospital after a car crash. His tales of December experiments at Bovolone with 1,200kph aeroplanes that would ram Allied bombers appear to have been chiefly aimed at impressing the Italian nurse he had befriended.

Nightfighters again?
A postwar RAF study says that Pohl obtained a 'first instalment of ten' Fw 190s for nightfighting in the last week of December, but that they stayed only one week. The authors have found nothing to support this beyond a sighting by 232 Wing medium bombers of two Fw 190s over Vicenza on the 27th. On the 30th

there was an enquiry from Italy to the aircraft park at Gablingen, Bavaria, regarding the dispatch of Fw 190 droptanks. Since 'no Fw 190 unit [had] recently [been] mentioned in Italy' the RAF surmised this was a belated indent for Einhorn, but SNSt.20 were probably the intended recipients.

Reconnaissance and 'Special Tasks'

Seebode's intelligence summary noted that a long spell of bad weather had held the level of operations rather below that of November. Some 120 missions were flown, almost exclusively over the sea and Allied ports, including some in Corsica and Southern France. Particularly commended in the summary were two Ju 188 crews, who while carrying out 'special tasks' brought back important information on the harbours of Naples and Palermo.

Our researches point to 14 daylight operations flown by the Me 410s of 2.(F)/122 and only limited activity down the east coast and over the front lines by NAGr.11. Ultra revealed Carmen's December fuel allocation of 61m^3, reckoned enough for 10-15 flights. FAGr.122 had a number of Ju 188s and Me 410s delivered from Riem.

NSGr.9 and Einhorn

Seebode said NSGr.9 operated on seven nights (we think more) against targets close behind the front lines. Long-range guidance systems meant that ops were no longer restricted to the full moon period and could proceed despite the seasonal weather. The main objectives were in the Faenza-Forlì district, and attacks were also made in the Serchio Valley and numerous fires and explosions were caused amongst transport and supply columns. For good measure, the Gruppe dropped 174,000 propaganda leaflets.

Munitions expended on the night of 22/23 December allow typical payloads to be pictured:

Ju 87s from Villafranca: 16 x SD 70 fragmentation; 6 x AB 36 incendiary cluster units; 2 x SD 500 fragmentation; 6 x AB 500 cluster units; 2 x Brand C 50 phosphorus incendiaries. (Suggesting that four of the aircraft carried a 500kg weapon on the centreline and four underwing SD 70, and the others a similar main load plus four underwing incendiaries.)

Ju 87s from Ghedi: 28 x SD 70; 2 x SD 500; 6 x AB 500. (Maybe eight aeroplanes, one of which carried only a centreline 500kg weapon – it might also have had flares or leaflets aboard – the others with the same plus four SD 70 on their wing racks.)

NSGr.9's operations were supplemented by those of Einhorn, which had probably its biggest success, before transferring to the Western Front. By the RAF's own admission, this attack sparked off a renewed spate of raids on Axis airfields, involving mainly P-47s by day and DAF night bombers. Many of these attacks were fruitless or hit only second-line Italian aircraft, but noteworthy results were achieved around Christmas.

During December, Villafranca was home to Einhorn and 1. and 3./9, while 2./9 was at Ghedi and the Stab probably at Bovolone.

The ANR

I° Gr.C., December 1944 to January 1945

The 'replacement' Bf 109G-12, flown by S.Ten. Di Santo of II° Gr.C., finally arrived on the afternoon of 2 December. Three days later training recommenced, but not for all of I° Gruppo's pilots, as Magg. Visconti had received an irresistible offer from the Germans. A group of his pilots would be trained on the Me 163 Komet in preparation for the probable allocation of this rocket-powered interceptor to the Italians. Hearing about 'secret weapons' was one thing, but an offer to fly them was something a fighter pilot could not resist, so Visconti asked for volunteers – single men only, because the training was so hazardous.

Seventeen pilots were chosen, and under the command of Cap. Robetto, Second-in-Command of I° Gr.C., they transferred during early December to Rangsdorf (Berlin) where they found a few Henschel Hs 126s and several gliders. The rocket-fighter course began with unpowered flight. Training began on 5 December, the syllabus comprising a two-seater Kranich, followed by a Grunau Baby and a Habicht 14 (= 14m wingspan), descending via the 8m model to the 6m to accustom the pilots to handling a short-winged glider, which is what the Me 163 was by the end of its flight.

Meanwhile, the group's other pilots continued training at Holzkirchen and on 9 December were visited by the Air Attaché of the RSI Embassy in Germany. He reported that 3ª Sq. had completed its training, while the other two had still two weeks to do. Most of the younger officers were, however, qualified only on old biplanes and needed more time to learn. A crucial factor was the incidence of good weather, permitting more flights and faster progress. By the end of December training was mostly complete, except for the 17 pilots at Rangsdorf and a handful in Holzkirchen.

Two events now delayed things. On 1 January 1945 the Luftwaffe launched Operation Bodenplatte, attacking Allied airfields in Holland, Belgium and France with around 900 fighters and ground attack aircraft, plus a few jet bombers. The results were disheartening, for although 200 or so Allied aircraft were destroyed or damaged on the ground, about 300 German aeroplanes were shot down and 237 pilots killed, hurting the Luftwaffe worse than the Allies. The following week OKL ordered a number of Italian pilots to help transport replacement Bf 109s to front-line units and on 9 January for example, S.M. Domenico Lajolo brought a G-14 (W.Nr.785894) from Straubing to II./JG 27 in Hopsten. This task lasted a week, and by mid-January all the pilots were back at Holzkirchen awaiting their return to Italy.

The second factor was the weather. A cold front hit Europe at the beginning of the year and the snow, besides stopping training, grounded the 17 pilots who had completed their primary course at Rangsdorf. They transferred to Liegnitz to practise on the 'real' Me 163, but snow and then the Soviet advance forced them to abandon the airfield and also their hopes of being the first Italian rocket pilots. Nor was their training on the Bf 109 complete and it was decided that they should finish it alongside II° Gruppo's 'Training Section' back at Aviano. In Italy, the first I° Gruppo Bf 109 was delivered from Orio al Serio to Lonate Pozzolo on 21 January.

II° Gr.C.

On the afternoon of the 1st the Gruppo transferred west to Lonate Pozzolo. This, like other base changes to come, was intended to avoid or deceive Allied reconnaissance and marauding USAAF strafers. The next day the whole unit deployed to Orio al Serio, returning to Lonate late that afternoon.

Back at Aviano, a group continued training on the Bf 109G-12 under the guidance of the experienced Ten. Filippi (2ª Sq.). Apart from this and the transfer of several repaired Bf 109s from Aviano to Lonate, little happened during the first third of the month. The first operation took place on the 10th, and the following day three tonnes of cannon and machine-gun ammunition were rushed to the Italian fighters at Lonate. On the 12th Marshal Graziani visited the Gruppo, and on the 13th it was back in Aviano and (in 5ª Sq.'s case) Osoppo. From the 14th to the 21st activity was confined to a lot of training flights with the G-12, S.Ten. Galetti doing the instructing.

Early in the month proposals had been issued to build 20 camouflaged dispersal pens for Italian fighters at 'Airfield 373', Thiene, this being the new dispersal base for Cap. Drago's pilots. On the 17th several 1ª Sq. Bf 109s flew there, joined by others over the next few days. If the pens were completed they failed to save the Gruppo from disaster on Christmas Eve. The year ended with the transfer of seven 2ª Sq. aircraft, two of 1ª and one from 3ª to Lonate. The remainder of 1ª and 3ª stayed behind at Aviano, the former awaiting new machines from Germany.

The Bf 109G-12 brought to Holzkirchen by S.Ten. Di Santo of II° Gr.C. Arriving on 2 December, it helped overcome the problems arising from damage to the only G-12 supplied to I° Gruppo for training and the Germans' refusal to supply the Italians with another.

II° Gr.C. was said to have operated on six days, had four combats and was credited by the Luftwaffe with shooting down four Mitchells, two Thunderbolts and a Spitfire, for no losses of its own. The MAAF version of events provides an instructive contrast:

> [The ANR] again proved to be a poor investment for its German backers, paying little or no dividend for the effort – the Me-109s and the even more precious fuel expended. On only one day, 10 December, did the Italian pilots engage our aircraft, and their results must have been disappointing. One B-25 was shot down for the loss of four Me-109s destroyed, one probably destroyed and four damaged. Fascist propaganda gave credit to the fighters for two additional B-25s (actually lost to flak) plus one fictional victory.

MAAF noted that the ANR fighters operated on other days without making contact and that the failure to respond to raids against the Brenner Pass in good flying weather during the last week of the month was probably due to fuel shortage. Reconnaissance cover of Aviano and Vicenza showed that most of the aircraft there did not change position during the last ten days of December. As usual, the Allies were inclined to disbelieve that determined attacks could possibly be Italian:

> Several attacks were made by pairs of Me-109s against Allied fighters and reconnaissance aircraft, with a few successes. These were probably German aircraft, normally employed on reconnaissance but capable of occasional aggressive attacks under conditions favourable to them.

'Poor investment' or not, the German High Command had recognised the need for 'II./Ital. JGr.' to be re-equipped with new Bf 109 models. Hitherto, the force had consisted overwhelmingly of G-6s with a handful of G-14s. An order signed by G.d.J. Galland had gone to Pohl on the 16th, saying that at least one ANR Staffel would get the G-10 and this proved to be Drago's unit.

Gruppo 'Faggioni'
By the 15th the Gruppo had amassed 18 serviceable S.79s at Lonate, considerably increasing its potential. It moved to Ghedi round about the 20th with a view to resuming operations in the full-moon period. On the 26th the unit suffered heavily when its base was strafed.

Fuel

There were 690m³ on hand when the month began. 340m³ were used by reconnaissance aircraft and 230m³ by other types. Deliveries of 660m³ meant that things had actually *improved* a little by the New Year. Koflug 10/VII noted on the 18th that its airfields had 100m³ of B4 and 150 of C3, and that 'the fuel situation has got considerably better'. Petrol was not everything, though, for the same diarist recorded that, against a need for 1,400 bottles of methane, deliveries totalled 600-650 at most.

The Ground War

The Allied Armies kept moving slowly forward, capturing Ravenna, Faenza and much of the east bank of the River Senio. The weather was mostly appalling, and troops dug in for cover from it as much as from the human enemy. German troops launched two sizeable counter-attacks: on the Canadian front on 8-9 December, and Wintergewitter ('Winter Storm') which hit the US 92nd Infantry in the Serchio Valley on the 26th. The Germans made progress for two days, and the 8th Indian Division was moved to Lucca to check them. MATAF fighter-bombers went in on the 26th, supplemented by light bombers the next day, and the Germans began to suffer reversals on the 28th. Air assaults on the now-stalled attackers went on for what remained of 1944.

Order of Battle

The Luftwaffe in Italy had the following on 30 November:

Unit	Aircraft	
	Number	Type
Stab/FAGr.122	0	
2.(F)/122	6(5)	Me 410A-3/B-3
4.(F)/122	6(4)	Ju 188D-2
	3(3)	Ju 88T-3
6.(F)/122	7(5)	Ju 188D-2
Kdo. Carmen	2/3	Ju 188D/F
Stab/NAGr.11	0	
1./NAGr.11	1	Bf 109G-6
	2	Bf 109G-6/R2
	8	Bf 109G-8/R5
2./NAGr.11	4	Bf 109G-14
	3	Bf 109G-5/R2
	1	Bf 109G-6
	1	Bf 109G-6/R2
	1	Bf 109G-6/U3
	2	Bf 109G-8/R5
SNSt.20	9(3)	Fw 190A-8
Stab/NSGr.9 } 1./NSGr.9	18	Ju 87D-5
2./NSGr.9 3./NSGr.9 }	7	Ju 87D-3
Einhorn	12(9)	Fw 190F-8

The ANR on 10 December had:

I° Gr.C. (in training)	6(6)	Bf 109G-14
	1(1)	Bf 109G-12
II° Gr.C.	40(33)	Bf 109G-6
	1(1)	Bf 109G-6/U4
	1(1)	Bf 109G-12
Gr. 'Faggioni' (forming)	20(20)	S.79

Notes

33. By the authors' count, 163 aircraft in operational units on 20 December and 99 on 30 October.
34. Authors' italics.

CHAPTER 9

Operations

1 December 1944

Near Lodi (MI) during the afternoon, 1st/Lt Walter R. Hinton of the 527th FS, 86th FG, shot down a Ju 88T-3 of 4.(F)/122 (W.Nr.330227, F6+FM), which was unwise enough to be out before dark. Of its crew, only Ofw. Erich Kramer was hurt however. At 1703, near Faenza and also still in daylight, W/O Baits and Flt Sgt Lothian of 600 Sqn met four Ju 87s in line astern with another below and to port; they were at 8,000ft and making about 200mph. The Beaufighter attacked in the face of return fire and was in turn set upon by some of the Germans, nonetheless claiming one probable and another damaged.

2 December 1944

At 0130 a Ju 188 piloted by Gefr. Mühlhoff landed at Ghedi from Bergamo and just over six hours later set off home again. This flight's purpose is not recorded but the aircraft was A3+TD of Kommando Carmen and will figure again in our story. Towards midday 2.(F)/122 resumed operations after a three-day break, Fhr. Sewald and Ogfr. Wachtfeidl flying a 2hr sortie in F6+GK.

Einhorn flew another mission, arriving over target at 1700; '6 or 8 aircraft, either Fw's or Me's' dive-bombed and strafed DAF's Advanced HQ and the road and bridge at Ronco (FO), just northeast of Forlì Aerodrome. No damage was reported by either the DAF or the Army although the attack is said to have caused some excitement – a not unreasonable reaction to the explosion of 1,000kg bombs in one's vicinity. Again there was evidence of radio guidance: traffic on 39mhz from Siegfried 1 and Paul 1. Villafranca recorded a total of 14 operational flights, suggesting that NSGr.9's Ju 87s were also up.

3-8 December 1944

Two incidents of strafing shortly after 0100 on the 3rd may have given rise to a British Air Ministry report that: '. . . an attack with aircraft armament was made by about eight Fw 190s against an Allied Headquarters south of Florence', while at 0750 a tactical recce pilot reported Allied AA and fighters. Next day F6+RK of 2.(F)/122 flew a 2½ hour sortie, then there seems to have been little other Axis activity before the 9th.

9 December 1944

At midday an He 111H-16 (W.Nr.8433), piloted by Maj Domokos Hadnagy, Head of the Technical Branch of the Hungarian General Staff, landed at San Severo (FG). It had been sent to Italy by the MFM resistance movement, which hoped to co-operate with the Allies and split Hungary from the Axis. In addition to the pilot's wife and two-year-old daughter, the Heinkel carried a lieutenant selected for his anti-German views; a sergeant mechanic not told of his destination; Gezer Soos, executive secretary of the MFM; and a Dutch PoW who had escaped from Germany into Hungary. The main purpose of the flight was to deliver Soos, who came prepared to supply names of contacts with Hungarian resistance members and to direct their activities in Hungary to fit Allied strategy.

They had taken off from Pàpa at 0900, climbing immediately into a cloud bank and flying by instruments towards the Austrian frontier. Just short of the border they altered course to cross Yugoslavia, clearing the coast south of Zara and making landfall 50km north of Ancona. While over the sea, Liberators were sighted and an escort fighter approached. Hadnagy promptly lowered his wheels, shot off signals and was not molested. Nearing Foggia they were surrounded by about 30 fighters and again the undercarriage was lowered and signal cartridges fired. After twice circling San Severo, the pilot put down.

The aircraft was one of 32 He 111s recently bought from the Germans. It carried the code 2B+DC and a red '4' low down on the rudder, and was fitted with long-range tanks in the bomb-bay and its full quota of guns. It was designated for shipment to Wright Field and eventually made its way to the USA under the care of Col Watson's captured aircraft unit, being assigned 'Foreign Equipment' number FE-1600.

At 1130 the Luftwaffe issued plans for twilight attacks by Ju 87s and Fw 190s from the Verona area against Allied roads in the eastern and central sectors. Marking of the front line was also requested. Additionally, single aeroplanes and pairs were to conduct Egon-directed harassment in the same areas and over Forlì, Grizzana (BO) and Castiglione (FO). In the event only three combat sorties left Villafranca, and no Egon signals seem to have been intercepted

The usual overwater reconnaissance was flown and 2.(F)/122's 'Viktor-Kurfürst' was heard homing from the east coast. This was F6+VK with Ofhr. Schiffels and Fw. Weber aboard, which safely completed a 2½ hour mission, the Staffel's first for five days.

Bringing a high-ranking Hungarian resistance delegation to Italy on 9 December 1944, this He 111H-16 (W.Nr.8433, 2B+DC) was subsequently taken to the USA for evaluation.

10 December 1944

Commanded by Cap. Bellagambi, 21 Bf 109s of II° Gr.C. scrambled at 1045 to intercept B-25s reported heading north from the Po Valley. The bombers were once again those of the 319th BG, now re-equipped with the more reliable, better-armed Mitchells, 18 of them meeting the Italians between Lakes Garda and d'Iseo at 1100.

As usual, Italian and Allied reports of the combat differ markedly, with four[35] B-25s claimed shot down on one side and four Messerschmitts on the other. The reality was one loss each. Comparing combat reports, it is evident that Cap. Bellagambi was first to intercept and attack 1st/Lt Herbert Herman's B-25J, leaving it separated from the others with its left engine on fire, the left undercarriage leg extended and men baling out. This B-25 was then attacked by three other Bf 109s before it crashed, each of the fighters probably claiming a kill.

On the other hand, of four Gustavs claimed by USAAF gunners, only Ten. Valenzano's 'Black 15' was shot down. When dozens of bullets struck his aircraft, first hitting the engine and then almost severing the starboard wing, he had no choice but to bale out, injuring an arm in the process. He reached the ground safely in the Melga Plaz area (a mountain district northwest of Lake Garda), where he was rescued by a woodcutter, returning to his unit a couple of days later.

Now eight P-47s of the 65th FS, 57th FG, providing area cover for the bombers, finally appeared on the scene. This caused the Italians to quit and Lt Atwood claimed a Bf 109 damaged after seeing pieces fall off an aircraft he fired at. It is not possible to determine which Italian he hit, but it is known that the Gustavs of Bellagambi, S.Ten Rosas and S.M. Baldi were damaged, the last-named being obliged to make an emergency landing at Orio al Serio. He brought his G-14 in on one leg, having had

several hits in a wing, and thanks to a skilful touchdown the aircraft sustained only minor damage. This was soon repaired, allowing him to fly back to Aviano.

From 1045-1200 a pair of Udine's tactical reconnaissance aircraft covered part of the northern Adriatic, taking in the harbours of Rimini and Ravenna. Three sorties were flown by 2.(F)/122 around midday, one of which photographed Livorno harbour at 1220. Aircraft F6+VK (Uffze. Wist and Rusch) and F6+MK (Ltn. Galle and Fw. Müller) were up for about an hour each and returned safely. Less fortunate were Ltn. Neumann and Uffz. Meister in F6+ZK, (Me 410B-3. W.Nr.190161) flying Mission No 3300. At around 1310 (German time) and 100min into their flight they were intercepted by P-47s of the 527th FS, 86th FG, and shot down near Mariana Mantovana (MN) by Capt Jesse R Core III. Both Germans were killed.

At midday the Luftwaffe broadcast its intentions for the afternoon and night to come: ferrying of two Bf 109s to Udine and a Ju 188 to Bergamo, and night harassment on the central and eastern fronts.

After what the Allies termed 'a quiet week', Villafranca logged 15 operational flights. From dusk to 1700 NSGr.9 and Einhorn were over Allied territory, the latter unit making perhaps its biggest impact – virtually unsung ever since – on the Allies. Indeed the Germans may not have known just what they accomplished or how close they came to causing far greater damage.

At dusk a few Ju 87s – estimated at no more than six – flew over the Forlì-Cesena locality. Two bombs were dropped near Forlì L/G and its dispersals were machine-gunned 'harmlessly', although vehicles on Highway 9 were hit. Then at 1652 Cesena town was attacked by Fw 190s with heavy bombs. One fell near an Officers' Mess without doing damage, but the other hit Eighth Army HQ. It fell on the Signal Office, knocking out nearly all line and radio communications. A postwar RAF study drily remarked: 'In view of an imminent Canadian attack, this was highly inconvenient'. It took an hour to restore communications to subordinate Corps and normal operations were underway again by midnight. Quoting the RAF again: 'There may have been an ingredient of luck in the operation, but the event does illustrate however that the enemy intelligence was not always comatose. The size of that mission was contemptible but its results came close to being really disturbing.' Indeed, it is not difficult to understand the righteous indignation with which the Tactical Air Forces reacted.

This attack was instrumental in sparking off a renewed spate of raids on Axis airfields. Rather than luck, Einhorn seems to have relied on technological advances, and that really should have disturbed the Allies – or, at least, anyone in the vicinity of an HQ at night. On the 10th radio traffic under callsign Armada was intercepted from 'three fighter-bombers' controlled by a station near Padua, clear evidence, when taken with previous Figaro traffic, that Einhorn was bombing under radar guidance and, what is more, doing so accurately and on the basis of good intelligence. It was perhaps as well that the Sonderverband had flown its last mission in the south.

From 2020-2300 a Ju 188 searched the Adriatic as far south as Ortona while another covered the circuit Genoa–Oneglia (IM)–Calvi–Cap Corse–Genoa between 2030 and 2210.

11-21 December 1944

On the 11th MAAF ATI had to reach for a copy of *Jane's All The World's Aircraft*. The curious specimen they were faced with was a 31ft-span monoplane with a long glasshouse canopy. Painted a basic light grey, it had a white rudder and elevators (their extremities colourfully adorned with the Hungarian red, white and green national stripes), yellow wingtip undersides and the civil registration HA-NAN on the wings and fuselage sides. Over all this were applied hasty approximations of the USAAF's stars and bars in white. The aircraft had been flown to the Adriatic coastal town of Tortoreto (TE) by a Hungarian civil test-pilot and a Polish workman and, after perusal of the recognition 'Bible', was pronounced to be an M-24 light aeroplane.

From 0615 two NAGr.11 aircraft flew a 55min. coverage of the Northern Adriatic. Just before midday Ofhr. Spöntjes and Fw. Zielenkiewicz of 2.(F)/122 left Ghedi on a mission of almost 2½hr duration. Unusually, they landed at Villafranca and neither their Me 410B-3 (W.Nr.190163, F6+MK) nor its observer seem to have flown with the Staffel again. Indeed, the aeroplane's fuselage was still at the airfield when the Americans arrived next April.

The 12th was quiet, but 2./122 put up a 2hr mission the following day, their last for nine days. During the afternoon of the 14th a Ju 188 coded +ZU was flown from Riem to Ghedi by an Ofw. Plake. It seems to have stayed put for another two weeks, by which time it was assigned to 6.(F)/122, before moving on to Bergamo. At Villafranca only five practice flights took place amid a string of air-raid alerts.

The next day at Villafranca a 'Bf 410' (possibly F6+MK, see above) took off at 1629 but damaged a tyre in the process. After a few circuits it landed, hit soft ground and swerved to the right, incurring 10 per cent damage. Junkers Ju 188 F6+EP deployed to Ghedi in the morning, returning to Bergamo next day. Although Villafranca was subject to harassment attacks throughout the night of 15/16 December and mounted no operations, other elements of NSGr.9 dropped anti-personnel bombs in the II Corps area, south of Bologna. Forty miles southeast of Saint Tropez a Ju 188 was claimed damaged by a 417th NFS Beaufighter.

Fw. Hans Deutsch (left) and Fw. Johannes Nawroth of 3./NSGr.9, pictured at Villafranca in late December 1944. Note the grey wave-mirror pattern sprayed over the pale blue undersides of their Ju 87D-5. (Nawroth)

Early in the afternoon of the 17th, NAGr.11 dispatched a Rotte to the Dalmatian Coast. Also that day, Einhorn left Villafranca, bound for Holzkirchen and then (it was intended) the Ardennes offensive. Six aircraft took off, but one veered off and suffered 80 per cent damage. This may have been Fw 190F-8/R1 (W.Nr.581447, A3+LX), of which the fuselage was found on the airfield postwar.

II° Gr.C. was back up on the 21st, flying an uneventful patrol. NAGr.11 sent two aircraft as far south as Ravenna early in the morning.

22-23 December 1944

From 1040 to 1140, ten Bf 109s of 1ª Sq. flew an unproductive interception mission in the Lake Garda area. At 1300, 12 Spitfires of 417 Sqn took off to patrol from Venice to Casarsa (PN), paving the way for a raid by medium bombers, and 22 Messerschmitts of II° Gr.C. scrambled from Thiene (1ª), Lonate (2ª) and Aviano (3ª) to oppose them. With 3ª providing top cover, the remaining Italians took on the Spitfires.

It was 1400, and intense flak from Verona had loosened the British formation. While it was reforming, two Bf 109s were seen attacking Blue Section and another went for Red Section. Fg Off A.D. Gibson's Spitfire Mk.VIII was hit, dived and headed for home. He had been attacked by Cap. Mario Bellagambi, who saw pieces fall off his pointed-winged adversary; he reported that the Spitfire exploded with fire as it spun towards the ground, trailing black smoke. In fact Gibson made it safely back to base, landing at 1425, uninjured but with Category III damage to his aircraft.

Another attack was made on Blue Section by a single Bf 109 without success. One of 3ª Sq.'s Messerschmitts was damaged during the engagement, M.llo Covre making a wheels-up landing at Thiene where the rest of his unit also set down, overcrowding this relatively small airfield. In addition, engine trouble had forced S.Ten Galetti to return to Aviano.

At 1424 a German tactical reconnaissance aircraft called in a sighting of Allied fighters.

The use of Thiene did not pass unnoticed by MAAF, as a section of 350th FG P-47s led by Lt Ed King spotted the camouflaged airfield for the first time. Photographs taken the next day showed a number of active aircraft on the field, leading the Americans to plan an immediate attack.

Later on the 22nd a Ju 87D-5 (W.Nr.131434, E8+BL) took off from Villafranca on an operation but had to make an emergency landing 4km south of the airfield at 1653 owing to engine trouble. The pilot, Ofw. Herbert Schick, was hurt (not seriously) and the aeroplane 50 per cent damaged. It was still at Villafranca when the war ended. Also from NSGr.9, a rare piece of unguarded radio traffic revealed that E8+KH was in the air. In all, eight combat sorties were flown by NSGr.9 from Villafranca, and perhaps a similar number from Ghedi and bombs were released through solid cloud south of Ravenna.

At 2130 1st/Lt Albert L Jones and his radar operator, Fg Off John Rudovsky of 414th NFS claimed a Ju 87 destroyed near Asola (MN), near both of NSGr.9's active airfields. It is likely that they shot down a D-5 (W.Nr.140750, E8+JK) which came down north of Cremona with its crew, Fhj.Ofw. Artur Heiland and Uffz. Artur Ballok, wounded. Rees and Beaumont of 600 Sqn destroyed two Junkers and damaged a third while patrolling between Forlì and

MAAF Intelligence needed their copy of 'Jane's' to identify this Hungarian M.24, a civil aircraft bearing a colourful combination of its native markings and improvised USAAF ones, when defectors flew it to Italy on 11 December 1944.

Bologna. Ofhr. Hans Kolster and Gefr. Gustav Leumann died when their D-5 (W.Nr.130532, E8+FK) was shot down 11km northwest of the latter city and Fw. Edgar Gerstenberger (who had survived a crash three months previously) was killed in W.Nr.140747, E8+KK but his gunner, Gefr. Hans Mechlinski, survived wounded.

6.(F)/122 lost a Ju 188D-2 (Fhj.Fw. Erwin Kresin's W.Nr.150534, F6+HP) in a crash 20km northwest of Bergamo, during a night when the Gruppe covered Ajaccio harbour.

24 December 1944

Eight aircraft of the 347th FS, led by Lt Kenneth Thomason, attacked Thiene with devastating results. Both the north and south ends of the runway were cratered, and two hits and four near misses were scored on a hangar, causing thick black smoke and considerable damage. Fifteen single-engined fighters were claimed destroyed and two more as damaged; a second hangar was repeatedly strafed and left smoking, as were several other buildings. In all, 56 cases of ammunition were used and 18 P-47 gun barrels ruined. A KTB entry of the previous day says that Thiene lacked any flak protection.

A vivid account from the receiving end is supplied by S.M. Cavagliano:

> . . . the ground crewmen were servicing the aircraft and doing the usual maintenance when eight P-47s began a "merry-go-round", first dropping the two bombs each carried, then strafing to the last round and destroying 14 of our new G-14s. Luckily no one was hurt . . . but we all had to dive into a couple of holes originally dug in the soft ground to bury petrol drums. Some of the P-47s orbited over these overcrowded "refuges" but apparently they had exhausted all their ammunition and soon departed, leaving our aircraft burning . . .

The mission's success was welcomed by telegrams from several top brass, including Brig Gen B. W. Chidlaw, OC XII Fighter Command. 'Please pass on to 350th Fighter Group our congratulations on their good show this date. Their destruction, on the ground, of one fourth of the known A/C fighter strength in Italy constitutes a severe blow to the enemy.'

In fact, on the 20th II° Gr.C's strength had reached 47 Bf 109s, so almost one third had been wiped out. The two surviving Messerschmitts, flown by Cap. Drago and S.M. Baldi, quit Thiene at 1115 for Aviano. The remaining pilots and personnel boarded buses, reaching Aviano that evening to celebrate their last wartime Christmas.

25 December 1944

German reconnaissance aircraft reported several ships off Ancona, and it was decided to attack that evening. Despite its increased strength, Gr. 'Faggioni' sent off only four aircraft[36] at 2130. Four more were held in readiness to attack following reports from the first wave. By the time the original group got home the others had been returned to their dispersals and could no longer be dispatched, even though Cap. Bertuzzi claimed a hit on a 7,000-ton vessel.

Also operating from Ghedi were Ju 87s of NSGr.9 (about 14 sorties), along with others from Villafranca (17 sorties), bombing targets around Ancona and Faenza. A Beaufighter chased a hostile to Ghedi where it landed without lights and, landing at Villafranca, a Ju 87 rolled into a slit trench, sustaining some damage, although nobody was hurt. 6.(F)/122 reported a Ju 188D-2 (W.Nr.150533, F6+GP) missing with four crew aboard during the night of 25/26 December, while a Ju 88 was held by searchlights over Ancona.

26 December 1944

A bizarre episode concluded II° Gr.C.'s operations for 1944. Eight Mustangs of 3 Sqn RAAF were ordered to cut a railway near Pordenone and, noting the dismay of his pilots who had been promised at least two days off, Sqn Ldr Murray Nash elected to lead the mission personally.

One pilot, not fully recovered from the previous night's festivities, was helped into his Mustang still wearing a war-trophy – full dress Carabiniere uniform, complete with sabre and scabbard, in which he had celebrated in the mess. He was strapped into the cockpit, his oxygen mask was secured and supply turned on, and he taxied out for take-off at 1435. That was W/O J.F. Quinn's last contact with his unit. En route to the target Nash noticed one aeroplane straggling and signalled him to close up, even breaking radio silence to order him to return to base, but all to no avail.

Meanwhile, at 1500 ten Bf 109s of 1ª and 3ª Sq. scrambled after warnings of approaching fighter-bombers. Twenty minutes later the lead Schwarm (Magg. Miani, Ten. Keller, S.M. Passuello and S.Ten. Galetti) reached Quinn's straggling fighter, Keller bringing it down with one accurate burst. Quinn baled out safely and had a lot of trouble explaining to the German troops that he was not some fancy-dress spy but an RAAF pilot.

After their first attack the Italian formation was split by a false move on Miani's part, and although Cap. Drago claimed another P-51 shot down (not confirmed), the Messerschmitts disappeared into the sun and the surviving Mustangs patrolled for at least 10min south of Aviano, waiting for their enemies to land.

The one who fell into the trap was S.Ten. Squassoni, who had become separated and was heading for base. He was attacked by Nash and his No. 2, Fg Off Andrews, who chased him across the airfield's southern boundary at zero feet. They were able to overtake the Bf 109 easily but being so close to the ground Nash had difficulty in keeping a bead. Closing to 100yd, he fired a 5sec burst while wallowing in Squassoni's slipstream, then his port undercarriage leg dropped of its own accord and forward vision was lost as the P-51's hood was covered with hydraulic fluid from the Messerschmitt. Nash instinctively broke away upwards.

Fg Offs Andrews and then Thomas joined in, and the former closed to 150yd, firing until forced to pull away at 20yd. He saw strikes on the port wing and cockpit, and both wheels came down. Notwithstanding this, the G-14 of the terrified, helpless Squassoni kept flying as he tried to lead his pursuers over Aviano's (as yet inexplicably silent) flak defences. He realised he could no longer withstand the attacks and, as Thomas's Mustang came in firing three more bursts, he saw a flat vineyard and pushed the stick hard, crashing his 'Black 8' at full speed. The aircraft continued for hundreds of feet, uprooting vines, stakes and small plants before coming to rest. The Italian jumped from the cockpit and ran, fearing both strafing and the explosion of his aeroplane, but nothing happened. The sudden crash-landing led Thomas to lose sight of the Bf 109 and it was thus claimed only as damaged, shared between the three Australians.

Amongst the victims of 'a 40-minute undisturbed beat-up' of Lonate Pozzolo by four P-47s were *14 S.79s of Gr. 'Faggioni' and every decoy aeroplane on the airfield, all burned and destroyed. Subsequently three flak batteries were drafted in, which 'caused the Allied fighters to be less enterprising'. NSGr.9 dispatched ten sorties from Villafranca and flares were dropped and bombing started large fires north of Forlì. At 2305, 10 miles east of Bologna, W/O Baits and Flt Sgt Lothian of 600 Sqn attacked a Ju 87, only to have their Beaufighter hit in the starboard engine by return fire.

This may connect to Johannes Nawroth's memory of how he and Deutsch had bombed Faenza when:

. . .we were chased by a twin-engined nightfighter which either had jammed guns or had run out of ammunition. We started twisting and turning wildly and my plane (E8+RH) flew east. Then we were over the Adriatic and [he] tried to drive us into the water. We managed to escape over Comacchio.

27-30 December 1944

On the 27th five Ju 87s set out from Villafranca at 1700 on a mission to Faenza. Forty-five minutes later an intruder dropped a fragmentation bomb and three HE on the airfield. An aircraft operating from Bergamo was warned of enemy fighters at 2122 and 2212. An unusual Axis loss was a P-38, strafed at Gallarate by P-47s, probably that which had crash-landed there on 16 August. Next day a Ju 87 was ferried to Thiene and seven Bf 109s to Bergamo, while 6./122's new Ju 188, +ZU, made its way to Bergamo from Ghedi. Me 410 F6+VK flew early morning and midday missions with different crews, and a Ju 188 suffered radar failure south of Toulon at 2252, an hour into its mission, and returned to base. Koflug 5/VII's HQ buildings at Pordenone were badly bombed.

On the 29th a KG 200 Ju 188 operated over the Gulf of Genoa/Civitavecchia area from 0105-0355 and two 5hr flights were sent out that night, taking in the ports of Naples and Milazzo, Sicily; II° Gr.C. dispersed ten aircraft from Aviano to Lonate. F6+VK was out for 2hr early in the morning, followed at 1558 by F6+GK (Me 410B-3, W.Nr.190165). The latter had made a short test-flight the previous day after a lay-off of almost four weeks; after 25min it was twice warned of fighters in its path and went down near Ancona, killing Ofhr. Spöntjes and Uffz. Schmauser. Except for a ½-hour test-flight for F6+AK, that was 2./122's last activity for 1944. Only one Ju 188 seems to have flown on the 30th, leaving at 2200 on a 'special task' for KG 200 and returning nearly 6hr later after passing over Naples and Palermo, reconnoitring those harbours on the way.

31 December 1944

In Villafranca at 0108 a Ju 188 landed from a mission with engine damage. From 0615 three tactical reconnaissance aircraft flew a 50min Adriatic coverage down to Ravenna. At Cameri, New Year's Eve festivities for the German personnel in the presence of the local Mayor were interrupted by an unexplained and violent explosion in the immediate vicinity. Uffz. Mittler (who had arrived only three days before) found himself under arrest for failing in his guard duty.

Notes

35. The figure given in a teletype report and German records. II° Gr.C.'s papers claim *five* B-25s, credited to Cap. Spigaglia, Cap. Bellagambi, Ten. Giorio, Ten. De Masellis and M.llo Mingozzi.
36. **F1-01**, Cap. Bertuzzi; **F1-03**, Ten. Del Prete; **F1-04**, Ten. Perina; **F1-06**, Ten. Neri.

The Mustang IV of 3 Sqn., RAAF, flown by Sqn Ldr. Nash on 26 December 1944 in the combat where he forced II° Gr.C.'s S.Ten. Squassoni to crash-land. (Nash)

In the half-light at Ghedi, a Ju 188 of FAGr.122 has just returned from its lonely mission. Under the wing are the antennae of the FuG 101 radio altimeter which permitted accurate low-level flying at night over the sea. The aircraft has "wave-mirror" camouflage sprayed over both its upper and lower surfaces. (Bundesarchiv)

Chapter 10

Old Year/New Year

As 1944 ended, the Axis had few grounds for optimism on any front. On 29 December Pohl had submitted his 'Proposals for the Conduct of Air Warfare in the Italian Theatre'. He had no illusions about regaining air superiority, but aimed to do his utmost in helping Army Group C hold its own. Had his and the whole Luftwaffe's situation not been so desperate, what he was asking for might have seemed modest. On 31 December he had:

Unit	Aircraft	Strength
Stab/FAGr.122	–	0
2.(F)/122	Me 410	2
4.(F)/122	Ju 88T-3	3(2)
	Ju 188D-2	5(5)
6.(F)/122	Ju 188D-2	5(3)
Kdo Carmen	Ju 188	2/3
Stab/NAGr.11	–	0
1./NAGr.11	Bf 109G-6	6
	Bf 109G-8	7
2./NAGr.11	Bf 109G-5/R2 MW 50	3
	Bf 109G-6	11
	Bf 109G-8/R5 MW 50	1
Seenotstaffel 20	Fw 190A-8	6(4)
NSGr.9	Ju 87D-3	7 } (12)
	Ju 87D-5	14 }

The ANR figures for 24 December were:

Unit	Aircraft	Strength
I° Gr.C.[37]	Bf 109G-6	8(3)
	Bf 109G-10	6(3)
	Bf 109G-12	2(1)
	Bf 109G-14	2(1)
II° Gr.C.	Bf 109G-6	27(12)
	Bf 109G-10	11(7)
	Bf 109G-12	1(0)
	Bf 109G-4	1(1)
In reserve	Bf 109G	9
I° Gr. Aerosil.	S.79	10(9)

Ultra revealed that, from 26-30 December, 11 Bf 109G-10s were delivered to II° Gr.C.: one to Thiene on the 26th, nine to Orio al Serio on the 27/28th, and one to Villafranca on the 30th.

By contrast, Pohl estimated that the Allies could send against him on a day of good weather approximately: 1,000 ground attack aircraft, 250 twin-engined bombers, 80 fighters (excluding escort fighters), 80 short-range reconnaissance aircraft, 20 night fighters, 20 intruders, and up to 700 strategic bombers which might occasionally attack Italian targets. As he put it, 'inadequate defences, especially as regards flying forces, oppose this increased enemy air activity'. He might have been heartened to know that MATAF counted 713 aircraft destroyed by flak during 1944.

Pohl hoped to force a change in Allied tactics and reduce the effectiveness of their attacks if OKL would grant him additional flying and flak units, and submitted detailed plans. The operation of a German Me 262 Gruppe (if provided) in conjunction with 'the

Italian Jagdgeschwader which is being formed' was not expected to bring any great numerical success against strongly-escorted bombers, but it would force MAAF to use more fighters on escort duty. Fighter-bombers would no longer operate with impunity, and the appearance of the most modern types would hearten the ground troops. Were the Italian Me 163 unit then under training be brought in, they might pick off individual heavy bombers returning over the Udine area from the Reich. Fearing that Co-Belligerent Italians (and perhaps others) might not treat RSI troops according to the Geneva Convention, he felt unable to send ANR units over enemy territory as, for example, fighter-bombers.

Future tactical reconnaissance would only be possible at heavy cost because of enemy air superiority, and difficulties were mounting in securing 'the necessary continuous photographic cover of enemy harbours'. To satisfy Kesselring's demands for intensified cover with existing types was impossible, 'and [reconnaissance] will probably peter out altogether, as has happened in the West'.[38] If continued cover was insisted on, Komm.Gen. wanted one of his tactical Staffeln re-equipped with the Me 262 and the allocation of an Arado Ar 234 unit soon – he had already asked OKL only to have the matter deferred. If he got what he wanted, his boundary with Luftflotte 4 could be redrawn and he could cover the harbours of Eastern Sicily and the Southern Adriatic.

The relinquishment of personnel had already reduced efficiency, and further measures now being ordered would only make things worse, eroding serviceability levels as well. The only remaining scope for small-scale combing out was in some flak units. If he was given more flying units he would need more operational airfields and improvements to his radar/reporting network. This would necessitate *more* personnel to garrison airfields and run signals units.

Provision of three light anti-aircraft batteries would help protect transport installations, especially the Brenner and the Po crossings, and the operational airfields. However, this alone would not guarantee the flow of supplies through the Brenner for all of the armed services; Luftflotte Reich had to increase defences at the northern end too. Protection of the pass would be more practical under one command.

Pohl looked at options for extending his jurisdiction as far as Innsbruck to meet OKL's requirement for dispersal of supply and reinforcement services over the Alpine region. MATAF raids from Italy into Austrian airspace reinforced his logic and he was given what he asked.

Perhaps linked to this was a request to higher authority on 22 December that Graz be made available 'extra-territorially' for use by FAGr.122. On the 30th seven Italian airfields were ordered to set up alternative command posts and signals arrangements by 1 January in view of the possibility of 'fairly large scale' Allied operations within the next few days. By 4 January it had been decided that airfields in the Vienna basin were unsuitable for use in the event of 'Threatening Danger South' and that Southern Bavaria should be investigated instead.

As for fuel, the year's closing entry in the Western Regional Airfield Command's KTB speaks volumes:

> Aviation fuel situation critical, no delivery from the Reich to be expected in the immediate future. Against stocks of 150m^3, daily consumption is 30m^3. Various airfields will probably have to be closed to make fuel available for the long range reconnaissance aircraft.
>
> Supplies of methane gas [for motor transport] have got very bad. Already three days with no methane.

Notes

37. Still in training in Germany
38. In fact both jet and conventional reconnaissance was still being mounted there daily.

CHAPTER 11

January 1945

Fuel – and Weather

Flying operations by the German and Italian units in Italy sank to probably their lowest level. Pohl's Ic blamed winter weather, but the desperately inadequate supply of fuel (780m³ of B4 and C3 at the beginning of the month, up to 1,176m³ by the 16th, then downhill for the rest of the war) and the low aircraft inventory were major factors.

The Luftwaffe

MAAF commented on:

> . . . occasional Ju 87 sorties, periodical sweeps (over their own territory) by the inconstant Italian Republican Fighter Group; and fairly regular reconnaissance flights by German aircraft over the Ligurian and Adriatic seas . . . The only formations that are to any extent efficient are the reconnaissance squadrons, whose flying is moderately consistent. The fighter squadrons do not seriously impair our interdiction of the northern rail systems and the Ju 87s are of little assistance to the enemy, beyond what they can contribute in attacks which are purely of a nuisance value.

Reconnaissance
2.(F)/122 was reduced to just two operational aircraft. It doubled its 'strength' after a few days, but flying remained at a minimum for the remainder of the war – the Staffel was entirely inactive from 4-19 January, for example. Seven operational sorties were flown during the month, five of them from Bergamo by Me 410B-3 W.Nr.190169, F6+NK (Oblt. v. d. Daele and Uffz. Blaschek) and W.Nr.190096, F6+KK (Fw. Bayer and Uffz. Lensing), which had redeployed there on the 20th.

The other Staffeln held their strengths at customary levels, way below full establishment. The Ic's commentary claims a total of 77 short- and long-range reconnaissance sorties flown, 'which again yielded important information on the enemy situation'. The Allies recorded no activity on at least 16 days, and monitored the cancellation of 18 planned sorties. No activity by 4.(F)/122's three Ju 88s was noticed, but Bergamo's Ju 188s put in a couple of very busy nights at the start of the month. On the 22nd Hptm. Weidman, Staffelkapitän of 1./NAGr.11, was posted away to command NAGr.12.

Night Attack
By the 15th NSGr.9 had concentrated all of its aircraft in the Stab and 2. and 3. Staffeln. Since only one of 1. Staffel's ten crews was rated operational, it seems likely that the decision had been taken to re-organise combat-ready men and machines into two rationalised formations. For some months Pohl had been pressing for the allocation of Fw 190s to NSGr.9, as their performance would give them a better chance against the guns and 'little owls'.[39] At the end of 1944 OKL conceded the re-equipping of one Staffel with Focke-Wulfs, although as late as 22 January MAAF intelligence could conclude that there was no evidence of their presence in Italy.

The Ic claimed 90 sorties over six nights, without loss, but there is reason to doubt these figures. Attacks were again made on army targets on the eastern and central sectors in the face of what were termed powerful AA and fighter defences. In several places bombs were seen to cause large explosions and fires. Further losses were claimed to have been inflicted by low-level bombing and strafing of supply columns, lorry traffic and artillery, AA and searchlight emplacements. MAAF's evaluation is less colourful; 'A small number of Ju 87s . . . flew over Allied forward areas on 7 to 8 nights during January and dropped a few bombs. The maximum effort for one night was probably 5 to 10 sorties.'

The Gruppe was at last using the Egon guidance system. On the 31st Komm.Gen. advised that, in future, special instructions for the marking of the front line for the safe execution of night attacks would not be given. Instead, ground troops would be requested from the beginning of the operation to mark the line by firing white Very lights as frequently as possible.

Jets?

MATAF's January assessment of the state of the opposition noted:

> . . . the apparent laying of the ground work for the introduction of a small unit of jet or rocket-propelled aircraft. A large number of credible ground reports . . . makes it appear probable that the enemy has considered employing such a unit, very likely for reconnaissance, in support of Army Group C. The possibility of a reconnaissance unit being crewed by Italians must be considered in view of reports from Germany that 10 Italians of the Primo Gruppo had been trained in jet/rocket aircraft, and supporting claims from Northern Italy that a few of Visconti's best pilots were trained on the 'Comet' (Me-163). However, the scarcity of jet/rocket types in the Luftwaffe makes it unlikely that they will be entrusted to the Italians. There was no evidence from photo reconnaissance of the arrival of these aircraft in January . . . Due to the long runways available at Ghedi and Bergamo, these airfields are likely candidates for use by jet/rocket aircraft, if and when they should arrive in Italy.

Facilities for the SS

In January 1945 5./Fliegergeschwader z.b.V. 7, was maintaining an outstation at Verona. This Geschwader had Staffeln scattered about Europe, with a selection of liaison aircraft at the disposal of the local SS/Police Chiefs.

Colosseo, Giulio and Carmen

Ltn. Joseph Thurnhuber and his crew joined Kommando Carmen in early 1944. It numbered two or three aircraft, dropping agents over Naples, Sardinia and Southern France, and gold to pay a spy in a British HQ. In the 1944/45 New Year moon period the Allies noted 13 saboteurs dropped.

On the 8th a young Italian was arrested in Rome and, with CSDIC at the Cinecittà film studios, his story emerged. An officer from a disbanded Alpini

Caught in Lonate Pozzolo by the snowfalls of January 1945, the aircraft of 2ª Sq. 'Diavoli Rossi' were grounded for two weeks. Bf 109G-14 'Yellow 16' is shown here at its dispersal. (Pagliano)

regiment, he had been recruited by the SD, codenamed Colosseo and in autumn 1944 returned home to Bologna with a 'stay-behind' network awaiting the city's fall. The Allies' offensive halted, plans changed and he was teamed up with an Italian radio operator, Giulio. About 9 December they were taken to 11 Via Milazzo, Bergamo – Dienststelle Carmen, the Kommando's HQ. There they saw a list of about 35 aircrew, small crosses indicating the missions each had flown: an officer and an Oberfeldwebel were marked as killed. Colosseo deduced that seven or eight crews made the clandestine flights and there had been two crashes.[40]

They awaited the next moon in Verona and on the 31st were driven back to Bergamo, changing their Fiat's SS number plate for a civilian one en route. At a New Year's Eve party Colosseo got drunk, threatening to shoot a German officer, and the two spies got to bed at 0600. They returned to Via Milazzo that evening, were kitted out for the jump and introduced to their aircraft's five crew. A 20min bus ride brought them to the airfield, where they boarded a Ju 188. Their flight went out over the Adriatic and then inland south of Ancona to drop them 35km north of Rome, near Bracciano, the Junkers returning via the Tyrrhenian. Colosseo landed without mishap, but could not find Giulio. He buried his parachute and wireless in a field, slept a while, then set off for Rome and captivity.

A new Jafü Oberitalien
The 'Mutiny of the Aces', the confrontation between prominent fighter commanders and Göring following G.d.J. Galland's dismissal, took place in Berlin on 22 January, but had repercussions in Italy. Oberst Günther 'Franzl' Lützow had been the pilots' spokesman, voicing the frustrations that had come to a head with the appalling losses in the Ardennes and Bodenplatte operations. The meeting broke up with threats to have him shot but nothing positive was achieved.

Eduard Neumann, who had been party to the 'conspiracy', was on leave in Berlin. On the day of his intended return he was telephoned by the Luftwaffe Personnel Office and told he would not be travelling after all. Lützow had been dismissed from command of 4. Jagddivision and told to take both Neumann's seat on the 2230 train from the Anhalter Station and his job – he had in effect been exiled to Italy. According to Galland this came within 48hr of the 'mutiny' and certainly Lützow was in post by 28 January.

On that date he began to make what are now faint and only intermittently legible notes in an exercise book. There are some from a meeting involving the ANR's T.Col. Foschini about basic fighter tactics and radio procedures; what to do on sighting a superior hostile force with strong fighter escort; staying in the sun when approaching the enemy; and so on. As events proved, the Italian units were dangerously weak in just these areas.

The ANR

II° Gr.C.
A new allotment of Bf 109G-10s arrived at the beginning of the month for 1ª Sq., delivered to Villafranca between 30 December and 1 January and brought across to Lonate by Italian pilots on the 2nd. These were not 'pure' G-10s, almost all being the /AS model, substituting the less powerful DB 605AS engine for the supposedly standard DB 605D[41]. However, the ANR pilots were only too happy with their new mounts, which were a great improvement over the G-6.

Following a transfer of 2ª and 3ª to Ghedi on the 4th, bad weather, heavy snow and Arctic temperatures grounded the unit for nearly two weeks. Sporadic training activity was maintained in Aviano, while Ghedi and Lonate stayed ice- and snowbound. On the 13th Flying Controller Oblt. Auer visited Cameri to investigate the possibility of dispersing 30 fighters there. Weather did not improve until the 20th and the events of that day are recounted below. After a lull of a few days conditions closed in again, preventing any flying for the rest of the month, and this pause was probably welcome to a unit that had just lost two of its most experienced pilots.

III° Gruppo Caccia: January/February 1945
On 12 January the Gruppo finally left for Germany, heading for the Flying School at Holzkirchen. En route to Bolzano the column of lorries was attacked by fighter-bombers by Lake Iseo, and although no one was hurt, much equipment was lost. This slowed things down and the Italians had an adventurous ten-day journey to their new base. I° Gr.C. had almost completely abandoned Holzkirchen and persistent problems with weather and logistics plagued the newcomers, so by the end of the month it was decided to move 1ª Sq. to the larger airfield of Fürth-bei-Nürnberg.

On 7 February 65 pilots were in Holzkirchen and 15 in Fürth, with ten more expected there. On the former field were 12 Bf 109s, a Bf 108 and a Klemm 35. Two days later S.Ten. Albani made the first training flight, others following. On the 10th came

AIR WAR ITALY 1944-45

Fuel supply was one of the worst problems for the Axis air forces in the last year of war. This forced operational units to cut missions to a much lower level than the situation would have warranted. Here, a German tanker refuels an Italian Messerschmitt of II° Gr.C. at Lonate Pozzolo.
(Pagliano)

the sole training casualty, Serg. Dachena being killed when his Bf 109 stalled while pulling up. As preliminary training was completed at Fürth the Italian pilots returned to Holzkirchen to complete the course and some of the better ones were made instructors to expedite matters.

I° Gruppo Aerosiluranti 'Faggioni', January/April 1945

During December discussions had gone on with a view to re-equipping the Group with torpedo-armed fighter aircraft, and the Fw 190 was suggested.

After the disaster at Lonate Pozzolo on the 26th, Magg. Marini asked that this plan should be adopted and inquired when he could expect the aircraft. He thereupon learned that, instead of Fw 190s, he would get Fiat G.55s, of which approximately 30 were ready for collection.

On 13 January, while working on this project, Marini had occasion to travel to Turin. Shortly after passing through Novara he was captured by partisans and remained their prisoner for about two months. During this period, and after his return, half-hearted efforts were made by the Group to retrain on the Fiats, continuously hampered by partisan attacks (on 14 March, near Gallarate, three pilots were ambushed and killed by machine-gun fire) and strafing of their airfields. These efforts continued until 26/27th April, when the Group surrendered to the partisans and ended its existence.

Notes

39. 'Kleine Eulen', Luftwaffe jargon for nightfighters.
40. See 13 August and 19 September 1944.
41. New research into Daimler-Benz documents by J.C. Mermet casts doubt on the 'official' existence of the G-10/AS sub-type and suggests that the external appearance of the G-14/AS and G-10 differed from what was previously thought. However the authors have adhered to their original descriptions while this interesting debate (mainly outside the scope of a campaign history) continues.

CHAPTER 11

Operations

1-19 January 1945

Perhaps the first mission of 1945 (but the Staffel's 3,312th) was flown at 1135 on the 1st, by Hennig and Berger of 2.(F)/122 in F6+AK. Meanwhile, the ANR welcomed the New Year by transferring another two Bf 109s of 5ª Sq. from Lonate to Aviano. That night, no fewer than seven Ju 188s were out – some on maritime reconnaissance but at least one, as we have seen, dropping agents.

Colosseo and Giulio landed at about 0130 on the 2nd. The next aerial activity that the authors can place with any confidence came nine hours later, when Hptm. Dietze and Fw. Bendorf undertook a 2hr sortie in F6+AK. Six Ju 188s were up after dark, and some were instrumental on this and the next two nights in dropping a total of four agents near Senigallia (AN), all of whom were caught.

On afternoon of the 3rd a new Me 410B-3 (W.Nr.150096, BR+RP) was delivered from Riem to 2./122; as F6+KK it would have a busy but tragically curtailed career. As it was, this delivery was the last flying in the Staffel for 17 days. That night the characteristic Egon radio traffic resumed under callsign Kasper, and an estimated ten Ju 87s were active around Bologna, bombs dropping south of the city. The aircraft reported on the 4th as brought down by AA fire at Pianoro may have been involved in this raid.

At 0323 on the 4th, the Mosquito of Plt Offs Hounslow and Lund of 256 Sqn attacked a Ju 188 doing 290mph over the Adriatic north of Falconara, and shot it down into the sea. The victim was a Ju 188A-2 (W.Nr.170622, A3+TD) from Kommando Carmen, returning home after completing a mission;

Gefr. Albert Mühlhoff and his four crewmates were all killed. The Germans learned what had happened when their monitoring service overheard traffic from Allied radar stations.

At 0615 a Rotte of tactical reconnaissance aircraft set off on a 60min flight over the northern Adriatic. Four P-47s of the 66th FS, 57th FG, were told by Cooler of bandits south of Lake Garda at 0930 but no contact resulted; four aircraft of the Group's 65th FS attacked Ghedi and left three 'Ju 88s' smoking in their revetments around midday. Allied bombers reported a group of 10 to 15 Bf 109s, four Fw 190s and a jet-propelled aircraft over Northern Italy but it is difficult to place much reliance on any but the first of these sightings and no combats ensued.

On the evening of 5 January two S.79s took-off on Gr. 'Faggioni's' last operation. The aircraft, flown by Cap. Mannelli and Ten. Del Prete, skimmed the waters of the Adriatic searching for targets and finally sighted a 5,000-ton vessel heading for the Dalmatian coast. Both torpedo-bombers attacked and the ship was claimed as sunk. Otherwise the day had seen only a NAGr.11 sortie and the transfer of 5ª Sq. from Aviano to Ghedi, while the 6th seems to have been devoid of aerial incidents.

There were three night sorties on the 7th, at least one of them by 6.(F)/122. The next day was again inactive but two Ju 188s were up after dark on the 9th. Back in Bavaria on the latter date, a Ju 52 transported a group of I° Gr.C. pilots from Holzkirchen to Plattling, from where over the next few days they helped deliver new Bf 109G-10s, G-14s and K-4s to Luftwaffe bases as replacements for those lost in the Bodenplatte attacks of 1 January.

On one such ferry flight on the 12th, 1ª Sq.'s Ten. Cesare Erminio was forced by bad weather to break off and return his Bf 109K-4 to Plattling.

On the 10th an unidentified aircraft, 'believed to be a single-unit jet' (which it surely cannot have been) was seen flying at 20,000ft north of Florence. Three reconnaissance Junkers operated on the night of 10/11 January, and from 0430 one was warned of Allied fighters. At 0502 a D/F fix put it 50 miles south-southeast of Venice and soon after it was making for Bergamo, only to report pursuit and attack by a fighter at 0532. It appeared from radio traffic to have sustained some damage and Bergamo asked the pilot if he wished to belly-land. He replied that he could land normally and was down safely by 0545. The following night two Ju 188s abandoned missions after warnings of Allied fighters.

On the 15th two Bf 109s flew dawn cover of the Northern Adriatic, 1./NAGr.11 reported a Bf 109 destroyed by strafing and the NSGr.9 returned to the fray on a small scale, dropping six bombs near Lucca. Two days later the Allies (but not the Germans) recorded an Me 410 sortie by day and three nocturnal ones by Ju 188s. A German aircraft was over Ancona at 0330, flash bombs were seen to fall and an attempt was made to photograph Rimini. The 18th saw two 'German fighters' airborne in the early morning between Villafranca and Padua, while four maritime reconnaissances were flown that night and an aircraft circling inland was thought to have parachuted agents. Just after 0700 next morning an Italian and a German fighter were up, the latter being ordered to land soon after. Two Ju 188s were out that night, plus a small formation of Ju 87s over the Eighth Army's lines.

20 January 1945

At 0700 German fighters were heard airborne between Padua and Villafranca, only to be ordered down within minutes. At 1008 more were detected and apparently saw Allied fighters but did not make contact. During the morning, separated by just a few minutes, two Me 410s (F6+NK and +KK) flew from Ghedi to Bergamo. After spending a couple of hours on the ground, each flew a mission at midday and returned to Bergamo where they would see out what remained of their operational careers.

Improved weather conditions were exploited by IIº Gr.C. to transfer aircraft from Lonate (two Bf 109s from 1ª Sq.) and Ghedi (nine from 2ª and 3ª) to Aviano during the morning. Flying almost blind with iced-up canopies, the latter group ran unexpectedly into eight P-47s from the 346th FS that had been attacking the Verona-Vicenza railway – in fact, some of the Italians did not even realise there had been a dogfight.

Cap. Bellagambi spotted the P-47s of Lts. Ellis and Morrow on the deck and alerted his pilots but could not himself attack because of frozen synchroniser gear. Unable to see clearly, the others were robbed of their initial tactical advantage and their attack failed completely. The five Bf 109s of 2ª Sq. and four from 3ª dived through the American formation, causing havoc but unable to score.

Six of the Messerschmitts climbed back up and headed north, while the aircraft flown by Ten. Alberto Volpi (3ª Sq.) and Ten. Brini (2ª Sq.) went through and stayed down. By now the American cover section dived on the two Bf 109s

Seen at Bergamo, the Ju 188 of Kommando Carmen's Ltn. Josef Thurnhuber. (via Gellermann)

and, as Lt Sulzbach (leading Minefield Purple section) recalls:

> All hell broke loose on the radio . . . By this time Elmer [Lt Belcher, leading Minefield Pink] was heading our way. He intercepted the two 109s that had gone through his flight. One . . . got away and after much confusion and the other . . . playing cat and mouse with the bunch of us, his engine was shot out. He crash landed but no sign of life emerged from the cockpit.

Ten. Volpi in 'White 5' was the one that got away, while Ten. Brini, was not so lucky. Not only his engine but his head and body had been hit. Despite his wounds he brought his aeroplane down but was found dead in the cockpit by rescuers arriving later that day. Volpi's aeroplane was damaged but he managed to reach Aviano in company with Ten. Ermete Ferrero.

In Aviano, by afternoon Volpi's 'white 5' had been repaired and Ferrero was landing it after a test flight when he swerved off track and hit a hangar. The pilot was unhurt but the Bf 109 was a write-off.

From 1500 an estimated six Ju 87s from Villafranca were strafing roads in the Ravenna area and 600 Sqn's Beaufighters claimed two destroyed and one damaged – their last successes for some time. One victim was a Ju 87D-5 (W.Nr. 140717) of 3./NSGr.9, in which Obfhr. Peter Stollwerk and Uffz. Franz Fischer were listed as missing. Allied crash investigators later found a parachute harness marked with Fischer's name. Tables were turned when 600 Sqn's W/O Ward was wounded in the neck by shots from an unseen assailant on his Beaufighter's tail. Four Ju 188s (including two radar reconnaissances) from Bergamo were plotted during the night.

21-28 January 1945

'German fighters' were heard in the Verona-Vicenza area early on 21 January and Italian ones between Verona and Padua in mid-afternoon. A Bf 109 was claimed destroyed in strafing at Villafranca. The day also saw the arrival of the first I° Gr.C. Bf 109 at Bergamo where a Bf 109G-6 of 1./NAGr.11 (W.Nr.230163) was damaged by strafing. At 1810 a bomb dropped near Castiglione caused 15 casualties, while bombs and chaff were reported falling in several places. At 1915 a 600 Sqn nightfighter saw a Ju 87 brought down by light AA near Alfonsine (RA), though the crew evaded capture. Nearer base, a 2./NSGr.9 Ju 87D-5 (W.Nr. 142082) crashed with engine trouble at Montichiari (BS), injuring Fhr. Bernd Jungfer and Uffz. Fritz Geide.

2.(F)/122's F6+NK was returning from a sortie over the Ligurian Sea when it was warned that P-38s were over its Bergamo base but v.d. Daele and Blaschek got down safely. Half an hour before, F6+KK (Bayer and Lensing) had set out on what was to be an 85min sortie, a now rare case of the Staffel having two aeroplanes aloft simultaneously. Following two Ju 188 flights on the 21st, none was detected for the next seven nights.

The next day, v.d. Daele and Blaschek, this time in F6+NK, flew a 90min morning reconnaissance from Bergamo (perhaps giving rise to the sighting of an 'Me 110' over Parma) but Bayer and Lensing were aloft for only a little over 10min that afternoon before aborting because F6+KK's machine-guns were unserviceable. After this 2./122 did not fly for a week.

At noon the Germans signalled intentions for day and night maritime reconnaissance, harassment on the central front and ferrying a Ju 188 to Bergamo. That evening they reported Aviano occupied by 26 Bf 109s and said that a flak battery was being brought in, to be ready next morning. Despite 350th FG's claimed destruction of four Ju 87s at Villafranca by bombing and strafing, NSGr.9 operated over the Faenza/River Senio sector and a British nightfighter chased and lost a Ju 87.

At least one ANR fighter stirred early on the 23rd, 'Yellow 5' of 2ª Sq. leaving Lonate at 0620 GMT. With 1ª Sq. still not operational (owing to slow deliveries of aeroplanes, acclimatisation to the Bf 109G-10/AS and bad weather), 2ª and 3ª were airborne together at mid-morning, south of Padua. Clouds covered the whole area, thick haze blotting out any detail in the distance, but after about 30min they were vectored on to Wg Cdr Bary and five Spitfire Mk.VIIIs of 417 Sqn, RCAF, making contact at 1053.

Fg Off Marshall wrote: 'All of us had long since lost hope of ever seeing the black cross in our sights . . . only one of us, the Wing Commander, had used his guns against a German aircraft . . . Eleven to six – let's get those bastards! The Jerries . . . didn't have a clue . . . '

The skirmish was brief, with only a few bursts fired. However, although neither side claimed hits, Bellagambi's wingman, Ten. Fausto Filippi of 2ª Sq., was mortally wounded in the head and his Bf 109G-6 (W.Nr.163466, Yellow 10) crashed near S. Giorgio delle Pertiche (VI). The Italians wrote-off another two aircraft in training accidents at Aviano, a 3ª Sq. Bf 109G-4 (W.Nr.19758) and S.Ten. Dell'Acqua's G-6 (W.Nr.660416).

Intentions for the 23rd included land and sea coverage by NAGr.11 and FAGr.122 but bad weather and attacks by 40 medium bombers on Udine and Gorizia airfields between them apparently precluded this.

Things went quiet until the 27th, when three Fw 190s were reported by MATAF to have dropped a 'fuel tank bomb' with a large detonator in its nose southwest of Bologna at 1020. Three other aircraft were reported dropping bombs or 'objects'.

By the end of January the de Havilland Mosquito was serving with 255, 256 and 600 Sqns. (RAF) and with the American 416th NFS. Although outperforming the Beaufighter, it was offered comparatively few targets by this time. German staff officers later claimed that one or two had been shot down by Fw 190s of NSGr.9. (IWM)

29 January 1945

The Me 410 of Ofw. Zimmerman and Uffz. Lenecke took off from Bergamo at 1148 but was back only 10min later. A P-38 of 3rd PRG reported an attack by an unidentified aircraft; eight P-47s of the 57th FG saw two Bf 109s 'on the deck' northeast of Milan at 1600 but were too low on fuel to attack; a German transport was seen at Bergamo, apparently set for take-off and with a fighter alongside. Strafing of the airfield destroyed a Ju 188D-2 of 4.(F)/122 (W.Nr.230147) and inflicted 15 per cent damage on two other aeroplanes of the Staffel (Ju 188D-2 W.Nr.230447, F6+HM and Ju 88 T-3 W.Nr.330237).

At about 1800, P-47s of Silver Section of the 346th Fighter Squadron, 350th FG, were vectored on to a formation of bogeys by Cooler (alerted in turn by RAF Sigint) while on dusk patrol near Bologna. They were five miles north of the city, low on fuel and returning home when they saw seven Ju 87s, 1,500ft higher and heading north. Unseen, the Thunderbolts climbed and opened up on the last of the group.

Lt Charles C. Eddy recorded in his diary: 'Dick [Lt Richard Sulzbach] and I both got in solid bursts and he was seen to crash. The rest . . . scattered like chickens.' After following their victim down they climbed back, to find another Ju 87 behind them. This they attacked head-on, continuing to fire as it evaded with a wingover, but were unable to observe any crash. Their Squadron War Diary continues: . . . 'the last the two aces saw of the enemy planes they were running like hell for home, on the deck . . . ' Eddy and Sulzbach saw the wreckage of one Ju 87 in the snow and claimed another probable.

Johannes Nawroth was in the back seat of E8+BK, compelled to jettison its bombs when:

. . .we had contact with two . . . Spitfires [*as he thought*], one of which shot at us. I returned fire and definitely hit [him] judging by the tracers. Since it must have been armoured on the sides, I can't have done any damage.

In 1994 Nawroth and Eddy established more friendly contact and Eddy recalled that, "fortunately for us your . . . machine-guns had too short a trajectory even to reach us. We suffered no hits."

The Ju 87s operated in groups of two or three from dusk through to 0300, attacking guns 20 miles south of Bologna and strafing and bombing vehicles. A Beaufighter of 600 Sqn. chased one of these aircraft but lost contact. On their second and third sorties that night, Deutsch and Nawroth bombed Fontanèlice and Loiano (BO) under Egon guidance. Four Ju 188 reconnaissances were flown during the night of 29/30th, one – by luck or judgement – following returning MAAF bombers in over Livorno. Despite showing no IFF response it was plotted as 'friendly, probably in distress' until it dropped its flash bombs at 0520 and escaped with photographs of the port.

30-31 January 1945

In the early hours of the 30th a parachutist was dropped behind Allied lines and two flash bombs fell over Livorno. On mid-morning patrol, a group of USAAF P-47s reported 'five He 111s' in revetments at Ghedi. Two Ju 188s were out by night, and one radioed that it had been detected by Allied fighters but apparently landed safely. A Ju 188D-2 of 6.(F)/122 (W.Nr.150515, F6+EP) experienced engine trouble and was wrecked in a crash-landing 5km south of Bergamo, Uffz. Happel, Fw. Steinkönig and Uffz Hänsler were injured.

At 0730 on the 31st, Ju 188 F6+CP arrived in Ghedi from Bergamo and during the day four Bf 109s were spotted near Udine.

Chapter 12

February 1945

The Ground War

An assault south of Bologna stalled after gaining half a mile. The weather was bad for much of the time and little could be achieved in the face of determined German defences although the Eighth Army 'improved their positions' on the east coast in the Faenza and Comacchio areas. Three German counter-attacks in the Serchio Valley all failed, and the Allies eventually retook Gallicano. On the 15th General von Vietinghoff was posted to command the cut-off German forces in Kurland, being replaced at Tenth Army by General der Panzertruppen Traugott Herr.

Fuel

The improvement of mid-January proved aberrant, and things soon got back to 'normal'. B4 was down to 280m^3 by the 28th, and no new deliveries of this or C3 were received, but by the 9th there was 320m^3 of J2 for the expected jets. The section on Italy in the OKL Chief of Staff's instructions of 21 February read:

> The Luftwaffe is being assigned a large number of tasks on all fronts. If these are carried out in their entirety, air activity will soon come to a complete standstill as, in view of the diffficult fuel situation, all reserves will be expended. Small-scale air operations will be carried out on the Italian front, the average daily fuel consumption amounting to nine tonnes.

A week later Major Walter Hutmacher, Pohl's Ia, wrote to Ob.SW on the matter. He wanted to keep a reserve of 580m^3 to sustain 14 days' operations at the following daily pitch in the event of 'large scale operations':
21m^3 for two Bf 109 reconnaissances with auxiliary tanks
112m^3 for one radar and one flash-bomb long-range reconnaissance
222m^3 for 21 night-attack sorties
225m^3 for 40 fighter sorties without auxiliary tanks

With further deliveries 'impossible in March and improbable in April', these reserves could only be amassed if all flying ceased forthwith. He therefore requested a decision on whether all air operations, including reconnaissance, should be suspended pending a big push. If not, he asked which of his list should be forgone when major fighting again erupted. The response is unknown but OKL meanwhile ceased to hold units ready to reinforce the Adriatic in the event of an enemy landing in Istria, citing Italy's low aviation fuel stocks as the reason.

The Luftwaffe

Jets

In February 1945 the first Luftwaffe jet aircraft was deployed to Italy; it was an Arado Ar 234 of the Versuchsverband Ob.d.L. and was based at Osoppo. How it came to be there is a complicated story, with several aspects still unresolved or open to dispute. We believe, however, that the evidence we have amassed is persuasive on these main points.

The tale could be said to have begun in late 1944 with Pohl's calls for jet fighters and reconnaissance aircraft, continuing through many false alarms among the Allies and culminating in a confusing postwar reference[42] that: 'the few German jet aircraft at Udine had done well against isolated Allied four-engined bombers returning from long-distance flights . . . [although] strictly a reconnaissance unit . . . we admitted the occasional loss of stragglers to their attacks.'

Reliable information really begins on 24 January, with OKL's agreement to allocate a small Ar 234 reconnaissance unit, followed by orders issued by Luftwaffenkommando West at 2100 on 1 February. Oblt. Erich Sommer's Kommando Hecht ('Detachment Pike') was disbanded and its Ar 234s were to be handed to 1.(F)/100, then at Biblis, near Worms. Hecht's air and ground personnel were to be renamed Kommando Sommer and transfer to Italy. An incomplete Ultra intercept on the 4th suggested that the unit would be going to Osoppo and this is confirmed by an entry in G.d.A.'s KTB the same day, stating that the movement was taking place by rail.

A Luftwaffe disposition map for 9 February has a note against Osoppo that Kdo. Sommer is being brought up but there was obviously some hold-up because the next information on the move comes a week later, when both Ultra and G.d.A. reported that Kdo. Sommer had suffered heavy material losses when its train was attacked by fighter-bombers near Worms on the 14th. What could be salvaged was being collected in the Biblis barracks. Two days later it was decided that Sommer's depleted Kommando would be reincorporated into the Versuchsverband, remaining at Biblis while its leader took the gear and personnel (but not the aircraft) of Kdo. Götz to Italy. Hptm. Horst Götz himself was posted soon after to command 1.(F)/123 on the Western Front.

On the 19th, the same day that Kdo. Götz confirmed that it had handed over to 1.(F)/123, Sommer was asked how far the stocking-up for his new unit had progressed. Next day came the somewhat negative Ultra intelligence that an advance detachment, headed by a 'pilot of Kommando Sperling in January', had *not* arrived at Osoppo. No runway was available and the length of the landing area was unknown, but Tornado D/F was available. However, five men, including one of Kdo. Hecht, had arrived. The landing area at Udine was 1,600m long but it was not known if preparations for Ar 234 operations had been made.

On the 21st Kdo. Götz's ground echelon began its train journey[43] from Münster-Handorf to Italy and a new plan was issued. Sommer, after handing over his aircraft, was to return to Kaltenkirchen (where the parent Versuchsverband had moved from Oranienburg) and Oblt. Muffey (Sperling's Technical Officer) was to go to Osoppo as the officer commanding 'Detachment South'. In fact, Muffey did not go and Sommer stayed on the Western Front a while longer, making operational flights on the 23rd and 24th.

On the 23rd, Cap. Bellagambi of II° Gr.C. wrote in his diary, 'a "Turbin-Jäger" [jet fighter] has come to Osoppo'. Subsequent questioning of Italian eyewitnesses, confirmed by reference to photographs and recollection that the aircraft took-off assisted by 'two canisters hung under the wings' – i.e. Walter RATO units – identifies this as an Ar 234. These witnesses were able to point to the hangar in which the aircraft was kept, the concrete foundations of which still exist.

Bellagambi may have had the wrong date: Kdo. Götz reported to G.d.A. that its first Ar 234 had arrived in Osoppo on the 24th, although the day's disposition map still marks the unit 'in transit'. An OKL status report of the 26th has one Ar 234 of Kdo. Götz in Osoppo and two more ready to start from Oranienburg as soon as the weather and air situation permitted.

MATAF summed up for the month:
. . . photo reconnaissance revealed what may possibly have been a jet . . . at Udine, and a ground report has mentioned Osoppo as the site of preparations to receive special aircraft from Germany. It is considered unlikely that even a small detachment of jet-propelled reconnaissance aircraft will become operational during March.

Seenotstaffel 20, NAGr.11 and FAGr.122
On the 1st OKL ordered the disbandment of SNSt.20 and the surrender of its aircraft to NAGr.11. Operationally, it is doubtful whether this made much difference as the two units seem to have worked in the closest co-operation anyway. As with so many of Berlin's instructions, this one was not put into immediate effect and February turned out to be a month when Fw 190s, almost certainly of this Staffel, began to be reported time and again in daytime encounters with Allied fighters.

Major Seebode noted that the 81 reconnaissance sorties flown were a slight increase on the January total but that frequent fog prevented more. The bulk of these missions were for sea and battlefield surveillance; the remaining 14 were photo-coverage of the harbours of Marseille, Toulon, Livorno, Ancona, Bari, Brindisi, Taranto and Naples. Flares were dropped over several of these ports. Photographed for the first time were the Allied-built airfields at Cervia, Cesenatico and Castellabate (SA). The Ju 188s of FAGr.122 staged through

Campoformido on several of their missions. Total reconnaissance unit losses were said to have been one Bf 109, two Me 410s and two Ju 188s, plus five pilots and eight other aircrew, but this was not the whole picture.

NSGr.9

The Stab was ordered to move from Bovolone to Villafranca on the 2nd, perhaps to oversee 1./NSGr.9 as it began to receive its Fw 190s. Fhj. Fw. Franz Züger[44] was one of the new pilots to arrive around this time, having converted to the Fw 190F-8 with Ergänzungskampfstaffel (Nacht) at Berlin-Staaken during January, only to be pitched into the assaults on the Red Army's Oder bridgeheads shortly afterwards.

The new aeroplanes offered numerous advantages: their greater speed enabled them to evade adversaries; the shorter flying time between waypoints made navigation more accurate; and reduced transit times meant that more sorties could be flown per night per aircraft. Their wide-track undercarriages were said to allow safer night landings but this was offset by faster approach speeds which caused a number of accidents. Twelve Fw 190Fs were delivered to Komm. Gen. Italien during the month according to OKL figures – the establishment of the re-equipped Staffel. Small groups of the new aeroplanes were active around dawn and dusk and during the night on at least eight days.

These developments were not lost on the Allies as new forms of radio traffic began to fill the night air with callsigns such as Ulrich-Anton, -Berta and so on through the phonetic alphabet to -Heinrich, appearing early in the month. There was also traffic giving rise to suspicion that the newcomers had a role as nightfighters, corroborated by a series of inconclusive encounters between A-20s of the 47th BG and unidentified single-engined aircraft showing lights of various colours. The diarist of 600 Sqn wrote on the 24th that 'enemy nightfighters are suspected to be operating, possibly from that area [Udine]. Nine Bostons [of 232 Wing] are missing in two nights and some of [them] report seeing nightfighters'.

In its primary role, the Gruppe seems to have been almost entirely out of action apart from 3. Staffel's unusual achievement in bringing down an enemy aircraft by small-arms fire. The British Air Ministry commented that, 'It is significant that despite improved weather conditions and the prevailing moonlight period, there are no reports of night-harassing bomber operations', and elsewhere it was conjectured that, were the Germans to stage a major withdrawal, the Gruppe might be sent against Allied airfields in an attempt to diminish MAAF's power to harry the retreat. In fact the Gruppe was being denuded of personnel. Men were being drafted into the ground forces and two, transferred from 2./NSGr.9 into 90. PG Div. on the 6th, later deserted to the Allies. They reported that 1. and 3. Staffeln were in the Verona area and that operations were curtailed by lack of petrol, but said nothing of conversion to the Fw 190 which an earlier prisoner had confirmed.

Flak (and V-Weapons)

The month's star performers were the various anti-aircraft gunners, although some individual battalions were being withdrawn in favour of other fronts. Luftwaffe and Italian gun crews claimed 104 enemy

Aviano, February 1945. The Bf 109G-14 (W.Nr.434444) of Magg. Miani, Deputy CO of II° Gruppo Caccia. The aircraft, belonging to Nucleo Comando, carries a somewhat asymmetrical, Italian-applied 'double chevron'.

aircraft, the Army two and the Navy 21. Another 14 came down in German-held territory for reasons other than combat damage.

After the war it was learned that the Germans had come to believe that the Allies were expecting V-1 launches from Villafranca. Noting the constant MAAF reconnaissance activity there, they sent up an aeroplane of their own to take a look, and decided that the shading of a section of concrete landing strip made it look like a launch ramp, and that stores of 1,800kg bombs and fuel tanks might have been mistaken for V-weapons by Italian civilians.

Cap. Ugo Drago, CO of 4ª Sq., IIº Gr.C., climbing into his Bf 109G-10/AS, 'Black 7'. By February 1945 the whole 4ª Sq. was re-equipped with this new sub-type which was the most widely used by the Italian fighter units in 1945.

Order of Battle
We have been unable to discover any Luftwaffe strength figures for Italy in February 1945.

The ANR

On the 8th Mussolini made 'a further request' to Pohl for a German Jagdgruppe to be moved to Italy. OKL refused but relied on the supply of modern aircraft and 'appropriate training' to the Italians to provide air defence 'at the highest possible quantitative and qualitative standard'.

Iº Gr.C.
The state of training of the 'Italian Jagdgeschwader' was summed up by the Germans on the 7th. Iº Gruppo had completed training at Holzkirchen and had 57 pilots ready for operations; its aircraft strength was 22 Bf 109s, including ten G-6s and two G-12 two-seat trainers. Four Bf 109s were still being brought up and in fact 20 of the total were in Bavaria, ready to transfer to Italy as soon as weather permitted. The planned bases were Lonate and later Gallarate (Malpensa-VA), only a few miles apart . While the ground personnel and some of the pilots returned to Italy by train, taking over their new bases and their quarters in Gallarate and Cardano al Campo respectively, a group of pilots remained in Germany, waiting to deliver new Bf 109s to Italy. Some delays were unavoidable but on the 15th the first two Bf 109s took off from Fürstenfeldbruck and Riem, reaching Lonate together with a third aircraft from Orio al Serio. The balance of the Gruppo's aircraft was flown to Lonate on 23 and 24 February, coming from Riem and Orio. This comprised 51 aircraft, two of them G-10/R2 reconaissance fighters (handed over to NAGr.11 in Udine on 27 February), and also three K-4s[45]. By the end of February all was ready for a new tour of operations.

IIº Gr.C.
This was the most active unit, and curiously MAAF credited it with more sorties and combats than its own side. For a loss of five aeroplanes and two pilots (Seebode's figures again) the Gruppo claimed destruction of five B-25s and three P-47s, plus severe damage to a further four heavy and 11 medium bombers. A new ground control station, Roma, took over from Caserma during the month, and would be used for the remainder of the war.

IIº Gruppo was at Aviano and Osoppo with 82 pilots, of whom 53 were ready for operations. They had 35 Bf 109s, including 23 G-6s and a G-12. With effect from 1 February SMAR, in view of Iº Gr.'s imminent return home, changed the numbering of the Squadriglie to conform to the German system. Within IIº Gr. 1ª, 2ª and 3ª Sq. became 4ª, 5ª and 6ª respectively. On the 2nd, thanks to improved weather, the whole of 4ª Sq. finally managed to complete take-over of their new Bf 109 G-10/AS's, while in Osoppo Cap. Bellagambi's Squadriglia received a visit by Oberst Lützow, reviewing his forces. Maybe the high-ranking German ace brought luck to the Italians as, when they returned to operations on the 4th, the results of this first combat were at last positive.

On 17 February 1945, Lt Edwin King of 347th FS, 350th FG, while escorting B-25 bombers, tried to pursue II° Gr.C. fighters that had attacked the formation. The result of the chase was a blown cylinder and a flood of oil over his P-47. Here, back at Pisa airfield, he describes the episode to two colleagues. (King)

Between the 9th and 11th several 4ª Sq. pilots completed their conversion to the G-10/AS, while the training section within the Group (once again headed by S.Ten. Di Santo, who was back at his job after his 'mission' in Germany ended in mid-December and he had taken a 30-day leave) continued to operate irregularly, owing to the frequent mechanical problems suffered by the old G-12 'White 20'. This section also instructed all the I° Gr.C. pilots coming back from Germany after being partially schooled on the Me 163 and thus not having completed their Bf 109 training.

On the 26th Cap. Bellagambi was awarded the Iron Cross 1st Class, and most probably on the same date he was promoted to Maggiore (no official data are available on this promotion, although it is certain that he ended the war with that rank).[46]

III° Gr.C.

Retraining was under way in Holzkirchen (65 pilots), although some activities (15 pilots) had been transferred to Fürth because of snow. In addition to ten Bf 109s included in I° Gruppo's strength (probably the obsolete G-6 models) the Holzkirchen training detachment had a Bf 108 and three Klemm 35s. The Geschwaderstab existed only as an administrative body.

Notes

42. In an RAF Air Historical Branch campaign history.
43. Officially, but Sommer comments, 'No way. They went by road under Oblt. Mänhard'.
44. Whose story is told in *Focke-Wulf 190 At War* by Alfred Price (Ian Allan, 1977)
45. This is the listing of the aircraft drawn up by I° Gr.C. on 28 February 1945:

1ª Squadriglia	2ª Squadriglia	3ªSquadriglia
1-1 W.Nr.491439	2-1 W.Nr.490265	3-1 W.Nr.491324
1-2 W.Nr.491497	2-2 W.Nr.491354	3-2 W.Nr.491325
1-3 W.Nr.491281	2-3 W.Nr.491398	3-3 W.Nr.491327
1-4 W.Nr.490761	2-4 W.Nr.491409	3-4 W.Nr.491356
1-5 W.Nr.491504	2-6 W.Nr.491480	3-5 W.Nr.491407
1-6 W.Nr.491464	2-7 W.Nr.491488	3-6 W.Nr.491425
1-7 W.Nr.785990	2-8 W.Nr.491493	3-7 W.Nr.491437
1-8 W.Nr.491485	2-9 W.Nr.491498	3-8 W.Nr.491456
1-9 W.Nr.785083	2-10 W.Nr.491499	3-9 W.Nr.491477
1-10 W.Nr.491461	2-11 W.Nr.785067	3-10 W.Nr.491479
1-11 W.Nr.786344	2-12 W.Nr.787465	3-11 W.Nr.490621
1-12 W.Nr.490266	2-13 W.Nr.412349	3-12 W.Nr.491444
1-13 W.Nr.782414	2-14 W.Nr.460367	3-13 W.Nr.785039
1-14 W.Nr.491485	2-15 W.Nr.462739	3-14 W.Nr.333878
1-15 W.Nr.461327	2-16 W.Nr.462995	3-15 W.Nr.333958
1-16 W.Nr.780904		3-16 W.Nr.440547
1-18 W.Nr.780356		3-17 W.Nr.330209

46. The strength of 5ª Sq. on 28 February, according to Magg. Bellagambi's diary, was as follows:
0- W.Nr. 163482 (G-6)
1- W.Nr. 464380 (G-14)
2- W.Nr. 491313 (G-10/AS)
3- W,Nr. 464430 (G-14)
5- W.Nr. 161428 (G-6)
6- W.Nr. 491319 (G-10/AS)
8- W.Nr. 490379(G-10 [/AS?])
10- W.Nr. 464456 (G-14)
13- W.Nr. 464446 (G-14)
15- W.Nr. 163197 (G-6)
16- W.Nr. 464464 (G-14)

The wreck of the Mustang IV of 112 Sqn. RAF, shot down on 18 February while strafing Aviano airfield by S.M.(Armourer) D'Ilario of II° Gr.C (right). The pilot, Flt Lt R.V.Hearn, was unable to bale out and died in the crash.

Chapter 12

Operations

1-3 February 1945

Over the Ligurian at 1030, P-47s of the 57th FG saw 'two possible Me-109's flying west at 7,500 ft . . . they were silver in colour with inline engines'.

On the 2nd ferry pilot Schaal brought Me 410 BU+SI (later F6+BK) to Ghedi. Messerschmitt works pilot Eberlein normally tested new Me 262s, but today (with an observer, Pankatz) ferried an Me 410 from Riem. Eberlein's logbook records his arrival with TI+WB at 1411, whereas 2.(F)/122's KTB has him landing in PS+TM (later F6+CK) at 1704! TJ+WB[47] (later F6+DK) was operating with 2./122 a fortnight later, but the KTB overlooks its delivery.

Intentions for the 3rd included ferrying a Ju 188 to Villafranca, a Bf 109 to Aviano and a Ju 87 to Vicenza.

4-5 February 1945

At 1130 eight Bf 109s of 4ª Sq. and six of 6ª took off from Aviano to intercept escorted bombers near Padua. At 1136 MAAF overheard an order to the Italians not to attack until reinforcements appeared and then one of the ANR fighters was called down with some kind of trouble (more of this later). The reinforcements were nine 5ª Sq. aircraft, arriving just before noon. A thick haze blanketing the northeastern part of the Po Valley had meanwhile split the bombers into two groups at 8,000ft, with the escort fighters 2,000ft above them also dividing to accompany their 'Big Friends'.

The first to make contact with the enemy were the Diavoli Rossi led by Cap. Bellagambi, attacking four P-47s of the 66th FS, 57th FG, and hitting the second of them, flown by Lt Guilford Groendycke. His '78' started to burn with black smoke, spinning earthwards to crash near Thiene. No parachute was seen to open.

The skirmish lasted less than a minute before both sets of fighters made for home, but a second victory was to be scored in an unusual way.

The Bf 109 ordered home just before the combat was that of Serg. Gualberto Benzi, of 4ª Sq. He was on his first mission and heading home in steadily worsening visibility. He was not alone, however, since another aircraft had become lost in the murky sky. When the Bf 109s had attacked the P-47s, Lt Edward Palovich, instead of breaking hard left, had made a full-throttle climb straight ahead, disappearing from his comrades' view, as they did from his, leaving him to wander the sky.

As Benzi recorded in his diary:

> . . . Suddenly, alerted by the radio, I saw an aircraft higher than me, 300m away, turning and diving slightly as if to attack me. I waggled my wings again to try and confuse him and closed my throttle . . . in a second I was on his tail, fired a burst and saw something fly off. I had hit him! A second burst with the cannon shot away one wing. I was a few metres from him when he began to fall, I tried to follow him with a split-S, but didn't manage it. The aircraft fell near the railway station of Valdagno (VI), while the pilot landed by parachute nearby . . .'

While the remains of P-47 *Peggy II* burned and Lt Palovich was captured by the Germans, Benzi continued receiving radio warnings about eight enemy fighters following him. Although not seeing anything, he preferred to try and land as soon as possible and, finding a small gap in the haze, put down at Treviso, almost crashing into a hangar. News of his landing as well as his first victory was welcomed enthusiastically back at Aviano, where everybody thought him either shot down or crashed in the mountains.

Cap. Mario Bellagambi, CO of 5ª Sq. 'Diavoli Rossi' and one of the most capable and aggressive ANR leaders. His daring style of combat led him and his unit to score several successes but inevitably brought a correspondingly heavy loss rate, with 15 pilots KIA in the period covered by this book.

6-7 February 1945

IIº Gr. was back in action, scrambling with 16 Bf 109s from all the Squadriglie at 1245 to intercept 18 B-25s of the 310th BG out to bomb a railroad bridge at Ala (TN). The Italians were themselves intercepted by P-47s of the 522nd FS, 27th FG and although several reached the bombers, Ten. Piolanti even claiming one (according to 310th BG's diary, ten of their aeroplanes were damaged), the main body of Messerschmitts clashed with the USAAF fighters.

The interception was brought about by No 10 FSU alerting the Americans to the hostiles' presence, and elicited thanks from 62nd FW:

... congratulating you ... for the splendid warning you enabled us to pass to [a] flight of eight aircraft on 6 February 1945, when Thunderbolts of 27FG, although greatly outnumbered by 42 Me 109s and six Fw 190s were able to use a valuable ten minutes after warning to gain altitude, destroying in the resulting engagement three Me 109s and damaging four more without loss to themselves.

Although the Americans overestimated the Italians' strength, the advantage of early warning was overwhelming in a fight lasting only a few minutes. The two P-47s claimed destroyed by Cap. Drago and S.M. Bianchini (the former admitted seeing no crash) were in reality badly damaged but able to reach base. Only one of the three Bf 109s claimed (by Lts. Williams, Hay and Rudd) was actually shot down; this was the G-6 (W.Nr.160411) of S.M. Fausto Fornaci, who fell to his death in the aircraft.

At 1515 southwest of Piacenza, 66th FS P-47s reported 'one Ju-88, clipped wing-tips, no markings, camouflaged with green and brown spots, and silver wings, flying west at 9,000ft'.

On the 7th three Bf 109s were sighted over the Lavis (TN) rail diversion by B-25s of the 321st BG. They closed to 800yd before (so the bomber crews reported) being driven off by P-47s, but the Thunderbolts flying area cover did not report seeing any hostiles.

8 February 1945

Sixteen IIº Gruppo aircraft scrambled between 1220 and 1240. As 5ª Sq.'s Messerschmitts rose from Osoppo there was an accident. Ten. De Masellis's aeroplane bounced heavily on the take-off run, damaging both its airscrew and droptank. He managed to come to a halt but leaking fuel suddenly ignited. The men rushing to the rescue pulled him from the blazing aircraft apparently burned only on his back. Sadly his condition proved far worse and he died a few hours later.

The Italians were again facing 310th BG's Mitchells, returning from bombing the Dogna (UD) railway bridge. The 27 bombers were intercepted over the Adriatic at 1315 and, in the ensuing combat the Bf 109s claimed either eight bombers (according to Group documents), six (S.Ten. Di Santo's diary) or four (official communiqué)! The USAAF reported no losses whatsoever, and the 'Group

History' says: '. . . ten or more Me 109s and FW 190s attacked the formation over the Adriatic Sea, and wounded one of the Group's radio gunners. One Fw 190 was destroyed in aerial combat by an upper turret and tail gunner in one of the Group's B-25s.' Victory reports filed by Cap. Bellagambi and S.M. Baldi both affirm that, after hitting the bomber they were shooting at, they saw '. . . two tall columns of water and foam rising from the sea . . .' Obviously they took these for the crash(es) of their victim(s), but they probably resulted from hung-up bombs being jettisoned. Nor is the 310th BG's claim substantiated. The only damage sustained by II° Gruppo was 15 per cent to the G-14 (W.Nr.464469) flown by Serg. Poluzzi (6ª Sq.), who was wounded but reached Osoppo.

Spitfires of 244 Wing, diverted to look for an Me 410 over the Adriatic, found nothing but east of Comacchio 93 Sqn was luckier:

> The first sensation came at lunch-time when an Me 410 stooged gently over the coast road at about 200 feet while many unbelieving eyes blinked with surprise. A section . . . was diverted from a bombing mission and after a chase Lt [H.P.] Anderson attacked it. The Hun was last seen diving into cloud at fifty feet with its starboard engine on fire. This is claimed as probably destroyed and it is hoped the gun camera will produce sufficient evidence to step up the claim.

In fact the Me 410B-3 (W.Nr.190096, F6+KK) was completely destroyed, and Ofw. Wilhelm Zimmerman and Uffz. Wilhelm Lenecke of 2.(F)/122 were killed.

At Riem an Me 410A-1 (W.Nr.420653) of Komm. Gen.'s Aussenstelle (out-station) suffered damage to its undercarriage. That night NSGr.9 dropped 'butterfly bombs' at several locations including Ferrara and the Cittadella (PD) marshalling yards.

9-11 February 1945

On the 9th an Allied P/R mission encountered five Bf 109s over Aviano and that night flash bombs lit up Livorno. The next day a 4.(F)/122 Ju 188D-2 (W.Nr.230445) was damaged in a belly-landing at Bergamo. An Ultra decrypt was taken to show that II° Gr.C. was in action against medium bombers over the mouth of the Isonzo on the 11th but other sources do not report this. That night 6.(F)/122 had a Ju 188D-2 (W.Nr.150513, F6+AP) destroyed in a crash after take-off at Grassobbio (BG), in which Fw. Biester and three crewmen were killed.

12 February 1945

Late that morning, 18 B-25s of the 310th BG took off from Ghisonaccia (Corsica) and, in three boxes of six, headed towards the Italian coast, their target a sugar refinery in Legnago (VR), adapted by the Germans into a synthetic fuel plant. No escort was provided despite repeated Axis fighter attacks in previous days.

At Aviano and Osoppo the alert was given at around 1315. Within half an hour 22 Bf 109s were in the air, assembling 15min later over Aviano, then heading towards the area where the bombers had been reported. At 1500 the refinery's AA defences opened fire on the B-25s beginning their bomb-run. Forty-four 1,000lb bombs were dropped and, as explosions and fires erupted, the Italians finally came on to the scene.

Two B-25 gunners (S/Sgts. Emil M. Strabac and Arthur S. Claypool) later told US Forces Radio:

> We had finished our first bomb-run when the Messerschmitts made their appearance. They came in at 7 o'clock and slightly high. From then on they were on our tail all the time. They would zoom in from 5, 6, 7 o'clock – straight at us – so we didn't have to worry about lead or deflection. Not until they were within 50 yards would they peel off. They were flying by the book, in formations of three or four, stacked neatly one above the other.
>
> Those Me 109s were the slickest planes I've ever seen. Kind of a light grey. When they made their third pass, I picked an Me, trained my guns on him, and gave him four bursts of fire. On the fourth burst, I saw a piece of the cowling rip away from his ship, and a thin streak of smoke followed it. He rolled off on his right wing and fell straight down . . .

This was probably S.M. Cavagliano who wrote in his diary:

> . . . it was my third attack but, as I began firing, my aircraft was shaken by a violent burst of bullets all along the cowling, the cockpit and the cannon's breech right between my legs. I was unable to see anything in the smoke and the oil covering my windscreen, only realising by some glimpses to my sides that I was flying amidst the enemy bombers! I immediately rolled my aircraft downwards and when I recovered from my dive realised that my engine was about to seize up. The only thing to do was to leave my "Black 12" [Bf 109G-10/AS, W.Nr.491320] and, although this was my first time, I managed somehow or

other to bale out and land safely near the village of Carceri (PD).

Ten. Leandro Bonara (6ª Sq.) was also hit, but was too low to bale out and was killed when his G-14 (W.Nr.464414) crashed. S.M. Bianchini (5ª Sq.) crash-landed his badly damaged G-6 (W.Nr.160319) in a field near Bovolone (VR). At least four more Gustavs were hit. Those of Cap. Drago (4ª Sq.) and Ten. Ferrero (6ª Sq.), though damaged, made it back to Aviano; S.M. Cusmano (5ª Sq.) and S.M. Zanardi (6ª Sq.) all had to land at Thiene.

Only one Italian, Cap. Drago, made a claim: one B-25 destroyed, although his victory report reads: '... after my third burst I noticed several explosions on the left engine but I was unable to follow the enemy bomber's fate because I was hit and forced to abandon the attack ...'. The bomber was almost certainly Claypool and Strabac's, since theirs was the only B-25 damaged, and their interview continued:

... the ship was hit badly, every gas tank was punctured. Two 20 millimetre cannon bursts exploded in the wings, one on each side of the fuselage. We had to feather our left engine because an oil line had been severed, and we were losing altitude ... after the Messerschmitts left, we were still sweating. Our hydraulic system was shot out and we had a wounded man aboard. At last we reached our base and when we got around to counting the holes in our ship, we got up to 400 – and quit. I bet there were a thousand.

An appropriate comment on the day's events is found in S.Ten. Di Santo's diary: '... a real disaster ... Really discouraging.'

A few days' pause followed while training of I° Gr. pilots continued and 5ª Sq. received two more aircraft to supplement the only four currently serviceable.

13-15 February 1945

In the Mantova area on the 13th a medium bomber formation turned back to the southwest, possibly, according to the Luftwaffe, because of contact with II° Gr.C. The authors have no information that the Gruppo flew a concerted operation, but some Bf 109s were certainly in the air. During the afternoon Ju 188s, F6+DM, +IM and +GP, left Bergamo, probably for Udine.

At 1455, six 241 Sqn Spitfires were over Lake Grado when Sqn Ldr A.J. Radcliffe saw two aircraft coming from the north and rapidly climbing to overhaul the Spits. When they swung in behind, Radcliffe ordered a turn: 'The E/A turned with our formation and were recognised as Fw 190s, radial engines, camouflage dark green, spinners possibly same colour'. Radcliffe and his wingman climbed to give top cover. One German broke away but was not chased because only three of the British could jettison their droptanks.

W/O A.J. Ray found that the other Fw 190 was tailing Fg Off L.A. Blake, manoeuvred behind it then lost sight of it while trying to get rid of his tank. Meanwhile, Blake had escaped his predicament, and when next seen the Focke-Wulf was:

... coming right into my sights. I gave three or four 1 to 2 second bursts ... and saw cannon strikes on engine cowling and fuselage. The E/A ... went into a ... spiral turn ... I followed him [and] blew 2-3ft off his port wing. I put in a further burst and saw strikes on the engine cowling causing a thin steady stream of dark smoke to come from the port side of his engine. The e/a continued to spiral down and I followed him, closing to about 20 yards and firing at will without obvious result ...

At about 250ft the Fw 190 suddenly dropped and was lost to view. They were now in ground mist and neither Ray nor Blake saw any crash. Radcliffe observed a large splash 'as though a 500lb bomb had been jettisoned' but which 'could have been caused by a Fw 190 crashing into the water'.

On the 15th three Fw 190s were delivered to Villafranca but F6+DK of 2.(F)/122 had to break off a mission because of bad weather.

16 February 1945

Early in the afternoon 'up to four squadrons' of ANR fighters sortied without contact. Near Trieste at 1340 an Fw 190 attacked a straggling bomber (and, so one German source suggests, shot it down), only to be set on in turn by 1st/Lt Walter K. Selenger of the 318th FS and shot down into the sea, 12km south of Grado (VE). Missing in this combat was Oblt. Heinz Langer, Kapitän of Seenotstaffel 20 (Fw 190A-8 W.Nr.680124). It was probably on the same sortie that another of the Staffel's A-8s (W.Nr.734006) suffered damage from engine trouble.

The only activity of 2.(F)/122 was to move TJ+WB from Bergamo to Ghedi during the late afternoon. Although it was aloft for only 20min, the Allies still detected it. Also during the afternoon, Ju 188 F6+FM was deployed to Aviano. A special operation was carried out on the night of 16/17 February by six aircraft (a record for the month), some of which staged at Aviano and Udine, probably for flights down the east coast of Italy. One of these was a Carmen

aircraft, up from 1720 to 1951, its route: Bergamo – the Po Valley – southwest of Pola – 10 miles south of Cattolica (FO) and back the same way. It was subsequently reported to have carried out its task without reaction from Allied defences. Another of the night's sorties was a 3hr radar surveillance of the Adriatic from west of Trieste to southeast of Ancona.

17 February 1945

On early-morning weather reconnaissance west of Udine, two Spitfires of 601 Sqn met three enemy aircraft flying northwest at 10,000ft. The hostiles, which turned out to be Bf 109s, moved in to attack the Spitfires, which responded by turning into them. A chase followed until the 109s began to climb and the DAF pilots were able to engage. Fg Off H.G. Proudman opened fire at 200yds and saw pieces fall off his opponent who pulled up, streaming black smoke; the pursuit continued right up to 16,000ft. When the Bf 109 turned to starboard and dived, Proudman began to close in for another attack but the Messerschmitt suddenly burst into flames, rolled over and crashed north of Udine.

Meanwhile, W/O W.W. Stratton, RCAF, fired on another of the enemy from astern, observing strikes on its cockpit and fuselage. White smoke poured out and the aircraft was last seen spiralling down. Stratton then went after the third German, chasing it up to 35,000ft before losing it in thick cloud. A MAAF radio intercept, apparently of this action, recorded one of the 'two-plus German fighters' breaking off the combat with an armament defect and

Although designated to take his Ar 234 to Osoppo, Werner Muffey (whose T9+KH is shown above) was not the pilot who arrived on 23 February. Eyewitnesses do not recall the man's name but have described scenes like that below of an Ar 234 taking off with rocket assistance. (via Creek)

that 'the last that was heard of them was that they were climbing into the clouds'.

The Spitfires claimed one destroyed and one probable, the Squadron later receiving information that the second aircraft was definitely destroyed. German records confirm only that Gefr. Eberhard Croce of NAGr.11 (Bf 109G-8, W.Nr.201439) was shot down and wounded in the Udine area, while another NAGr.11 G-8 (W.Nr.201054) suffered minor damage from engine trouble during a non-combat flight.

At midday 15 Gustavs of II° Gr.C. took off to intercept a group of B-25s escorted by P-47s. They met near Ghedi, but Cap. Bellagambi's diary records that 4ª and 6ª Sq. unaccountably failed to attack, leaving 5ª to make a firing pass at the P-47s, fly through the bombers and peel back into the sun with no result. Lt Ed King of the 346th FS, 350th FG, tried unsuccessfully to pursue the Bf 109s, blowing out a couple of cylinders in the process and returning to base with an oil-covered P-47.

Eight more P-47s of the same unit had strafed Aviano during the morning, claiming one Bf 109 destroyed and three more damaged. Otherwise during the day there were only ferry or transfer flights. Ju 188 F6+IM arrived at Udine early in the morning but returned to Bergamo later that afternoon; Bf 109 'Yellow 8' left Bergamo after 0700, 'White 15' made the Bergamo-Udine journey during mid-afternoon and four more Messerschmitts left Vicenza around the same time.

Overnight, two Ju 188s were to be ferried to Bergamo and three reconnaissance sorties apparently included photography of shipping at Bari, Taranto, Brindisi and Ancona. A Ju 188 flew radar cover on the route Genoa – southeast of San Remo – north of Cap Corse – southeast of La Spezia – Genoa. Another FAGr.122 aircraft that had taken off at 2100 to cover the Adriatic radioed in at 2326 to say it had only an hour's fuel remaining. Fifty-five minutes later it reported that it was in difficulties, and requested that the runway at Aviano be lit up. No more was heard, and it seems to have got down safely on the last of its petrol.

18 February 1945

While II° Gruppo's pilots were in Pordenone for a meeting with Jafü Oberitalien, the ground personnel had their own moment of glory. Eight Mustang IIIs and IVs of 112 Sqn were attacking targets of opportunity after bombing a bridge near Dogna. Crossing Aviano airfield, they saw aircraft in the revetements and Flt Lt R.V. Hearn ordered the formation to strafe.

In one corner of the field several groundcrewmen ran for cover, S.M. D'Ilario, an armourer, jumping into an empty machine-gun post where a 12.7mm Breda-SAFAT seemed to be waiting for him. Almost instinctively D'Ilario grabbed the gun and began firing at an oncoming Mustang. Flt Lt Hearn's aeroplane was hit just after crossing the perimeter. It trailed white smoke, then burst into flames, climbing to 2,000 ft before crashing in a flat spin in the middle of the aerodrome. Hearn had no chance to bale out; his comrades could hardly believe their eyes, D'Ilario likewise. The DAF pilots flew disconsolately home while jubilation reigned in Aviano – in one way or another II° Gruppo had gained another victory.

19-20 February 1945

At Osoppo during a test-flight the engine of Ten. Di Fiorino's Bf 109G-6 failed on landing approach. It crashed in a wood and was destroyed, the 5ª Sq. pilot being hospitalised with multiple fractures.

Two tactical reconnaissance Rotten were active in the afternoon, returning from the central front area and homing on Vicenza and Villafranca. A photographic mission was flown over Livorno harbour at 2355, Bastia was covered 20min later and radar cover was flown over the Adriatic. The next day saw 'unusual German activities' suggesting new fighter-bombers or nightfighters to MAAF radio monitors. Ferrying in the afternoon included an Fw 190 to Villafranca and two Bf 109s and a Ju 88 to Bergamo. A German aircraft reported undercarriage trouble at 2021.

21 February 1945

Three or four German fighter-bombers (surely Fw 190s of 1./NSGr.9) were on early-morning bombing practice around L. Garda when warning was passed of Allied fighters. They were told to evade or put down and at 0634 one with undercarriage problems was ordered to crash-land. A Bf 109G-8 (W.Nr.200620) from 1./NAGr.11 experienced engine failure during a mission over the Adriatic and was destroyed in the resulting crash at Punta-Salvore, Istria (now Savudrija, Croatia); its pilot was unhurt.

II° Gruppo completed its series of encounters with the 310th BG's Mitchells; 20 Bf 109s scrambled at 1220 to intercept, over Chiusaforte (UD), 21 B-25s escorted by ten Spitfires of 241 Sqn. The weather was cloudy, with 9/10ths strato-cumulus, and the Spitfires saw the Italians first, Sqn Ldr Radcliffe spotting vapour trails above and giving the order to switch to main tanks. Shortly after, ten enemy aircraft were seen approaching from 10 o'clock, so droptanks were jettisoned and the Spits turned towards them in a climb.

The Bf 109s of 4ª and 6ª Sq. were (erroneously again) identified as being mixed with Fw 190s 'with silver cowlings and undersides', while the Bf 109s had 'complete dark camouflaging'[48]. They held course towards the bombers until Red Section's Spitfires dived on them but before contact could be made the Italians half-rolled and dived for the clouds. Plt Off Jenner followed the last Bf 109 (flown by Serg. Patton of 6ª Sq.), closing to 250yd and firing two short bursts from dead astern. He saw the pilot jettison his canopy while disappearing into clouds at 4,500m, trailing smoke.

Meanwhile, Patton had baled out of 'White 3' (nicknamed *Idelma*), landing on a snowy mountainside and getting back to his unit only three days later, after a long journey steering clear of local partisans.

While Cap. Drago's fighters climbed back through the clouds to attack the bombers, Blue Section's Spitfires were attacked by four 'FW-190s' of 5ª Sq., but after a short turning match the Italians disengaged and were lost. After this the Spits noticed another ten hostiles above and to the east (the regrouped Bf 109s of 4ª and 6ª Sq.) but elected to stick by the bombers. A few minutes later, however, Radcliffe radioed to the bombers that he must return to base owing to fuel shortage. They did not reply and the departing Spitfires noticed the Bf 109s still following the B-25s.

Although the RAF reported a subsequent call from the bombers confirming that all was well, 310th BG's diary records six passes by fighters, luckily without result. The Italians nevertheless claimed a Spitfire and a Mitchell (unconfirmed) and the bombers hit the Bf 109 of S.M. Ancillotti (5ª Sq.), who baled out safely. It was another bad day for the Italians; two aircraft lost for no real gain.

The only intended night flight was to transfer F6+KP from Bergamo to Udine.

22 February 1945

At about midday a tactical reconnaissance aircraft abandoned its mission to the central front on sighting Allied bombers and their escort and an hour later another turned back with equipment failure. These may have been the bandits reported by 'Cooler' to the 66th FS: one ten miles north of Pistoia at 26,000ft, the other north of Bologna.

There were three separate instances where German aircraft were heard on night-flying training round Villafranca and Ferrara, one being ordered to lose height and warned of Allied intruders over its base. The latter were eight P-47s of the 66th FS, up to dive-bomb Villafranca. Their leader saw two red smoke pots, one at each end of the runway, and then, at 3,000ft and heading north over the field's southeast corner, an Fw 190. The Americans jettisoned bombs and gave chase, but lost the Focke-Wulf in haze and ground fog.

'The usual long range recce' was plotted 45 miles east of Rimini and chased by a 600 Sqn aeroplane at 26,000ft.

23 February 1945

This was successful day for the 350th FG, and a particularly bad one for the Luftwaffe, bringing the last combat fatalities in 2.(F)/122. It began inauspiciously when Me 410 F6+CK took off for the front at 0844, crewed by Ltn. Franz Girlich and Uffz. Walter Kemna. About half an hour later, using the phonetic callsign Cäsar-Kurfürst, they radioed Bergamo, requesting illumination of the flarepath, apparently because of fog, and landed with some kind of technical breakdown. At 1037 they were off again in F6+NK (Me 410B-3, W.Nr.190169). Warnings of Allied fighters were broadcast to them at 1120 and 1134 and at 1207 they were south of Piacenza, heading north.

Twenty miles south of Parma they ran into the P-47s of Orchid Section, 347th FS, 350th FG, returning from dive-bombing the Ora (BZ) rail diversion. 2nd/Lt Jim Young takes up the story:

> . . . it was my 15th mission . . . we were getting low on gas and ammo, so started home at 10,000 feet. Somebody in the flight spotted a bogey at 2 or 3 o'clock at the same altitude, so we turned and gave chase. When the German saw us he hit the deck. Flight Leader Powers[49] fired the rest of his ammo and there was a thin stream of grey smoke coming from [the German's] port engine.
>
> I remember using water injection to get "enuf" speed to keep up with the 410. The enemy 'plane tried to use evasive action by pulling straight up from the deck to 900-1100 feet, then pushed the nose back to the deck. I kept firing small bursts . . . and could see some hits on the 410. I remember we flew 10-15 minutes (it seemed that long) at top speeds . . . and I kept firing short bursts at him. Finally he was at treetop level with his port engine trailing smoke, and my ammo finally hit his starboard engine. The plane dipped his right wing and hit the ground in a big ball of flame.

Nordpol-Kurfürst exploded in a field just 15 miles from the comparative safety of Ghedi aerodrome. Both crew were killed.

Just after 1400, two NAGr.11 Bf 109s, Bettler ('Beggar') 1 and 2, had to abort their mission to the eastern part of the front on encountering four Spitfires. At 1424 one of the Messerschmitts reported engine trouble. An Allied reconnaissance aircraft reported an attack by three Bf 109s over Udine.

A P-47 flight from the 346th FS on armed reconnaissance ran across what it believed at first to be a pair of SAAF P-40s with belly tanks, then either Fw 190s or Fiat G.55s, near Vicenza and apparently heading for either Campoformido or Aviano. The bogeys carried black crosses outlined in white on their wings and 1st/Lt Ed Kregloh and his wingman

Fg Off 'Bull' Hosey, whose first combat mission this was, jumped them. As Hosey tells it: '. . . we were about 100 feet above the ground. . . . there were two airplanes flying side by side . . . They were painted different than our airplanes and they appeared to be camouflaged. I . . . heard [Kregloh] say, "They're Germans!"

I immediately opened fire on the left 'plane [and] pieces began to fly off . . . I was about 75 yards behind and closing rapidly [and] saw that he had been shot up very badly . . . on his back, nosing down towards the ground.'

It was 1515, about 10km northwest of Cittadella and Hosey had shot down a Bf 109G-6/R2 (W.Nr.230164, Black 10) of 1./NAGr.11, killing Fw. Ludwig Soukup.

Kregloh pursued the other Bf 109 for about 50 miles, claiming to have flown so low that he could look up at the windows of houses as he passed, while his wingman recalls: '. . . trying to decide which side of the smokestacks to go around . . . I always thought this was a hell of a way to start a new man on his first mission.' They were into tree-covered Alpine foothills before the German gradually pulled away and, thanks to his camouflage, lost them.

A group of Fw 190s had been heard that morning, probably training, and from 1505 Allied monitors again overheard German fighter-bombers in the Lake Garda area. Shortly after 1524 two of them landed, reporting fuel shortage and engine trouble. A 1./NSGr.9 Fw 190F-8 (W.Nr.584549) which incurred 30 per cent damage from 'technical deficiencies' at Villafranca was probably one of this pair.

When Allied fighters were detected approaching from the west, the Germans were ordered to disperse and to fly low over an airfield. This matches a report from eight 57th FG P-47s which, about to dive-bomb Villafranca, saw four Bf 109s flying south at low level over the field. After bombing they searched unsuccessfully for these hostiles in the thick haze. These were more likely to have been Fw 190s than Messerschmitts and at least four of the same unit were up again on a night training flight. During the day, several I° Gr.C. pilots went to Orio al Serio to take delivery of Bf 109s, briefly interrupted by three P-47s strafing and bombing the field at 1600. None of the Messerschmitts was damaged and soon the Italians left for Lonate. Cap. Barioglio crashed on take-off but emerged unscathed from the wreck.

In Osoppo there was great excitement as an Arado Ar 234 landed and Cap. Bellagambi had to run and stop Italian groundcrew from shooting at the strange machine. A new Ju 188, CZ+BR (W.Nr.0590, later

I° Gr.C. had the privilege of being probably the first non-German fighter unit to receive Bf 109K-4s, with three delivered by February 1945. One of these is depicted at Lonate Pozzolo just after its arrival, with personnel swarming inquisitively over it. This particular aircraft was later coded '3-17' and assigned to the 'Sezione di Gruppo', a sort of Staff flight like II° Gr.C. already had.

F6+CM) was delivered to Ghedi from Riem during the evening; it was to achieve the rare distinction of surviving the war intact and in Italy. Three Ju 188 night sorties were mounted, and a D-2 (W.Nr.150544) of 6.(F)/122 suffered 50 per cent damage in a bad landing at Bergamo.

24-27 February 1945

Compared with the previous day, the 24th was relatively calm, although the 66th FS again lost two single-engined bandits in haze, 10 miles southwest of Villafranca. A Bf 109G-10/AS with MW 50 injection arrived in Osoppo, and T.Col. Alessandrini went there to bid farewell to the members of 5ª Sq. before handing over command of IIº Gr. to Magg. Carlo Miani.

Between 1525 and 1604, Riem signalled to Lonate the departure of nine Bf 109s, probably new aircraft for Iº Gr.C. MAAF Sigint noted four night reconnaissance sorties, and the dropping of a parachutist near Siena points to one of these being a Carmen operation. Number 600 Sqn sent five intruders to Udine in search of the nightfighters now believed to be operating from there.

The 25th saw the start of a run of accidents when a pair of Bf 109s was heard homing on Fiume (now Rijeka, Croatia) from 1038, one of them with engine trouble crashing just short of its destination. Ultra later revealed that it had been hit by German flak during a reconnaissance of the Yugoslav coast. A later signal implied that these were Yugoslav-based aircraft that had, on account either of bad weather or technical trouble, strayed into Italian airspace without clearance.

The 26th saw just three night reconnaissances and four suspected fighter-bombers homing and landing in the Ghedi area. One of the reconnaissance aeroplanes escaped a 600 Sqn Mosquito at low level, releasing chaff in the chase.

The next evening a defecting Hungarian Fw 58 (K3+58), with lowered wheels and trailing a white cloth from the cabin window, made landfall between Fermo and Pescara, unchallenged by Allied fighters or AA. Its pilot, Generalmajor Ladislaus Hary, bringing along his wife and children and the managing director of an aircraft company, landed at an emergency field just south of San Vito (TE).

The intense activity of IIº Gr.'s training section led to a small mishap when Serg. Archidiacono (6ª Sq.) crashed one its seven G-6s on take-off. W.Nr.161798 suffered only 10 per cent damage, but this was enough to render it u/s and cause a lot of trouble for S.Ten. Di Santo, who as training Leader was held responsible for all accidents.

An Fw 190 of 1./NSGr.9 crashed at Villafranca and four others spent an hour practising formation flights over the Po Valley during the afternoon. From 1837 two were again airborne, apparently on a defensive sortie against Allied bombers in the Verona-Ferrara region. Radio traffic included talk of bomber flares and orders to attack and there is some evidence of engagements taking place. There were two night reconnaissances – one entailing the low-level evasion of a pursuing Mosquito – and Ju 188 CZ+BR made the short trip from Ghedi to its permanent base at Bergamo in the hands of a pilot named Anders.

28 February 1945

While Carmen operated successfully on the night of 28 February/1 March, trouble hit two of FAGr.122's sorties[50], one being curtailed by engine trouble in a 6. Staffel Ju 188D-2 (W.Nr.150512). The aircraft belly-landed at Bergamo with 40 per cent damage and injuries to two crew members, pilot Uffz. Happel and wireless operator Fw. Steinkönig, both of whom had been hurt in a crash a month earlier.

Worse was to follow for Ltn. Fritz Wöllert's Ju 188D-2 (W.Nr.230412) of 4. Staffel, returning from a photographic mission over Naples. He evaded a Mosquito XIX of 255 Sqn, dropping Düppel during the chase, but was picked up again by the Mosquito NF Mk.30 of Capt Lawrence E. Englert and 2nd/Lt Earl R. Dickey of the 416th NFS and shot down northwest of Cremona at around 2300. Wöllert was killed with three of his crew. The sole (wounded) survivor was Fw. Heinz Schlenaider, one of the two wireless operators. One of them may have been a special 'early-warning' operator, carried to listen out for threatening enemy signals.

Ground control called the missing aircraft for some time afterwards and there was a dramatic sequel for Englert and Dickey. As a result of sustained high-speed climb during the pursuit their starboard engine caught fire and they had to bale out over home base. Theirs was the 416th NFS's only victory for 1945, despite 370 sorties and eight lost aircraft.

Notes

47. I and J were then practically interchangeable in handwritten German.
48. These differences may be explained by the presence of both 'old' and 'new' Bf 109s: the later versions painted in dark greens, the older ones in greys.
49. Lt John E. Powers, killed in action only three days later.
50. However another visited Corsica and Sardinia, achieving full coverage of La Maddalena at 2125.

An artfully composed shot of a 6ª Sq. pilot. Although still retaining the 4ª Sq. badge on its engine cover, this Bf 109G-10/AS had, by the time of the photo, been incorporated in 6ª Sq., as confirmed by the 'White 11' repeated on the nose.

Chapter 13

March 1945

Italy's place among Luftwaffe priorities is well summed up by a telegram dated 9 March from General Christian of the OKL Operations Staff to Komm.Gen. Chief of Staff, Oberst Paul Gottschling:

> Luftwaffe forces in the Reich and on the Eastern Front are so heavily engaged . . . that the transfer of units to other fronts is no longer possible. Moreover, transfers on any appreciable scale could not be carried out owing to the difficult fuel situation.
>
> The plan to dispatch reinforcements to [Italy] in the event of an enemy landing must therefore be cancelled. Defensive operations will be carried out with the forces at present available . . . in Italy.

Ten days later OKW was ordering Ob.SW to surrender further elements from his flak forces. A protest was lodged on the 21st that, aside from two Italian fighter Gruppi and the two Fw 190 Staffeln being brought up, the whole air defence burden fell upon the flak. Moreover only limited fighter operations were possible given the fuel situation. Presumably Ob.SW was referring to the Fw 190s already in Italy: Stab NAGr.11 and 1./NSGr.9, although the former was well below Staffel strength. Both could perhaps be described as 'being brought up' to full operational status and there were many reports of the type operating as a fighter by day and night over Italy at this time.

The Ground War

There were no major developments, although Kesselring was transferred to become Ob. West with effect from 9 March. To succeed him, Vietinghoff was recalled from Kurland, flying back via OKW's Zossen HQ on the 12th and formally taking over both the Southwest Theatre and Army Group C from the 19th. Allied preparations for the spring offensive continued, with an intensified air effort against substitute fuel sources and transport links to the front. Railway lines in Austria were interdicted and diplomatic pressure exerted on the Swiss to stop the passage of German trains carrying food and non-warlike supplies through their neutral country.

Fuel

The remorseless deterioration continued. Stocks of B4 sank from $317m^3$ on 1 March to $218m^3$ on the 26th; A3 for aircraft such as the Fi 156 stood at $56m^3$ on the 11th; C3 fell from $310m^3$ at the start of the month to $138m^3$ on the 26th. The consumption of J2 was enough to fill the internal tanks of an Ar 234 about 11 or 12 times.

An intriguing oddity was the message on the 19th from Komm. Gen. to Operations Staff Croatia that 10 tonnes ($14m^3$) of B4 had been made ready for ferrying Caproni aircraft at Milan-Taliedo; confirmation was requested that a similar amount was available at Zagreb, but we have no idea what all this was for.

The Luftwaffe

Jets

Luftwaffe jet aircraft became fully operational in Italy during March. On the 1st the Komm.Gen. strength return showed one Ar 234 of (as the British translated it) 'Special Staff Götz' on hand, although unserviceable, and 382m³ of J2 available for it. We assume that this was the same Arado that had flown into Osoppo on 24 February, and all our evidence leads us to guess that it must have departed during the early part of March. It has not been possible to establish the exact date but the 4m³ drop in stocks of jet fuel between the 1st and the 11th would have fuelled an Arado with a little to spare.

There is much firmer evidence regarding the arrival of a permanent jet reconnaissance presence in the theatre. Erich Sommer recollects receiving fresh orders to establish a Kommando in Italy on 28 February. Equipment to replace that lost in the train-strafing had arrived from Kdo. Sperling, in the charge of Oblt. Mänhard. During a visit to Oranienburg on 10 March, Sommer had taken the precaution of equipping his aircraft with a Magirusbombe centreline pack, containing two MG 151/20 cannon, acquired from the stocks of the Versuchsverband's experimental Ar 234 nightfighter flight. The next day he reported to Gen.d.A Barsewisch at Würzburg and had his aeroplane's gunsight calibrated on the 12th. By this time Oblt. Loah had left for Italy in charge of the new Kommando's ground personnel and his intended posting as Staffelkapitän of 1.(F)/33 never took effect. Indeed, Sommer only learned of it some 44 years later!

Sommer flew from Biblis via Lechfeld to Campoformido on 14 March and found his other two pilots, they having come down from Oranienburg by way of Riem, which was both the base of the Ar 234 unit 1.(F)/100 and out-station of Luftwaffe Italien. Probably these two Arados were the ones referred to in the G.d.A.'s 26 February note as being in readiness at Oranienburg. The pilots and aircraft of new detachment were:

Oberleutnant Erich Sommer   W.Nr.140344   T9+EH
Leutnant Günther Gniesmer   W.Nr.140142   T9+DH
Stabsfeldwebel Walter Arnold   –   T9+FH

The Kommando's arrival had been well prepared for. Carefully camouflaged dispersal areas and blast shelters had been constructed at Campoformido and Lonate, and alternate landing grounds were apparently made ready at Bergamo, Ghedi and Villafranca, although it is doubtful that these were ever used and Sommer himself says that there was J2 only at home base, Lonate and Osoppo. Specially trained ground crews were on hand to tend the jets. Berlin noted that the Kommando was present and at full strength[51] on the 17th.

Close attention was also paid to security procedures. The unit's sorties were regulated by the Jafü organisation and if their base was threatened while they were aloft the Arados would be diverted to land elsewhere. Once on the ground (at Lonate, if not Campoformido), in addition to the usual camouflage netting, the nacelles were fitted with dummy wooden propellers in an attempt to delude Allied reconnaissance. Furthermore, Sommer ordered that, wherever one of his aeroplanes landed, Flying Control should erase both times and aircraft markings from its logbook. This distrust extended to the loyalties of the civilian population adjoining the dispersal areas and to the security of the telephone system (e.g. an Ar 234 take-off was notified simply as '986').

The first few days were also spent establishing liaison with Jafü staff and radio interception units in the Tagliamento Valley. There was much scavenging and/or improvising of all manner of necessary supplies. Kommando Sommer had no photo-processing facilities of its own, and was dependent on those of NAGr.11, for example. Personnel were quartered in Ceresetto (UD), about 3 miles north of the airfield, although a document of 20 March refers to 'Kommando Götz . . . Torreano, NW Udine'.

Reconnaissance
Elsewhere in the reconnaissance forces there was a lot of upheaval. On the 8th Obstlt. Domnick was posted from FAGr.122 to command FAGr.4, and was succeeded by Hptm. Maetzel. On the 14th the disbandment was ordered of 2.(F)/122 and Stab and 1./NAGr.11. The reasoning behind some of this is set out in a signal of 13 March from General Christian to Ob.SW. Responding to a query from Kesselring dated 4 March, Christian explained that the tasks of 2.(F)/122 and some of those of NAGr.11 would be assumed by the new Ar 234 Kommando, and that accordingly 2./122 and *2./11* (the latter is obviously an error) were to be disbanded right away. The disbandment of 4.(F) and 6.(F)/122 was not envisaged in the short term, but was ultimately inevitable. OKL would try to keep one Staffel in being for as long as possible, and collect within it specialist aircraft and crews for both Hohentwiel and night photography operations. In this way it would probably be possible to sustain the Staffel's existence until late Autumn of 1945.

To strengthen reconnaissance in the Italian theatre, it was planned to bring in 1.(F)/22 about the end of April. This unit had left Norway on 21 January, to convert to the Ar 234 at Jüterbog-Waldlager, and Hptm. Fuchs had been named as its Kapitän on 8 March. Once in Italy it was to absorb and take over from Kdo. Sommer, which would be disbanded.

Reality differed, 1./22 never arrived[52], 1./11 lasted another three weeks, and 2./122 flew three abortive and one successful operational sorties *after* its 'immediate disbandment', radio traffic suggesting that Villafranca was used as an advance base for these missions. The last new Me 410 (BS+CG/F6+EK) was delivered to Ghedi from Riem on 2 March, its 'career' in Italy consisting of one abortive sortie on the 20th, lasting 8 min. However, the success of Sommer's jets was such that Berlin was asked on the 29th to permit the photographic staff released by the proposed disbandments to fill vacancies in the remaining units. The improved coverage being achieved by the Ar 234s had considerably increased the technicians' workload.

NAGr.11's Bf 109s were active in Schwarm and Rotte strength in the first half of the month, achieving up to eight sorties a day. Photo coverage was flown of both the east and west coasts as well as sea surveillance. Fw 190s flew armed reconnaissance on the 6th (two aircraft in the Bologna area) and 9th (four, central front area). A total of only 38 nocturnal sorties was recorded between the 2nd and the 25th (none was flown during the remainder of the month), all attributed – erroneously – by MAAF to 4.(F)/ and 6.(F)/122. Sixteen flights were detected over the Adriatic and four over the Ligurian, with Aviano and Campoformido[53] serving as advanced bases, although Bergamo retained its pre-eminence.

The southern extent of the Adriatic sorties could not be determined, but positions off Istria were sometimes quoted and returning aircraft frequently crossed the coast between the Po Estuary and Venice. Knowing this was one thing, preventing it another and 600 Sqn's ORB noted on 2 March, after the third unsuccessful pursuit of a low-level contact in a week:

> These reconnaissance aircraft have had a long spell of success, their chief advantage appears to be that they are equipped with every aid . . . their ability to fly right down low is due to their being equipped with a really efficient Radio Altimeter. They have a fast aircraft . . . plotted at 385 mph on the deck, and . . . backward looking AI of a range from 3 to 6 kilometres. Plus all this, there is no doubt that their crews are well trained and really know their business.

Not to mention using Düppel. The luck of the nightfighters, if not of 600 Sqn itself, improved a little during the month however.

Kommando Carmen

The Germans recorded operations by the Kommando on the nights of the 2/3rd, 5/6th, 6/7th and 7/8th; the Allies arrested agents dropped on the 6th and 22nd. One apprehended in Rome confessed to having been among a party of four dropped in a container by parachute. This was the PAG (Personenabwürfgerät = personnel dropping device), a 4m x 1m plywood cylinder with four parachutes at one end and coiled, inflated rubber tubing under a domed cap at the other to absorb landing shock. In between was 'accommodation' for three passengers[54] suspended in woven, elasticated hammocks. The device was carried on an external bomb rack, with only minimal ground clearance at its tail end, and a (supposedly reassuring) telephone link to the aircraft's crew.

On 12 March Carmen's Ltn. Thurnhuber was awarded the Ritterkreuz in a ceremony at Bergamo.

Mistel

On the 18th KG 200's Navigation Officer signalled II. Gruppe (the Mistel composite aircraft unit) that aircraft security data for the Italian theatre were being sent to them immediately. Since similar material had already been promised for other fronts, the Allies deduced that the unit was simply building up a

---

A Bf 109G-10/AS of 4ª Sq. This 'Black 12' replaced the aircraft with the same number shot down on 12 February and was flown by S.M. Cavagliano until almost the end of the war. The most noticeable detail is the complete absence of ANR markings, something that became increasingly common within IIº Gruppo.

complete collection rather than specifically intending to operate in Italy.

Night Attack

NSGr.9 operated on only about six or seven nights, evaluated by MAAF as involving training on new aircraft. There was again suspicion of Fw 190s flying as nightfighters, one such unsuccessful sortie being logged over the Po Valley on the the 18th. Werner Hensel of 1./9 is said to have shot down a nightfighter (a Mosquito according to Pohl) in March or April. On 31 March, Capt. Webster of CSDIC (Air) wrote to a colleague: 'There has been considerable interest . . . at DAF in possible new methods of radar control of German nightfighters. I wish they might be able to lure some of them sufficiently far south to fall into our hands.'

The ANR

The two operational ANR fighter Gruppi saw combat on a limited scale, and yet again the Italian pilots were denigrated, this time by MAAF. Even after allowing for the 'dry tank blight': '. . . the intention of the Italian Republican pilots to engage our aircraft must be questioned, as a minimum of combats occurred, and several sightings were reported in which the enemy fighters were going the other way.' Adding insult to injury, there was even a theory to cover cases of indisputable courage and aggression: 'There was some evidence that these were Italian pilots flying swastika-marked aircraft, but the operation was un-Italian in nature, and the possibility of a small German unit of day fighters being based in Northeastern Italy must be considered.'

Whilst we too, believe that German aircraft did double as day fighters on a small scale, it seems to have been easier for some to believe that the Luftwaffe – with the Anglo-Americans crossing the Rhine and the Red Army across the Oder – was able to spare a fighter unit for Italy, than to acknowledge Italian bravery. There were a great many factors bearing on the relative ineffectiveness of the ANR but there is no reason to believe that an endemic lack of courage was among them.

I° Gruppo Caccia

March began with pilots completing their acclimatisation to the new airfields. The somewhat rugged taxying and take-off surfaces did not suit the Bf 109's delicate undercarriage, engendering a string of problems, small and large. Another major source of trouble was strong partisan activity in the area around I° Gruppo's airfields and quarters. This had increased in intensity in recent weeks, clashing both with strict security measures in force on the bases and Magg. Visconti's temper.

On the 5th, following the disappearance of Ten. Mangiapane, a Staff Flight pilot, Visconti led a group of armed aircraftmen with two trucks to cordon off the villages of Cardano al Campo, Ferno and Samarate while searching for the officer. No particular violence occurred and only seven out of 40 people arrested were finally detained, but such episodes, combined with the charismatic figure and strong temperament of I° Gr.C.'s Commander, clearly made him a target for revenge.

German pilots ferried replacement aircraft from Bergamo and München-Riem, and on the 7th the unit made its first formation flight. On the next day they had a visit from the experimental torpedo-carrying Fiat G.55 (MM.97084), flown to Lonate from Venegono by Cap. Mantelli, its test pilot.

On the 22nd the two Bücker Bü 181s previously with II° Gr.C. (see below) arrived in Lonate to improve I° Gruppo's pilots' gunnery also.

II° Gruppo Caccia

The first of March was the first anniversary of the unit's creation and the event was celebrated with a dinner involving the ANR's Under-Secretary, Gen. Bonomi and its Chief-of-Staff, T.Col. Baylon. At the same time T.Col. Alessandrini relinquished command of the Gruppo to Magg. Miani.

Oblt. Erich Sommer, CO of the sole jet unit to operate in Italy. From 19 March 1945 the Ar 234s of Kommando Sommer carried out reconnaissance flights over the front line and the main Allied ports in Italy, Corsica and Southern France.

There was little to celebrate, operations being necessarily constrained by the constant presence of enemy fighter-bombers watching for the slightest sign of activity on the Italian bases and thoroughly bombing all the targets around Pordenone. Nonetheless, training flights and the delivery of new aircraft continued both in Aviano and Osoppo.

Following the combat on the 3rd, things were quiet until two accidents on the 7th. In Osoppo a Bf 109G-6 (W.Nr.161428, Yellow 5) crashed during a training flight, seriously wounding S.M. Neri[55], while at Aviano a I° Gruppo pilot, Serg. Taberna, damaged the dual-control G-12 (W.Nr.162331, White 20) halting training yet again. Meanwhile (probably because of the meagre 'real' results of recent combats), a couple of German instructors arrived at Aviano with two Bücker Bü 181s to give an aerial gunnery training course. The aircraft carried gun-cameras and each Italian pilot had to try and keep his sights on the 'enemy' Bücker as long as possible while its German pilot flew complex manoeuvres. It is not known whether this training had the desired results, since deficient marksmanship was only one among many adverse factors the Italian pilots by now had to face but it is remarkable that the Germans felt it necessary, even at this late stage.

On the 13th good news arrived for 5ª Sq. in the shape of ten new Bf 109s. These, with three more on the following day, transformed the Diavoli Rossi line-up, and they now disposed of 20 Messerschmitts. The Bü 181s continued their classes in Osoppo, although a sudden decision on the 16th stopped the training section's flights at Aviano.

The following week brought forth a strange revival of interest by the 'Top Brass' in the unit; Oberst von Borg, T.Col. Vizzotto, Maj. Zahn (Jafü Operations Officer), T.Col. Bonzano and T.Col. Alessandrini all visited the Group on separate occasions. Two accidents occurred in Osoppo, to S.Ten. Spreca on 16 March and S.Ten. Dinale on the 19th. Both escaped unhurt.

Battle was rejoined on the 23rd, but there then followed another lull up to the end of the month, with only two events on 28 March worth reporting. The Training Section resumed its flights with M.llo Covre in charge, and four pilots of 4ª Sq. were deployed to Osoppo to operate with 5ª Sq.

III° Gruppo Caccia

On 2 March Oberst Lützow visited the Gruppo in Holzkirchen. There he found 45 pilots, of whom 14 had flown the Macchi C.200 and 17 the Cr.42 – but not since September 1943. He assessed training needs in relation to the men's experience and the time each needed to spend on the Bf 108, Bf 109G-12 trainer (18 landings was the norm) and Bf 109G-6. What by Allied standards would have been a drastically abbreviated programme would require 36,000 litres of aviation fuel – a figure he underlined twice and followed by two exclamation marks.

Order of Battle

Strengths on 1 March were:

Unit	Aircraft	
	Number	Type
Stab/FAGr.122	0	
2.(F)/122	3(3)	Me 410B-3
4.(F)/122	2(1)	Ju 188D-2
	2(2)	Ju 88T-3
6.(F)/122	8(6)	Ju 188D-2
Kdo. Carmen	2/3	Ju 188
Stab/NAGr.11	4	Fw 190A-8
1./NAGr.11	13(6)	Bf 109G
2./NAGr.11	19(11)	Bf 109G
Sonderst. Götz	1(0)	Ar 234B-2
Stab/NSGr.9	1(1)	Ju 87D
1./NSGr.9	7(4)	Fw 190F-8/F-9
2./NSGr.9	10(9)	Ju 87D
3./NSGr.9	15(13)	Ju 87D
I° Gr.C.	29	Bf 109G/K
II° Gr.C.	36(29)	Bf 109G[56]
III° Gr.C. (training)	16(6)	Bf 109G
I° Gr. Aerosil. (forming)	13?	S.79ter.

Notes

51. 54 officers and men, according to Sommer.
52. It was ordered disbanded at Lübeck-Blankensee on 19 April.
53. A detachment of FAGr.122 was addressed there on the 30th, for example.
54. There was a one-person version as well.
55. The authors' researches accidentally revealed that this pilot was not the 'real' Neri, but one Armando Briglia who had come into possession of Neri's documents (the true owner not having answered the call of the newly-forming ANR) and impersonated him. He thus became a pilot, training at Venaria Reale, then being assigned to II° Gr.C.
56. Further interesting information comes again from Magg. Bellagambi's diary, recording the strength of his 5ª Sq. on 14 March:

0 – W.Nr. 782309 (G-14[AS?])	11 – W.Nr. 784933 (G-14[AS?])
1 – W.Nr. 464380 (G-14)	12 – W.Nr. 785910 (G-14[AS?])
1 – W.Nr 785749 (G-14[AS?])	13 – W.Nr. 464446 (G-14)
2 – W.Nr. 491313 (G-10/AS)	13 – W.Nr 785731 (G-14)
3 – W.Nr. 464430 (G-14)	14 – W.Nr 784118 (G-14)
3 – W.Nr. 785061 (G-14)	15 – W.Nr. 413685 (G-14/AS)
4 – W.Nr. 787470 (G-14[AS?])	16 – W.Nr 464464 (G-14)
5 – W.Nr. 464480 (G-14)	
6 – W.Nr. 491319 (G-10/AS)	
8 – W.Nr. 780838 (G-14)	
9 – W.Nr. 780869 (G-14)	

Dispersed in the woods around Osoppo, Magg. Bellagambi's Bf 109G-14 'Yellow 1' is serviced. This aircraft shows some interesting details, like the tall tailwheel, the rudder camouflage and the Squadriglia's badge applied on a dark green patch, but the unique feature is the black fuselage Balkenkreuz, to date the only example ever seen on a Bf 109.

BELOW:
During March 1945, German instructors with two Bü 181s made the rounds of the ANR fighter units to test the Italians' level of air-to-air marksmanship. The results were less than encouraging and here M.llo Forlani of 1ª Sq., I° Gr.C. is about to receive further instruction. (Forlani)

Chapter 13

Operations

1-2 March 1945

On the night of 1/2 March a lone aircraft strafed Highway 65 south of Bologna and one reconnaissance sortie was flown. Two Ju 188s were out the next night, one unsuccessfully chased at low altitude by a 600 Sqn Mosquito; Allied night bombers in their turn reported seeing 12 single-engined hostiles, one of which attacked.

3 March 1945

While two pairs of NAGr.11 Bf 109s accomplished their respective missions over the sea and to the Po Estuary, a Schwarm sent to photograph Ancona was driven back by bad weather.

During an attack by Marauders from Nos. 12, 24 and 30 (SAAF) Sqns on the Conegliano (TV) marshalling yards, a 'mixed dozen Fw190s and Me109s' intervened. Twenty-two Bf 109s of II° Gr.C. had scrambled from Aviano and Osoppo at 1030. At 1041, near Pordenone, they radioed in a sighting report and three minutes later 5ª and 6ª Squadriglie opened the attack, soon followed by 4ª. They went for a 12 Sqn box escorted by four Spitfires of 4 (SAAF) Sqn. As 12 Sqn's report related:

> ... the third box was attacked by enemy fighters on the bombing run. The leader succeeded in dropping his bombs on the Western approach to the yards. No.2 had his starboard engine made unserviceable, as a result first of a hit by flak and then of strikes by enemy cannon shells.
>
> The enemy fighters ... 1 Fw 190 and 9 Me 109s went on to attack the first and second boxes ... two minutes after bombing, a running fight ensued between our gunners and the fighters, which lasted about 10 minutes. The aircraft of the third box who had been split-up, were followed for about 15 minutes until they reached the coast at Tagliamento Point. 1 Me 109 is claimed probably destroyed and 2 Me 109s damaged ...

In the meantime the remaining Messerschmitts surprised the escorts, shooting down Lt Reim who, as 'Tail-end Charlie', was naturally the first to be attacked. He was able to bale out successfully at 16,000ft. In the ensuing combat two enemy aircraft (identified as Fw 190s) were claimed as damaged by the Leader, Lt Pretorious, and Lt Neser.

Meanwhile, over the Adriatic, a section of aircraft of 4ª Sq. led by Cap. Drago (Bf 109G-10/AS/U4, W.Nr.491353, Black 7) took on a group of six bombers. S.Ten Squassoni (Black 13) and Ten. Valenzano (Bf 109G-10/AS, W.Nr.491323, Black 3) each claimed a Marauder. The claimants from 4ª and 6ª Sq. were *Capitani* Bellagambi (his tenth and final kill) and Luccardi; Ten. Ferrero; S.M. Mazzanti and Zanardi. By 1056 the Italians had been outdistanced over the sea and were back on the ground a quarter of an hour later.

None of the Marauders was lost in these actions, but two landed with wounded aboard and an engine out (HD649 'P' at Ravenna and HD612 'N' at Cervia), hardly matching the Italians' claim of seven bombers.

The confusion of combat is well illustrated by Ten. Betti (4ª Sq.) who followed his prey out over the Adriatic, finally scoring hits and turning back only when: '... the bomber dissolved in a cloud of debris that I barely escaped!' The way 3 (SAAF) Wing saw it was: '. . . while limping home, B-26 'P' was followed by a single Me 109 which was eventually shaken off by throwing in his face a bundle of the latest "FRONT POST".' The 'debris' had been propaganda leaflets, influencing the enemy a bit faster than usual.

S.M. Cusmano (Bf 109G-6 W.Nr.163842, Yellow 0) was shot down and killed by the bombers' defensive fire north of Castelfranco Veneto (TV). M.llo Covre's aircraft lost its canopy after being hit by Spitfires, and was forced to return to Aviano, where M.llo Girace's Bf 109G-6 (W.Nr. 163197, Yellow 15) was 40 per cent damaged in an emergency landing. That of the wounded S.M. Sanson (Bf 109G-10/AS, W.Nr.490379, Yellow 8) suffered similarly when it came down a few miles away. Fate was perhaps especially cruel to S.M. Wladimiro Zerini of 6ª Sq., who had emerged unscathed from his first combat and was returning at low level to Aviano when his aircraft (Bf 109G-6, W.Nr.160766) overflew German Panzers on the road near Pordenone. Fearing a strafing attack, the Germans opened up with machine-guns, bringing down the Messerschmitt and killing its young pilot.

Once again, claims and losses are hard to reconcile. The Italian teletype claimed six Marauders and a Spitfire for the loss of two Bf 109s, but IIº Gr.C.'s records make no mention of the South African fighter – the only genuine kill achieved! Perhaps a German-piloted Fw 190 *was* responsible; some were based nearby, and Ultra reported 28 fighter sorties on this date, whereas we are sure of only 22 by the ANR.

That evening at least three night attack sorties were mounted, two of them as a range calibration test for the Egon system, and NSGr.9 lost probably its first Fw 190 in combat. Midwood Copper, the 350th FG's dusk patrol, was aloft around 1717 GMT when No.10 FSU warned of approaching hostiles which appeared some *13 minutes* later,[57] allowing ample time to get into a favourable position.

There were two Fw 190s, and Lt Sigmund E. Hausner and his wingman, Lt Wylder, spearheaded the attack. While engaging one Focke-Wulf (reported by Wylder as a P-47!) which split-S'ed then blew up, Hausner hit flying debris and lost control of his Thunderbolt. Both aircraft fell burning and one parachute opened, that of Hausner, who was taken prisoner. (He was imprisoned in Nuremburg but, on his third escape attempt, got back to his Squadron). Less fortunate was Hptm Willi Wilzopolski, Staffelkapitän of 1./NSGr.9, killed when his Fw 190F-8 (W.Nr.583576) exploded about 20 miles north of Bologna. In the rapidly gathering darkness the second Fw escaped, radioing at 1741 that its companion had probably fallen prey to enemy fighters, and landing back at Villafranca at 1756.

NSGr.9 soon had some inadvertent revenge, as described in the diary of Lt. Oscar Wilkinson of 347th FS for 3 March: 'Jerry bombed us tonight. It was the first time I had heard bombs from ground. Our field threw up a lot of flak.'

The following night's spectacle was more pleasant, a showing of Bogart and Bacall's *To Have and Have Not.*

During the night of 3/4 March, Allied night bombers on the way to Pola reported sightings of three Fw 190s, and three long-range reconnaissance missions were flown. These included search cover of the Ligurian and Adriatic Seas and flash photography of Livorno harbour. Attempted photography of Ancona harbour had to be broken off twice owing to technical trouble.

4-11 March 1945

On the 4th the pilot of one of the eight NAGr.11 Messerschmitts out that day reconnoitred the east coast battle area shortly after midday and was homing by 1302, first checking the air situation en route with his controller. The next day, early morning cover was flown on the circuit Pola–Ravenna–Venice–Marano (UD). An Adriatic radar reconnaissance took place that night, and one or two aircraft were out almost every night until the 25/26th.

In daylight on the 6th Fw 190s strafed Highway 65 in three separate incidents, and another, an A-8 of Stab/NAGr.11 (W.Nr.172706), suffered 30 per cent damage at 'Airfield 705', apparently owing to pilot error. Next day the Gruppe's 1. Staffel lost two Bf 109G-6s to engine failure; W.Nr.410531 in an emergency landing southeast of Latisana (UD) and W.Nr.230272 crashed at Campoformido.

Kdo. Carmen operated from 0130-0501 on the 8th and reported success. An unusual flight, 'possibly connected with agent-dropping activity', was again plotted on the night of the 8/9th, when what was thought to be a Ju 188 came inland from the Adriatic near Termoli, crossed the west coast near Naples and returned to the Adriatic by way of Foggia.

On the 9th 1./NSGr.9 had an Fw 190F-8 (W.Nr.584577) 10 per cent damaged in a belly landing at Mantua during a training sortie. North of the city another two 'probable' Focke-Wulfs intercepted an Allied reconnaissance aircraft. That night a German victory of a sort was achieved off Cap Corse when a Mosquito of 255 Sqn flew into the sea while chasing a low-level reconnaissance aeroplane. The score was paid off to a degree next day, when Bergamo was shot up and a Ju 188D-2 (W.Nr.150514) of 6.(F)/122 was destroyed.

The series of accidents that was to plague I° Gr.C.'s second tour of operations continued on this date when 25 Bf 109s set out at 1410 to intercept eight P-47s reported in the Pavia-Stradella area. On take-off Ten. Santoli veered off track, so damaging his Bf 109G-14/AS (W.Nr.785039, "3-13") that it needed 14 days' repairs in the main workshops.

After searching unsuccessfully for 45 minutes, the machines returned to their airfields, where more accidents occurred in the landing pattern. At Malpensa Ten. Rosati's engine cut out just before touch down and his Bf 109G-14 (W.Nr.782474, "1-13") broke its undercarriage, with only minor injury to its pilot. At Lonate a mistaken manoeuvre by a wingman forced Cap. Barioglio to open his throttle abruptly, causing his Bf 109G-10/AS (W.Nr.491499, "2-10") to nose up, stall and dive inverted into the ground, cartwheeling on impact.

The aeroplane was a total write-off, the pilot sustained multiple fractures, and command of 2ª Sq. was taken over by Cap. Rovetta. Four days went by before the Gruppo had the chance to face the enemy again, seven months after its last combat.

Before dawn on the 11th, in what was to prove the last offensive action for some while, a lone aircraft dropped anti-personnel bombs south of Bologna. A 255 Sqn Mosquito attacked an unidentified hostile but no claim resulted; two nights later the same squadron had a fruitless high-level chase.

12-13 March 45

II° Gr.C. was again scrambled against medium bombers. Ten Bf 109s of 4ª Sq., eight of 6ª and the aircraft of Magg. Miani took off from Aviano, while seven of 5ª Sq. scrambled from Osoppo. On take-off an accident befell Ten. Valenzano's Bf 109G-10/AS (W.Nr.491323, Black 3) but he was unhurt and the aircraft sustained only 10 per cent damage. The mission was uneventful until, on the way home, just north of Padua, Drago's *Squadriglia* intercepted a lone F-5E of the 32nd Photo Recon. Sqn at 1243.

Lt Clyde T. Allen had been warned by Commander sector control of bogeys in the area and right afterward observed four single-engined black aircraft at 9 o'clock high and curving round behind him.

Drago reported:
> ... at about 100 metres' range I opened fire right on his tail. After a short burst (only five 30mm and 30 x 13mm shells were expended) the enemy aircraft, hit between the right engine and the fuselage, emitted a dense white trail and dived to the left. I didn't follow him because I had only 15 minutes' fuel left ...

Drago was credited with a victory, but Allen managed to increase power and dive into a cloud, losing his opponents. He nursed his badly damaged aircraft back to base at Florence where, with his hydraulic system shot out and unable to lower his landing gear, he safely crash-landed on the runway after both engines cut out over the field.

Returning home after the combat, the Bf 109G-6 (W.Nr.161798) of Serg. Quasso (6ª Sq.) developed serious engine trouble and he baled out successfully.

An armed photo-reconnaissance of the Pisa-Lucca area by two Bf 109s of NAGr.11 had to be broken off in the face of strong fighter defence, but another pair carried out their mission to Forlì, Faenza and Bagnacavallo (RA) and a German aircraft was over Naples that night.

14-17 March 1945

At 1145 on the 14th a formation of 321st BG B-25s was returning from bombing a rail bridge at Vipiteno (Bolzano), escorted by eight P-47s of the 346th FS, 350th FG (Minefield Green and Yellow Sections). From Lonate and Malpensa, on their first operational sortie since returning from Germany, 19 of I° Gruppo Caccia's Bf 109s, alerted by Tactical Command at Verona, scrambled to intercept, taking off in clouds of dust.

There was an accident at the outset when 3ª Sq.'s CO, Cap. Guido Bartolozzi (Bf 109G-10/AS, W.Nr.491324, "3-1"), taking off last and slightly late, lifted off before his speed had built up, trying to avoid some unevenness in the runway. His aircraft side-slipped into the ground from 50ft and the pilot was pulled from the cockpit only to die a few hours later in Busto Arsizio (VA) hospital. The rest of the Group, reduced to 17 after Ten. Cesare Erminio experienced engine trouble, headed towards Lake Garda in a climb.

2nd/Lt Charles C. Eddy was first to sight the Italian fighters, then still climbing, but despite alerting Capt. Belcher, was ordered to hold position. He therefore had to watch them gain a height advantage and prepare to attack the B-25s. Only then was Minefield Yellow ordered to engage. 1st/Lt Bergeron was first to hit a Bf 109 – M.llo Giuseppe Chiussi's G-10/AS (W.Nr.491485, '1-8') – forcing it to crash-land near S. Vigilio (BS) where it ran into a wall, its pilot dying when his head hit the gunsight.

Eddy's diary charted the developing dogfight:

> ... immediately an Me got on Bergeron's tail, so I hopped on him with a burst and got him off.... Ellis called in saying he had been hit in the engine and was losing oil. Bergeron and Ellis then broke off for home. This left Walt Miller and myself alone to tangle with the sixteen Jerries.
>
> They circled above us ... breaking off individually to make passes ... Miller stayed close on my wing and we broke into them as they would dive on us. Usually they would break off when we gave them a squirt. At one time a Jerry got on my tail and opened up on me from a very small deflection shot. Miller called me to break but he was blocked on the RT. [He] opened up on this guy really laying lead into him. I happened to notice an Me 109 in a steep dive off to my right. When he got down to about 5,000ft. he went into a spin and went into the ground. It surprised me, so I asked Miller if he had just shot at an Me. He said: "Hell yes, I just shot one off your tail!".

Miller had fatally damaged Serg. Domenico Balduzzo's Bf 109G-10/AS (W.Nr.491437, '3-7').

Balduzzo baled out but his parachute opened too low and he died of head injuries sustained on impact with the rocky ground.

By now Magg. Visconti realized the necessity of a determined assault, opting for a personal attack on the leader:

Due to lack of fuel, operations normally carried out by vehicles were done instead by muscle power. Here, a Bf 109G-10/AS of I° Gr.C. at Lonate Pozzolo is pushed back to its revetement by several Italian groundcrewmen.
(Pagliano)

Next I spotted a Jerry at 2 o'clock high going into a wing-over to make a frontal attack. I squared off on him for a straight head-on. We both opened up at extreme range and fired long bursts. We closed on each other fast and it was evident one of us would have to give way. I could see my bullets hitting him solidly. Finally at the very last second when it seemed we were both too stubborn to give, he pulled up over me and passed only five feet over my nose. All the time I could hear the sound of his cannon over my machine-guns. After he once passed we didn't turn to observe what happened to him, but the crews of the bombers confirmed that he had baled out.

G-10/AS, W.Nr.491356, hit by scores of bullets, could no longer fly and Magg. Visconti, with several shoulder and facial splinter wounds, jettisoned his canopy and jumped. He landed in the mountains west of Lake Garda, near the village of Costa, and was taken to the German military hospital in Gardone (BS). He was discharged a few days later.

Meanwhile Minefield Green escorted the bombers well clear of the combat zone then came back after I° Gr.C., catching them over Orio al Serio airfield. In this action only one Bf 109 was claimed as damaged (by 2nd/Lt Thompson), but the damage sustained by the Italians in the two combats was actually far worse. Cap. Cesare Marchesi's G-10/AS (W.Nr.491407, "3-5") crashlanded at Ghedi; S.M. Isonzo Baccarini's "3-9" (W.Nr.491477) turned over in an emergency landing at Orio al Serio but he was safely rescued a few minutes later in the middle of a strafing attack by Minefield Green's P-47s, as fuel leaked all around him. M.llo Danilo Billi's "3-2" (W.Nr.491325) while landing at Malpensa hit the crane recovering the remains of Bartolozzi's aeroplane, lost a wing and cartwheeled to a halt, the pilot miraculously unhurt.

I° Gruppo Caccia was in the red. Three Bf 109s shot down, six more wrecked in accidents or crash-landings; three pilots killed and one wounded. All for

just one P-47 damaged (the ANR's communiqué of 15 March credited Visconti with destroying the P-47 he had attacked head-on, however).

Two NAGr.11 Bf 109s broke off an armed photo-reconnaissance to the eastern front-line area at 1350 owing to engine trouble; they were aloft for only 20min. A Ju 188 was over the Ligurian from 2030-2200. On the 15th and 16th Italian and German pilots ferried eight new Bf 109s[58] from Orio as attrition replacements for I° Gr.C. At 1300 on the former date an F-5 was reportedly set on by two unidentified black single-engined aeroplanes over Faenza, possibly the two NAGr.11 Bf 109s whose photographic mission to the area at that time was greatly hampered by poor visibility. On the 17th, rocket-firing P-47s of the 350th FG claimed to have destroyed two Fw 190s in a strafing attack.

18-19 March 1945

During the afternoon 2.(F)/122 twice tried to get an aircraft away on its first operation since 23 February. In the event F6+VK broke off after 42min and F6+DK after 50min. Over the Po Valley from 1845, a 'German nightfighter' was guided toward Allied bombers but, unable to find any, it soon landed, probably at Villafranca.

The next day four Allied photo-reconnaissance aircraft were assailed by a pair of probable Fw 190s while operating in the Trento-Padua-Gorizia region, and 'two Me 262s' were reported 20 miles north of Udine. These last were almost certainly a case of mistaken identity, as it is known that Oblt. Sommer successfully carried out a mission in his Ar 234 – quite possibly his unit's first in Italy.

20 March 1945

The P-47s of the 79th FG made a spectacular claim of three aircraft destroyed and 19 damaged when strafing Campoformido on the 20th. Ob.SW signalled that in attacks on the Udine airfields 'six more Me 109s were reported destroyed', though any losses appear to have been made good by the beginning of April. Nevertheless, Kdo. Sommer operated again. An Ar 234 landed at Lonate from Udine at 0640, heading off west 90min later. Security was observed to some extent this time, at least – neither the aeroplane's markings nor its pilot's name were logged. The Arado's unit was noted, then and subsequently, only as 'NAG.' A team of ten men was waiting for the jet. They towed it out of sight, fitted fake wooden airscrews on the engines, and refuelled its tanks with J2. The pilot was surely Sommer; he did not let his two subordinates loose for some time, both on account of their inexperience in the west and the need to strip down and rebuild their aircraft to operationally acceptable standards.

In Furth III° Gr.C. continued training. On 10 February 1945 Serg. Dachena was killed when his Bf 109 crashed on landing, its wreckage being scattered over the airfield.
(Versolato)

The recently-delivered (and subsequently unflown) Me 410 F6+EK aborted a morning sortie after just eight minutes, but at 1127 Bayer and Lensing took F6+BK out on 2./122's final mission (No. 3326), returning safely just over two hours later.

One of the campaign's more unusual engagements occurred that night, when an A-20 of the 47th BG found itself in a 20min running battle with a twin-engined enemy aircraft showing lights over Northern Italy. Fire was exchanged until the mystery aeroplane caught fire and crashed.

21-22 March 1945

Between 0547 and 0825, three or four 'fighter-bomber' aircraft – probably 1./NSGr.9 Fw 190s – were heard on a bombing exercise near Lake Garda. Warned of approaching fighters, they were ordered to land or evade. One apparently experienced undercarriage problems and was told to crash-land. After a stay of almost two weeks, Cap. Mantelli took his Fiat G.55 from Lonate to Gallarate at 1800.

On the 21st, a Ju 188D-2 of 4./KG 200 (W.Nr.180444) went missing over the Italian war zone and the fate of Hptm. Heinz Domack and his four crew remains officially unknown. MAAF Sigint had forecast two German reconnaissances that night and 'two Ju 188s from Bergamo' were duly overheard. The first (F6+KP) landed at Udine and fighter-warnings were broadcast to the second at

2130 and 2140. It was reported overdue at 0038 by Control.

A 255 Sqn Mosquito was vectored on to a hostile contact in the Ancona-Fano area but ran low on fuel. A second, that of Fg Off Scollan and Flt Sgt Blundell of 256 Squadron, was then scrambled. The hostile recrossed the coast, heading northeast, and after a 270mph chase they made contact in the Pola-Trieste area. After visual confirmation they opened fire, setting both its engines ablaze and recognising it as a Ju 188 by the light of the flames. Scollan's third kill, it fell into the sea and broke up about three miles offshore at 2245.

The circumstantial evidence is persuasive that it was Domack's aircraft, in all probability belonging to Carmen. There was a sequel to this loss. On the 26th a signal, most likely from KG 200, explained that increased Allied nightfighter activity was making operations from Bergamo impossible, and only after FuG 217 (tail-warning radar) had been installed would flights again be made.

23 March 1945

At 0213 and 0216 a Ju 188 on reconnaissance over the Adriatic was warned of Allied fighter activity in the vicinity. Repeated calls were made until 0412 without response. This aircraft, one of two heralded by indiscreet radio traffic, was pursued at a height of 100-200ft by a Mosquito of 255 Sqn from 60 miles east of Ancona to 2 miles north of the Po Delta, where it was shot down in flames 1½ miles offshore at 0228. The successful airmen were Flt Lt Pertwee and Flt Sgt Smith, scoring their unit's last victory of the war.

At Campoformido, an Allied PR aircraft saw what was described as a 'probable Me 262' being towed from its pen to take-off position and DAF Spitfires later reported another 'arrow-shaped aircraft' heading north. Kdo. Sommer did fly a mission, with airfield protection patrols provided by seven Bf 109s of 4ª Sq., six of which were up at 0850 from Aviano.

While over the Campoformido area at 0925, Cap. Drago spotted and attacked a long file of bomb-laden P-47s from the 85th FS, 79th FG, catching them completely by surprise and, as 2nd/Lt De Witt Morton reported: '... several Me109s came in out of the sun and shot Lt. Faires plane. At that instant he did a split 'S' and dropped his bombs upon recovering ... His plane did a roll similar to a barrel roll and he baled out. From the instant he was hit, white smoke was seen coming out from the plane. I saw ... Lt. Faires' parachute open.' It is difficult to determine who shot down 2nd/Lt Jack Faires' P-47, which crashed near the village of Tarcento (UD). No fewer than three Italian pilots claimed the victory, while the official communiqué claimed two P-47s shot down and one probable. From Drago and S.M. Baldi's reports, it seems the kill belongs to the former, although there must have been some talk in the squadron when Baldi refused to sign an eyewitness confirmation of Drago's claim.

Later, 11 Messerschmitts (two of Nucleo Comando, one of 4ª Sq. and eight of 6ª Sq.) scrambled to intercept 310th BG B-25s headed toward Aviano, escorted by Spitfires. The opposing forces met over Pordenone at 1000, and the Allied airmen believed they were attacked by 15 to 20 Fw 190s and Bf 109s. These held off until the escort withdrew, low on fuel, then made: '[a] determined attack ... remarkable for the aggressive character of the passes made ... these e/a were dark green or grey and had swastikas[59] on wings and fuselage. The leader had a red spinner – others were white.'

Cap. Spigaglia, M.llo Covre and Serg. Patton each claimed destruction of a bomber, though in fact only one was lost (that of Lt. James J. Summers, who baled out safely, along with his R/T operator and a gunner) and three damaged. The Americans claimed two fighters shot down and two damaged, but there were no Italian losses.

Otherwise during daylight, P-47s attacked Aviano airfield, claiming hits on Bf 109s, Fw 190s and Ju 52s, as well as the control tower, which was left smoking. One German aircraft photographed Salerno during the evening.

24-31 March 1945

On the 24th a report to 66th FS of bandits in the Verona area brought no contact but a reconnaisance aircraft released five flash bombs over Naples that night. The sole long-range reconnaissance on the night of the 25th was the last for some days.

Flown by two Hungarian Air Force officers from an army courier unit, and with an army captain as passenger, an Fw 58 landed in Italy at 1045 on 27 March. It crossed the coast 15 miles north of Pescara and, with only a few litres of fuel remaining, quickly made a wheels-down landing in a rough wheatfield, tearing its fabric in a few places but otherwise remaining intact. The trio had come from Beled, Hungary, and had been planning their move since January, but acquiring enough petrol had taken some time. They had made the trip at 50m, with an interim landing in a field to top up from jerricans. Some Hungarian soldiers had helped them out when they got bogged down. They headed for Ancona, alternating engines to save petrol, and a Spitfire found them and shepherded them to a landing.

The aircraft (W.Nr.2672, K3+12) had passed to the Hungarians in December 1944 but still carried the rear fuselage inscriptions (and telephone numbers) of its former owners, successively Pilot School A14, Klagenfurt, and Bomber Observer School 2, Hörsching.

On the 29th a Boston saw a Bf 109 east of Trieste. The next day at Lonate, Ten. Santoli of 3ª Sq. destroyed his Bf 109G-14/AS (W.Nr.781121, 3-7) on take-off.

Near Marina di Ravenna on the 31st, two Hungarian Air Force officers landed in a Bücker Bü 131D Jungmann training biplane (W.Nr. 1955, I5+01). On each side of the nose was painted the head of a black terrier with a red collar and the slogan *Erö Huseg*. It had come from the Hungarian Fighter School at Zeltweg, Austria, and its crew believed that a second would-be escaper had crashed in bad weather en route. Evading guards and skipping an engine warm-up, they had set off with only 90 litres of petrol. Around Comacchio they were fired on by Allies and Germans alike. Unable to find an aerodrome, they put down in a field just before 0830.

At Campoformido, and at the other end of the technological scale, Allied aircraft saw a 'probable Ar 234' being towed out, despite all the Luftwaffe's precautions. The ANR had a 2ª Sq. Bf 109G-10 destroyed by strafing.

Notes

57. Major Kasun, CO of 62nd FW, wrote to the RAF full of appreciation for this performance and for corroborating plots from an American unit.
58. These were:
    2-10 W.Nr.491333
    3-1 W.Nr.461512
    3-2 W.Nr.464502
    3-4 W.Nr.490736
    3-5 W.Nr.491495
    3-7 W.Nr.781121
    3-9 W.Nr.781127
    3-10 W.Nr.785753
59. Many Allied pilots termed all German crosses 'swastikas.'

Maintenance of a Bf 109 of I° Gr.C. parked inside its revetment. The extensive dispersal area around Lonate Pozzolo conferred relative safety on the Italian aircraft even this late in the war.

ABOVE:
Aviano, 1945. Bf 109G-10/AS 'Black 11' flown by S.M. Baldi is one of the 4ª Sq., II° Gr.C. aircraft with a girlfriend's name painted on it. Lack of photographic documentation precludes an estimate of how widespread this practice was. 'Silva' will be shot down on 2 April, with Baldi baling out wounded.

BELOW:
Pisa, 2 April 1945. Two stills from an unofficial movie document the return of 346th FS pilots after they and 347th FS had fought against II° Gruppo Caccia. Their 13-0 score was an all-time high for the USAAF in Italy. While Maj. Gilbert expresses his joy to the surrounding personnel at two victories scored, Lt. Sulzbach, still in the cockpit of his P-47, grabs an identification manual to be sure of his own two claims.

CHAPTER 14

April 1945

The Ground War – Final Offensive

Flying weather improved, but the main spur to reviving Axis air activity was the opening of the Allied offensives. The pattern of slow Allied progress and grudging Axis retreat shattered, and it was all over in three weeks. A war of movement developed which the German and Italian armies could no longer fight, their mobility fatally compromised by fuel shortages and Allied airpower. The Fifth Army struck for La Spezia on 5 April, and the Eighth Army attacked the massively fortified Senio and Santerno River Lines on the 9th, after a devastating fragmentation bombing by the strategic bombers. The Fifth Army's main assault on the central front went in on the 14th, soon outflanking Bologna.

On the 17th OKW directed Vietinghoff to yield not an inch of ground, but on the 20th he nonetheless ordered a retreat across the River Po.

The Luftwaffe

An RAF study pays this tribute to Pohl's airmen: 'The small, experienced body of aircrews made the most of their hopelessly inadequate material with the reduced rations of fuel'. However, apart from a few large-scale bombing raids: '. . . Thunderbolts paid attention at times to the enemy's remaining air bases, but only on a low priority basis.'

Probably few on the receiving end were conscious of having an easy time and numerous aircraft were claimed by strafers. Erich Sommer has understandably vivid memories of almost daily attacks on Campoformido: '. . . by Thunderbolts, Lightnings, Spitfires, Bostons and B-24s . . . A lot of attacks were copped by the dummy airfield just to the west . . . nasties consisting of napalm and anti-personnel bombs [with] steel spring fuses which stuck in the runway undetected and slashed my tyres on landing, several times'.

Jets
Information came from an infantry PoW that on 2 April German ground troops had been issued with recognition information on the Ar 234, and more next day on 'another jet type'. Orders were given that neither should be fired on.

Reconnaissance
Restructuring continued. Komm. Gen. announced that from the 5th 2./NAGr.11 and Kdo. Sommer would be subordinated to FAGr.122 for disciplinary purposes but remain directly under his HQ's operational control. Malcesine announced Stab and 1./11's disbandment on the 8th, adding that 2./11's establishment would now be 12 Bf 109s and four Fw 190s. It seems that the nocturnal Staffeln did not operate until the night of 10/11 April, with only seven sorties plotted after that. NAGr.11 'made a small effort' over the battlefront and continued covering the Adriatic Coast. The last four serviceable aircraft of 2.(F)/122 left Italy early in the month.

The jets began to monopolise the reconnaissance scene but even for them conditions were next to impossible. Although the Kommando had but three pilots, Stabsfw. Arnold never got to fly a mission, his every attempt to get off the ground being curtailed by Allied fighter-bombers. A punctured fuel tank resulted from one such encounter and was mended in an Udine tyre-repair factory (the proprietor being paid in cigarettes) failing more conventional maintenance back-up.

Kdo. Carmen

KG 200 was, for all its mythologised reputation, in the same boat as the rest of the Luftwaffe. The entire Geschwader was allocated 276m³ of fuel for April, of which just 17m³ went to Carmen – good for about five sorties.

NSGr.9

On the 1st NSGr.9 advised G.d.S. that its 2. and 3. Staffeln averaged ten crews each and, owing to personnel given up, were not fully operational. It was proposed to merge these units and bring them up to strength (presumably the 20-aeroplane establishment of a single Staffel), thereby releasing groundcrew. 1./9 was listed as operational though still re-equipping. The Gruppe's Egon detachment was ordered to start loading in Villafranca on the 6th for transfer to Kamenz, Saxony. Since the Allied offensive provoked a 'strong reaction in the form of Egon-controlled ground-attack operations', either the transfer did not happen or an alternative was available. Sorties were controlled two Freya radars – a fixed installation near Este (PD) and a mobile unit at Custoza, just northwest of Villafranca.

The use of ground control ended the Gruppe's customary radio silence, and MAAF plotted complete sorties from Rakete ('rocket' = take-off) to Ente ('duck' = target) and back to Bahnhof ('railway station' = home base). Aircraft were frequently ordered higher because they had dropped below control's radar horizon and the presence of nightfighters was also broadcast. Not content merely to listen, the Allies broadcast appeals to defect over Luftwaffe R/T frequencies. This necessitated pilots' constantly changing channels to escape these unwelcome interruptions.

NSGr.9 followed its bombing by strafing with machine-guns or cannon, although Franz Züger said that bursts were sometimes fired into empty air, avoiding both exposure to ground fire and reprimand for returning with no ammunition expended. Even so, strafing frequently accompanied the scattering of cluster bombs on Allied troops and transport during the Po Valley fighting. The bombing itself was made from a shallow dive after approaching at about 4,000m. All-out operations resumed during the final offensive, continuing until collapse overtook the Axis air forces.

The ANR

I° Gruppo Caccia

There was little activity before a combat on the 10th and a scramble the next day. A week passed with only Bü 181 gunnery training at Lonate and the delivery of 11 new Bf 109s there from Riem between the 15th and 16th.

The situation outside the airfield deteriorated steadily as partisan activity grew, and on the 15th Magg. Visconti, following the disappearance of two of his officers, ordered another sweep of neighbouring villages. Beyond five arrests little came of this but a hardening of the populace's feelings against Visconti.

Final operations took place on the 19th and 20th.

II° Gruppo Caccia

The first of April was Easter Sunday but this celebration was prelude to a tragedy, for next day – the so-called 'black Easter Monday' – the Group suffered the worst blow since its constitution.

The days following saw only a meeting at Pordenone between Magg. Miani and the COs of the three Squadriglie to discuss the grave situation. Inactivity on the airfields was only interrupted in Aviano from 5-10 April by a few flights of the Bf 109G-12, now flown by M.llo Covre, completing the

Near Alfonsine (RA). What remained of Lt. Gneismer's Ar 234, T9+DH, after it was shot down and the wreck burned by German troops. In the tailplane leading edge can be seen bullet holes; the square opening in the fuselage bottom is the aperture for one of the plane's reconnaissance cameras.

near-pointless training of a few young pilots. On the 10th four P-47s of the 347th FS strafed Aviano, claiming at least two Bf 109s destroyed in their revetements and several other aircraft (or dummies) damaged.

In Osoppo on the same day, with 5ª Sq. drawing up only five serviceable Messerschmitts, Magg. Bellagambi decided to begin transferring personnel to Pordenone, a decision eased by the Allies bombing Osoppo on the 11th, completely destroying the Fort, atop a rocky hill, where the pilots were quartered. Nobody was hurt, but here was proof that 5ª Sq. could no longer stay and it was time to shift the aircraft elsewhere.

That evening, after a telephone discussion with Magg. Miani, the decision was taken and on 12 April Bellagambi and four of his pilots flew their Bf 109s from Osoppo to Villafranca, leaving behind some pilots and a few Messerschmitts still under repair. The rest of the Squadriglia (pilots, ground personnel and their families) reached Villafranca after three days on the road, under continuous threat of Allied strafing.

Meanwhile, at Aviano the Gruppo had begun receiving new aircraft to make good its losses. Among these were at least three brand-new Bf 109K-4s, inexplicably assigned to 6ª Sq., whose pilots were certainly not the most experienced.

On the 14th a few 4ª Sq. aircraft made an inconclusive interception of P-47s near Ostiglia (MN), and three days later the last four repaired Bf 109s of 5ª Sq. reached Aviano from Osoppo.[60] Nothing more occurred before the 19 April action, and talks continued at Aviano to decide when and how to transfer the whole of II° Gruppo to Villafranca or another more westerly airfield.

III° Gruppo Caccia: March/April 1945

Gen. von Pohl had visited the unit in Holzkirchen at the beginning of March and told the pilots – none too diplomatically – that they would be equipped with old Bf 109G-6s. Responding to a chorus of protests, on the 24th OKL informed the Italian Air Attaché that G-10 and K-4 models would now be supplied. This stayed mainly on paper, as two days earlier the first small groups from the unit had begun returning to Italy by road.

Members of 7ª and 8ª Sq., their training completed, were first to reach quarters between Desio and Seriate (BG). Orio al Serio was their intended base but the only aircraft to arrive there was a Bf 109G-10 flown in by CO Cap. Malvezzi in early April. Despite having 21 aeroplanes on charge in the first part of the

S.Ten. Aurelio Morandi was killed on 19 April 1945 at 1120 hrs by Swiss AA fire while trying to intercept a USAAF B-24 subsequently shot down by his colleagues. He was the last pilot of I° Gruppo Caccia to die in action.

month (serviceability ranging from 10-13) only four Bf 109s were flown to Italy by III° Gr. pilots.

On 9 April OKL was enquiring how long it would be before the Gruppo was trained and on the 17th allocated 30 tonnes of B4 to Luftwaffenkommando West for the Italians' 'final training'. In the conditions of the time this was a major investment but one without a pay-off. Political considerations may have played a part, as five days earlier the Germans had turned down the latest request from Mussolini for the allocation of more fighters to defend his fast-shrinking puppet Republic. Getting another Italian unit into action was seen as partial consolation for this refusal.

Fuel

It is hardly necessary to look any further for an explanation of the Luftwaffe and ANR's limited response to the climax of the campaign, although fuel was just one of their rapidly multiplying problems. The month began with 226m³ of B4, 125m³ of C3 and 341m³ of J2 on hand. C3 hit an all time low of 93m³ on the 10th,[61] but a rare delivery on the 14-15th brought it back up to 132m³. At the prevailing consumption rate, J2 would have held out for about eight months!

Air War Italy 1944-45

Order of Battle

Strengths on 1 April were:

Unit	Aircraft Number	Type
Stab/FAGr.122	0	
2.(F)/122	4(4)	Me 410B-3
4.(F)/122	6(5)	Ju 188D-2
	2(1)	Ju 88T-3
6.(F)/122	7(7)	Ju 188D-2
Kdo. Carmen	1	Ju 188
Stab/NAGr.11	3(2)	Fw 190A-8
1./NAGr.11	14(12)	Bf 109G
2./NAGr.11	19(12)	Bf 109G
Kdo. Sommer	3(2)	Ar 234B
Stab/NSGr.9	1(0)	Ju 87D
1./NSGr.9	11(10)	Fw 190F-8/F-9
2./NSGr.9	10(10)	Ju 87D
3./NSGr.9	16(15)	Ju87D
I° Gr.C.	45(34)	Bf 109G/K
II° Gr.C.	45(37)	Bf 109G
III° Gr.C. (training)	21(10)	Bf 109G
I° Gr. Aerosil. (forming)	13(7)	S.79

In reserve were:

Bf 109 fighters	20	
Bf 109 recce	1	
Ju 87D-5	2	
Fw 190F	2	

By 4 April, eight Bf 109 fighters had been drawn from reserve, as well as the reconnaissance machine; reserve Fw 190 attack models had *increased* to eight.

Bf 109G-10/AS W.Nr.491333 '2-10' steered by Cap. Rovetta, CO of 2ª Sq., I° Gr.C. along the rough taxiways of Lonate Pozzolo. This aircraft, flown by Ten. Colonna, was damaged in the combat of 19 April during which the unit scored its last victory.

Notes

60. Ten. Tramontini destroyed his aircraft on landing, escaping unhurt.
61. On this date it was noted that 12 tonnes of B4 (this is probably the allocation to Carmen mentioned above) and 100 of C3 were en route to Italy, and that the latter was the entire April allocation of this type of fuel.

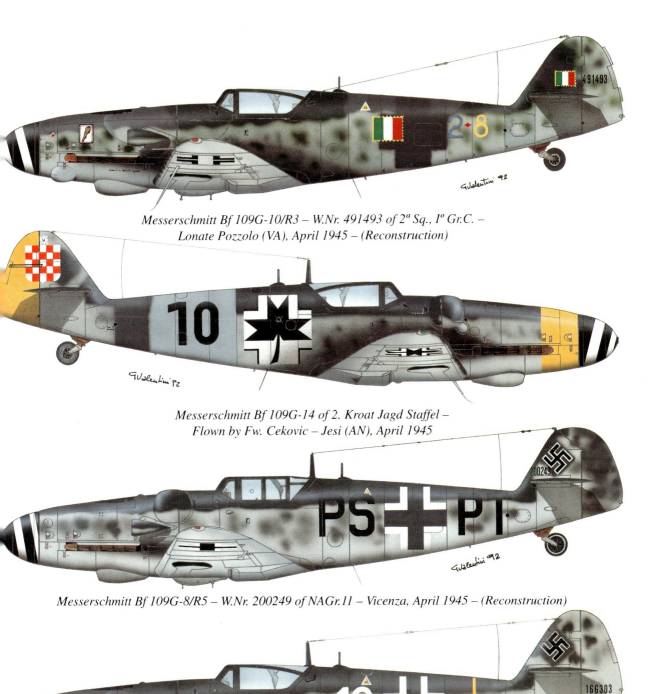

Messerschmitt Bf 109G-10/R3 – W.Nr. 491493 of 2ª Sq., I° Gr.C. – Lonate Pozzolo (VA), April 1945 – (Reconstruction)

Messerschmitt Bf 109G-14 of 2. Kroat Jagd Staffel – Flown by Fw. Cekovic – Jesi (AN), April 1945

Messerschmitt Bf 109G-8/R5 – W.Nr. 200249 of NAGr.11 – Vicenza, April 1945 – (Reconstruction)

Messerschmitt Bf 109G-6/AS/R3 – W.Nr. 166303 of 6ª Sq., II° Gr.C. – Orio al Serio (BG), April 1944 – (Reconstruction)

Arado Ar 234B-2 – W.Nr. 140142 of Kommando Sommer – Flown by Lt. Gniesmer (shot down on 11 April 1945) – Campoformido (UD), April 1945

Junkers Ju 188D-1 – W.Nr. 230499 of 4.(F)/122 – Bolzano, May 1945

Junkers Ju 188D-1 of Kommando Carmen, 4./KG 200 – Bergamo, Autumn 1944.
This aircraft had '5254Q' painted in small white characters below the cockpit on the port side (hidden by the engine nacelle when viewed in profile).

Junkers Ju 87D-3 – W.Nr. 132230 of 3./NSGr.9, reportedly the aircraft of Staffelkapitän, Hptm. Eduard Reither – Vicenza, April 1945
Shown with a typical load of two fragmentation bombs with a long fuse under each wing and an AB500 anti-personnel weapons dispenser under the belly.

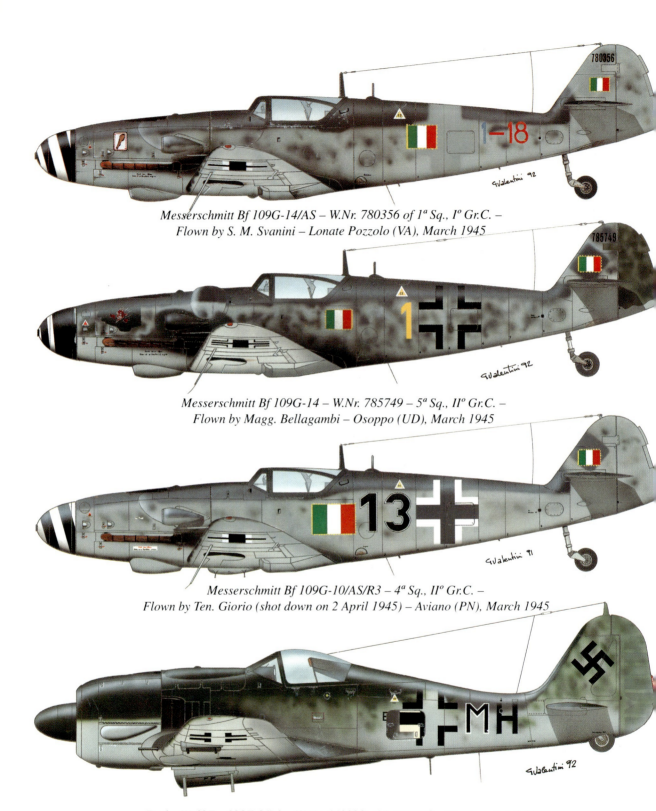

*Messerschmitt Bf 109G-14/AS – W.Nr. 780356 of 1ª Sq., Iº Gr.C. –
Flown by S. M. Svanini – Lonate Pozzolo (VA), March 1945*

*Messerschmitt Bf 109G-14 – W.Nr. 785749 – 5ª Sq., IIº Gr.C. –
Flown by Magg. Bellagambi – Osoppo (UD), March 1945*

*Messerschmitt Bf 109G-10/AS/R3 – 4ª Sq., IIº Gr.C. –
Flown by Ten. Giorio (shot down on 2 April 1945) – Aviano (PN), March 1945*

Focke-Wulf Fw 190F-9/R1 – W.Nr. 440323 of 1./NSGr.9 – Vicenza, April 1945

CHAPTER 14

Operations

1 April 1945

After ten days' inactivity, 2.(F)/122 stirred again, but not for an operation. Shortly after 0600, v.d. Daele and Blaschek flew F6+DK out of Ghedi, bound for Munich, followed 15min later by Bayer and Lensing in F6+BK. The Staffel was at last bowing out from Italy, its role assumed by the jets.

In Lonate, Oblt. Sommer's +EH arrived from Udine I at 0823, the flight logged as 'mission-transfer'. At 0840 Ltn. Gniesmer arrived in +DH, on a similar errand from Osoppo; both aircraft departed westward, at 1014 and 1019 respectively. Sommer is adamant that the Gniesmer entry must be wrong, since the latter was not yet operational.

Sommer's mission lasted from 1014-1221, covering Corsica, several airfields and Pisa, where an AA unit sighted his Arado, estimating its speed at 500mph. RAF eavesdroppers also plotted: 'a German aircraft probably engaged on tactical reconnaissance . . . south of Lake Comacchio . . . '.

2 April 1945

The 350th FG's Thunderbolts were assigned two almost simultaneous missions. Eight from the 346th FS (Minefield Green and Yellow sections) were to bomb a rail bridge in the Brenner Pass at Ora (BZ), thereafter providing area cover for B-25s bombing a bridge at S. Michele sull'Adige (TN), 25 miles further south. Sixteen 347th FS aeroplanes (Midwood Black, Crimson, White and Buff sections) were to escort other B-25s raiding the Brenner.

The 347th FS rendezvoused at 1350 with 36 B-25s from Corsica, and were soon joined by the 18 Mitchells headed for S. Michele. The 346th FS took off at 1350 and followed a direct route cutting across the Po Valley.

In Aviano, 18 Bf 109s were on alert; three from Nucleo Comando, eight from 4ª Sq., and seven from 6ª Sq. In Osoppo, ten 109s were made ready; seven from 5ª Squadriglia and three from 4ª Sq., detached there a few days before. At 1345 both groups were ordered to scramble.

The rendezvous point for the entire II° Gruppo was over Aviano, where the 18 Bf 109s already circling were joined by nine from Osoppo (ten had scrambled, but 4ª Sq.'s S.M. Guido Minardi aborted with engine trouble). Two more soon landed from the Aviano contingent; the Bf 109 of S.M. Rolando Ancillotti (5ª Sq.), whose cockpit had filled with fumes from a cracked exhaust, and that of M.llo Tullio Covre (6ª Sq.), whose engine ran rough.

As the remaining Messerschmitts flew westwards, Roma control advised Magg. Miani that a large number of medium bombers with fighter escort was coming from the south. Roma gave the estimated interception point, leaving Miani free to attack at his own discretion, and II° Gruppo Caccia headed toward one of the blackest days in its history.

By 1415 the B-25s and 347th FS P-47s were about 35 miles southeast of Ghedi. II° Gr.C.'s 25 Bf 109s were just passing Verona, approaching Lake Garda. The 346th FS was 15 miles southwest of Villafranca. The USAAF fighters had been warned at 1400 by Cooler of bandits approaching from the Udine area. This advice, repeated at 1410 and 1415, was confirmed by Lt Richard P. Sulzbach (Minefield Yellow Leader) of 346th FS: '. . . Cooler did a fantastic job for us that day! Maj. Gilbert's radio had malfunctioned and I was leading the formation. Cooler directed us so that we made contact with the enemy aircraft just as he told us we would.' The 347th FS's combat report continues: '. . . at 14.20 hours, 3 miles east of Ghedi, a flight of 16 Me-109s were sighted at 3 o'clock coming in from the east at 13,000 ft between the 2 bomber formations . . .'.

The Italians were simultaneously spotted by the 346th FS. Lt. Eddy: 'I was observing a group of B-25s proceeding north twenty or thirty miles south of Brescia, when I sighted twenty bandits at two o'clock at our same level headed west on a course that would cross our line of flight. I called them in to Green leader.

Maj. Gilbert:

. . . two or three miles west of Villafranca . . . at about 14.20 hours, I observed about sixteen bogeys at two o'clock headed west on the same level as my flight. Their course would place them at twelve o'clock to us about 1,200 yards away.

Meanwhile, among the Italians (according to Cavagliano's diary):

Just after sighting the enemy bombers on our left, 3,000 ft below us, we heard Miani curse . . . and tell Bellagambi to take the lead, as his airscrew pitch control had jammed, forcing him to abort. Miani turned sharply to the left and – I'll never understand why – all of Nucleo Comando and 6ª Sq. followed him, disappearing from my sight.

Not all of 6ª Sq.'s aeroplanes had followed Miani (whose radio had meanwhile failed), however. There had been a heated exchange between Cap. Spigaglia and Ten. Alberto Volpi. The former wanted the whole Squadriglia to follow Miani and land at Villafranca, while the latter, seeing no reason for this, refused to comply. Thus, while the Messerschmitts of Miani, Spigaglia, Serg.'s Caimi, Tampieri and Archidiacono and M.llo Moratti headed for Villafranca, Volpi and his section (Serg. Patton and M.llo Fumagalli) prepared to attack.

Bad luck doesn't come singly, however, and Cavagliano's diary continues:

. . . immediately after, while in a shallow dive to attack, Bellagambi throttled back abruptly and we heard him . . . say that a sudden wash of oil over his windscreen had completely blinded him. His manoeuvre forced us to throttle back too, to avoid a collision. At that precise, confused moment, out of the corner of my eye I noticed the bombers passing below us, but also . . . to our right – 1,500 ft higher than us – a "cloud" of enemy fighters, four of which were diving into

us . . . I screamed over my radio to Sarti to pull up and face their attack, while ramming my throttle forward and starting the tightest possible turn to the right.

At this point eight P-47s of the 347th FS were just about to attack 4ª Sq. head-on, while four of the 346th FS Thunderbolts were closing on the tails of 5ª Sq. The 347th's combat report continues: 'Midwood Black and Crimson sections dropped all external fuel tanks and Black section broke into the enemy aircraft closely followed by Crimson . . . .. As Black section broke, the 109s started a climbing turn to the right, and by using full throttle and water [injection], our pilots were able to climb with the enemy . . .'.

The climbing Messerschmitts were those led by Drago, who did the only thing possible: engage methanol injection and pull up.

The 346th FS's P-47s reacted by splitting into pairs. Lt Sulzbach and his wingman Flt Off Jennings were first to close the pincers, turning left and diving on to the tail of the Diavoli Rossi formation, which was clearly disvantaged by its loss of speed. Maj Gilbert and his wingman, Lt Thompson, (Minefield Green 1 and 2) followed after a few seconds, enough to be left several hundred yards behind. Lts Barton and Eddy (Minefield Green 3 and 4), having meanwhile sighted six e/a above them and become separated by Maj Gilbert's manoeuvre, climbed at full power to intercept. Also outdistanced, Lt Bergeron and Flt Off Miller (Minefield Yellow 3 and 4), turned right and tried to gain height.

At this point battle had commenced in earnest, split into a series of 'duels' very difficult to follow. Sulzbach fell on Cavagliano and Sarti's tails, and though the former managed to evade, the latter was immediately hit by the American's fire. The shooting down of 'White 8' and the death of Ten. Aristide Sarti (crashed near Goito (MN)) was witnessed by Maj Gilbert: 'The pursuing P-47, whom I found later to be Lt. Sulzbach, broke off the engagement while I continued to dive with the Me 109. I was closing rapidly, at about 5,000 feet, when I observed him attempt an aileron roll slowly to the left but he did not pull out, crashing into the ground about twelve miles west of Villafranca.'

While the 'Red Devils' and the three 6ª Sq. fighters scattered at Cavagliano's warning cry, the eight Bf 109s led by Drago were performing a deadly spiral with the four P-47s of Midwood Black led by Capt Heckenkamp, closely followed by Lt Brandstrom's Crimson section.

Heckenkamp closed on the Italian 'tail-end Charlie' (Ten. Bruno Betti) and opened fire, scoring hits which started his 'Black 8' smoking. Betti's instrument panel suddenly exploded and smoke poured into the cockpit. After a last radio message to alert his comrades, he jettisoned the canopy and jumped.

Continuing his climb, Heckenkamp framed a second Messerschmitt in his gunsight and after one burst it, too, began to smoke badly. In the earphones of Italians flying for their lives echoed a desperate cry. Everyone recognised the voice of Ten. Mario Giorio, whose 'Black 13', out of control, was seen by Lts Taylor and Olson (Midwood Black 2 and 3) to crash and explode south of Villafranca.

The two 347th FS sections now split into pairs and continued fighting, while the Messerschmitts of 4ª Sq., despite their losses, finally managed to climb away from the P-47s. Drago, gaining a momentary height advantage, suddenly executed a half roll and dived on the pursuing Americans. This broke up the Gigi Tre Osei formation and only S.M. Loris Baldi, Drago's wingman, was able to follow. Of the others, Ten. Raffaele Valenzano, S.M. Stefano Camerani and S.Ten. Alessandro Abba (on his first combat mission) regrouped and, after quickly assessing the situation, decided to head for Aviano. S.Ten. Felice Squassoni, finding himself suddenly alone, continued climbing, intending to escape the fighting.

Drago and Baldi did not notice that their dive had taken them past Heckenkamp and his wingman. With a sharp turn and steep dive, the Thunderbolts were on the Italians' tails, Heckenkamp closing in for the kill and repeatedly hitting Bf 109 G-10/AS 'Black 11' of S.M. Baldi, who baled out and, despite wounds and a damaged parachute, came down safely.

With the downing of Baldi, Heckenkamp had got three victories inside 60 seconds. He could have scored a fourth if his ammunition had not run out moments later. In his sights was the unsuspecting Ten. Volpi, who had evaded the 346th's first attack, clearing a way between the enemy aircraft by firing at anyone crossing his path. Volpi had been hit in the engine, and it was while diving toward Villafranca airfield, trailing smoke, that the two P-47s caught him. After a few rounds Heckenkamp's guns quit, and it was the turn of Lt Taylor, who overtook his leader. His eight 0.5in guns truncated the right wing of 'White 5' and, with his engine on fire too, Volpi parachuted, landing safely near the airfield.

The second Midwood Black pair – after Wilkinson had regained position on Olson's wing – encountered Serg. Margoni, who had just escaped another Thunderbolt. Olson gave chase and hit the Messerschmitt, which rolled over in flames and went straight in. Margoni's aeroplane, like Baldi's, crashed near Pozzuolo sul Mincio (MN). This victory was apparently a 'double claim'; Brandstrom and Wilson (Midwood Crimson) fired at a Bf 109, seeing it smoke, roll on its back, crash and explode in the same place as Margoni.

Meanwhile, Maj. Gilbert noticed that he was at 3,000ft over Villafranca airfield, just as Miani's group were about to land:

> I looked again and saw six Me-109s preparing to land . . . They were at about 800 feet and . . . circling to the left. It was very difficult to see them against the ground because they were camouflaged dark blue. I turned to the left and dived on them, firing at each one in quick succession on the initial pass. I observed as I did so that all had their wheels and flaps down and that no flak was being fired from the airdrome. As I pulled up to the left for my second pass, I looked for my wingman but did not see him. On the second pass, I again fired at each successive aircraft but concentrated mainly on the fifth one, giving him two to three short bursts from 400 to 200 yards range, decreasing deflection from 45 degrees to 25 degrees. Again I broke hard left and came around for my third pass. I did not observe but four aircraft on this pass.

The fifth aircraft was M.llo Giuseppe Moratti's, hit by Gilbert in the landing pattern, just as Miani's aeroplane touched down. Moratti's Bf 109 was set afire, and despite his desperate attempts it clipped three trees at the runway's edge and turned upside down on a fourth. Groundcrewmen ran to the burning aircraft and managed to extract him from the cockpit. Although he was burned and wounded, Moratti survived.

Gilbert's attack was not yet over:

> . . . this time I concentrated on the number four. I gave him a good burst from a 45 degree overhead pass, observing strikes around the engine [which] ceased to function and his propeller started to windmill. Instead of turning left towards the field he continued on to southwest while I continued on above him at 1,000 feet trying to reduce my speed. It appeared that he was going to crash-land but made no effort to retract flaps or wheels. When about ten feet off the ground, a P-47, later found to be my wingman, Lt. Thompson, came in and gave him a short burst from 30 degrees on the port side. I observed strikes on the ground off to the Me's right wing. The Me 109 then crashed into a ploughed field two miles south southwest of

Villafranca. His left wing was broken off by a tree. I did not see the aircraft burn, nor the pilot get out.

In fact, Serg. Raffaele Archidiacono was badly wounded in the abdomen and unable to get out. He nonetheless found the strength to ask rescuers who arrived a few minutes later if his crash-landing had hurt any of the peasants working in the fields. He then fainted. Archidiacono died a few hours later in hospital from a serious internal haemorrhage.

Maj. Gilbert was joined by his wingman and both headed back to Pisa.

Four US pilots witnessed the presence of a P-47 among the enemy.

Maj. Gilbert: '. . . it was my impression when we first attacked the first westbound group of enemy fighters . . . over Villafranca, that there was an olive drab camouflaged razorback P-47 in the enemy formation. I believe that this was an enemy piloted P-47 . . .'

Lt Sulzbach: '. . . we jettisoned our bombs and belly tanks and started turning to give pursuit. I was low and out of range but I fired on and missed a plane in the center of the group. The aircraft I had mistakenly fired on was a P-47 razorback with olive drab camouflage. No distinguishing marks were observed.'

The mysterious P-47 was then met by two more pilots, as described by the 347th FS combat report:

During the engagement a camouflaged razorback P-47 was encountered among the enemy aircraft. Lt. Pickerel . . . gave it calls on 3 channels in an effort to identify it, but received no answer. [He] pulled in close and wagged his wings and the camouflaged '47 did likewise. As Lt Pickerel broke away, the camouflaged '47 made a pass on him and his wing man (Lt. Poindexter). . . Pickerel broke and got into a "Lufbery" with the '47, and as he closed in [it] "Split-S-ed" and [he] lost sight of him. [He] was never close enough to see the markings on the tail, but he did notice that there were no markings on the side of the fuselage, as on our aircraft.

The conclusion was that this was a 'close encounter' with a captured, German-flown P-47. Its companions were two Focke-Wulf Fw 190s engaged by Lt Sulzbach, who claimed one of them. The Fw 190 identification and the victory were confirmed by wingman Flt Off Jennings. The second Focke-Wulf, grey with black crosses on its upper wing surfaces, was claimed as damaged by Lt Bergeron.

We thus have a 'pirate' P-47 and two Fw 190s, apparently well corroborated. Apart from mistaken identity, one hypothesis is that two Focke-Wulfs were escorting a captured Thunderbolt and joined the Italians for part of their flight. They might have been flying separately and joined up when warned of approaching hostiles (although heading for the nearest airfield would seem safer). We do not believe that the Luftwaffe ever used captured US fighters against their former owners. There would have been no advantage in doing so – indeed, there were many drawbacks, such as dependence on salvaged ammunition and the lack of spares and super high-grade fuel.

Between 1 and 4 April, 1./NSGr.9's complement of Fw 190s fell by two, so, if correctly identified, the one claimed damaged by Bergeron could have come from this Staffel, based at nearby Villafranca. The sole documentary source giving a German view is an Ultra decrypt for 2 April reporting 'German fighters scrambled' against medium bombers. This, however, is an English paraphrase of an unreleased original;

Two Bf 109G-10/AS of 4ª Sq., IIº Gr.C., ready to take off from Aviano for one of the unit's last missions. Both the nearer aircraft and 'Black 5' in the background are devoid of any Italian markings. In fact, several Bf 109s of this unit found at Orio al Serio after the war (see Appendix) bore no Italian Tricolour.

did it in fact use the customary term "eigene Jäger" (= 'our own fighters') covering both Luftwaffe and ANR? All this is still open to question and only Italian fighter traffic was overheard during the action.

By now S.Ten. Squassoni was far from the combat area, and on the same route was another Bf 109, that of Ten. Michelangelo Piolanti (5ª Sq.), struggling with his damaged aircraft and flying at reduced speed. The two Italians continued toward Aviano, unaware of one another.

Meanwhile, Lts Barton and Eddy had climbed to 24,000ft and started circling near Verona. No sooner had they arrived than they sighted Bergeron and Miller. Barton also noticed, ten miles away, Piolanti and Squassoni's Bf 109s. The two Americans, ascertaining that no more enemy fighters were around, set off after the unsuspecting Italians, Bergeron and Miller covering their tails. Barton chose the Messerschmitt slightly behind (Piolanti's), while Eddy took on Squassoni's 'Black 5'. Barton wrote:

> ... Me 109 made a steep turn to port towards an opening in the overcast. I cut him off in astern. At 3,000 feet range I opened fire but was chagrined to find my tracers falling short so held my fire for a few seconds. I raised the nose a little on the second burst at 2,000 feet and observed many strikes in the fuselage and wing roots. As I continued to close I fired short bursts and observed that most of my strikes were in the vicinity of the cockpit. On the third burst at about 300 yards distance dead astern, smoke billowed out from behind the cockpit and the Me started to roll to the right and down. When he reached the inverted position, 1,500 feet from the ground, I ceased firing and broke to the left then back to the right in time to see [him] strike the ground and explode in the vicinity of Cittadella.

Barton's victory had actually occurred over 20km northwest, near Thiene, where Piolanti was trying to land.

Piolanti's last moments were also witnessed by Squassoni, who suddenly saw, emerging from under his wing, the smoking Messerschmitt and pursuing P-47. Instinctively Squassoni grabbed his radio and screamed 'break left, break left!', but at that moment Eddy reached firing range on Squassoni's tail:

> I gave him a burst from dead astern, range about 3,000 feet. He started weaving back and forth. This slowed him down considerably and I closed rapidly to 1,000 feet before firing again. My second burst bracketed the fuselage with a multitude of strikes. Throttling back to avoid overrunning him, I concentrated on firing. Heavy black smoke and white coolant resulted as I closed to 100 feet firing short bursts. At this point . . . the Me start[ed] to roll, and at the completion of the roll [it] pulled up and the pilot baled out in the vicinity of Cittadella. I had to dump the nose of my P-47 to avoid hitting the body of the enemy pilot, then I came back passing close to him as he hung in his parachute. He seemed unhurt.

While the USAAF fighters, now low on fuel, formed small groups to fly home, II° Gruppo's survivors looked for somewhere to land. In addition to the aircraft shot down, two others were missing: those of M.llo Mario Fumagalli and S.Ten. Ferdinando Spreca. The former, badly hit in the engine and chased by several P-47s, had escaped by slipping into a cloud. He then hedge-hopped to Treviso airfield, arriving as the first tongues of fire appeared in his cockpit. This was a true emergency landing, Fumagalli jumping out of the cockpit as soon as the aircraft halted and with the airfield personnel running towards him.

Spreca had just landed on the same airfield. Taking advantage of the confusion among the Diavoli Rossi after the enemy attack, he arrived safely. No sooner had the air-raid alert ceased than Spreca returned to his aeroplane, wanting to get to Osoppo as soon as possible and find out what had happened to his comrades. His take-off was perfect, but as the Messerschmitt's undercarriage retracted the aircraft was suddenly surrounded by explosions. The Gustav tottered, kept climbing for a few feet and then, out of control, crashed into the ground with a loud explosion and a ball of fire rising from behind the trees at the airfield perimeter. In their haste, nobody had advised the surrounding German flak posts of his take-off.

Three hours after the combat, three of the Messerschmitts that had landed in Villafranca took off for Aviano, flown by Magg. Miani, Ten. Volpi (taking over Serg. Patton's 109) and Serg. Tampieri. In the meantime, Lts Horace W. Blackeney and Darwin G. Brooks of the 345th FS, 350th FG, were on dusk patrol, flying towards the same area.

The first to notice the two Thunderbolts was Volpi. He rocked his wings to alert Miani, who acknowledged, and started climbing for a better position. At a nod from Miani the two Bf 109s jettisoned their droptanks, rolled and dived. Serg. Tampieri could not release his tank and went into a spin. On regaining control he had lost too much altitude, and decided to land at Treviso. The Italians failed to catch the Americans off guard, as Brooks recalls: '. . . as I pulled off a strafing pass I looked behind and there were Me 109s turning in on us. We dropped the belly tank, shoved it all forward and turned into them.' A short dogfight ensued but, while Miani managed to disengage and got to Aviano, the Thunderbolts' fire soon hit Volpi's Messerschmitt, forcing the him to bale out for the second time in a few hours, while his aircraft ended its last dive by crashing into a lonely barn.

Volpi's second shooting down brought the day's total of Messerschmitts lost by II° Gr.C. to 14 (shot down or damaged beyond repair) with six pilots killed, two wounded and five parachuted. Even so, the Gruppo officially claimed three victories, and unofficial unit documents claimed at least five. The day's ANR HQ communiqué reported two B-25s and a P-47 shot down. The two bombers were credited (in II° Gr.C.'s documents) to Ten. Sarti and Ten. Giorio, while the three P-47s were (unofficially) credited to M.llo Fumagalli, Serg. Caimi and a third, unknown, 5ª Sq. pilot. Thorough examination of all the available USAAF reports and documents allows the authors positively to rule out any American losses in this combat.

Also on 2 April a jet was spotted flying at around 400mph from south of Bologna along the front lines to the Adriatic coast near Rimini. Spitfires of 1435 Sqn, were scrambled in pursuit of this 'Me 262' – in fact an Ar 234.

3-5 April 1945

After the disasters of the previous day, the ANR and Luftwaffe were apparently inactive on the 3rd. On the 4th, the 79th FG reported three sightings of 'possible Me 262s' in the Udine area, one allegedly making a pass at them. Radio traffic suggested that two Rotten of Bf 109s were placed on one hour's readiness for a sea search, and at least one pair from NAGr.11 did operate.

On the next day DAF recorded that: 'An enemy jet-propelled aircraft was seen over our bases this morning. Radar plots gave a height of 35,000 feet and a speed of 400mph. after a good look round it moved north towards Venice.'

A Spitfire reported an Me 262 over Venice and, over Lake Comacchio, an F-5 claimed that an Me 262 attacked but was 'driven off by friendly flak'.

Erich Sommer remembers an eventful day, corresponding with this and various other Allied reports in many respects. Campoformido was assailed all day by fighter-bombers at 30min intervals. Returning from a mission, he attacked one of them (he thought it a Spitfire) at around 3000ft, 'with consequent evasive action'. Later on, in the dispersal pens, he in turn was attacked by rocket-firing aircraft (certainly not the Typhoons he then believed them to be) which set ablaze the Bf 109 opposite. The heat detonated its ammunition and his Arado was hit, putting it out of action for a couple of days. Sommer's comment: 'nice deflection shot . . .'.

Campoformido was raided by 168 B-24s and their escorts. MASAF claimed 11 aircraft destroyed or damaged on the ground, while German sources give three Bf 109s destroyed and nine damaged, plus two Fw 190s and three Fi 156s damaged. The main loser was NAGr.11, reduced from 36 to 24 aeroplanes.

6-9 April 1945

No operations took place on 6-8 April (rendering anti-jet patrols over the Po Valley by 239 Wing's Mustangs superfluous), but on the 6th S.Ten Semperboni flew a Bf 109 to Aviano from Germany. Ltn. Gniesmer arrived at Lonate from Udine in Ar 234 T9+DH at 1215 on the 8th. At 1505 the next day he left on a mission taking him southeast, but not before Allied flyers had noticed the Arado's presence on the airfield. Returning to Campoformido, he managed to evade intruding Spitfires and land safely. Komm. Gen. also reported an Ar 234 reconnaissance of the western part of the front from 1250 to 1405, broken off following damage to one of the aeroplane's power units. Sommer was the pilot concerned.

10 April 1945

In the Milan-Lake Como area at 0545 three Bf 109s of I° Gr.C., operating out of Gallarate, intercepted four weather reconnaissance P-47s from the 65th FS, 57th FG. In the short engagement that ensued, the Americans damaged M.llo Veronesi's Bf 109G-14/AS (W.Nr.785990, '1-7') and S.Ten Gallori's K-4 (W.Nr.333878, '3-14'). M.llo Forlani claimed a P-47 damaged in return.

Early in the day, Ltn. Gniesmer's Ar 234 flew photo cover of Forlì. Sommer remembers *this* as his subordinate's first operation, necessitated by his own Arado's unserviceability after the previous day's mishap. Once again an Ar 234 was spotted on Campoformido airfield.

Radio traffic indicated 'German-piloted fighters' in action against Allied aeroplanes at midday. Two hours later, German pilots 'Heine 1, 2, 3 and 4' (probably from NAGr.11) were homing in a northeasterly direction and called in a sighting of enemy fighters. During the day, strafing Mustangs claimed destruction or damage to seven Fw 190s and a Ju 88 but, even so, two Focke-Wulfs were reported on patrol that night. Three Ju 188s were dispatched, marking FAGr.122's resumption of operations. One intended to cover the Adriatic 'but evidently encountered Allied fighters' and returned early, making a one-engined landing at Udine at 2012.

11 April 1945

At about 0545, traffic was heard from Italian aircraft, callsign Rosso (= 'Red'). For an hour, from 1015, aircraft were active in the Vercelli-Alessandria-Milan areas, under callsign Acqua (= 'Water'). Nineteen I° Gr. aircraft scrambled without reward, but S.Ten. Gallone badly damaged his G-10/AS (W.Nr.490265, '2-1') in a landing accident.

At 0925 Ltn. Gniesmer arrived back at Lonate from Udine, refuelled, and left at 1310 on what was to be his last flight. The 15th USAAF had sent 112 B-17s, escorted by 30 P-51s, to bomb the rail bridge at Vipiteno, on the approaches to the Brenner Pass. It may have been this raid or (more likely) the MATAF mission to Padua that reported seeing an Ar 234 east of Verona, but it was definitely the 15th AF which encountered Gniesmer. The incident is logged as: 'Ar 234 made ineffective pass at bomber SW Bologna, destroyed by escort.'

At 1330 Lt Benjamin W. Hall III (2nd FS, 52nd FG) and his wingman, Lt Cooper, escorting a lone B-17 from the target area at 22,000ft, saw an aircraft two miles away at similar altitude. It was approaching a group of bombers and, on seeing the fighters veered north, Hall manoeuvred to about 800yd dead astern and fired, hitting the Arado's port nacelle.

A full-boost chase ensued, the P-51 achieving 380mph IAS, but unable to gain until the jet gradually lost power. Until then the German had taken no evasive action, seemingly trying to outdistance his pursuers straight and level. From about 500yd and – finding it difficult to hold position in the jetwash dead astern, Hall fired sustained bursts from 5 to 7 o'clock, scoring hits on the tail, fuselage and port wing. There was a ball of flame from the left engine and the Arado went into a gentle dive. Cooper then hit the wings and fuselage, and reported that the aircraft crashed before the pilot could get out.

It is now generally understood that Gniesmer did bale out, but struck his aircraft's tail, suffering serious injuries. He came down behind Axis lines but died in a Ferrara military hospital two days later. The Arado fell on flat, open ground about ten miles northwest of Alfonsine, near Lake Comacchio, where it was found by Field Intelligence on the 16th. They were under the impression that it had come down on

Serg. Renato Patton of 6ª Sq., II° Gr.C. had the sad distinction of being the last ANR pilot to die in action in World War 2. He was shot down on 19 April 1945 at 1235 hrs by P-51s of 325th FG and compelled to bale out from his Bf 109K-4, but his parachute didn't open fully and he fell to his death.

the evening of the 14th and were puzzled at the absence of a corresponding victory claim, despite the abundant evidence of damage from fighter gunfire. It appeared to them that it had made a controlled belly-landing (this may have been thanks to its autopilot) and had later been set alight by retreating German troops. Hall had correctly reported underfuselage glazing, which he attributed to reconnaissance cameras, but what he thought were radar dipoles round the tail were more probably the mass-balances on the control surfaces. In a thorough examination of the burnt-out remains the FIU found no evidence of radar.

The 11th was the first day of Operation Impact, a British amphibious assault across Lake Comacchio, and it was possibly this or (since he thinks that he did not fly on the day of Gniesmer's death, although there is evidence that two jet sorties may have been flown) the follow-up two days later that Sommer witnessed from the air. Heading home, he saw a Lightning about a mile ahead and decided to try an attack. Then he spotted amphibious craft coming north along the coast and turning into a lagoon. Feeling duty-bound to photograph them, he broke off his stalking. Sommer remains convinced that the

Magg. Visconti photographed a few days before the war's end. The tense expression on his face and the presence of a sub-machine-gun exemplify the heavy climate of those April days around the bases of I° Gr.C., surrounded by partisan units. The CO of the Italian Group did not survive to the war; he was shot by the partisans after his unit's surrender on 29 April 1945.

Lightning, which he attributes with some confidence to the Anglo-US 682 Squadron, did not see him.

A German aircraft was out taking photographs of Allied airfields, including obliques of Fano, between 0545 and 0730, and NAGr.11 sent out a pair of Bf 109s. Allied reports of an Me 410 over Forlì at 1400 are wrong – none remained flyable in Italy – but during the evening a 4.(F)/122 Ju 188 deployed to Udine in preparation for a mission over the Adriatic. There was cover of Naples, Salonika and Capodichino on the 11th, flash bombs falling at the first of these before midnight.

Three NSGr.9 aircraft were active for an hour from 1819, one attacking a target in the Bologna area at about 1838, and Allied bombers reported two encounters with Fw 190s. About 15 Ju 87 and Focke-Wulf sorties were mounted, and one Junkers very nearly came to grief. Fg Offs Denby and Raisen of 600 Sqn had already lost a contact near Bologna at 2045. Three minutes later they were vectored after another, and obtained a visual on a violently-weaving single-engined aircraft ten miles north of Imola, clearly silhouetted against the light portion of the western sky. Three cannon bursts produced no strikes as the target continued evasive action, but some flashes were taken to be return fire. As Denby fired again the Ju 87 peeled rapidly to starboard and was lost to view.

12 April 1945

MAAF reported a possible jet over the eastern/central front, and there were indications of Fw 190 activity near Ferrara around 1100. Two more were at 25,000ft over Corbola (RO) at 1300, jumping an F-5C which managed to evade them. The American pilot reported that his opponents had orange cowlings, suggesting they came from NAGr.11 (it had a tradition of yellow nose markings, and recorded two sorties on this date).

13 April 1945

General von Pohl requested from OKL the 'immediate allocation of two Ar 234s for maintaining and carrying out urgent operational tasks'. One Arado had been lost two days before and this signal may pinpoint the loss of another – Sommer wrote off T9+EH in a belly landing at Campoformido but forgets the exact date. The aeroplane's hydraulics had always been troublesome and now only the nosewheel would deploy: caught in a severe crosswind, the Blitz was smashed. He took over Stabsfw. Arnold's aircraft for subsequent operations; no replacements were sent.

German orders during the day called for dusk to dawn night attack operations on the front of LXXVIth Pz.Kps. and Ju 87s and Fw 190s duly flew from Villafranca under Egon control to targets in the Eighth Army's zone.

A 600 Sqn Mosquito XIX met a pair of Focke-Wulfs near Alfonsine. At 2030 Sqn Ldr Hammond and Fg Off Moore were directed on to a bogey coming southeast at 9,000ft. Visual and AI contact was obtained with two climbing Fw 190s, the rear one about 70yd behind the other and weaving slightly. Hammond opened fire on the leader from 350yd: '. . . a good concentration . . . caused bits to fly off the e/a. What appeared to be a long-range tank centrally-underslung, burst into flames. There was an explosion as the e/a turned over to starboard and went straight down, still burning.'

By now the No.2 was taking evasive action and a high-speed chase through cloud ensued, relying on AI. Regaining visual contact, the Mosquito scored hits on the German's starboard wing. Then vibration from the four cannon moved the reflector-sight switch to 'off' and the Fw 190 entered 10/10ths cloud, broke away to port, and escaped. The downed Focke-Wulf had been the second of three whose Egon traffic was monitored and its control station called it in vain for some time after it fell. On five subsequent nights 600 Sqn had contacts but this was to be its last combat in the Second World War and the RAF's last in Italy. The night's only other activity was the return home from Udine of the Ju 188 that had arrived from Bergamo two days earlier.

14-18 April 1945

On the 14th at least two night-attack aircraft operated around Lake Comacchio. The next morning two Italian fighters patrolled the Gallarate area, while that evening an attack aircraft homing in the Ghedi-Villafranca region, its bombs still aboard, jettisoned them near its airfield before landing at about 1953.

On the afternoon of the 16th two unarmed Bf 109s of the 2nd Croatian Fighter Squadron were flown in by their defecting pilots. On seeing landing facilities, each lowered his undercarriage, waggled his wings and fired red and white flares, following the instructions given in Allied propaganda broadcasts. Fw. Vladimir Sandtner landed his G-10 'Black 4' at Falconara; Fw. Josip Cekovic put G-14 'Black 10' down at Jesi. Joining their unit in March, they had flown five and eight missions respectively. At 1450 on this day they had set out from Lucko as part of a four-plane reconnaissance over the Senj area. After circling the target they had gradually fallen behind the others on the homeward leg and aimed for the Italian coast.

That night an estimated five to ten attack sorties were flown and it is possible to follow how Egon plotting-control Regent (apparently at either Este or Monselice (PD)) guided 'Nero-Anton' (aircraft 'A') to its target:

1848	Regent to Nero-Anton:		Come 10° left.
	"	"	: Now 5° right.
	"	"	: 4 minutes to target.
	"	"	: A bit more to the right.
	"	"	: Again a little left.
1900	"	"	: 50 seconds to target.
	"	"	: Target dead ahead of you.
	"	"	: Prepare to release on my signal.
	"	"	: Attention! Drop now.
	"	"	: I've lost radar contact with you.
	"	"	: You're too low: course 320°.
1910	"	"	: I've regained contact.

Look out for nightfighter.
10km to go, the airfield's right in front of you.

After evacuating Thiene (VI) on 27 April 1945, the Ju 87 of Ofw. Herbert Kehrer and Fw. Alfons Eck (3./NSGr.9) was shot down by American fighters over the Inn Valley, Austria. (Nawroth)

On the 17th a possible jet was reported east of Bologna and an Ar 234 was seen by MAAF reconnaissance aircraft at Campoformido; a German aircraft apparently reconnoitred Ancona. After sunset two aeroplanes strafed targets near Ravenna, one outclimbing a pursuing Mosquito. From 1809 to 1831 another three aeroplanes were plotted but abandoned their mission owing to faulty instruments.

At 0047 next morning an A-20 reported coming under air attack west of Ferrara. Four German aircraft dropped bombs in the Portomaggiore-Argenta (FE) area at about 0300 before returning to Villafranca. Italian fighters (under four different callsigns, including 6ª Sq.'s 'Gamba') patrolled in the Milan-Ghedi region just before midday, and at mid- and late afternoon. Something of a straw in the wind was the intelligence that two Ju 188s of 4.(F)/122 had left Bergamo and landed at Neubiberg, Bavaria. From 1832 to 1944 four ground-controlled Luftwaffe aircraft strafed and bombed around Bologna, while another reached its target at 2100.

19 April 1945

At 0925 two B-24Hs of the 849th BS(H), 2641st Provisional Group (Special), took off from Rosignano (LI) to drop supplies to Italian partisans harassing the Germans in the Alpine passes. By now the usual night missions were giving way to unescorted daylight ones. Only the dorsal and tail turret gunners protected each bomber, assigned to make a drop over the Valtellina, a valley south of Bormio (SO). Their route was partly over the sea and then over land, circumnavigating the Alps clockwise.

Meanwhile, at Lonate, 2ª Sq. was holding five aircraft at readiness. Towards 1030, as German radar confirmed that two unescorted four-engined aircraft were separately following the same Alpine route, Magg. Visconti ordered them to scramble. The ready-room telephone rang and the pilots ran for their Messerschmitts as mechanics removed camouflage netting.

Led by Ten. Oddone Colonna, the first three Bf 109s taxied out. S.Ten. Aurelio Morandi's aircraft refused to start, so he dismounted and ran towards the aeroplane of Serg. Alberto Bernardi, the last of the five, whose aircraft was just beginning to roll from its shelter. Pulling rank, Morandi ordered the NCO out of his Messerschmitt, jumped in, and sped off to join to the three already climbing away.

Meanwhile, the first B-24, flown by Capt Walter 'Tod' L. Sutton, cut across Swiss territory to continue towards Sondrio, a procedure unofficially followed by most 2641st Prov. Gp. pilots to shorten their journeys, relying on the Swiss gunners' limited belligerence and poor aim. Although the Americans apparently were not shot at, the Italians (also traversing a short stretch of Swiss airspace, near the Chiasso rail junction) certainly were.

Three of the four Gustavs quickly escaped with a swift right turn but Morandi had still not quite caught up and was bracketed by a salvo. The explosions caused the droptank (later found on Swiss soil) to release and hit the aeroplane's cockpit, causing it to side-slip and dive out of control. Morandi, probably wounded, released his canopy in an attempt to jump, but unavailingly. Moments later, at 1120, the Messerschmitt crashed near Cassina Rizzardi (CO).

The three other Italians, in line astern, carried on, and when the B-24 emerged from Swiss airspace forced it to change course southward, allowing them to cut inside and close on its tail. Capt. Sutton radioed an emergency call that was heard by the second B-24 and then, warned by tail gunner Sgt. Veazey that the fighters were reaching a firing position, tightened his turn and began evasive action.

Ten. Colonna's Bf 109G-10/AS (W.Nr.491333, '2-10') was first to attack, expending nearly all of its ammunition. With the bomber's sharp turns and accurate fire from its turrets, he apparently did not score any hits but was himself struck in the wing. Inside the B-24, however, Sgt. Burke's top-turret guns jammed, while Veazey was short of ammunition. Colonna radioed his base that the bomber was still airborne. Visconti's irate voice, already shocked at the loss of Morandi, sounded in the pilots' earphones, ordering the B-24 down shot down at all costs.

S.M. Brunello, Colonna's wingman and second in line, took his leader's place, positioning his Bf 109G-10/AS/U4 behind and slightly above the bomber. After two machine-gun bursts he saw that the tail turret had ceased firing. Manoeuvring to stay with the B-24, Brunello fired four more bursts, opening up with his 3cm cannon once his tracers were on target. The cannon's shells were devastating. A long tongue of flame burst from the ruptured starboard wing tanks. Aboard the bomber Capt. Sutton ordered his miraculously unharmed crew to bale out, and parachutes began to cascade from the bomb doors. Sutton was last out and the B-24 spiralled down to crash in a wood between the villages of Mozzate and Cislago (7km south of Tradate (CO)[62].

After a last pass over the flaming wreckage, the three Messerschmitts returned to base. S.M. Franciosi landed at Malpensa, and Brunello and Colonna put down moments later at Lonate, the latter with his brakes almost useless owing to bullet damage. Once down there was an acrimonious dispute, Colonna claiming the B-24 for himself and Brunello refusing to give up his victory. This was settled by Visconti assigning the kill posthumously to Morandi.

That morning at Aviano, Nucleo Comando, 4ª and 6ª Sq. were on the move, having been ordered a few

On 16 April, two Bf 109s of 2. Croat Staffel escaped to Italy. A G-10, landed at Falconara and was seized by US troops, while the second, a G-14 (shown here with its Croat markings overpainted) landed at Jesi. After the war this aircraft was offered to the Italian government but aroused no interest and was soon scrapped. (Gori)

days earlier to transfer to Villafranca. Groundcrewmen had been busy since dawn; almost 30 Messerschmitts equipped with droptanks had to be refuelled, armed and checked before take-off, and these operations had to be concealed from increasingly frequent enemy patrols that never missed a chance to strafe the aerodrome.

At 1140 the roar of 26 DB 605 engines shook the field. Moments later a green flare started a series of take-offs. First were the aircraft of Nucleo Comando, flown by Magg. Miani, S.M. Bianchini and M.llo Varacca, plus the three remaining serviceable 5ª Sq. Gustavs, recently arrived from Osoppo; 4ª Sq.'s 12 Messerschmitts followed, and last were the seven of 6ª Sq. Among the assembling formation were two of the three Bf 109K-4s just received by 6ª Sq. (the other was unserviceable), flown by S.M. Ferdinando Zanardi and Serg. Renato Patton. These aircraft, with their high performance and firepower (an engine-mounted 3cm cannon was standard), had been assigned to cover the rear against surprise attack.

At the same time, 270km further south, 16 P-51Ds of the 317th FS, 325th FG, (the famed 'Checkertail Clan') rendezvoused with B-25s from 340th BG off to bomb a bridge at Ora.

II° Gr. C. was climbing to 6,000m when, from 1200 to 1210, six Gustavs of 4ª Sq. developed a series of faults and malfunctions, forcing them back to Aviano[63].

At 1220 the 340th BG Mitchells were entering their bomb-run and in minutes it was all over. Leaving Ora's bridge shattered beneath heavy columns of smoke, bombers and escort made a wide turn on to their return route. Ten minutes later the converging American and Italian formations were nearing visual contact. As Lake Garda appeared in the distance, Magg. Miani received a call from 'Roma' control that enemy bombers would be crossing his path. The presence of hostile fighters was a matter of conjecture.

Tactical conditions seemed favourable. The Messerschmitts were higher and had the sun behind them. Miani weighed up the situation and then, perhaps over-estimating his unit's effectiveness, waggled his wings to signal his decision to attack. Meanwhile, another aircraft left the formation, that of S.Ten. Gianfranco Dinale, whose engine appeared about to seize, forcing him to throttle back and turn towards Aviano.

At 1235 Miani, Bianchini, Varacca and the 4ª Sq. aircraft jettisoned droptanks and dived to attack, leaving 6ª Sq. as top cover. The ten Messerschmitts side-slipped, quickly closing the distance to the bombers, but the sudden and (for most of the Italians) unexpected appearance of two flights of P-51s up ahead caused chaos.

Conversely, the Americans' reaction was swift and near-automatic. Eight of the 16 Mustangs headed for the Bf 109s and, led by 1st/Lt Frank W. Schaefer, split into pairs, diving after those Messerschmitts trying to run from them.

Lt Wendell B. Bagley had also noticed the enemy, and when they made a 180° turn was able to gain on the rear element. Firing at a Bf 109 as he closed in, Bagley observed hits on its engine; shortly afterwards it started smoking and, after doing a split-S, the Italian levelled out, rolled his aeroplane over and baled out. The Messerschmitt was seen to crash and burn.

This was Ten. Betti's 'Black 8' and its pilot, unaware that Serg. Zanetti, who should have been covering his back, was absent, had held formation, heedless of Bagley's approach. A hail of bullets and the explosion of his instrument panel convinced Betti that someone was on his tail. He tried evasive action but, realising his engine was out, released the canopy and jumped for the second time in two weeks.

S.M. Bianchini's aeroplane was in Lt. Schaefer's gunsight:

> I followed the Me 109 in a diving left turn . . . fired a burst at him from about 300 yards and saw some strikes on his left side around the wing root. I closed to about 100 yards and was just about to fire another burst . . . when he suddenly baled out, going right over the top of me (in fact I had to pull down a few feet to miss him) and about two seconds later the left wing separated from his aircraft. I climbed back up where it all started, but couldn't find a single aircraft. I circled a few times and then started home.

As Bianchini slowly descended, the other P-51s climbed and, as Lt. Bagley recalls: 'The Me's scattered, my right wing tank did not release and, as I wasted time to shake it off . . . I lost sight of Lt. Schaefer, our leader. Finally the tank released and I suddenly saw one Me flying alone straight to my left.'

The Italian top-cover section had lost cohesion when Serg. Patton's K-4 experienced engine trouble, losing height and speed. He was followed by S.M. Zanardi, slowing down to keep his comrade in sight. Patton was a sitting duck, and a desperate call from Zanardi to alert him to the attacking Mustang was to no avail. 'I pulled in behind and fired a long burst with 40° to 0° deflection, and observed hits on the left side of the fuselage. An explosion was observed at the left wing root and pieces were observed to fall from the aircraft. The Me 109 rolled over and went straight down, burning when it crashed.' The Italian jumped but his parachute failed to open fully, forming a so-called 'candle', and the unfortunate pilot fell to his death near Ponti sul Mincio (MN) at 1235. Serg. Renato Patton thus became the last ANR pilot killed in action.

Zanardi, jettisoning his K-4's droptank, joined the fight, but Lt Frank M. Bolek got on his tail, helped by the fact that the 109's DB 605D suddenly began 'coughing'. A quick glance by Zanardi at his fuel gauges showed a disconcerting 'zero', although his main tank was still full: the system was malfunctioning. Firing from 6 o'clock, Bolek noted many hits on his target's fuselage and cockpit; the Bf 109 burst into flames and its pilot baled out. Zanardi landed shaken but safe about 1km south of Desenzano (BS).

By this time the surviving top-cover Messerschmitts were under attack from Lts Baldwin and John Barrett. While M.llo Fumagalli and Ten. Ferrero (the latter wounded) managed to disengage, M.llo Covre and Serg. Tampieri fought desperately to free themselves from the mêlée. Bagley closed in to 60ft from 6 o'clock low on Covre's aeroplane, firing a long burst with 0° deflection. Although he saw no hits on the fuselage, there was an explosion shortly afterwards in the cockpit area and the Bf 109 pulled up, stalled, and was lost in the haze, out of control, smoking and burning furiously.

Although Covre was already almost completely out of his aeroplane, he re-entered its burning cockpit to radio Serg. Tampieri to disengage from Lt Barrett's Mustang. Then, burned on his hands and face, he jumped successfully, seconds before his aircraft hit the ground.

The warning saved Tampieri's life. Barrett fired a series of short bursts, observing hits at the base of the left wing. The Bf 109 began to smoke, but then snapped over suddenly and went down almost vertically. Barrett had to break away when other Bf 109s came at him but claimed the Gustav as destroyed as when last observed it was diving in flames at 1,500ft and smoking heavily. In fact Tampieri regained control and headed his badly damaged aircraft towards Villafranca.

As suddenly as it had begun, the action ceased. The eight Mustangs found themselves each in a quiet corner of the sky, all radio channels jammed by excited chatter. At about 1330 they rejoined those who had stayed with the Mitchells and 15min later they touched down at base, claiming six Bf 109s destroyed without loss.

Actually, II° Gruppo had suffered five aircraft lost with four pilots safe and one killed by a faulty parachute, plus several Bf 109s damaged, including 'White 12' of Ten. Ferrero, who had a leg fractured by a bullet – all in less than 15min.

As soon as the surviving Messerschmitts had reassembled, Cap. Drago led the six 4ª Sq. aircraft in to land at Ghedi, while Miani and the other six survivors headed for nearby Villafranca, where they landed at 1300. News of Serg. Patton's death only reached the other pilots later in the day, and sadness at his death was mixed in some with suspicions of sabotage.

At 1830, five[64] of the 4ª Sq. pilots who had 'evaded' the morning transfer left Aviano for Villafranca. Ten minutes after take-off Serg. Zanetti's engine again developed trouble and he landed at Thiene, the others reaching Villafranca at 1930. While taxying towards the dispersals, Cavagliano and Cavagnino burst their tyres on some of the thousands of nails that British bombers had dropped the previous night. This apparently minor damage was in fact extremely serious, given the prevailing spares shortages. The accident kept them in Villafranca for several days, and ended the second worst day in II° Gruppo Caccia's history.

There was one more combat that day, when the Checkertails' Lt. Leo A. Gertin (319th FS) went out late in the afternoon to run-in a newly-fitted engine. He had never before encountered a hostile aircraft, but ran into an Fw 190 near Florence. After each had attempted a head-on pass against the other, the Focke-Wulf ran for home on the deck, Gertin following to shoot it down as it came into land at Villafranca.

Notes

62. Capt. Sutton, Lt. Robert W. Brimmer (bombardier) and Sgt. William V. Marck (engineer), were captured by Italian paratroops based near Tradate; Sgt. Edward J. Veazey (tail gunner) and 1st/Lt Earl D. Cartmill (observer) were taken by the Germans. Lt Frank A. Stoehrer (co-pilot), Lt Ralph A. Anderson (navigator), S/Sgt. Kenneth C. Lail (radio operator), Sgt William J. Burke and T/Sgt Charles Schaeffer (waist gunners) landed in a partisan-controlled area and were taken to Switzerland.
63. They were: 'Black 14' (S.M. Passuello) and 'Black 11' (Serg. Benzi) – pilots' illness; 'Black 16' (M.llo Cavagnino), 'Black 19' (S.M. Cavagliano), 'Black 6' (M.llo Mingozzi) and 'Black 2' (Serg. Zanetti) – all claiming engine trouble. It is hard not to suspect a pact by 4ª Sq's NCOs to avoid the flight; all of these coincidences seem highly improbable.
64. Serg. Benzi (Black 11); S.M. Cavagliano (Black 14); M.llo Cavagnino (Black 16); S.M. Passuello (Black 5) and Serg. Zanetti (Black 2).

OPPOSITE:
This Ju 188 (probably F6+DP of 6.(F)/122) was photographed at Innsbruck. Together with five other aircraft of 4. and 6. Staffel it had reached this airfield on 25 April 1945 from Bergamo. As with many other aircraft operating primarily by night, this one shows a very hazy camouflage that almost completely hides its markings.

BELOW
Also at Innsbruck, a Ju 87D-5 of NSGr.9. In the background is an Me 262 of JV 44. (via Hildebrandt and Crow)

Covered by camouflage netting, Ju 188D-1 W.Nr.230499, F6+DM of 4.(F)/122 photographed at Bolzano after its arrival from Orio al Serio on 25 April 1945. A week later, on 2 May, with all Luftwaffe markings painted over and a makeshift civil registration, D-CEDM, it took off for Barcelona, Spain, carrying Vichy Prime Minister, Pierre Laval. After being allowed only a three-month stay, the Ju 188 (and M. and Mme. Laval) was flown back to Linz, Austria on 31 July 1945, into the hands of American troops. (Ries & via Crow)

CHAPTER 15

Collapse, Capitulation, Clear-up: 20 April – 2 May 1945

The Ground War

Mobile warfare returned and the Axis defence fell apart. On 21 April Bologna was finally taken; between the 23rd and 25th the Fifth and Eighth Armies linked up at Finale Emilia, trapping 100,000 German Tenth Army troops south of the Po. On the 24th the Americans took La Spezia and the Germans pulled out of Genoa. On the 25th the Gestapo, murderous to the last, shot six Jews in Cuneo. There was insurrection by up to 150,000 citizens of Milan and Turin; workers' councils took over the factories and hundreds of suspected fascists were put to death. The fleeing Mussolini was captured by partisans, shot, and his body exhibited in Milan on the 28th and 29th. Venice and Ghedi airfield were captured on the latter date and Army Liguria surrendered.

The major development of the 29th was the signing of the surrender of the Wehrmacht in Italy. German officers flew to Caserta, near Naples, to sign the instrument, to take effect on 2 May. Those involved in this unauthorised capitulation were ordered to be removed from their posts and various groups tried to arrest each other. Luftwaffe Chief of Staff Koller was initially supicious – '. . . one always had to be careful when dealing with Maxi Pohl' – but soon realised that the Kommandierender General could not fight on if the ground forces did not. In the event Kesselring, commanding the severed southern half of German-held territory, made the whole thing official, allegedly to avoid chaos. During the night of 1/2 May, the Luftwaffe in Italy was subordinated to Lfl. 6 'with immediate effect' – and to no purpose.

The Luftwaffe

Plans
Before the collapse, airfields in the 'Pre-Alpine Position' had been allocated for use *in extremis*:

FAGr.122	Graz, Austria
NAGr.11	Graz
NSGr.9	Sluderno (BZ)

The Italian fighters were to divide between Bolzano and Innsbruck, Gruppo 'Faggioni' going to Munich. Bolzano had a complete underground operations room where Jafü Oberitalien's staff were established at the war's end but it was never used.

In captivity in Rome in late 1945, General von Pohl began writing an account (from memory, for he had no access to files) of his time in Italy from the day in June 1940 when he and Oberst Gottschling arrived as a liaison mission to the Regia Aeronautica. Aside from the largely unrealised potential of the Fw 190 as a nightfighter, he had wanted to develop a pathfinding capability using Egon in conjunction with a Ju 87 carrying Erstling IFF and a 500kg marker bomb. Recognising that attacks on heavily defended objectives such as Ancona were not feasible, he nonetheless planned to send Egon-controlled aeroplanes on blind-bombing missions showering small-calibre fragmentation bombs on to Allied fighter airfields. Problems with fuel, manpower and weather supervened.

Oberst Neumann's memories were of plans to operate Me 163s from airfields around Verona and Brescia, with powerful flak to screen the rocket interceptors during their unpowered landings. These aircraft would presumably have been Italian-manned, had the training programme been completed. He also told his captors that work was under way to prepare Gallarate as a base for 'the projected JG 44', since its runway, dispersals and camouflage were ideal but that this fell through in the face of supply and fuel difficulties[65] and the general progress of the war.

Something of a mystery was this Fw 190F-9, W.Nr.440340, that landed at Villafranca on 25 April 1945, just after American troops had overrun the base. No Allied report reveals the origin of this brand-new aircraft, most probably destined for NSGr.9.

In March a PoW, recently stationed at Ghedi, had claimed that 80 jets were due to arrive there and at Villafranca from Germany during early April, 40 being based at each field. Maintenance equipment was being installed in a schoolhouse at Borgosatollo (BS), and personnel would be billeted in an underground barracks at Ghedi II. A 100-bed hospital had also been established underground. Heavily camouflaged dispersal bunkers had been constructed at Borgosatollo, Villafranca and in woods and farmyards near Castenedolo, Ghedi. New taxying strips had been laid between Borgosatollo and Ghedi I since mid-December 1944 and depressions at crossroads levelled out so that existing roads could be incorporated into the system. Along these strips, potted evergreens had been arranged to simulate ordinary roads and a park. The prisoner described the composition of the nine-man maintenance crews for each aircraft and named the workshop units from which other technical staff would be drawn.

Despite many reported sightings, we know of no hard evidence that Me 262s were ever in Italy. OKL in April had notified the Italian Embassy that pilots of II° Gr.C. would be trained on the type in Germany but no more came of this than of rumours within the Gruppo that they would be getting the He 162.

Order of Battle

Pohl's staff compiled the following on 22 April:

Unit	Base	Aircraft Number	Type
Stab/FAGr.122	Bergamo	0	
4.(F)/122	Bergamo	5(4)	Ju 188D-2
		1(1)	Ju 88T-3
6.(F)/122	Bergamo	6(6)	Ju 188D-2
2./NAGr.11	Udine II	8(5)	Bf 109G-10/R2
Kdo. Götz	Osoppo	1(1)	Ar 234B-2
Stab/NSGr.9	Villafranca	1(0)	Ju 87D (trainer)
1./NSGr.9	Villafranca	3(2)	Fw 190A-8
		4(4)	Fw 190F-8
2./NSGr.9	Ghedi II	3(3)	Ju 87D-3
		7(7)	Ju 87D-5
3./NSGr.9	Villafranca	6(6)	Ju 87D-3
		10(7)	Ju 87D-5

Other evidence suggests that as well as a number of liaison aircraft we should add:-
Kdo. Carmen   Bergamo   1(1)   Ju 188

The table indicates that at some time after 9 April 2./NAGr.11 gave up its surviving Fw 190A-8s to 1./NSGr.9. Two were found burned out in a revetment at Villafranca, one (E8+BB) with Stab/NSGr.9's markings and, what is more, *two* Ju 87s with Stab markings were found (E8+MB at Villafranca and E8+LB at Ghedi).

From the evidence of the identifiable wrecks found at Campoformido, 2./NAGr.11 operated only a single Bf 109 G-10/R2, the balance of its strength being G-8s and a G-6/R2.

The ANR

I° Gr.C.

From 22-25 April the few flights just shifted aircraft from Lonate to Malpensa, the last being at 0835 on the latter date and involving ten Bf 109s led by Visconti and the two Bü 181s.

After this, Visconti and his men occupied schools in Gallarate, digging in and opening negotiations with the local partisan units and others that had descended from the mountains. He aimed to surrender only to Allied troops and to have his men's lives guaranteed but the talks immediately proved difficult, as the disparate politics of the various partisan groups led to misunderstandings and hardening of positions. Meanwhile, on 27 April, an agreement allowed four trucks led by Cap. Robetto to Malpensa, to try and prevent German troops destroying the Messerschmitts. They were too late; Maj. Stamm, the airfield's Kommandant, had already given the order and the Italians could do nothing but watch their aircraft burn and explode.

In the ensuing 24hr the situation got even worse and, given that the partisans completely controlled the area, and that in the event of conflict there were thousands of civilians all around, Visconti finally decided to sign a surrender that at would least safeguard his men against reprisals. However, unknown to him, a partisan tribunal had already decreed his death and when all of I° Gruppo's officers were brought to Milan's 'Savoia Cavalleria' barracks on 29 April, he and his aide-de-camp, S.Ten. Stefanini, were summoned for interrogation. This was a ruse to separate them from the others and no sooner were they in the barracks courtyard than the sentence was executed with a few bursts of machine-gun fire. Thus died Adriano Visconti, one of the Italian Air Force's most gallant pilots; with six aeroplanes claimed in the ANR and 19 in the Regia Aeronautica, he was one of the top-scoring Italian pilots of the Second World War.

The lives of the other airmen were saved first by the intervention of an Army officer, then the arrival of British troops.

II° Gr.C.

On the 20th the Gustavs of Serg. Benzi and S.M. Passuello took off from Villafranca and joined the rest of the Squadriglia in Ghedi. The paths of II° and III° Gruppi finally crossed when, on that day, two Bf 109G-10s, flown by Ten. Ramponi and S.M. Tonini, took off from Holzkirchen (where III° Gr.C. was still training) and flew via Riem to Aviano, where the aircraft were handed to II° Gruppo.

Two more Messerschmitts were due to be delivered by III° Gr.C. on the 21st, but, while Serg. Somadossi's G-10 reached Aviano safely, M.llo Alessandri's G-12 crashed in the Alps for unknown reasons, killing both him and 1° Aviere Mellano in the back seat. On 22 April four Messerschmitts (probably the three from Germany and one repaired in Aviano) left Aviano for Ghedi.

According to S.Ten. Di Santo's diary, until 22 April the intended destination of the Training Section was Ghedi, but in Villafranca there were new discussions between Oberst Neumann and Magg. Miani about where II° Gruppo should go. The Germans proposed the planned transfer to Bolzano or Innsbruck but the Italians, realising the war was ending, wanted to go west and await the Allies' arrival.

The next day agreement was reached. All of II° Gruppo's aeroplanes would fly to Orio al Serio and pass to the Germans, and the Italian pilots and personnel would await the end in the nearby town of Alzano Lombardo (BG). On the 24th the transfer began; at 0530, under cover of thick haze, the first aircraft began taking off from Villafranca for Orio al Serio.

With the intervals between take-offs and the impossibility of operating in full daylight, only nine effected the transfer. At dusk, eight more reached Orio: six from Ghedi and two from Aviano.

The events are well described by Di Santo:

> Reveille at 2 o'clock. All is ready to leave: I have to transport one plane. On the airfield. Enemy aircraft continuously on our heads dropping bombs. Ten. Larese has taken off in my place. The younger men have collapsed, we of the old guard try to keep spirits high. We have reached Desenzano in our bus. Always bombardments. At 1700 departure with the Commander for Valeggio to take other aircraft. Most adventurous journey.

At dawn on 25 April the last aircraft reached Orio: six came from Ghedi, while a section comprising M.llo Cavagnino, Serg. Zanetti and Di Santo (the latter flying a G-12) left Villafranca at 0530, landing 20min later.

According to Magg. Bellagambi's diary, this left a total of 26 aircraft in German hands. Some were destroyed immediately, as S.M. Cavagliano remembers:

> While in the circuit . . . I noticed a lot of small flags scattered all over the airfield that didn't signify anything good. I chose a strip of ground with fewer flags and was lucky to avoid the unexploded 'frags' they denoted, dropped a few hours earlier by a British night bomber. I taxied up to a corner of the airfield following the signals of an old German officer, completely drunk, who kept saying "Deutschland kaputt" and ordered me to take my parachute away from the plane, then bathed it with petrol and set it afire, repeating his refrain and weeping . . .

Other Messerschmitts had their wings partly sawn through, yet others were left intact. All of the Italian units were grounded from that day on.

Since the evening of 25 April II° Gr.C's personnel (excepting those few in Aviano with the aircraft still under repair) were billeted in schools at Alzano

Lombardo. The situation is described by the diaries of Magg. Bellagambi and S.Ten. Di Santo.:

26 April
(Bellagambi) The situation is chaotic. We are still united. It seems that we should co-operate for the sake of public order.

27 April
(Bellagambi) Chaos continues. It seems that there is an agreement between our HQ and the Bonomi Government. Many think it's time to leave. Nobody harms us.
(Di Santo) The Commander [Miani] has reached an agreement with the leader of the CLN, we will co-operate to maintain public order. At 1400 Col. Baylon reached agreement with a General of the Regia Aeronautica. We must remain here and wait for British troops.

28 April
(Bellagambi) . . . we give the personnel the choice of remaining or leaving. Seventy go. Some 250 elect to remain. We are threatened by two partisans of the Garibaldi units because we refused to turn our weapons over to them. We pay all the personnel with cheques. There are disturbances in Bergamo. I am worried.
(Di Santo) . . . Nothing new. the Americans passed not far from here. In the evening the Commander said that whoever wants to go will be supplied with a safe-conduct. I don't know what to do. I am uncertain like everyone. To leave our Commander is unworthy of an officer. I have been paid my salary.

29 April
(Bellagambi) . . . The situation is quieter.
(Di Santo) I awoke late. At 0900 I decided to leave. I made the journey by foot and near Ponte S. Pietro I was humiliated. Partisans wanted to kill me. I didn't believe it all could end like this. Luckily they finally set me free. At 1500 I was home at last.

The troubles of Miani, Bellagambi, Drago and the other officers of II° Gr.C. were not over yet, for on 30 April all were arrested and brought to Milan and the presence of Gen. Sala, official representative of the Air Force of the Italian Government. After a short and futile interrogation they were released at 2100.

The officers went back to Alzano Lombardo and organised the disbanding of the unit. This passed off without problems, apart from those caused by the conflict among the partisans about taking over the unit's property. This was officially handed over on 4 May to a representative of the Regia Aeronautica and various partisan units, a document signed by Magg. Bellagambi, Cap. Drago and Ten. Bettinardi (Gruppo treasurer) marking the final dissolution of II° Gruppo Caccia.

III° Gr.C.
As the month, and the war, ended, the Germans let 9ª Sq.'s pilots go home, their bus reaching Molveno (TN) in peacetime. Meanwhile, on 25 April the men of 7ª and 8ª Sq. holed up in the schools of Desio and Seriate respectively, successfully negotiated safe conduct with the partisans for themselves and their families and disbanded without further incident.

Order of Battle

The ANR's strength recorded on the 22nd was:

Unit	Base	Aircraft Number	Type
I° Gr.C.			
Stab I° Gr.C.	Lonate	2(2)	Bf 109K-4
1ª Sq.	Gallarate	7(5)	Bf 109G-10
		4(2)	Bf 109G-14
2ª Sq.	Lonate	7(6)	Bf 109G-10
		6(4)	Bf 109G-14
3ª Sq.	Lonate	7(5)	Bf 109G-10
		4(2)	Bf 109G-14
II° Gr.C.			
Nucleo Comando	Villafranca	1(1)	Bf 109G-10
4ª Sq.	Ghedi I	9(6)	Bf 109G-10
	Villafranca	3(2)	Bf 109G-10
	Aviano	2(1)	Bf 109G-10
5ª Sq.	Aviano	1(0)	Bf 109G-14
	Thiene	1(1)	Bf 109G-14
	Villafranca	4(3)	Bf 109G-14
		2(1)	Bf 109G-10
6ª Sq.	Aviano	2(0)	Bf 109G-14
		1(0)	Bf 109K-4
	Villafranca	5(4)	Bf 109G-14
Sez. Addestramento	Villafranca	7(7)	Bf 109G-6
		2(1)	Bf 109G-12
III° Gr.C.	Bergamo	1(1)	Bf 109G-10
	Holzkirchen	[no figure given]	
I° Gr. Aerosil.	Ghedi II	8(6)	S.79
	Lonate	4(1)	S.79

Since only one Bf 109 in Aviano is listed as serviceable, this may reflect the situation a few days earlier than the 22nd, before the arrival of the other aeroplanes from III° Gr. The II° Gr. Villafranca figures show that the training section had apparently grown to Squadriglia-size, probably using all the old

Messerschmitts supplanted in the front line by newer versions.

Fuel

The statistics (in m³) for the last days of the Campaign are:

Date	B4	C3	J2	A3
23.04	147	116	326	52
28.04	130	80	280	
29.04	47	10	267	
30.04	50	13	85	
01.05	10	7	85	

It is easy to see the effects of aircraft evacuation and the distribution (official or otherwise) of aviation fuel for use by earthbound transport in full retreat. MAAF found no fuel dumps at all after fighting ceased, just 200 tons of various types (aviation spirit included) being used at unit level for local movement.

Notes

65. Although Italy was well provided with J2 for three Ar 234s, it would not have lasted 20+ Me 262s for long.

Inside a sandbagged blast pen at Campoformido, the only Bf 109G-10 reconnaissance model found in Italy was pictured on 19 May 1945. Bf 109G-10/R2 W.Nr.770338 was found together with the wrecks of 11 more reconnaissance Gustavs of NAGr.11, whose withdrawal to Bolzano had been prevented by a short spell of bad weather, leading the unit to destroy all its aircraft at Campoformido. (NASM)

The remains of two Bf 109s of IIº Gr.C. found by Allied troops at Villafranca di Verona. The wreck with the US officer standing beside it was Bf 109G-6 W.Nr.160660, while the second Gustav was a G-10/AS most probably belonging to 4ª Sq., as the size of the fuselage flag suggests. (NASM)

CHAPTER 15

Operations

20 April 1945

According to M.llo Forlani's logbook, ten Bf 109s of I° Gr.C. scrambled at 1000, and in combat with P-47s near Piacenza he claimed one shot down. These would be the Gruppo's last combat and victory, although neither has yet been corroborated from other sources.

Luftwaffe radio monitors once gave Erich Sommer a transcript of P-51 pilots trying to intercept him and frustratedly reporting, 'he's too bloody fast!': perhaps this was the P-51 that tried to chase his Ar 234 over Padua on the 20th. Jet sightings were made over Bologna, Ravenna and Venice, all around midday.

Italian fighters patrolled during early evening and a Ju 188 flew a short operation after dark. About five NSGr.9 aeroplanes operated around Bologna, supporting 1. FJ Div. At 2014 traffic was heard from two Fw 190s operating as nightfighters, claiming they had shot down a Liberator over the Adriatic, but the authors have been unable to confirm that a B-24 was lost.

21 April 1945

At 0303 one of a pair of NSGr.9 aeroplanes reported 'bombs gone' but was probably short of its target. A Croat biplane with two aboard made a last-minute defection to the Allies at Falconara; NSGr.9 dropped 'butterfly-bombs' on traffic near Budrio (BO) and FAGr.122 operated over the Adriatic. A 255 Sqn nightfighter fired on a radar contact but lost it.

22 April 1945

Oblt. Sommer flew T9+FH over the Po Valley, covering the German retreat. After what appeared to be a solo weather reconnaissance about 30 night-attack sorties were mounted round Bologna. Four or five aircraft strafed II Corps HQ and a single aircraft shot up Fifth Army HQ around midnight. A lone Ju 188 flew a short mission. That night an aircraft in Croat markings took off from Milan-Linate for Spain. This was an S.83T (factory number 34013, formerly civil registration I-ARCA) of the RSI Air Ministry, carrying VIPs[66] and political documents to a neutral haven. The 'disguise' had been adopted to circumvent political/diplomatic restrictions on landing rights and the transport landed safely at Barcelona airport.

23 April 1945

Six Egon-directed aircraft were operating in the early hours and an Ar 234 was seen under tow to take-off position at Campoformido; 2./NAGr.11 attempted four sorties to cover the central front but all were turned back by the defences or weather. Just as a 30min armed reconnaissance marked the ANR's last mission, so that night's Ju 188 reconnaissance was the last recorded in Italian skies. NSGr.9 flew dusk to dawn attacks entailing 21 Ju 87 and Fw 190 sorties in front of the Fourteenth Army in the Viadana-Modena-Mirandola area. Hans Deutsch in Ju 87 E8+EL bombed and strafed the river crossing at San Benedetto Po (MN). A Baltimore evaded an Fw 190 and, in a signal to Lfl.6, Pohl reported one Fw 190 missing on ops.

24 April 1945

At 0300, nightfighters obtained a number of AI contacts but were unable to follow through; an hour later a Rotte from 2./NAGr.11 was placed at readiness. Six enemy aircraft reported sighted by MAAF may have been those of II° Gr.C. in transit. At 1100 an F-5C reported two Spitfires pursuing a Bf 109 over Lake Garda. NSGr.9 quit Villafranca for a new base, Thiene's Parish Diary recording that: 'On the airfield there are more than 30 aircraft, German bombers of various models.'

Oblt. Sommer took T9+FH on a sortie covering Viadana, Reggio Emilia, Bologna and Bergantino (RO). At 1600 a tired column of 100 men from NSGr.9's ground echelon reached Thiene, bringing three lorry-loads of bombs. At 2130 aircraft took off to bomb towards the Po, one returning an hour later to crash to destruction near the church.

It is probable that 24 April saw Carmen's finale. Lt. Raymond L. Knight[67] led P-47s of the 346th FS on a reconnaissance and, finding nothing at Ghedi or Villafranca, went on to Bergamo. In this attack and another the same day they claimed destruction of flak positions, a building, three single-engined types and *nine* Ju 88s: 'All of the enemy aircraft must have been fully gassed up, for all of them burned and four of the Ju 88s blew up with a terrific explosion, which indicated full bomb loads.'

Compare this with the account of Carmen's Ltn. Thurnhuber[68]: 'In mid-April 1945 the whole crew stood on the roof of their quarters and watched an attack on their airfield by American fighters, during which their Ju 188 was shot up. One of the bombs that had been loaded on the plane for a planned attack on a bridge exploded and tore the machine apart.'

Having no more serviceable aircraft, Thurnhuber and his men set off home overland, reaching Southern Germany by way of the South Tyrol. That night, 4. and 6.(F)/122 at last left Bergamo, ordered to Sluderno and Bolzano. In the event just two went to the latter airfield and six across the Alps to Innsbruck-Hötting.

25 April 1945

The RAF noted a possible Ar 234 reconnaissance over the battle area and there were sightings by Spitfires, near Venice and in the Ostiglia-Udine area, of a jet going north. 2./NAGr.11 put up two sorties but Erich Sommer is categorical that his Kommando's last flight was made the day before. Shortly after American troops had overrun Villafranca an Fw 190F-9 landed there, whether by accident or design is unknown. It bore no unit markings, only the normal crosses and W.Nr.440340, but presumably it was intended for the now-departed NSGr.9. Its equally pristine sister, 440341, was found by the Americans at Neubiberg-bei-München.

26 April 1945

At 0300 there was homing activity which Sigint associated with NSGr.9. Northeast of Verona at 1310, a pair of P-47s from the 66th FS were strafing when, as Capt Richard L. Johnson put it: 'To our great surprise an Me 109 came towards us. We think at first he only saw [2nd/Lt Roland E.] Lee who was on a strafing pass.' The Bf 109, coming from the northeast, made a pass at Lee but he was out of range. It tried again but Lee evaded, leaving his companion to cut the German off on his third pass. Johnson kept his sights on the bandit for about a minute: 'I decided he perhaps, knowing they had had it, would not be very aggressive. That perhaps we could induce him somehow to come our way and then we would have his aircraft to play with. Each time he would turn [in] a wrong direction I would fire left of him [to make him] turn right . . . right to cause left guiding.'

The German pulled up, nearly stalling, and made a split-S to starboard. Lee fired, closing to about 500ft before the Bf 109 was hit in the rear fuselage. The pilot jettisoned his hood and baled out on a dark green parachute, his aeroplane rolling thrice before spinning in and breaking up on impact (but not exploding).

The Bf 109 carried dark camouflage, German crosses and yellow bands round its nose. This last item (and the circumstances) point strongly to it coming from 2./NAGr.11. This was the last combat over Italy and another chapter closed around midday when American pilots saw burning, demolished hangars at Ghedi and a 'large column of our troops on highway two miles east'.

27 April 1945

A short spell of bad weather beginning on the 27th prevented NAGr.11's withdrawal to Bolzano and all of its Bf 109s were reported destroyed at Campoformido, barring a G-8 apiece at Aviano and Vicenza. There were no NAGr.11 pilots among the aircrew remaining in Italy at the Surrender, however.

The Germans began destroying stores, documents and installations at Thiene and the base CO fled in civilian clothes. At 1100 NSGr.9's flyable aeroplanes set off for Innsbruck; the rest were burned. A Ju 87 could not make it over the mountains and was forced to return, also to be set on fire by its crew. A local boy later scavenged several fragments from the wreck, including an airscrew blade, a wing panel and part of the chassis plate[69]. Five Fw 190s and 13 Ju 87s made their escape and once in Austria the Focke-Wulfs were reportedly destroyed, as was at least one Junkers

At 1845 the aircraft safety station transmitter at Verona, which had long served FAGr.122, finally shut down.

28 April 1945

An attack on Thiene led to the destruction of a remaining Fw 190.

Erich Sommer tells us that his last Arado, T9+FH, left Campoformido on this date. Its pilot, Stabsfw. Arnold, had orders to make for Bolzano or Feldkirchen according to the weather but opted for Holzkirchen while in the air. Sommer was then among the witnesses to a spectacle unmentioned by our other sources:

> . . . a squadron of Me 109s took off while there were some Thunderbolts circling some kilometers south at about 2,000ft. Shortly afterwards there was a mêlée and a Thunderbolt fell burning from sight. The gun noise stopped [but] the circling went on . . . getting gradually wider. It looked as if a friendly meeting was taking place and finally both Messerschmitts and Thunderbolts, flying together disappeared southwards . . . Everyone shook his head and I left, telling Hptm. Eckerscham of NAGr.11 . . . of my decision.

Sommer had secured written orders (a prudent measure, given the summary 'justice' being dispensed by death-squads to suspected deserters) to withdraw to Bolzano. His own Ar 234 remained in pieces at Campoformido, its engines stored in the town, to be found later by the Allies. Learning of this only in 1989, he was somewhat surprised: 'This means that instead of blowing them up as I had directed before driving home, my men just left them there. In the end it did not matter a bit. Only it could have cost me my head, especially at this crazy moment in time . . .'

He and his ground echelon set off by road for their intended new home. Their route over the Alps, via Lienz in Austria, was circuitous but the only one open. Their journey was eventful, including a gun battle with partisans (who had also been killing or abducting unwary Germans around Campoformido)

and the loss of Sommer's logbooks and diaries in a trailer that fell over a mountainside. Also, many documents and aerial photographs were deliberately destroyed – no one wished to mark himself out as belonging to a special unit and the men even carried fake pay books to conceal their identities. Sommer and Arnold were reunited in an internment camp after the war. The latter told his commander that he had landed safely at Holzkirchen, where he blew up his aeroplane the following day.

29-30 April 1945

Probably the only flying involving the Axis was the surrender delegation's journey to Caserta on the 29th.

1-2 May 1945

Some faint vital sparks remained in FAGr.122. In the early hours of the 1st a 4. Staffel aircraft (one of the pair that had left Italy on 18 April) was in radio contact with Lübeck. At 0915 next day a 4.(F)/122 Ju 188 (W.Nr. 230499) left Bolzano for neutral Barcelona; it carried the Prime Minister of the collaborationist French Vichy régime, Pierre Laval, and his wife. Granted only a three-month stay, they were flown back to Linz, Austria on 31 July, then delivered to the French occupying forces at Innsbruck.

It has been claimed that the two (now ex-) Luftwaffe crew, Gerhard Boehm and Helmut Funk, chose the aircraft's destination, giving Laval little say in the matter. A contemporary newspaper report suggests that the Junkers was devoid of all national markings and painted black all over. It did, however, retain its W.Nr. in white on the fin and white spirals on the spinners.

Probably the last casualty of the Italian airwar was the CO of the 345th FS, Maj. Edward Gabor. While strafing near Udine on 2 May his P-47 was hit by light flak, went out of control and crashed. Major Gabor was killed.

Notes

66. Among them were the parents and some relatives of Claretta Petacci, Mussolini's mistress, who had been shot alongside him (the circumstances are unclear) on 28 April by partisans in a village near Lake Como.
67. An audacious and successful strafer, Knight was killed the next day, when his flak-damaged aeroplane failed to make it home across the Apennine mountains. He was awarded the Congressional Medal of Honor.
68. Given to Dr G.W. Gellermann (NB's translation).
69. He has preserved these items to the present day, but a corroded section (carrying the aircraft's Werk Nummer) was snipped from the plate and discarded.

Chapter 15

Peacetime

MATAF dispatched a liaison party to Pohl's HQ at Malcesine, meeting the General himself on 6 May. They then set about gathering the information needed to disarm the Luftwaffe in Italy. There were 18,300 personnel, 119 of them aircrew (including eight air gunners of the hitherto unheard-of 4./NSGr.9), and the following flyable aircraft (all at Bolzano):

Type	W.Nr.	Code
Ju 188 D-2	0590	F6+CM (ex CZ+BR)
Fi 156 C-3tr.	5138	DH+MZ
Fi 156 C-3tr.	1400	V1+TF
Fi 156	110416	SV+SF
Bf 108	865	–

All were taken south on Allied instructions and F6+CM went to Naples via Florence, being intended for evaluation at Wright Field, but apparently this plan fell through, as did another less official one.

A few days after the end of the war, Lts Sulzbach and Morrow of the 346th FS, 350th FG, flew to Orio al Serio:

. . . we landed with our P-47s at Bergamo with the thought that we might be able to fly a 109 back to Pisa. While we were taxying, a couple of German personnel came towards us riding bicycles. We made a short bargain with the two and for a few dollars each, they loaned their bicycles to us, while mounting guard to our aircraft. We then reached some buildings and identified ourselves with a German Colonel. He gave us a jeep and a driver to guide us. We located the 109s. All . . . had been sabotaged. The wings were chopped off just outside the wheel wells. I never did get to fly a 109.

For MAAF's Intelligence men the work went on of interrogating prisoners, many of them now Staff Officers, sifting captured documents and picking over wrecked aeroplanes. Without their unsung labours and the reports and histories they wrote, this book would not have been possible in its present form.

Milan, 29 April 1945. The first US troops enter the city, welcomed by cheering crowds and here shown passing the Duomo, the city's cathedral. The war in Italy is over and only wrecks remain of the Axis equipment.
(Istituto Nazionale per la Storia del Movimento di Liberazione in Italia.)

Appendix

Camouflage and Markings

This section is intended to be read with reference, where appropriate, to the colour paintings and photographs elsewhere in this book. Paintings labelled '(reconstruction)' are based primarily on documentary rather than direct photographic evidence. The main text contains numerous examples of markings and Werk Nummer and this appendix gives only a few supplementary examples to illustrate specific points. Exotic colour schemes 'seen' in the heat of combat are not covered, simply because documentary and photographic evidence for them is lacking.

Luftwaffe

Day Fighters and Tactical Reconnaissance Aircraft

In the early part of the campaign, fighters seem to have carried standard camouflage in greys 74/75/76, frequently with the addition of a white tail band as a Mediterranean Theatre marking; Geschwader emblems were common on Bf 109s of JG 77 and JG 53. By the early summer of 1944 a scheme had been developed apparently to offer better ground concealment in Italian terrain. All upper surfaces were densely oversprayed, with a scribble of dark green and brown paint almost obliterating the tail band and frequently national markings as well. Aircraft of I./JG 4 offer the most extreme example of the practice, while a Bf 109G-6 delivered to II./JG 77 was more lightly oversprayed and with all its crosses (outline type) clearly visible. By late summer the aircraft destined for JG 77 (e.g. the two that landed in Switzerland) were again conventionally painted. As on the Invasion Front, unit emblems seem to have been done away with in summer 1944. Orders were issued to this effect for aircraft in the Luftflotte 3 area and the same may well have applied elsewhere.

The Bf 109s of NAGr.11 again wore the 74/75/76 scheme, but during summer 1944 (if not later) a white tail band (and, for the short-lived 3. Staffel, a yellow one) was carried. As with other recce units, the panel beneath the engine could be painted yellow and there are numerous reports right up to the war's end of aircraft (both Bf 109s and Fw 190s) with a yellow (or 'orange') ring around the nose. The Gruppe was peculiar in that aeroplanes of 1. Staffel carried their individual numbers in black and those of 2. in white, with 3. using the normal yellow. Available photographic evidence suggests that these numbers were quite small.

Night Attack
NSGr.9

NSGr.9's Fiat Cr.42s seem to have been painted with a scheme of 76, green and brown. The colours were either applied as blotches or in a sort of 'wave-mirror' pattern, in some cases extending even under the wings. The E8 code was in small characters and the aircraft and Staffel letters were large with thin black or no outlines at all.

When Ju 87s were first delivered in early 1944 they arrived in standard 70/71/65 or 70/65 and factory code letters, and some carried a white (or yellow?) tail band, possibly from their former employment. The photograph on page 38 shows this early scheme which may have been used operationally for a short time.

By the end of the war aircraft E8+GK looked quite different – an Allied report describes its finish as 'night camouflage: mottled brown and green'. Photographic and wreck evidence suggests that this new scheme was in use during the summer of 1944. When 2./NSGr.2's aircraft arrived in Italy in July they were (to quote a prisoner from the Staffel) 'painted brown'. Photographs show Ju 87s oversprayed on their upper surfaces with a scribble pattern in a light brown[70] (possibly Luftwaffe 'sand yellow' 79 or a close Italian equivalent, depending on stocks available).

The overspray might partially obscure national markings and 'feathers' of it were sometimes sprayed over the wheel spats, while 'feathers' of a dark colour (green?) could be extended under the wing leading edges or a grey scribble applied right across the pale blue undersides.

Upper surface national markings were of the late-war outline type and underwing crosses were often lacking. Some machines had a black spinner with a one-third segment of the forward section in white. In other cases the camouflage paint was carried over on to the spinner. Most aircraft had their individual letter in the appropriate Staffel colour (examples of white and yellow are known from photographs) on the front of one or both wheel spats.

Camouflage of the Gruppe's Fw 190s was apparently 74/75/76 – at least for the F-8 models. The unmarked F-9 (W.Nr.440340) arriving at Villafranca at the war's end was – to judge from the cursory description given – in the later grey/green scheme of 75/83/76 with much of the rear fuselage and vertical tail surfaces in the latter colour. On all types the E8 code was in characters one fifth the size of the individual and Staffel letters. The marking system within the Gruppe was as follows (examples of representative Ju 87s and Fw 190s can be found in the next Appendix):

Gruppenstab (code E8+_B): A burnt-out Ju 87 (E8+MB) reportedly had a yellow third letter. One would have expected green (or just possibly blue) so perhaps fire had discoloured the paint. No reference to colour is made on any other Stab aircraft, which may indicate that all four code characters were black.

1.Staffel (code E8 + _H): Individual letter in black with a narrow white outline on Ju 87s and Fw 190s.

2.Staffel (code E8+_K): Individual letter in red with a narrow white outline on Ju 87s. E8+JK, a Cr.42 at Aeritalia, Turin in late April 1944 had no outline to the J.

3.Staffel (code E8 + _L): The Staffel letter was in yellow. When 2./NSGr.2 (forerunner of 3./9) arrived in Italy its aeroplanes were reported as "White 1, White 2" etc., and later that day as D3+AK, D3+BK and so on, suggesting that each carried a number corresponding to the alphabetical position of its code letter. In common with other night attack units this number may have appeared in a circle or diamond, high on the rudder.

Sonderverband 'Einhorn'

At Villafranca in May 1945 the Allies found just the fuselage of an Fw 190F-8/R1 (W.Nr.581447 A3+LX). No other information has come to light on the unit's aircraft.

An aircraft of 1944 vintage would *probably* have carried 74/75/76 camouflage and been fitted with the old-type cockpit canopy. The carriage of 1,000kg weapons would imply use of the ETC 504 bomb rack. By analogy with A3+LV (an F-8/R16 photographed in Northern Europe after the war), the lettering would have been all-black, with the first two characters one fifth the size of the last two.

Long Range Reconnaissance
1.(F)/123 and Westa 26

The Ju 88T-1 (+BH) pictured on page 35 probably belonged to 1.(F)/123. The '4U' Gruppe code is not visible in the photograph, but loss reports show that it was carried by the unit's aeroplanes. The black individual letter is noteworthy.

Westa 26's code, 5M, was in small characters, and the individual aircraft letter was large and black. Only three characters were used: 5M+A etc. The unit badge – a white shield with an owl sat on a yellow crescent moon – was inherited by 6.(F)/122 and reportedly carried as late as September 1944.

Both units' Ju 88s carried a pale scribble over a dark background on their top sides and were either 65 or 76 underneath.

2.(F)/122

The unit's Me 410s were painted in 74/75/76, mottled on the fuselage and segmented on the wing upper surfaces. The codes were F6+_K with the F6 in small characters, the third and fourth letters were large and black. Some aircraft had a red ring on one or both spinners; the unit's badge was apparently not seen after 1943 and nor were yellow panels beneath the engine nacelles.

4.(F) and 6.(F)/122

Information on 4.(F) (coded F6+_M) and 6.(F)/122 (coded F6+_P) is inconsistent. It seems likely that their Ju 88 and 188 aircraft began life in 70/71/65, most receiving a brown, pale-grey (02) or light blue scribble on their topsides, supplemented in some cases with a dark (66 or 22) scribble on the pale blue undersurfaces. The overspray toned down national markings to a considerable extent in some cases, and this may have become standard practice, as with bombers. The aircraft that brought Pierre Laval back from Spain was all black 22 underneath. Black and white spirals on spinners were common. No report from Italy mentions coloured Staffel letters but F6+KM, found in Greece, had a blue third letter.

Kommando Sommer

The wreck report on Ltn. Gniesmer's aircraft notes 'a dark olive-drab' on the upper surfaces (photographs show a two-tone splinter) and light blue beneath: clearly the standard 81/83/76 scheme. The *Hakenkreuz* was partially obscured by paint. A battery cover among the wreckage was marked SI+BP, which was assumed to be the aeroplane's factory callsign.

Only the Balkenkreuz and DH in large black letters could be discerned on the remaining fuselage sections. The common practice on 1./Versuchsverband OKL aircraft was for the unit code T9 to be applied in small white letters, and Kommando Sommer probably followed suit. Large black Ds were applied outboard of the underwing outline-type crosses. No letter is reported on the detached wing found at Campoformido, but this cannot be taken as confirmation of its absence. Only a cross and large black H remained of the fuselage markings of the latter aircraft.

If the F3 code logged by Lonate was indeed real, one might have expected it also to have been small and white but this can only be conjecture. This code was attributed to both Sommer's and Gniesmer's Arados up to and including 1 April. It is reasonable to assume that Arnold's +FH would have conformed.

The Werk Nummer of T9+DH was in the standard format, black with the first three figures of a reduced size.

Kommando Carmen

The scant photographic evidence (see page 148) suggests an uppersurface scheme similar to that of FAGr.122's Ju 188s but the presence of a dark scribble on the undersides is impossible to confirm. It is quite possible that KG 200 did not standardise the paintwork of the aeroplanes it inherited. A Ju 188E-1 that crashed in Holland had '. . . light green predominant on a faint background of blue/grey/mauve', while its undersides were black.

Transports

The S.82s of II./TG 1 seem to have been plain black-green 70 on their upper sides and pale blue 65 underneath. Many bore a white tail band, over which (on the port side) the aircraft's individual letter was painted in the appropriate colour. In 8. Staffel (and probably the others) each aircraft carried its individual and Staffel letters in white, high on the rudder. National markings seem to have been of the outline type except on the wing undersides, where 'full' Balkenkreuze were carried.

Nightfighters

For II./NJG 6 our best available evidence comes from photographs of Ofw. Treynogga's Bf 110G (W.Nr.5545, 2Z+OP) interned in Switzerland in March 1944. The remains of its sister, W.Nr.5546, were found in Perugia. The segmented arrangement of the two greys (75 and 76) is not a common permutation of the standard nightfighter camouflage, however. Also, the extent of the black paint under the starboard wing may have varied from one aircraft to another.

The painting between pages 120 and 121 follows the scheme of Treynogga's aeroplane, but uses the codes of an aircraft identified in Italy by Ultra. The W.Nr. we have used is that of Hptm. Habermayr's aircraft on the basis that he signed 6. Staffel casualty reports (usually a CO's prerogative) and may well have flown 2Z+AP (aircraft 'A' often being the unit leader's). Both code and W.Nr. are therefore authentic, but their application to the same aeroplane is educated guesswork. While 2Z+OP had FuG 202 radar, the plate shows a FuG 220/212 array as the older system had apparently been all but supplanted in use against the Western Allies by June.

Bombers

All of the available photographic evidence from Sicily onwards suggests that 'wave-mirror' camouflage was universal. Upper surfaces carried a pale overspray on a darker background, and there was an inverted version on the undersides. Some aircraft had tail bands, national markings and unit code letters either covered by the scribble or blacked out.

Schlachtgeschwader 4

In 1944 it seems that most of the unit's Fw 190s were painted in the 'desert' colours of blue 78 undersides and sand yellow 79 upper surfaces, blotched with olive green 80, the latter often partially obscuring national markings and the Mediterranean Theatre white tail band. Unit emblems were common on both sides of the engine cowling, and coloured tactical numerals had almost entirely supplanted the earlier system of coloured letters.

New, factory-coded aircraft delivered in June may well not have been repainted in the local scheme before the unit pulled out of Italy.

Aeronautica Nazionale Repubblicana

I° Gruppo Caccia
(June–August 1944)
The camouflage of the unit's Macchi C.205s and Fiat G.55s had been 'unified' with the German scheme since April 1944. This meant a 74/75/76 scheme with the 75 only applied on the top fuselage, a mottled overspray of 74/75 on the fuselage sides, and a splinter of 74/75 on the wings. During June the white tail band was deleted from all Italian aircraft, while the yellow undercowling panel was retained, most probably as an identification marking.

National markings consisted of fasces on the wings inside a square black frame and the Italian flag with a yellow fringe on the fuselage and tail. The unit insignia of each Squadriglia were applied on both sides of the cowling.

Numbering
This was almost always applied between the cockpit and the fuselage flag in figures 1m high, following the 'individual no.-Sq. no.' scheme, coloured as follows:

(1ª Sq.) Red-White; (2ª Sq.) Yellow-White; (3ª Sq.) Saxe Blue-White.

(February–April 1945)
The unit's Bf 109s had late-war German camouflage with a mix of 74/75/76, 81/83/76 and 82/75/76 schemes. The unit badge was standardised on the 'Ace of Clubs' and was officially applied on the left side of the cowling only.

National markings were, in contrast to II° Gruppo, all Italian, in the usual positions, except for the use of underwing Balkenkreuze, probably for flak identification purposes.

Numbering
Slightly different from the first period. The numbers were smaller and applied following the 'Sq. No.-Individual No.' scheme between the fuselage flag and the tail in this way[71]:

(1ª Sq.) Saxe Blue [Blue]-Red; (2ª Sq.) Saxe Blue [White]-Yellow [White]; (3ª Sq.) Saxe Blue-White.

II° Gruppo Caccia
(June–August 1944)
(For camouflage see Luftwaffe section). The first period of use of the Bf 109 saw the application of all Italian markings on the aircraft, overspraying the German ones. The white tail band was deleted during June, while most aircraft had the lower nose panel painted yellow (see I° Gr.C.). Squadriglia insignia were applied on both sides of the cowling.

(October 1944–April 1945)
The camouflage followed the evolution of the Luftwaffe's and so, besides 74/75/76, 81/83/76 and 82/75/76 schemes were also gradually introduced by 1945.

National markings, following the rules set out by the Germans in September 1944 (see page 101), were replaced by standard Luftwaffe ones on the fuselage and under the wings with the application of a smaller Italian flag behind the cockpit (within 4ª Sq. the flag was enlarged by January 1945).

As the war dwindled to a close, on several occasions the Balkenkreuze were left also over the wings and sometimes also the Hakenkreuz was to be seen, ending up with some cases where Italian markings were not applied at all.

Squadriglia badges continued to be applied on the nose up to the end of the war only by 2ª (later renamed 5ª) Sq., while 1ª (4ª) Sq. apparently applied them only up to the first months of 1945 and 3ª (6ª) Sq. had replaced its insignia since October 1944 by repeating the individual aircraft number in its place.

Numbering
This remained the same throughout the war, consisting of an individual number (from 0-21) usually around 1m high applied between the cockpit and the fuselage flag until August 1944, and then between the fuselage flag and the German cross up to the end of the war.

Nucleo Comando: <<, <|, < in black or black (blue) with white outline.

1ª (4ª) Sq.:   Black number with white outline.
2ª (5) Sq.:   Yellow.
3ª (6ª) Sq.:   White.

Torpedo-Bombers

Although originally painted dark green on their upper surfaces and light grey under, by June 1944 most of the operational S.79s of I° Gruppo Aerosiluranti 'Buscaglia' were painted dark green overall, since they operated mainly by night. National markings were all Italian in the usual positions and no unit badge was applied. Often these markings were obliterated by black (or dark) paint for night operations.

It is interesting to note that, even after the resumption of operations in October 1944, no German markings ever appeared on the aircraft of this unit.

Numbering

The codes consisted of two parts: B for Buscaglia, 1, 2, 3 for the corresponding Squadriglia, a hyphen and the individual two-digit number (01, 02 . . .), for example: B2-05.

In the first period of activity the codes painted on the S.79s were coloured:

B (black), Sq.No. (white), – (white), Ind.No. (red).

From April onwards the whole code was painted in light blue-grey. From October 1944 the Squadriglie were reduced to two and the unit was renamed Gruppo 'Faggioni', the first letter of the code changing to 'F'.

Transports

Camouflage (as for most of the non-fighter units) consisted of dark green upper surfaces and light grey undersides.

Being incorporated within the Luftwaffe, both I° Gr. Aerotrasporti 'Terracciano' and II° Gr. Aer.'Trabucchi' mainly followed German rules for their markings. In fact, the only Italian presence was a small flag usually applied just behind the cockpit or (in Gr.'Trabucchi') under it, while the rest of the insignia were Luftwaffe ones.

Unit codes

Gr.'Terracciano' had its 8Q code painted smaller than the rest of the letters and its codes were black (except for the colour of individual letter here indicated within parentheses):

1ª Sq. – 8Q+_(white) H; 2ª Sq. – 8Q+_(red with white outline) K; 3ª Sq. – 8Q+_(yellow) L.

The code of Gr.'Trabucchi' was P6 with similar Sq. letters. Although quoted in signals traffic, no example of these codes was seen applied to an aircraft.

Notes

70. Although modern sources have inferred a blue 76 scribble from photographs, contemporary accounts always speak of brown.
71. The colours in brackets are different examples found in MAAF reports from captured airfields.

Aircraft Found on Italian Airfields by No. 1 Field Intelligence Unit in May 1945

Aviano aerodrome

Aircraft found by No.1 F.I.U. (Party 'B') on 31 May 1945

Type	Unit	W.Nr.	Markings	Notes
Bf 109	II° Gr.C.	?	?	Burnt-out fuselage; mainplane with ANR markings
Bf 109 G-6	II° Gr.C.	163476	?	Burnt out
Bf 109 G-8/R5	NAGr.11	?	?	Burnt out
Bf 109 G-6	II° Gr.C.	166093	Italian & German	Burnt-out fuselage
Bf 109 G	?	–46077	?	Burnt out
Bf 109 G-14	?	784118	?	Burnt out
Bf 109 G-14	II° Gr.C.	—5719	19 (black w.o.)+	*
Bf 109 G-	?	782309	?	Burnt out
Bf 109 G (K)?	?	?	?	Burnt out – DB 605D engine
Br.20	?	?	?	Six badly damaged airframes in blast shelters used as decoys

* (black w.o.) denotes a black character outlined in white.

Osoppo airfield
Aircraft found by No.1 F.I.U. (Party 'B') on 25 May 1945

Type	Unit	W.Nr.	Markings	Notes
Bf 109 G-14	II° Gr.C.	?	?	Completely wrecked in Southern dispersal

Campoformido aerodrome
Aircraft found by No.1 F.I.U. (Party 'B') on 25 May 1945

Type	Unit	W.Nr.	Markings	Notes
Bf 109 G-10/R2	NAGr.11	770338	?	Demolished
Bf 109 G	?	?	?	Completely burnt out
Bf 109 G	?	?	?	Demolished – 1 x MG 151 only
Bf 109 G	?	?	?	Completely burnt out
Bf 109 G-8	NAGr.11	230144	?	Demolished and looted – wooden rudder
Bf 109 G	?	?	?	Completely burnt out – 1 x MG 151 only
Bf 109 G	?	?	?	Completely burnt out – 1 x MG 151 only
Bf 109 G-8	1./NAGr.11	230292	+11 (black)	Demolished and burnt out
Bf 109 G-8	NAGr.11	230132	?	Completely demolished
Bf 109 G-8	NAGr.11	201134	?	Forepart completely burnt out
Bf 109 G-8	NAGr.11	201129	?	
Ar 234	Kdo Sommer	140344	?+H	Burnt and demolished – jet units missing
Ju 188	?	?	ESL-JU (on tail unit)	Demolished and burnt
Ju 188	KG 40 (?)	0251	F8+ED	Demolished
Ju 88	?	?	?	Demolished and burnt – Jumo 213

Ghedi airfield
Aircraft found by No.1 F.I.U. (Party 'A') on 2 May 1945

Type	Unit	W.Nr.	Markings	Notes
Me 410 B-3	2.(F)/122	190167	F6 (small)+RK all black	Fuselage and centre section of wing only
Me 410 B-3	2.(F)/122	190127	F6 (small)+HK all black	Fuselage and centre section of wing only
Ju 188	6.(F)/122	—5466	F6 (small)+BP	Fuselage only
Ju 87 D-3	Stab/NSGr.9	3-1009	E8 (small)+LB	Stripped
Ju 87 D-3	NSGr.9	3–1159	?	Stripped
Bf 109 G-10/AS	I° Gr.C.	491407	3 (saxe blue)-5 (white)	Fuselage only – Italian tricolour
Bf 109 G-14	II° Gr.C.	464428	4 (yellow)+	Italian tricolour – rudder damaged
Bf 109 G-14	II° Gr.C.	464464	4 (white)	Remains under crashed building – Italian tricolour – white spinner
Bf 109 G-14	II° Gr.C.	464469	3 (white)+	Remains under crashed building – Italian tricolour
Bf 109 G-10	II° Gr.C.(?)	—5208	?	a/c badly burned – remains of GM apparatus
Bf 109 G	?	?	?	Completely burned – engine DB 605
Bf 109 G	?	?	?	Completely burned – engine DB 605
Bf 109 G-6/U4	?	441168	4 (yellow)+ –	Dismantled
SM.79	?	?	?	Portion of fuselage – German markings
Go 242 (glider)	?	?	30+21	Part of fuselage only

Lonate Pozzolo airfield
Aircraft found by No.1 F.I.U. (Party 'A') on 5 May 1945

Type	Unit	W.Nr.	Markings	Notes
Savoia Marchetti	?	?	?	Several burned-out **examples of different types in scrap dump**

Malpensa airfield

Type	Unit	W.Nr.	Markings	Notes
Bf 109 G	I° Gr.C.	?	?	30 burned-out aircraft scattered on the airfield

Vizzola Ticino airfield

Type	Unit	W.Nr.	Markings	Notes
Bf 109 G-10	I° Gr.C.	491493	2 (blue)-8 (yellow)	Italian tricolour – cockpit burned and stripped
Bf 109 G	?	?	?	Four aircraft burned and stripped

Casorate Schools

Type	Unit	W.Nr.	Markings	Notes
Bf 109 G-10	?	491490	?	Fuselage only
Bf 109 G-14	I° Gr.C.	462739	2-15	Fuselage only
Bf 109 G-10	I° Gr.C.	490761	1-4	Fuselage only
Bf 109 G-10	?	491500	?	Fuselage without engine
Bf 109 G-10	?	491435	?	Fuselage without engine
Bf 109 G	?	?	?	Fuselage without engine

Orio al Serio aerodrome
Aircraft found by No.1 F.I.U. (Party 'A') on 2 May 1945

Type	Unit	W.Nr.	Markings	Notes
Ju 188 D-2	4.(F)/122	230447	F6 (Small) +HM	Jumo 213 A-1 engines
Ju 188 D-2	4.(F)/122	230492	F6 (Small) +BM	Engines and tail unit removed
Bf 109 G-10	II° Gr.C.	491506	<<(black with white outline) +	Italian tricolour
Bf 109 G-10/AS	II° Gr.C.	491322	2 (black w.o.) +	Italian tricolour*
Bf 109 G-10/AS	II° Gr.C.	491323	3 (black w.o.) +	Italian tricolour
Bf 109 G-10/AS	II° Gr.C.	491325	5 (black w.o.) +	Italian tricolour
Bf 109 G-10	II° Gr.C.	491474	10 (black w.o.) +	
Bf 109 G-10	II° Gr.C.	491501	11 (black w.o.) +	
Bf 109 G-10	II° Gr.C.	491313	2 (yellow) +	Italian tricolour
Bf 109 G-14	II° Gr.C.	785061	3 (yellow) + 2' yellow band	Italian tricolour
Bf 109 G-10	II° Gr.C.	491358	12 (yellow) +	Italian tricolour
Bf 109 G-14	II° Gr.C.	785731	13 (yellow) + 2' yellow band	Italian tricolour
Bf 109 G-14/AS	II° Gr.C.	413685	15 (yellow) +	Italian tricolour
Bf 109 G-10	II° Gr.C.	130370	0 (white) +	
Bf 109 G-10/AS	II° Gr.C.	166303	12 (white) + 2' yellow band	
Bf 109 G-6	II° Gr.C.	781096	18 (white) +	
Bf 109 G-14/AS	II° Gr.C.	785875	21 (white) + 2' yellow band	

* (black w.o.) denotes a black character outlined in white.

Vicenza airfield
Aircraft found by No.1 F.I.U. unit (Party 'B') on 4 May 1945

Type	Unit	W.Nr.	Markings	Notes
Bf 109 G-8/R5	NAGr.11	200249	PS+PT	Completely demolished
Fw 190 F-9	1./NSGr.9	440323	E8 (small) + M (black w.o.) H	Wrecked and looted – 2x50 VIIId under each wing + 1xETC 501 under belly – FuG 25a + FuG16ZY
Fw 190 F-8/R1	?		E8+EH (as above)	Wrecked and looted – as above
Ju 87 D-5	3./NSGr.9	132230	+A (yellow) L	Wrecked and looted – 1 triple-slip bomb carrier under each wing +1 ETC 501 under belly – FuG 25a + FuG 16ZS
Me 410 A-3	2.(F)/122	?	?	Dismantled and looted
Me 410 A-3	2.(F)/122	?	F6 (small) +FK all black	Dismantled and looted
He 111	?	?	CN+B	Dismantled and looted – without engines
Ju 52	?	584562	?	Completely burnt out
Fw 58 C-2	?	?	?	Built in 1941 – completely demolished

Villafranca di Verona aerodrome
Aircraft found by No.1 F.I.U. (Party 'A') on 2 May 1945

Type	Unit	W.Nr.	Markings	Notes
Fw 190 F-9	NSGr.9(?)	440340	none	Landed on the airfield shortly after capture
Fw 190 F-8/R1	1./NSGr.9	581632	E8 (small) + D (black w.o.) H	Stripped in hangar
Fw 190 F-8/R1	Svbd. Einhorn	581447	A3+LX	Fuselage only
Fw 190 A-8	Stab/NSGr.9	734018	E8 (small) +BB	Burned in revetment – FuG 101
Fw 190 A-8	NSGr.9	734014	?	Burned in revetment – FuG 101
Ju 87 D	3./NSGr.9	131434	E8 (small) + B (yellow) L	Stripped in hangar
Ju 87 D	3./NSGr.9	3-1193	E8+KL (as above)	Damaged in hangar
Ju 87 D	Stab/NSGr.9	?	E8+M (yellow) B	Destroyed in revetment
Ju 87 D	NSGr.9	130782	E8 (small) + L	Burned
Me 410 B-3	2.(F)/122	190163	F6 (small) + MK	Fuselage only
Bf 109 G-6	II° Gr.C.	160319	14 (yellow) +	Italian tricolour – fuselage only
Bf 109 G-6	II° Gr.C.	160660	?	Italian tricolour – fuselage only
Bf 109 G-6	II° Gr.C.	464380	11 (white) +	Destroyed in revetment – Italian tricolour
Bf 109 G-(?)/AS	?	?	?	DB 605AS – burned

Bovolone airfield
Aircraft found by No.1 F.I.U. (Party 'B' on 5 May 1945

Type	Unit	W.Nr.	Markings	Notes
Ju 87 D-5	2./NSGr.9	2600	E8 (small) +GK	Demolished – GSL K81Z rear turret

Sources and Acknowledgements

For the Luftwaffe and ANR there is almost no one reliable, detailed source which covers even one aspect of their operations in Italy over the period of this book. Very little Luftwaffe material survived a sort of documentary scorched-earth policy in the last days of the war, and then some of what was captured by the Allies has since disappeared (much to the authors' frustration). The political divisions and upheavals in Italy from 1943 to 1945 had similar consequences for ANR material. On both sides, a useful source will tend come to a stop or change emphasis and format; one covering the whole period will give little detail. To identify even the pilot, markings, date and fate of a single lost aircraft may entail cross-referencing four or five sources.

The Allies themselves periodically changed the format or content of their intelligence reports, and intelligence data is by its nature not consistent in availability or quality. The same goes for the famous Ultra decrypts. While they contain a lot of information, ranging from the strategic to the domestic, and are perhaps the best surviving source on how the Germans saw things, they are just a small section of the signals traffic of the Wehrmacht. Moreover, the original messages are not available, only the Allied reports based on them.

Underlying this book is a mosaic, pieced together from the fragments that we could find into what we hope is a reasonably coherent whole. Inevitably there is information that we can give on one unit at one time that will be lacking at another. Whilst the book does not contain absolutely everything we have found out about the subject, and choices have been made about which events merit the greatest attention, inconsistencies in the amount of detail given on Axis aircraft and units are generally not deliberate. For example, if we do not give the tactical marking of a German or Italian aeroplane it is because we do not yet know it. The names of aircrew present another problem: with four- or five-seater aircraft we have often named only the pilot, simply for reasons of space, and mean no disrespect to those who flew with him.

We have tried to be honest about guesswork and gaps in our knowledge – having read too many books that pretend to complete certainty – but if any reader knows something we do not, please tell us.

The following sources were consulted in researching this book:-

Public Record Office, London
Files of: Air Directorate of Intelligence; Mediterranean Allied Air Forces (in particular those of Signals Intelligence and Field Intelligence units); operational summaries of MASAF, MATAF, MACAF, BAF and DAF; reports to Allied commands based on decrypted Enigma traffic; Operations Record Books of RAF units.

In establishing the framework of events, volume 2 of the UK Air Ministry Air Historical Branch 'History of MAAF' was particularly helpful.

University of Keele, Keele, UK
Aerial photographs of Italian airfields in the Second World War.

Deutsche Dienststelle (WASt.), Berlin
Personnel casualty reports of Luftwaffe flying units.

Imperial War Museum, London
Department of Documents: Microfilm records of Luftwaffe aircraft losses for 1945 (fragmentary) and other captured German documents. Department of Photographs. Department of Printed Books.

Air Historical Branch (RAF), Ministry of Defence, London
Information on specific incidents and guidance as to avenues of investigation.

Archivi di Stato, Roma, Italy
ANR documents; personal documents of deceased ANR officers.

Ministero dell'Aeronautica, Ufficio Storico, Roma
ANR historic diary and official documents.

Bundesarchiv-Militärarchiv, Freiburg i. Br., Germany
Surviving records of Kogen Italien and Luftflotte 2; unit and airfield war diaries; Luftwaffe High Command staff correspondence; strength returns; disposition maps.

Bundesarchiv Koblenz, Germany
Photographs.

USAF Historical Research Center, Maxwell AFB, Alabama, USA
Documents from MAAF and subordinate units; microfilm copies of German documents.

US National Archives
Photographs.

National Air and Space Museum, Smithsonian Institution, Washington D.C., USA
Photographs.

Service Historique de L'Armée de l'Air, Vincennes, France
French Air Force units' diaries; documents.

The following published sources also helped:
G. Aders: *History of the German Night Fighter Force* (Ian Allan); *Close Up No. 8: Focke-Wulf 190 F* (Monogram).
G. Bocca: *La Repubblica di Mussolini* (Mondadori).
F. D'Amico & G. Valentini: *The Messerschmitt Bf 109 in Italian Service, 1943-45* (Monogram); *Regia Aeronautica Vol. 2* (Squadron/Signal).
John R. Beaman: *Last of the Eagles* (self-published), *Messerschmitt Bf 109 in Action, Part 2* (Squadron/Signal).
W. Dierich: *Die Verbände der Luftwaffe 1935-45* (Motorbuch Verlag).
B. Filley: *Junkers Ju 88 in Action – Parts 1 & 2* (Squadron/Signal).
J-B Frappé: *La Luftwaffe En France, 2. – Normandie 1944* (Editions Heimdal).
Dr. G.W. Gellermann: *Moskau Ruft Heeresgruppe Mitte* (Bernhard & Graefe Verlag).
M. Gilbert: *The Second World War* (Weidenfeld & Nicholson, 1989)
Dr. K. Gundelach: *Die Deutsche Luftwaffe im Mittelmeer, 1940-45* (Peter D. Lang, 1981).
Joseph Heller: *Catch-22* (Corgi).
T.H. Hitchcock: *Close Up No. 6, Gustav part 1* (Monogram) and *Close Up No. 7, Gustav part 2* (Monogram).
George G. Hopp: *Close Up No. 18: Bf 110G* (Monogram).
Edwin Kregloh, Harold Jenkins and George Grove: *The Memory is Still Fresh* (Grove).
V. Kühn: *Die Deutsche Seenotdienst* (Motorbuch Verlag).
G. Lazzati: *Ali nella tragedia* (Mursia);
J-Y Lorant & B. Frappe: *Le Focke-Wulf 190* (Editions Docavia).
E.R. McDowell and W.N. Hess: *Checkertail Clan, The 325th Fighter Group In North Africa and Italy* (Aero Publishers).
Frank J. Olynyk: *USAAF MTO Credits for Air Victories 1943-1945* (Olynyk).
F. Pagliano: *Storia di 10.000 aeroplani* (Longanesi).
G. Pisanò: *Gli ultimi in grigioverde* (FPE).
A. Price: *Focke-Wulf 190 at War* (Ian Allan).
G. Schlaug (Ed.): *Geschichte Einer Transportflieger-Gruppe Im II. Weltkrieg* (Kameradschaft Ehemaliger Transportflieger, 1989).
C.J.F. Shores: *Illustrated History of the Mediterranean Air War, Vols. 2 & 3* (Ian Allan); *Luftwaffe Fighter Units in the Mediterranean* (Aircam); *USAAF Fighter Units in the MTO* (Aircam).
J.R. Smith and E.J. Creek: *Jet Planes of the Third Reich* (Monogram); *Close Up No. 24: The Arado 234 B* (Monogram).
J.R. Smith, A. Kay and E.J. Creek: *German Aircraft of the Second World War* (Putnam).
J.R. Smith and K.A. Merrick: *Luftwaffe Camouflage and Markings Vol. 3* (Kookaburra).
P. Stahl: *KG 200* (Ian Allan).
G. Venè: *Coprifuoco* (Mondadori).

The help of the following individuals is gratefully acknowledged:-

Australia
Russell Guest; Neil Mackenzie; Sqn Ldr Murray Nash; Erich K. Sommer; Ken Watts; Air Marshal Archie Wilson.

Belgium
Jean-Louis Roba.

Canada
David Brown and David Wadman (both of 'Experten'); George G. Hopp.

France
Olivier Canon; Col Georges Gauthier; Jean-Michel Guhl; Roger Guillaume; Pierre Hentgäs; Jean-Yves Lorant; Gen. Emile Thierry.

Federal Republic of Germany
Arno E. Abendroth; Ulf Balke; Winfried Bock; Manfred Boehme; Frau Busekow (of the Deutsche Dienststelle); Hans-Joachim Deicke; Theodor Lindemann; Flugkapitän Hartmut Küper; Dipl. Ing. Werner Muffey; Johannes Nawroth; Eduard 'Edu' Neumann; Peter Petrick; Dr Jochen Prien; Dieter Reichardt; Karl Ries; Frau Scholl (of BA-MA, Freiburg); Martin von Vacano; the Editor of *Flugzeug* magazine.

Great Britain
Members of the 'Staffel 90' Luftwaffe Research Group – Steve Coates, Eddie Creek, Robert Forsyth,

Mike Norton, Martin Pegg, Richard Smith, Tom Willis. William H. Blake; The Staff of the Public Record Office; Mr J.S. Cox of the Ministry of Defence; Phil Reed (IWM Department of Documents); Phil Irwin; Geoff Thomas; the Editor of *RAFA Air Mail*.

Italy
Gregory Alegi; **Famiglia** Ancillotti; Giorgio Apostolo; Isonzo Baccarini; Loris Baldi; Gen. Mario Bellagambi; Gualberto Benzi; Bruno Betti; Danilo Billi; Giuseppe Biron; **Famiglia** Bonopera; **Famiglia** Brunello; Stefano Camerani; Carlo Cavagliano; Carlo Ceccardi; Ottone Colonna; **Famiglia** Covre; Pietro De Benedetti; Gen. Ezio Dell'Acqua; Armando D'Ilario; Luigi Di Cecco; Giorgio Di Giorgio; Gianfranco Dinale; Giuseppe Di Santo; Ugo Drago; Angelo Emiliani; Cesare Erminio; Amedeo Fagiano; Artidoro Galetti; Giancarlo Garello; Roberto Gentilli; Paolo Gianvanni; Luigi Gorena; Cesare Gori; Giuseppe Grande; Gino Künzle; **Famiglia** Longhini; Guido Luccardi; Carlo Lucchini; Giuseppe Maffioli; **Famiglia** Mancini; Cesare Marchesi; Sergio Mazzi; Alfonso Mino; **Famiglia** Morandi; Pietro Orio; Maurizio Pagliano; **Famiglia** Patton; Spartaco Petrignani; Franco Ragni; **Famiglia** Robetto; **Famiglia** Rodoz; Emanuele Rosas; Enzo Rovetta; Attilio Sanson; Felice Squassoni; Pietro Stivanello; Giuseppe Torre; Raffaele Valenzano; **Famiglia** Volpi; **Famiglia** Zanardi; Gian Mario Zuccarini.

South Africa
Rodney G. Simmonds.

Switzerland
Hans-Heiri Stapfer; The Swiss Air Force.

United States of America
Shuford M. 'Al' Alexander; Woodrow P. Baldwin; Howard Barton; Steve Blake; Darwin G. Brooks; James V. Crow; Henry L. 'Larry' de Zeng IV; Carl Hildebrandt; Richard W. Dambrun; Hugh 'Rowdy' D. Dow; Charles C. Eddy; Herschel H. Green; Frank W. Heckenkamp; Bill Hosey; Harold W. Jenkins; Chester Jennings Jr.; Richard L. Johnson; Ed King; James H. Kitchens III (of USAFHRA and the 'Luftwaffe Circle' Research Group); Edwin R. Kregloh; Ernest McDowell; Dr Frank J. Olynyk; Edward Olson; Bob 'P.D.' Poindexter; Barry C. Rosch; Kenn C. Rust; Frank W. Schaefer; Durward M. Stayton; Richard P. Sulzbach; Walter and Virginia Sutton; Robert C. Tomlinson; Carl J. Weisemberger; Oscar M. Wilkinson.

Yugoslavia
Dragisa Brasnovic'.

Apart from the help of the above people, all word-processing, translation, illustrations and archival research were by the authors.

Another aircraft of NSGr.9 abandoned at Vicenza. Fw 190 F-9 W.Nr 440323 "E8+MH" of 1. Staffel was almost new but had its radio inspection panel replaced by one from another plane. (NASM)

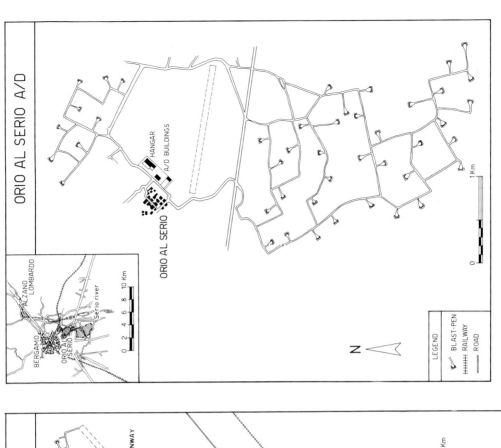
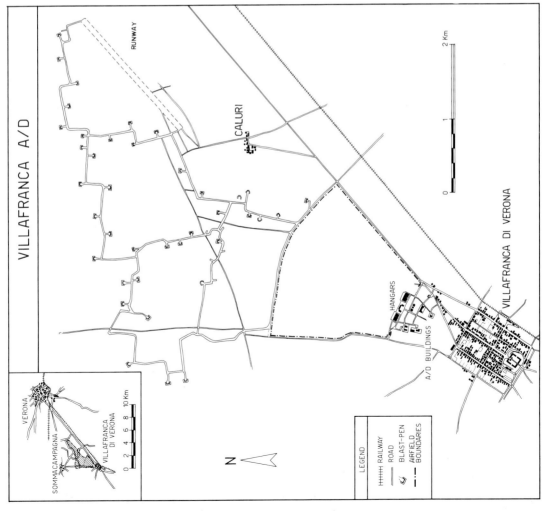

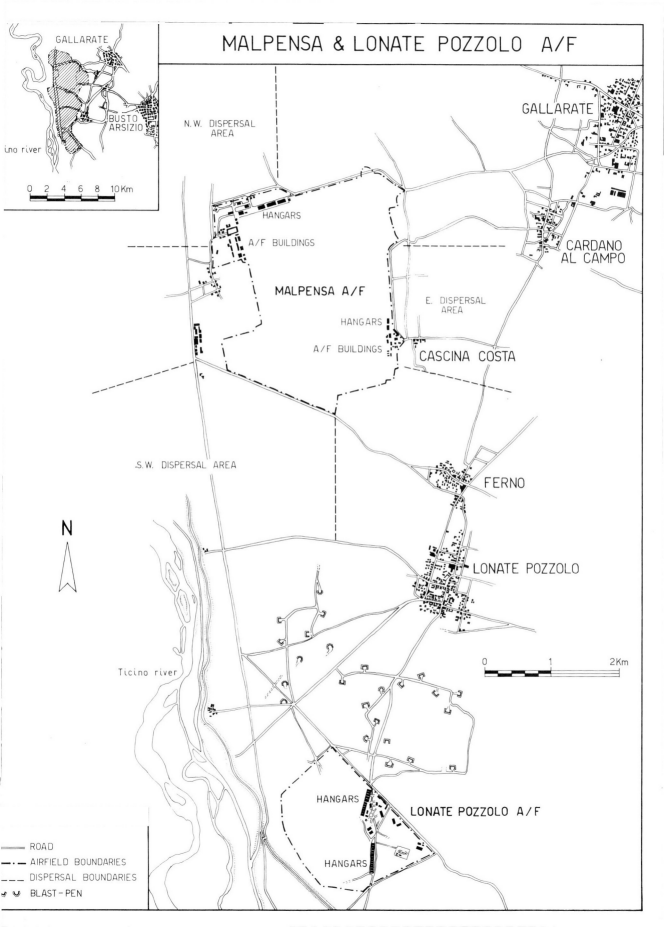

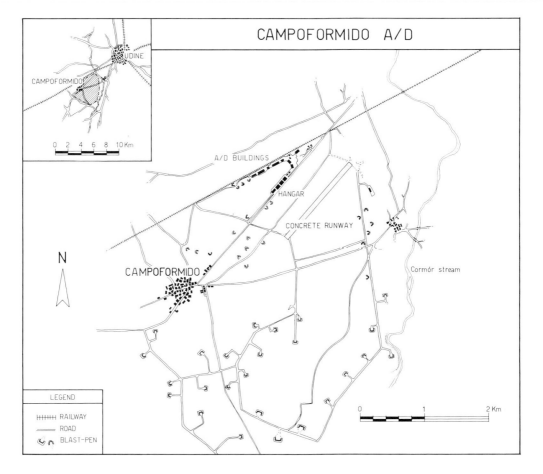
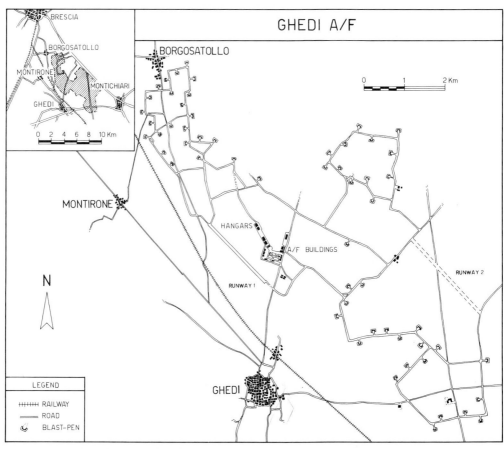

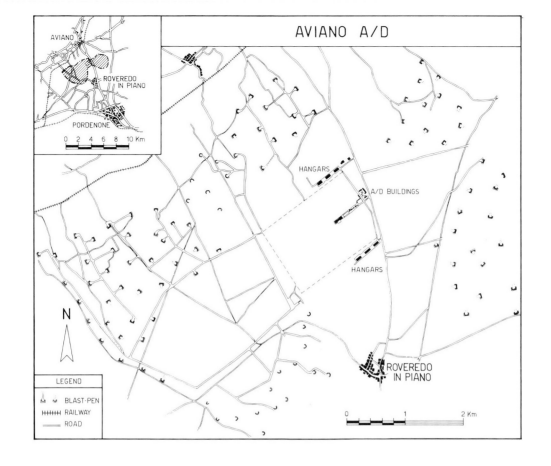

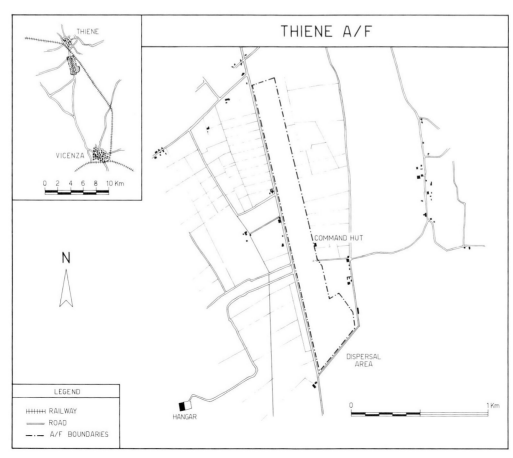

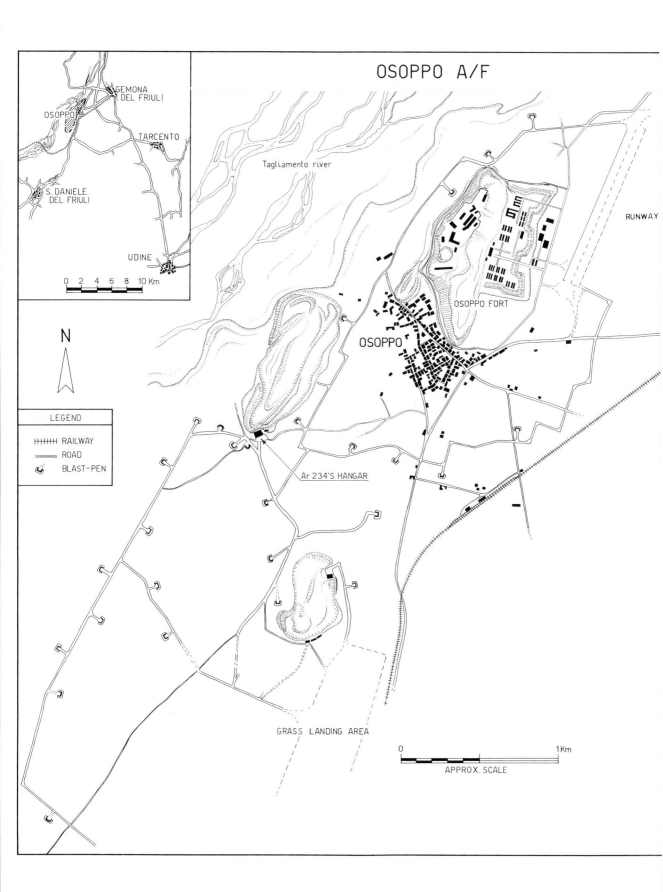

Index

INDEX OF NAMES

Allied Personnel

Adams, *Lt* 111
Allen, *Lt* Clyde T. (32nd PRS) 175
Allen, *Lt* Hyrum J. (417th NFS) 114
Anderson, *Lt* Ralph A. (849th BS) 197
Anderson, *Lt* H.P. (90 Sqn.) 159
Andrews, *Fg Off* 138
Archer, *Sqn Ldr* O. 128
Armstrong, *W/O* 63
Atger, *S-Lt* (France) 66
Atwood, *Lt* 134

Bagley, *Lt* Wendell B. 196
Bailey, *Sqn Ldr* Jim R. 40, 66
Baits, *W/O* 133, 138
Baldwin, *Lt* 197, 219
Barrett, *Lt* John 197
Barrington, *Flt Lt* 128
Bartlett, *Fg Off* D.C. 40, 104
Barton, *Lt* 186, 189, 219
Bary, *Wg Cdr* E.R., DFC 149
Beaumont, *Fg Off* G. 74, 84, 93, 104, 136
Belcher, *Lt (later Capt.)* 149, 175
Bell, *Sgt* 115
Bergeron, *1st Lt* 175, 186, 188
Bettinger, *Lt* 61
Blackeney, *Lt* Horace W. 189
Blake, *Fg Off* L.A. 160
Blundell, *Flt Sgt* (256 Sqn.) 178
Blundell, *Sgt* (255 Sqn.) 62
Bolek, *Lt* Frank M. 196
Boy, *Lt* V 52
Boyle, *Flt Lt* 66
Brandstrom, *Lt* 186, 187
Bray, *Fg Off* 52
Brebner, *Capt* 104
Bretherton, *Fg Off* B.A. 64, 75, 84, 85
Brewer, *Fg Off* 65, 94, 104
Brezas, *Lt* 69
Brimmer, *Lt* Robert W. 197
Brooks, *Lt* Darwin B. 189, 190, 219
Burke, *Flt Lt* (243 Sqn.) 48, *101*
Burke, *Sgt* William J. (849th BS) 194, 197
Burke, *Sqn Ldr* (600 Sqn.) *101*, 104
Burls, *Lt* 48
Bush, *1st Lt* Bobby A. 125

Caple, *Maj* 68
Carpenter, *Lt* Elbert R. 48
Cartmill, *1st Lt* Earl D. 197
Charles, *Sgt* 84
Chenery, *Flt Sgt* 62
Chidlaw, *Brig Gen* B.W. 137
Clark, *Gen* Mark 15, 29
Claypool, *S/Sgt* Arthur S. 159, 160
Cleveland, *Lt* 61
Cole, *2nd Lt* Truman C. (441st BS) 121
Cole, *Flt Sgt* (600 Sqn.) 41, 75, 104
Cooper, *Fg Off* (154 Sqn.) 66
Cooper, *Lt* (52nd FG) 191
Cordell, *Lt* Dan B. 84
Core III, *Capt* Jesse R. 135

Cornet, *Lt* (France) 66
Cox, *Sqn Ldr* 70
Crooks, *Plt Off* 84
Cunningham, *Flt Lt* 75, 84, 85

Dailey, *Lt* 115
Daniels, *Sqn Ldr* 104
Daveson, *W/O* 48
Davidson, *Flt Lt* 104
Davis, *Lt* 61
Deakyne, *Lt* 128
Denby, *Fg Off* D.S. 192
Despinoy, *Adjt* (France) 66
Dickey, *2nd Lt* Earl R. 165
Dinham-Peren, *Flt Sgt* 93
Dixon, *Capt* E.R. 94
Doherty, *W/O* 48
Dorris, *Maj* 69
Dorval, *Lt* 111
Draper, *2nd/Lt* Joe F. 54
Duke, *Sqn Ldr* Neville 103
Dunford, *Flt Sgt* 127

Eddy, *2nd/Lt* Charles C. 150, 175, 176, 186, 189, 219
Ellis, *Lt* 148, 176
Englert, *Capt* Lawrence E. 165
English, *Plt Off* 51
Ewing, *Maj* 69
Ewing, *W/O* 62

Faires, *2nd/Lt* Jack 178
Fawkner Corbett, *Flt Sgt* 93
Forrest, *Plt Off* 66

Gabor, *Maj* Edward 207
Galitzine, *Flt Lt* E. 115
Gardner, *Flt Lt* B. 52
De Gaulle, *Gen*. Charles (France) 93
Gertin, *Lt* Leo A. 197
Geyman, *1st Lt* Richard J. 45
Gibson, *Fg Off* A.D. 136
Gilbert, *Maj* *180*, 185, 186, 187, 188
Goebel, *Lt* 69
Goff, *Flt Sgt* 74
Goodman, *Lt* A.E. 73
Gould, *Flt Lt* G.R., DFC 47
Green, *Maj* Herschel H. 47, 68, 219
Green, *W/O* (232 Sqn.) 53
Griffiths, *Flt Sgt* T.C. 64
Grinnell, *Lt* William E. 114
Groendycke, *Lt* Guilford 157
Gunn, *Lt Col* James A. 93

Hackett, *Plt Off* 94
Hall III, *Lt* Benjamin W. 191
Hamar, *Fg Off* 103
Hammond, *Sqn Ldr* G.W. 193
Hancock, *Lt* 73
Hansen, *Fg Off* (238 Sqn.) 51
Hanson, *2nd/Lt* Junior R. 125
Harland, *Flt Lt* A.H. 74
Hausner, *Lt.* Sigmund E. 174
Hawkes, *Fg Off* W.D.C. 73
Hay, *Lt* 158

Head, *Lt* 73
Hearn, *Flt Lt* R.V. 104, *156*, 162
Hearne, *2nd Lt* 70
Heckenkamp, *Capt* 186, 187, 219
Hendry, *Fg Off* 115
Hentges, *Col* (France) 66
Herman, *1st Lt* Herbert 134
Hilgard, *Lt* 73
Hinton, *1st Lt.* Walter R. 133
Hosey, *Flt Off* "Bull" 164, 219
Hounslow, *Plt Off* 147
House, *Lt* 52

Inglis, *Fg Off* 70

Jackson, *Lt* 115
James, *Fg Off* (451 Sqn.) 45
James, *W/O* (255 Sqn.) 85
Jefferey, *Fg Off* 65
Jefferson, *Plt Off* 84
Jenner, *Plt Off* 162
Jennings, *Fg Off* 186, 188, 219
Johnson, *Fg Off* T.E. (255 Sqn.) 64
Johnson, *Lt. (later Capt.)* Richard L. (57th FG) 61, 206, 219
Johnson, *Fg Off* (238 Sqn.) 66
Johnstone, *Fg Off* 51
Jones, *1st Lt* Albert L (414th NFS) 136
Jones, *Fg Off* (451 Sqn.) 47
Judd, *Plt Off* 94, 104

Kamanski, *1st Lt* Charles 122
Kasun, *Maj* Nicholas J. 179
Kimberley, *Flt Sgt* E.R.. 64
King, *Lt* Ed 48, 136, *155*, 161, 219
Kirkham, *Sqn Ldr* 45
Knight, *Lt* Raymond L. 206, 207
Kregloh, *1st Lt* Ed 163, 164, 219

Lail, *S/Sgt* Kenneth C. 197
Larsen, *Capt* William E. 54
Lee, *2nd Lt* Roland E. 206
Lesieur, *Sc.* (France) 66
Longsdon, *1st Lt.* James R. 121
Lothian, *Flt Sgt* 133, 138
Lovell, *Wg Cdr* A.D.J. 48
Lund, *Plt Off* 147
Lyon, *Lt* R.V. 70

McCann, *W/O* E.A. 63, 68, 74, 75
McDonald, *Fg Off* 84
McGibbon, *Sgt* 85
McLaren, *Sqn Ldr* J. 64, 66
Manne, *Lt* 70
Mannon, *Lt* 52
Marck, *Sgt* William V. 197
Marshall, *Fg Off* S.A. 149
Mercer, *Fg Off* 47
Michel, *Capt* 123, 124
Michie, *Flt Lt* N.P. 62
Miller, *Flt Off* Walt 176, 186, 189
Millican, *Lt* Vincent 83
Monard, *Fg Off* D.S. 73, 86
Montgomerie, *Flt Lt* 88, 93
Monti, *2nd Lt* Martin J. 112

225

Moore, *Fg Off* L.R.   193
Morris, *Wg Cdr* E.J.   44, 47
Morrow, *Lt*   148, 208
Morton, *2nd Lt* De Witt   178
Moubray, *Fg Off* "Dinks"   62
Mulholln, *Lt* Ralph   128

Nash, *Sqn Ldr* Murray   138, *139*
Neser, *Lt*   173
Newman, *W/O*   94
Nice, *Plt Off*   51

O'Bryant, *1st Lt*   113
Odd, *Sgt*   41, 75, 104
Olson, *Lt*   187, 219
Ormerod, *Flt Lt*   69
Palovich, *Lt.* Edward   157
Patten, *Sqn Ldr* (255 Sqn.)   62
Perkins, *Lt*   128
Pertwee, *Flt Lt*   178
Pickerel, *Lt*   188
Powers, *Lt* John E.   163, 165
Pretorious, *Lt*   173
Proudman, *Fg Off* H.G.   161

Quinn, *W/O* J.F.   138

Radcliffe, *Sqn Ldr* A.J.   160, 162
Rahn, *Lt*   61
Raisen, *Fg Off* G.H.   192
Ray, *W/O* A.J.   160
Rees, *Fg Off* D.W.   40, 104, 136
Reim, *Lt.*   173
Reynolds, *Fg Off* R.E.   65, 74
Rimes, *Flt Sgt*   63
Robert, *Flt Lt*   45
Roberts, *1st Lt*   113
Robinson, *Sub Lt*   52
Ross, *Lt*   104
Rudd, *Lt*   158
Rudovsky, *Fg Off* John   136

Schaefer, *1st Lt* Frank W.   195, 196, 219
Schaeffer, *T/Sgt.* Charles   197
Schareck, *Lt*   48
Schindler, *Maj* Andrew R.   106
Scollan, *Fg Off*   178
Selenger, *1st Lt* Walter K.   160
Sidney, *Fg Off*   52
Simmonds, *Fg Off*   66, 219
Small, *Flt Lt*   51, 66
Smith, *Flt Lt* L (92 Sqn.)   52
Smith, *Flt Sgt* (255 Sqn.)   178
Smith, *W/O* (600 Sqn.)   127
Spencer, *Sgt*   41
Spencer, *Plt Off* (600 Sqn.)   84
Steiner, *Lt*   73
Stoehrer, *Lt* Frank A.   197
Strabac, *S/Sgt* Emil M.   159, 160
Stratton, *W/O* W.W.   161
Styles, *Wg Cdr* L.H., DFC   94
Sulzbach, *Lt* Richard P.   149, 150, *180*, 185, 186, 188, 208, 219
Summers, *Lt* James J.   178
Sutton, *Capt* Walter "Tod" L.   194, 197, 219
Sutton, *Flt Lt* R.   44, 45

Tatman, *2nd Lt*   47
Taylor, *Fg Off* (92 Sqn.)   88, 93

Taylor, *Lt* (346th FS)   187
Taylor, *W/O* (238 Sqn.)   66
Thomas, *Fg Off*   138
Thomason, *Lt* Kenneth   137
Thompson, *2nd Lt* (350th FG)   176, 186, 187
Thompson, *Flt Lt* D.A. (600 Sqn.)   74, 84, 93, 104
Tolmie, *Lt*   49
Tomlinson, *1st Lt*   115, 123, 124
Towell, *Sgt*   84
Tozer, *Fg Off* A.W.   64, 66
Treadwell, *1st Lt*   113
Trelford, *Plt Off*   104
True, *Fg Off*   75
Turkington, *Flt Lt* R W., DFC   69, 70, 72, 73, 74
Tutill, *W/O*   53

van Niekerk, *Lt*   52
van Rensburg, *Lt*   66
Veazey, *Sgt* Edward J.   194, 197
Vintner, *Flt Sgt*   52
Voll, *1st Lt (later Capt)* John J.   105, 125

Waitman, *Flt Sgt*   74
Wallace, *Lt*   104
Walton, *Fg Off* J.E.   71
Ward, *W/O*   149
Watford, *Sgt*   104
Watson, *Col*   134
Weathers, *Capt* Luke J., Jr.   125
Webster, *Capt* Truman M.   170
Whaley, *Flt Lt*   *101*, 104
White, *Plt Off* D.F.   62, 86, 94
Wilkinson, *Lt* Oscar   174, 187, 219
Williams, *Lt*   158
Williamson, *Lt.* William R.   84
Wilmer, *Fg Off* H.J.   94, 111
Wilson, *Sqn Ldr* Archie.   62, 219
Wilson, *Lt* (350th FG)   187
Wingham, *Plt Off* M.A.   65, 74
Wint, *Flt Sgt* N.   40, 66
Wylder, *Lt.*   174

Young, *2nd Lt* Jim   163

Italian Personnel

Abba, *S.Ten.* Alessandro   187
Agostini, *M.llo* Serafino   84, 85, *87*
Albani, *S.Ten.*   146
Alderighi, *T.Col.*   31
Alessandri, *M.llo*   201
Alessandrini, *Magg. (later T.Col.)*   26, 90, 119, 165, 170
Ambrosino, *Ten.* Vinicio   124, 125
Amore, *S.Ten.*   73
Ancillotti, *S.M.* Rolando   73, 113, *116*, 122, 124, 163, 185, 219
Archidiacono, *Serg.* Raffaele   80, 165, 186, 188
Arrabito, *Magg.*   35, 59, 69
Arrigoni, *Serg.* Gianni   51

Baccarini, *S.M.* Isonzo   176, 219
Baldi, *S.M.* Loris   80, 113, 118, 122, 123, 134, 137, 159, 178, *180*, 187, 219

Balduzzo, *Serg.* Domenico   83, 176
Barioglio, *Cap.*   175
Bartolozzi, *Cap.* Guido   175
Bellagambi, *Cap. (later Magg.)* Mario   35, 40, 52, 66, 113, 115, 121, 124, 125, 126, 134, 136, 148, 149, 152, 154, 155, 157,158, *158*, 161, 164, 171, *172*, 173, 183, 186, 201, 202, 219
Benzi, *Serg.* Gualberto   80, 157, 197, 201, 219
Beretta, *Ten.*   61, 69, 74
Bernardi, *Serg.* Alberto   194
Berti, *S.Ten.*   124
Bertuzzi, *Cap.*   42, 91, 138, *139*
Betti, *Ten.* Bruno   173, 186, 187, 196, 219
Bettinardi, *Ten.*   202
Bianchini, *S.M.*   158, 160, 195, 196
Biasi, *Ten.*   115, *116*
Billi, *M.llo* Danilo   176, 219
Biron, *Ten.*   69, 219
Bolzoni, *M.llo*   52
Bonara, *Ten.* Leandro   160
Bonet, *Cap.*   24
Bonomi, *Gen.*   170
Bonomi, Ivanoe   202
Bonopera, *S.M.*   126, 219
Bonzano, *T.Col.*   100, 171
Borgogno, *Magg.*   25
Boscaro, *S.M.*   61
Botto, *T.Col.* Ernesto   35, 89
Briglia, Armando   171
Brini, *Ten.*   112, *116*, 148, 149
Brunello, *S.M.*   194, 219
Buscaglia, *Magg.*   110

Cacciola, *S.Ten.*   59
Cadringher, *T.Col.*   91
Caimi, *Serg.*   186, 190
Camaioni, *Ten.* Antonio   40, 122
Camerani, *S.M.* Stefano   123, 187, 219
Canavese, *Ten.*   115
Cavagliano, *S.M.*   50, 66, 121, *122*, 137, 159, *169*, 186, 197, 201, 219
Cavagnino, *M.llo*   69, 121, 197, 201
Chinca, *Cap.*   67
Chiussi, *S.M. (later M.llo)* Giuseppe   45, 176
Cimatti, *Serg.*   83
Colonna, *Ten.* Oddone;   *184*, 194, 219
Covre, *M.llo* Tullio   115, 136, 171, 174, 178, 182, 185, 197, 219
Cusmano, *S.M.*   160, 174

D'Ilario, *S.M.*   *156*, 162, 219
Dachena, *Serg.*   146, *177*
De Biagi, *1° Av.*   51
De Camillis, *Cap.*   81
De Masellis, *Ten.*   139, 158
Del Prete, *Ten.*   139, 147
Dell'Acqua, *S.Ten.* Ezio   112, 149, 219
Di Cecco, *S.M.* Luigi   47, 84, 86, 219
Di Fiorino, *Ten.*   162
Di Santo, *S.Ten.* Giuseppe   49, 89, 123, 130, *131*, 155, 158, 160, 165, 200, 201, 202, 219
Dinale, *S.Ten.*   171, 195, 219
Drago, *Ten. (later Cap.)* Ugo   35, 50, 68, 69, 70, 73, 119, 122, 125, 131, 132, 137, 138, *154*, 158, 160, 163, 173, 175, 178, 186, 187, 197, 202, 219

Erminio, *Ten.* Cesare   148, 175, 219

Faggioni, *Cap.*   26, 27
Fagiano, *S.Ten.*   124, 219
Fagnani, *Col.*   90
Falconi, *T.Col.*   90, 91
Feliciani, *S.M.* Luigi   70
Ferrero, *Ten.* Ermete   149, 160, 173, 197
Fibbia, *M.llo*   49
Filippi, *Ten.* Fausto   115, *116*, 125, 131, 149
Fissore, *Ten.*   67
Forlani, *M.llo*   48, *172*, 190, 205
Fornaci, *S.M.* Fausto   113, 158
Foschini, *T.Col.*   90, 145
Franciosi, *S.M.*   194
Fumagalli, *M.llo* Mario   186, 189, 197

Galetti, *M.llo (later S.Ten)*   53, 110, 122, 136, 138, 219
Galli, *1° Aviere*   112
Gallone, *S.Ten.*   191
Gallori, *S.Ten.*   190
Gamberini, *S.Ten.* Gino   50, 51
Gentile, *Ten.* Francesco   84, 85
Gianelli, *Ten.* Giuseppe   35, 59
Giorio, *Ten.* Mario   139, 187, 190
Girace, *M.llo*   174
Graziani, *Marshal*   131
Graziani, *S.Ten.* Alberto   101
Guidi, *Cap.* Amedeo   35, 49

Lajolo, *S.M.* Domenico   131
Larese, *Ten.*   201
Lombardo, *S.M.* Antonio   51
Longhini, *Ten.*   124, 125, 219
Luccardi, *Ten.*   59, 173, 219
Luziani, *S.Ten.*   51

Machi, *S.Ten.*   52
Magagnoli, *Cap.* Dante   34
Malvezzi, *Cap.*   183
Mancini, *Cap.* Massimino   61, 219
Mancini, *Ten.* Giovanni   53, 68
Mangiapane, *Ten.*   170
Mannelli, *Cap.*   147
Mantelli, *Cap.*   170, 177
Marchesi, *Cap.* Cesare   35, 59, 70, 176, 219
Margoni, *Serg.*   187
Marin, *Serg.* Luigi   48, 69
Marini, *Cap. (later Magg.)*   27, 34, 42, 65, 67, 91, 110, 118, 119, 146
Marinucci, *S.Ten.*   54
Mazzanti, *S.M.*   125, 173
Mazzei, *S.Ten.*   41
Mazzi, *Serg.*   69, 75, 219
Mellano, *1° Av.*   201
Merani, *Ten.*   42
Miani, *Cap. (later Magg.)* Carlo   35, 66, 73, 138, *153*, 165, 170, 175, 182, 183, 185, 186, 187, 189, 190, 195, 197, 201, 202
Minardi, *S.M.* Guido   125, 185
Mingozzi, *M.llo (later Ten.)* Renato   125, 197
Molfese, *Col.* Manlio   89
Monaco, *Ten.*   67
Morabito, *S.M.*   72, 74
Morandi, *S.Ten.* Aurelio   *183*, 194, 219

Moratti, *M.llo* Giuseppe   186, 187
Morettin, *S.Ten.*   48
Morino, *Ten.Col.*   91
Morselli, *Ten.*   65, 87
Mussolini, Benito   24, 84, 89, 91, 110, 154, 183, 199, 207

Nardi, *Sig.*   84
Neri, *S.M.*   171
Neri, *Ten.*   75, 139

Pacini, *S.M.*   75, *119*, 121, 123
Palermi, *Ten.*   63
Pandolfo, *Ten.*   75
Parisi, *S.M.* Angelo   51
Passuello, *S.M.*   138, 197, 201
Patton, *Serg.* Renato   162, 178, 186, 189, *191*, 195, 196, 197, 219
Perina, *Ten.*   63, 139
Petacci, Claretta   207
Petrignani, *Serg.*   49, 219
Pezzi, *S.Ten.*   61
Pignatti di Morano, *Ten.*   72
Piolanti, *Ten.* Michelangelo   158, 189
Pollo, *Ten.* Luigi   49
Poluzzi, *Serg.*   159

Quasso, *Serg.*   175

Ramponi, *Ten.*   201
Robetto, *Ten. (later Cap.)* Giuseppe   35, 45, 130, 201, 219
Rosas, *S.Ten.*   121, 122, 134, 219
Rovetta, *Cap.*   175, *184*, 219

Saccani, *M.llo* Elvio   49
Sajeva, *S.Ten.*   48
Sala, *Gen.*   202
Saletti, *Serg.*   65
Sanson, *S.M.*   113, 115, 174, 219
Santoli, *Ten.*   178
Santuccio, *Serg.*   68
Sarti, *Ten.* Aristide   186, 190
Secchi, *M.llo*   63
Semperboni, *S.Ten.*   190
Sgubbi, *S.M.*   69
Somadossi, *Serg.*   201
Spazzoli, *M.llo*   61
Spigaglia, *Cap.*   *114*, 139, 178, 186
Spreca, *S.Ten.* Ferdinando   171, 189
Squassoni, *S.Ten.* Felice   138, *139*, 173, 187, 189, 219
Stefanini, *S.Ten.*   201
Stella, *Serg.*   53

Taberna, *Serg.*   171
Taen, *Serg.*   51
Talamini, *Ten.* Renato   25
Talin, *Serg.*   66, 68, 113, 114
Tampieri, *Serg.*   80, 186, 189
Tessari, *Gen.* Arrigo   35, 89, 90, 91
Tomaselli, *Cap.* Pio   35
Tonini, *S.M.*   201
Torresi, *Cap.*   35, 61
Tramontini, *Ten.*   184

Valenzano, *Ten.* Raffaele   66, 70, 121, 134, 173, 175, 187, 219
Varacca, *M.llo*   195
Veronesi, *M.llo*   190

Visconti, *Magg.* Adriano   25, 35, 59, 83, 101, 119, 130, 144, 171, 176, 177, 182, *192*, 194, 200, 201
Vizzotto, *T.Col.*   171
Volpi, *Ten.* Alberto   148, 149, 186, 187, 189, 190, 219

Zanardi, *S.M.* Ferdinando   160, 173, 195, 196, 219
Zanetti, *Serg.*   197, 201
Zerini, *S.M.* Wladimiro   174
Zigiotti, *Magg.*   81
Zuccarini, *Ten.* Gian Mario   72, 73, 219

German Personnel
(Note: We apologise for any inaccuracies arising from the gaps in, conflicts between or Gothic script of our source documents)

Abendroth, *Fhj.Fw.* Herbert   64
Ackermann, *Uffz.* Erich   64
Adami, *Uffz.* Alois   127, 128
Albert, *Fw.*   68
Aller, *Maj.*   77
Altmann, *Oblt.*   103, 105
Arnold, *Stabsfw.* Walter   168, 181, 192, 207, 211

Ballok, *Uffz.* Artur   65, 136
Barsewisch, *Gen.*   168
Bayer, *Fw.*   87, 143, 149, 177, 185
Beck, *Uffz.* Rudolf   83
Beherend, *Oberst*   90
Behrens, *Oblt.*   30
Bendorf, *Fw.*   44, *49*, 147
Begemann, *Oblt.* Rolf   63
Berger (2./(F)122)   147
Berkemeyer, *Uffz.* Artur   127
Berndt, *Uffz.* Rolf   43
Biester, *Fw.* Konrad   159
Blaschek, *Uffz.*   44, 48, 86, 126, 143, 149, 185
Boehm, Gerhard (ex 4.(F)/122)   207
Böhm, *Ltn.*   47
Bomke, *Ofw.* Horst   105
Borg, *Oberst* von   171
Bork, *Ogefr.* Fritz von   65
Borrmann (2./(F)122)   88, 111, 125
Böwing, *Ofw.* Wilhelm   64, 104
Braitsch, *Ofw.* Emil   65
Brinkmann, *Fw.* Otto (3./NSGr.9)   94
Brinkmann, *Oblt.* (6.(F)/122)   58, 109, 119
Brücker, *Maj.* Heinrich   21
Buckow, *Ofhr.* Bernhard   127
Bunje, *Fw.* Helmut   41
Burgstaller, *Gefr.* Rudolf   104
Büttner, *Ogefr.* Walter   61

Carstens, *Ogefr.* Emil   93
Christian, *Gen.* Eckard   167, 168
Christians, *Uffz.* Gerhard   41
Clemm, *Hptm.* von   30
Close, *Gefr.*   103
Croce, *Gefr.* Eberhard   161
Czibulski, *Ofhr.* Josef   45

Daele, *Oblt.* v.d.   44, 48, 74, 86, 126, 143, 149, 185

Darbois, *Uffz.* Renè 59, 72
Defele, *Uffz.* Karl 46
Deicke, *Oblt.* 51, 218
Deubner, *Oblt.* Kraftmut 41
Deutsch, *Fw.* Hans-Joachim 73, 111, *136*, 138, 150, 205
Dieckhoff, *Uffz.* Walter 45
Dietrich, *Obstlt.* 90
Dietze, *Hptm.* *49*, 147
Dirich (2.(F)/122) 88
Domack, *Hptm.* Heinz 177, 178
Domnick, *Obstlt. i.G.* Ernst 55, 119, 168
Dörffel, *Obstlt.* Georg 21
Dümcke, *Oblt.* Horst 105

Eberlein (Messerschmitt works pilot) 157
Ebert, *Gefr.* Gerhard 88
Eck, *Fw.* Alfons *193*
Eckerscham, *Hptm.* 21, 119, 297
Eickhoff, *Uffz.* Heinz 121
Entress, *Ltn.* Günther 30

Fährmann, *Fhj.Uffz.* (later *Fhj.Fw.*) Gottfried 50, 64, 68
Fietz, *Uffz.* Herbert 84
Fink, *Ofw.* Toni 49, 106
Fischer, *Ltn.* Gerhard (2.(F)/122) 88
Fischer, *Uffz.* Franz (3./NSGr.9) 149
Flindt, *Fw.* Rudolf 45
Franken, *Ofw.* Josef 112
Freisenhausen, *Oblt.* Bodo 112
Frey, *Uffz.* Adam 41
Freytag, *Fw.* Gerhard 85
Freytag, *Hptm.* Günther (II./JG 77) 22
Frost, *Hptm.* (later *Maj.*) Rupert 19, *36*, 56, 80, 98, 119
Fuchs, *Hptm.* 168
Funk, Helmut (ex-4./122) 207

Gabauer, *Ogefr.* Karl 73
Galland, *Genlt.* Adolf 43, 57, 71, 132, 145
Galle, *Ltn.* 69, 74, 83, 135
Geide, *Uffz.* Fritz 149
Gerstenberger, *Fhj.Fw.* Edgar 106, 137
Gerstner (2.(F)/122) 69, 74, 83
Gieger, *Ofw.* Otto 73
Girlich, *Ltn.* Franz 163
Gladeck, *Ofw.* Ewald 105
Glas, *Uffz.* Michael 41
Gniesmer, *Ltn.* Günther 168, *182*, 185, 190, 191, 192, 211
Göring, *Reichsmarschall* Hermann 56, 145
Goosmann, *Uffz.* Ernst 65
Gottschling, *Oberst i.G.* Paul 167, 199
Götz, *Hptm.* Horst 152
Götz, *Maj.* Franz 20, 23
Graf, *Hptm.* Hans-Horst 65
Grahl; (2.(F)/122) 44
Gravath, *Oberst* 90
Gressler, *Fw.* Horst 39
Griese, *Hptm.* (II./NJG 6) 31
Griese, *Maj.* Heinrich (NJG 6) 31
Grigoleit, *Ofhr.* Walter 95, 103
Gutowski, *Hptm.* Werner 52
Haas, *Ogefr.* Walter 85
Habermayr, *Hptm.* Alfons 41, 211
Habicht, *Uffz.* Wolfgang 95, 103
Hallensleben, *Obstlt.* 30
Hammel, *Oblt.* Kurt 68
Handrick, *Oberst* 57

Hansch, *Uffz.* 64, 68, 69
Hansen, *Ltn.* Broder 43
Hänsler, *Uffz.* Alfred 150
Happe, *Gefr.* Wilhelm 62
Happel, *Uffz.* Heinrich 150, 165
Harbauer, *Oblt.* Hans 47
Heene, *Ltn.* Gottfried 105
Hegenbarth, *Hptm.* 98
Heid, *Hptm.* 30
Heiland, *Fhj.Ofw.* Artur 136
Heinert, *Oblt.* 56
Helbig, *Obstlt.* 30
Heller, *Ltn.* Richard 52
Hellmann, *Uffz.* Siegfried 111
Hennig (2.(F)/122) 147
Henscl, *Fw.* Werner 84
Herr, *Gen. d. Panzertruppen* Traugott 151
Herrmann, *Ltn.* 45
Hesse, *Fhr.* Richard 87, 88
Hirdes, *Hptm.* 109, 119
Hitler, Adolf 89, 91
Hitschold, *Gen.* 21, 56
Hoeb, *Oblt.* Heinz 122
Hoffmann, *Uffz.* Harald 75
Hollborn, *Hptm.* 31
Holstein, *Oblt.* 103
Holz, *Uffz.* Rudolf (5./JG 77) 45
Holz, *Uffz.* Walter (2./JG 77) 48
Holzapfel, *Oblt.* 119
Horn, *Fw.* Kurt 53
Hug, *Fw.* Oskar 104
Huntjeur, *Hptm.* 31
Hutmacher, *Maj. i.G.* Walter 151

Itzstein, *Ltn.* Fritz 64

Jackstadt, *Ofw.* (later *Ofhr.*) 47, 71, 104, 127
Jägers, *Uffz.* Adolf 62
Jantos, *Ogefr.* Josef 104
Jungfer, *Fhr.* Bernd 149

Kapahnke, *Uffz.* Ewald 62
Karsch, *Uffz.* Arthur 86
Kasbar, *Oblt.* 70
Kasper, *Uffz.* Hermann 64
Kaufmann, *Ogefr.* Erwin 73
Kehrer, *Ofw.* Herbert *193*
Kemna, *Uffz.* Walter 88, 163
Kesselring, *Feldmarschall* Albert 16, 29, 41, 55, 77, 88, 97, 114, 142, 167, 168, 199
Kier, *Uffz.* Siegfried 45
Kirchner, *Uffz.* Helmut 105
Klamke, *Maj.* 24
Klein, *Ofw.* Günter 51, 62, 64
Klemm, *Uffz.* Rudolf 83
Klette, *Maj.* 32
Klingohr, *Ltn.* Otto 88
Klinka (2.(F)/122) 104
Köbring, *Hptm.* 120
Koch, *Gefr.* Hermann; (1./NSGr.9) 74
Koch, *Maj.* 17
Köhler, *Uffz.* Horst 45
Kolb, *Ltn.* 62
Koller, *Gen. d. Flieger* Karl 56, 199
Kolster, *Ofhr.* Hans 137
Kornhoff, *Ofw.* Heinz 88
Kramer, *Ofw.* Erich 133
Kranz (2.(F)/122) 125
Kresin, *Fhj.Fw.* Erwin 137

Krieg, *Fw.* Hans 128
Krüger, *Uffz.* Helmut 84
Kuchenbuch, *Oblt.* 98
Kuhle, *Hptm.* 119, 127
Kurz, *Uffz.* Richard 45, 66

Lang, *Fw.* 61
Lange, *Oblt.* 108
Langer, *Oblt.* Heinz 108, 119, 160
Lankenau, *Oblt.* 62
Lankes, *Gefr.* Hans 66
Lässig, *Uffz.* Gottfried 74
Laufenberg, *Uffz.* Heinrich 84
Lehr, *Uffz.* Hermann 63
Lenecke, *Uffz.* Wilhelm 150, 159
Lensing, *Uffz.* 87, 143, 149, 177, 185
Leuchs, *Maj.* Rolf 31, 41
Leumann, *Flg.* (later *Gefr.*) Gustav 74, 137
Lindemann, *Hptm.* Theodor *81*
Lotsch, *Ogefr.* Werner 106
Lütjens, *Hptm.* 18
Lützow, *Oberst* Günther "Franzl" 145, 154, 171

Mader, *Ltn.* Josef 85
Maetzel, *Hptm.* 168
Mahncke, *Gen. d. Flieger* 104
Mahr, *Ltn.* 45
Maltzahn, *Oberst* Günther *Freiherr* von 20, 21, 57, 58, 90, 99
Manhard, *Oblt.* 155, 168
Martin, *Maj* 77
Martini, *Oblt.* Rolf 19
Mechlinski, *Gefr.* Hans 137
Meister, *Uffz.* 46, 105, 135
Metz, *Ltn.* (1./NAGr.11) 74
Metz, *Uffz.* Konrad (6./122) 70
Meyer, *Oblt.* 70
Meyer, *Staffelführer*(1./JG 4) 72
Misch (2.(F)/122) 104
Mittler, *Uffz.* 139
Möbius, *Uffz.* 70
Möhrke, *Ogefr.* Rolf 104
Mokrus, *Uffz.* Erwin 65
Möller, *Uffz.* 103
Mrusek, *Uffz.* Alfred 31, 41
Muffey, *Oblt.* Werner 152, *161*, 218
Mühlhoff, *Gefr.* Albert 133, 147
Müller, *Fw.* (2.(F)/122) 135
Müller, *Oblt.* Fritz (4./122) 70, 83
Müller, *Uffz.* (3./NAGr.11) 41

Nägele, *Ltn.* Franz 45
Nawroth, *Fw.* Johannes 49, 64, 111, *136*, 138, 150, 218
Nehrenheim, *Flg.* Karlfriedrich 76, 88
Neubert, *Fw.* Kurt 45
Neubert, *Maj. i.G.* Frank; 56
Neumann *Ltn.* Kurt (2.(F)/122) 46, 135
Neumann, *Oberst* Eduard 99, 100, 102, 199, 201, 218

Obentheuer, *Fw.* Rudolf 104
Oettel, *Uffz.* Helmut 88
Orlowski, *Maj.* 17

Pankatz (2.(F)/122) 157
Pannwitz, *Maj.* Günther 33, 48, 49, 55, *58*, 70

Patta, *Fw.* 44
Pendel, *Uffz.* Egon 61
Pieper, *Fw.* 63
Plake, *Ofw.* 135
Pläschke, *Uffz.* 47
Platte, *Ltn.* 46
Pohl, *Gen. d. Flieger* Maximilian *Ritter* von 16, *17*, 19, 20, 97, 107, 108, 118, 129, 132, 141, 142, 143, 151, 154, 170, 181, 192, 199, 200, 205, 208
Polak, *Ofw.* 45
Przykling, *Ogefr.* Paul 47

Rasinski, *Fw.* Karl 84
Rautenburg, *Ofw.* Kurt 114
Regitz, *Ogefr.* Friedrich 112
Reihlen, *Uffz.* Wolf 45
Reither, *Hptm.* Eduard 80, 119, 120
Richthofen, *Generalfeldmarschall* Wolfram *Freiherr* von 16, *17*, 77, 90, 97
Rissmann, *Uffz.* Günther 85
Rohlfing, *Gefr.* Helmut 75
Rohlfs, *Gefr.* August 53
Rohn, *Maj.* 98, 119, 120
Rudel, *Oberst* Hans-Ulrich 20
Rumholz, *Gefr.* Wilhelm 64
Rusch, *Uffz.* 135
Rüth, *Fhj.Uffz.* Hans 69

Sachs, *Obstlt.* 126
Schaal, (ferry pilot) 157
Schäfer, *Fw.* Herbert 53
Scheer, *Uffz.* 45, 47, 54
Scheibel, *Ltn.* Werner 62
Scheithauer, *Ofw.* 122
Schemel, *Uffz.* Joachim 62
Scherpf, *Ofhr.* Heinz-Arnold 44
Schertel, *Gefr.* Erwin 104
Scherzer, *Uffz.* Franz 94
Scheuer; (2.(F)/122) 88
Scheven, *Oblt.* 80
Schick, *Ofw.* Herbert 136
Schiedel, *Hptm.* 18
Schiffels, *Ofhr.* 39, 65, 105, 134
Schlenaider, *Fw.* Heinz 165
Schlichting, *Gefr.* Günter 73
Schmauser, *Uffz.* 139
Schmidt; (2.(F)/122) 44
Schmoller, *Hptm.* 57
Schönauer, *Ogefr.* Heinz 111
Schreiterer, *Uffz.* Johannes 41
Schulz, *Uffz.* Heinz 40
Schulze, *Uffz.* Kurt 127
Schummer, *Uffz.* Ewald 67
Schuntermann, *Oblt.(later Hptm.)* 108, 118
Schuster, *Fhj.Fw.* August 122
Schütz, *Uffz.* 127
Schütze, *Uffz.* 104
Schwarz, Helmut 46
Schwobe, *Uffz.* Richard 63, 73
Seebode, *Hptm. (later Maj.) i.G.* Erich 108, 117, 130, 152
Seegert, *Uffz.* Helmut 74, 87, 88
Sewald, *Fhr.* 124, 133
Sliwa, *Fw.* 75
Sommer, *Oblt.* Erich K. 152, 155, 168, *170*, 171, 177, 181, 185, 190, 192, 205, 206, 207, 211, 218
Sonnenberg, *Ogefr.* Paul 104
Soukup, *Fw.* Ludwig 164

Spöntjes, *Ofhr.* Ernst 135, 139
Spörr, *Ogefr. (later Uffz.)* Franz 74, 128
Spousta, *Ltn.* Herbert 104
Stamm, *Maj.* 201
Stämmler, *Ltn.* Dietrich 40, 86
Stauch, *Uffz.* 47, 88, 111
Steinhoff, *Obstlt.* Johannes "Macky" 22, 44, 45, 47, 57, 58, 68, 69, *81*, 90, 104
Steinkönig, *Fw.* Walter 150, 165
Stollwerk, *Obfhr.* Peter 149
Stölting, *Ofw.* 49
Strehl, *Ofw.* Robert 61
Stuber, *Fw.* Kaspar 128

Tanck, *Fw.* Paul 76, 88
Thomsen, *Uffz.* 115
Thurnhuber, *Ltn.* Joseph 119, 144, *148*, 168, 206
Till, *Ogefr.* Franz 73
Tomschegg, *Ltn.* Hans 45
Tornow, *Ltn.* 21
Treynogga, *Ofw.* Helmut 42, *53*, 211
Tröster, *Ogefr.* Ulrich 65
Tschirch, *Ogefr.* Günter 84

Ullrich, *Fw.* Albert 66, 67
Urban, *Uffz.* Kurt 74, 104

Vietinghoff, *Gen.* Heinrich von 151, 167, 181
Volke, *Fhj.Ofw.* Maximilian 104
Voss, *Uffz.* Günther 94
Vossen, *Uffz.* Hans 94

Wachtfeidl, *Ogefr.* 125, 133
Wagner, *Gefr.* Hans 65
Waissnor, *Uffz.* Werner 63, 74
Weber, *Fw.* 39, 65, 134
Weidman, *Hptm.* 119, 143
Weinand, *Hptm.* 18, 32, 48, 49, *50*, 55, 83, 88, 119
Wentzlaff, *Uffz.* Franz 83
Wilk, *Gefr.* Hans 84
Wilzopolski, *Hptm.* Willi 174
Wist, *Uffz.* 135
Wolff-Rothermel, *Ofhr.* Klaus 66
Wolfsen, *Ofw.* Hans 84
Wöllert, *Ltn.* Fritz 165
Wolters, *Fw.* Heinrich 52

Zahn, *Maj.* 171
Zander, *Ofw.* Karl 121
Zantow, *Ogefr.* Egon 106
Zein, *Gefr.* Karl 44
Zielenkiewicz, *Fw.* 135
Zimmerman, *Ofw.* Wilhelm 150, 159
Zimmermann, Wilhelm 63
Züger, *Fhj.Fw.* Franz 153, 182

Other Nationalities

Cantacuzino, *Cap.* Constantin (Romania) 93
Cekovic, *Fw.* Josip (Croatia) 193
Hadnagy, *Maj.* Domokos (Hungary) 133, 134
Hary, *Generalmajor* Ladislaus (Hungary) 165
Kovacevic, *Fhr.* Nonrad (Croatia) 103

Kulenovic, *Ofw.* Sulijman (Croatia) 86
Laval, Pierre (Vichy France) 207, 211
Michael, *King* (Romania) 93
Mihalovich, *Fhr.* Ivan (Croatia) 103
Ratkovicic, *Ltn.* Dragou (Croatia) 67
Sandtner, *Fw.* Vladimir (Croatia) 193
Schweiger, *Ofw.* Zvonko (Croatia) 86
Soos, Gezer (Hungary) 133
Vouk, *Ltn.* Albeiu (Croatia) 74

INDEX OF PLACES

Achmer (Germany) 108
Adria (RO) 73
Airasca (TO) 30, 43, 47, 61, 74, 88
Ajaccio (Corsica) 118, 137
Ala (TN) 158
Albano Laziale (Roma) 40
Alberobello (BA) 68
Albino (BG) 101
Alessandria 68
Alfonsine (RA) 149, *182*, 191, 193
Algeciras (Spain) 42
Algiers (Algeria) 83
Alzano Lombardo (BG) 201, 202
Amendola (FG) 103
Ancona 44, 50, 52, 54, 55, 62, 63, 64, 65, 66, 69, 70, 73, 75, 83, 85, 98, 111, 120, 134, 138, 139, 145, 148, 152, 161, 162, 173, 174, 178, 179, 193, 199
Ansbach (Germany) 108
Anzio (Roma) 15, *17*, 18, 19, 20, 21, 22, 30, 40, 41, 45, 46, 83, 98
Arezzo 48, 55, 74, 75, 84, 85, 93, 94
Argenta (FE) 194
Argos (Greece) 84
Arlena (VT) 33
Arnhem (Holland) 108
Arno river 29
Artena (Roma) 39, 40
Asola (MN) 136
Athens (Greece) 65, 84, 85
Avezzano 39
Aviano (PN) 30, 33, 37, 39, 44, 46, 47, 52, 69, 108, 118, 121, *122*, 123, 124, 125, 126, 127, 136, 137, 138, 139, 145, 147, 148, 149, *153*, 154, *156*, 157, 158, 159, 160, 162, 163, 169, 171, 173, 174, 175, 178, *180*, 182, 183, 185, 187, *188*, 189, 190, 194, 195, 197, 201, 202, 206, 213
Avignon (France) 30, 41

Bad Voeslau (Germany) 52
Bagnacavallo (RA) 175
Bagno a Ripoli (FI) 55
Baltringen (Germany) 72, 85
Baranovici (USSR; now Belarus) 58
Barbi (SI) 53
Barcelona (Spain) 205, 207
Bardi (PR) 69
Bari 16, 17, 32, 46, 63, 65, 68, 74, 78, 103, 127, 152, 162
Bastia (Corsica) 61, 84, 162
Bautzen (Germany) 81
Beled (Hungary) 178
Belgrade (Yugoslavia – Serbia) 65, 67, 75, 83

229

Belgrade-Semlin (Yugoslavia – Serbia) 75, 86, 87
Bellagio (CO) 90
Belluno 105
Benghazi (Libya) 84
Bergamo 18, 23, 32, 33, 39, 40, 41, 44, 46, 48, 49, 52, 53, 55, 64, 70, 74, 78, 79, 82, 83, 84, 85, 86, 88, 93, 95, 98, 101, 103, 105, 106, 109, 112, 114, 121, 122, 125, 126, 127, 128, 129, 133, 135, 136, 137, 139, 143, 144, 145, 148, *148*, 149, 150, 159, 160, 161, 162, 163, 165, 168, 169, 170, 175, 177, 178, 193, 194, *196*, 200, 202, 206, 208
Bergamo-Seriate 33, 77, 85, 109, 111, 112
Bergantino (RO) 206
Berlin (Germany) 22, 57, 71, 128, 130, 145, 168
Berlin-Staaken (Germany) 152
Berlin-Tempelhof (Germany) 24
Berne (Switzerland) 88
Bettola (BS) 33, 53, 57, 58, 82, 88, 90, 99, 126
Beundenfeld (Switzerland) 88
Biblis (Germany) 227, 251
Bizerta (Tunisia) 32, 44, 75, 83
Bobbio (PC) 75
Bologna 16, 20, 23, 33, 43, 44, 46, 48, 51, 52, 53, 61, 62, 63, 65, 68, 79, 83, 85, 98, 102, 104, 108, 110, 111, 115, 121, 123, 137, 138, 145, 150, 151, 163, 169, 173, 174, 175, 181, 190, 192, 193, 194, 199, 205, 206
Bolzano 51, 52, 72, 85, 145, 175, *198*, 199, 201, *203*, 206, 207, 208
Bonn-Hangelar (Germany) 47
Borella (FO) 85
Borgosatollo (BS) 200
Bormio (SO) 194
Bovolone (VR) 75, 98, *99*, 105, 108, 118, 127, 128, 129, 130, 153, 160, 216
Bracciano (Roma) 145
Brenner Pass 120, 122, 123, 131, 185, 191
Brescia 39, 73, 186, 199
Bresso (MI) 26
Brindisi 16, 32, 152, 162
Brioni Island (Yugoslavia; now Croatia) 45
Brolio (AR) 31
Brussels-Melsbroek (Belgium) 46, 48
Bucine (AR) 74, 75
Budapest (Hungary) 113
Budrio (BO) 53, 205
Buonconvento (SI) 54
Busto Arsizio (VA) 175

Cagliari/Elmas 51
Calcinato (BS) 115
Calderara di Reno (BO) 52
Calvi (Corsica) 135
Cameri (NO) 77, 85, 93, 103, 104, 106, 122, 139, 145
Campoformido (UD) 25, *25*, *110*, *116*, 126, 153, 163, 168, 174, 177, 178, 179, 181, 190, 192, 193, 200, *203*, 205, 206, 207, 211, 214
Canazei (TN) 79
Cannes (France) 128
Cap Corse (Corsica) 48, 74, 135, 162, 175
Cap de Fer (Tunisia) 84
Cabo de Gata (Spain) 42

Cabo de Palos (Spain) 42
Cabo de la Não (Spain) 42
Capodichino (NA) 192
Capraia island (LI) 48
Carceri (PD) 160
Cardano al Campo (VA) 112, 154, 170
Carpi (MO) 68
Casabianca (TO) 27, 31, 39, 56
Casale Monferrato (AL) 91
Casarsa (PN) 136
Casciana Terme (PI) 75
Cascina Vaga (PV) 23, 26, *26*, 36, *37*, *42*, *43*, 49, 50, 52, 53, 58, 62, 89
Caselle (TO) 19, 22, 31, 39, 46, 49, 52, 56, 61, 62, 64, 71, 74, 79, 82, 105
Caserta 199, 207
Cassina Rizzardi (CO) 194
Cassino (FR) 15, 21, 23
Castano Primo (MI) 90
Castelfranco Veneto (TV) 174
Castellabate (SA) 152
Castellarano (RE) 70
Castenedolo (BS) 200
Castiglione (FO) 134, 149
Castiglione del Lago (PG) 20, 22, 31, 40, 47
Catania 16, 62
Cattolica (FO) 104, 161
Cavriago (RE) 35, 43, 73, 79, 94, 98
Cazaux (France) 47
Cecina (LI) 55, 62, 71
Centocelle (Roma) 19, 20
Ceresetto (UD) 168
Cerignola (FG) 74
Certaldo (FI) 75
Cervarezza (RE) 70
Cervere (CN) 27, 49, 80, 90
Cervia (RA) 103, 152, 173
Cesano river 70
Cesena (FO) 52, 104, 110, 111, 135
Cesenatico (FO) 62, 64, 103, 152
Chiasso (Switzerland) 194
Chiusaforte (UD) 162
Chiusi (SI) 44, 53
Cicogna (AR) 75
Cislago (VA) 194
Città di Castello (PG) 84
Cittadella (PD) 154, 164, 189
Civitavecchia (Roma) 31, 139
Colle di Val d'Elsa (SI) 74
Colonna (Roma) 41
Comacchio (FE) 67, 127, 139, 151, 159, 179
Conegliano (TV) 173
Corbola (RO) 68, 192
Cori (LT) 39
Costa (BS) 176
Côte d'Azur (France) 114
Courmayeur (AO) 88
Cremona 71, 103, 114, 123, 136, 165
Crete (Greece) 84
Cuneo 199
Custoza (VR) 90, 182
Cyrene Island (Greece) 65

Desenzano (BS) 34, 115, 123, 196, 201
Desio (MI) 183, 202
Dogna (UD) 158, 162
Dolo (VE) 59
Dresden (Germany) 105

Eisenstadt (Germany) 24
Elba (LI) 29, 43, 47, 48, 56, 64
Eleusis (Greece) 65, 83, 84, 85, 86
Erding (Germany) 52, 65, 115
Eschborn (Germany) 97
Este (PD) 182, 193

Fabrica di Roma (VT) 33, 39
Faenza (RA) 62, 128, 130, 132, 133, 138, 139, 149, 151, 175, 177
Falconara (AN) 64, 74, 86, 104, 112, 125, 128, 147, 193, *195*, 205
Fano (PS) 73, 93, 178, 192
Feldkirchen (Germany) 207
Fels-am-Wagram (Austria) 23, 57
Fermo (AP) 62, 70, 165
Ferno (VA) 170
Ferrara 23, 30, 33, 36, 43, 46, 49, 50, 52, 62, 65, 67, 68, 94, 98, 104, 115, 123, 159, 163, 165, 191, 192, 193
Ferryville (Tunisia) 44
Finale Emilia (MO) 106, 199
Finsterwalde (Germany) 79
Firenzuola (FI) 111, 122
Fiume (Yugoslavia; now Croatia) 165
Florence 16, 20, 31, 33, 44, 45, 47, 49, 53, 56, 65, 75, 77, 84, 93, 94, 111, 115, 117, 128, 133, 148, 175, 197, 208
Foggia 86, 93, 112, 174
Foligno (PG) 41, 43
Follonica (GR) 48
Fontanélice (BO) 150
Fontanella (BG) 106
Forcngai (Yugoslavia; now Croatia) 86
Forlì 18, 20, 30, 31, 39, 40, 46, 49, 51, 52, 56, 61, 62, 64, 65, 66, 79, 82, 117, 122, 127, 128, 130, 133, 134, 135, 136, 138, 175, 190, 192
Fornaci (BS) 128
Fornovo di Taro (PR) 68
Frascati (Roma) 43
Frosinone 17, 41
Fürstenfeldbruck (Germany) 154
Fürth-bei-Nürnberg (Germany) 146, 155, *177*
Futa Pass 102

Gablingen (Germany) 130
Gaeta (LT) 15, 21
Gallarate (VA) 24, 34, 47, 73, 75, 77, 83, 87, 88, 111, 139, 146, 154, 177, 190, 193, 200, 202
Gardone (BS) 176
Gattinara (VC) 49
Genoa 29, 39, 41, 50, 87, 117, 128, 135, 139, 162, 199
Ghedi (BS) 20, 30, 31, 33, 39, 40, 41, 42, 46, 47, 48, 52, 53, 57, 58, 62, 64, 66, 67, 68, 69, 72, 73, 78, 79, 82, 85, 86, 87, 88, 91, 93, 94, 95, 98, 99, 103, 104, 105, 106, 108, 110, 111, 112, 113, 115, 118, 119, 121, 122, 123, *124*, *140*
Ghedi I 88, 200, 202
Ghedi II 200, 202
Ghisonaccia (Corsica) 159
Gibraltar 16, 34, 42, 43
Giebelstadt (Germany) 105
Giulianello (LT) 39, 40
Goito (MN) 113, 186
Gorgona Island (LI) 62, 70

Gorizia   26, 27, 51, 78, 150, 177
Gorla (MI)   114
Goslar (Germany)   44, 81
Gracciano (SI)   42, *53*
Grado (VE)   160
Grassobbio (BG)   159
Graz (Austria)   109, 142, 199
Grizzana (BO)   139
Grosseto   29, 41
Grottaferrata (Roma)   43
Holzkirchen (Germany)   101, 108, 130, 131,*131*, 136, 145, 146, 147, 154, 155, 171, 183, 201, 202, 207
Hopsten (Germany)   131

Il Giogo Pass   102
Imola (BO)   51, 123, 192
Innsbruck (Austria)   115, 142, *196*, *197*, 199, 201, 206, 207
Innsbruck-Hötting (Austria)   206
Isola Dovarese (CR)   66
Isonzo river   159
Istres (France)   40, 42, 43, 44, 48, 74

Jesi (AN)   39, 46, 49, 114, 193, *195*
Jüterbog-Waldlager (Germany)   168

Kaltenkirchen (Germany)   152
Kamenz (Germany)   182
Karachi (Pakistan)   112
Kassel-Rothwesten (Germany)   79
Kaufbeuren (Germany)   77
Klagenfurt (Austria)   179
Königsberg (Germany; now Kaliningrad, Russia)   55

La Jasse (France)   39
La Maddalena (Maddalena) Island (SS)   55, 70, 72, 165
La Spezia   29, 41, 47, 51, 74, 87, 88, 93, 162, 181, 199
Labico (Roma)   41
Lagnasco (CN)   23, 25, 31
Lake Bolsena   44
Lake Bracciano   41
Lake Comacchio   185, 190, 191, 193
Lake Como   190, 207
Lake Garda   16, 57, 62, 97, 114, 121, 122, 123, 134, 136, 147, 162, 164, 175, 176, 177, 185, 195, 206
Lake Grado   160
Lake Iseo   134, 145
Lake Trasimeno   29, 44, 53, 56, 61, 62, 66
Lake Vico   40
Landsberg (Germany)   77
Latisana (UD)   174
Lavariano (UD)   23, 33, 45, 46, 48, 52
Lavis (TN)   158
Le Culot (Belgium)   52
Lechfeld (Germany)   168
Legnago (VR)   62, 159
Levaldigi (CN)   30, 43, 61, 72, 88
Lida (Poland)   31
Liegnitz (Germany)   80, 131
Lienz (Austria)   207
Linz-Hörsching (Austria)   45
Lippspringe (Germany)   24, 58
Liri river   15
Livenza river   125

Livorno   29, 47, 48, 65, 69, 73, 135, 150, 152, 159, 162, 174
Ljubljana (Yugoslavia; now Slovenia)   51
Locarno (Switzerland)   73
Lodi (MI)   133
Loiano (BO)   150
Lonate Pozzolo (Lonate) (VA)   27, 40, 44, 51, 52, 59, *60*, 63, 67, 75, 77, 82, 87, 90, 91, 93, 129, 131, 132, 136, 138, 139, *144*, 146, *146*, 147, 148, 149, 154, 164, *164*, 165, 168, 170, 175, *176*, 177, 179, *179*, 182, *184*, 185, 190, 191, 194, 200, 202, 211, 215
Lonato (BS)   115
London (England)   122
Lonigo (VI)   83
Loreto (AN)   56, 62, 63, 64, 66, 73
Lübeck (Germany)   207
Lübeck-Blankensee (Germany)   171
Lucca   33, 53, 132, 148, 175
Lucko (Yugoslavia; now Croatia)   193
Lugo (RA)   61, 104
Lyon (France)   47, 74, 75

Macerata   56, 62
Malcesine (VR)   16, 97, 108, 181, 208
Malpensa (VA)   154, 175, 176, 194, 200, 201, 215
Malta   85
Maniago (PN)   *10*, 23, 33, 41, 45, 51, 58, 69, 72, 75, 126
Mantua   66, 72, 83, 88, 105, 113, 174
Marano (UD)   174
Marcianise (CE)   40
Mariana Mantovana (MN)   135
Marina di Pisa (PI)   84, 85, 87
Marina di Ravenna (RA)   179
Marseille (France)   111, 114, 152
Marzabotto (BO)   60, 66
Melsbroek (Belgium)   46
Memmingen (Germany)   77, 101
Merano (BZ)   64
Metkovic (Yugoslavia; now Croatia)   103
Metz (France)   72
Milan   20, 39, 57, 86, 90, 91, 93, 99, 112, 114, 120, 150, 190, 191, 194, 199, 201, 202, *208*
Milan-Linate   88, 112, 205
Milan-Taliedo   167
Milazzo (ME)   139
Minerbio (BO)   61
Mirandola (MO)   104, 205
Modena   63, 66, 68, 72, 74, 111, 205
Molveno (TN)   202
Monselice (PD)   16, 193
Montanara (MN)   68
Monte Aleso   45
Monte Belvedere   127
Monte Castellaro   127
Monte Oggioli   111
Monte Riceo   16
Monte S. Pietro (BO)   51
Monte Soratte   16
Montecristo Island (LI)   70
Montefiascone (VT)   47
Monteriggioni (SI)   65
Monticello Conte Otto (VI)   90
Montichiari (BS)   149
Montopoli in Val d'Arno (PI)   57
Mozzate (CO)   194

München-Riem (Germany)   41, 56, 61, 77, 170
Munich (Germany)   34, 47, 53, 67, 69, 78, 86, 185, 199
Münster-Handorf (Germany)   152

Naples   32, 61, 64, 78, 93, 110, 112, 130, 139, 144, 152, 165, 174, 175, 178, 192, 199, 208
Nettuno (Roma)   15, 18, 19, 27, 30, 46
Neubiberg-bei-München (Germany)   206
Neuruppin (Germany)   86
Niedermendig (Germany)   78
Nijmegen (Netherlands)   108
Nish (Yugoslavia; now Serbia)   83
Novara   146
Novi Ligure (AL)   74

Oder river   153
Oldenburg (Germany)   79
Ombrone river   54
Oneglia (IM)   135
Ora (BZ)   163, 185, 195
Orange (France)   88
Oranienburg (Germany)   153, 168
Orbetello (GR)   16, 29, 43, 47
Orio al Serio (Orio) (BG)   27, 33, 44, *49*, *86*, 131, 134, 141, 154, 164, 176, 177, 183, *188*, 201, 208, 215
Ortona (CH)   46, 135
Orvieto (TR)   44, 53
Osoppo (UD)   21, 30, 47, 72, 83, 118, 127, 131, 151, 152, 154, 158, 159, *161*, 162, 164, 165, 168, 171, *172*, 173, 175, 183, 185, 189, 195, 200, 214
Ostiglia (MN)   63, 70, 75, 183, 206
Otocac (Yugoslavia; now Croatia)   75
Ovada (AL)   50

Padua   88, 114, 118, 123, 135, 148, 149, 157, 175, 177, 191, 205
Palata (BO)   79, 94
Palazzolo (MI)   93
Palermo   130, 139
Pàpa (Hungary)   134
Paris (France)   93
Parma   16, 51, 68, 69, 72, 83, 88, 94, 149, 163
Pavia   88, 108, 175
Peri (VR)   123
Perpignan (France)   42
Perugia   16, 17, 18, 23, 26, 27, 29, 31, 32, 39, 40, 41, 42, 44, 45, 46, 53, 71, 211
Pesaro   50, 71, 74, 93, 94, 103, 104
Pescantina Veronese (VR)   122
Pescara   16, 18, 29, 31, 72, 88, 93, 165, 178
Piacenza   21, 30, 32, 41, 43, 47, 48, 49, 66, 68, 69, 70, 71, 73, 74, 79, 83, 87, 88, 98, 158, 163, 205
Pianoro (BO)   123, 147
Pianosa Island (LI)   48, 54
Piave river   121
Piccione (PG)   61
Pieve (BS)   63
Piombino (LI)   48, 65, 84, 85, *87*
Pisa   16, 29, 41, 48, 49, 55, 115, 124, *155*, 175, *180*, 185, 188, 208
Pistoia   41, 44, 46, 47, 104, 163
Plattling (Germany)   147, 148

231

Po river   59, 70, 73, 89, 94, 111, 129, 142, 181, 199, 206
Po Delta   178
Po Estuary   16, 112, 121, 169, 173
Po Valley   78, 89, 107, 115, 122, 134, 157, 161, 165, 170, 177, 182, 185, 190, 205
Poggio Renatico (Poggio) (FE)   30, 33, 43, 46, 50, 52, 56, 58, 79, 82
Pola (Yugoslavia; now Pula, Croatia)   45, 70, 111, 121, 126, 161, 174
Polesella (RO)   43, 104
Pomigliano (NA)   112
Ponte del Diavolo (VT)   22
Ponte Di Piave (TV)   69
Ponte S. Pietro (BG)   80, 202
Pontedera (PI)   57, 74, 75
Pontelagoscuro (FE)   62
Ponti sul Mincio (MN)   196
Pordenone   22, 69, 138, 139, 162, 171, 173, 174, 178, 182, 183
Porto Recanati (MC)   63
Portogruaro (VE)   45
Portomaggiore (FE)   194
Pozzuolo sul Mincio (MN)   187
Provesano (PN)   69
Punta Ala (GR)   48
Punta de Almiña (Algeria)   42
Punta Salvore (Yugoslavia; now Savudrija, Croatia)   162

Rangsdorf (Germany)   130, 131
Ravenna   20, 31, 41, 50, 52, 53, 56, 62, 65, 66, 69, 70, 80, 82, 85, 93, 122, 132, 135, 136, 139, 149, 173, 174, 193, 205
Redona (BG)   109
Reggio Calabria   15
Reggio Emilia (Reggio)   25, 34, 35, 43, 45, 47, 51, 52, 59, 61, 62, 68, 69, 89, 94, 206
Reno river   52
Rhein-Main (Germany)   47
Rhine river   170
Rhône river   47
Riem (Germany) see also München-Riem
Riesa-Canitz (Germany)   105
Rieti   19, 44
Riga (Latvia)   33
Rijeka (Croatia)   165
Rimini   29, 31, 46, 51, 52, 55, 56, 61, 62, 64, 65, 66, 68, 73, 74, 82, 102, 104, 105, 106, 111, 115, 117, 121, 135, 148, 163, 190
Rome   15, 16, 19, 20, 21, 29, 30, 31, 32, 32, 39, 40, 41, 44, 72, 84, 85, 89, 144, 145, 169, 199
Ronco (FO)   133
Ronco river   110
Rosignano (LI)   194
Rovato (BS)   104
Roverbella (MN)   111
Rovereto (TN)   104, 121
Rovigno (Yugoslavia; now Rovinj, Croatia) 115
Russi (RA)   46

S. Bonifacio (VR)   127
S. Giorgio delle Pertiche (PD)   149
S. Martino (VR)   127
S. Michele sull'Adige (TN)   185
S. Vigilio (BG)   176
Saint Tropez (France)   128, 136

Salerno   15, 17, 178
Salonika (Greece)   65, 67, 192
Salsomaggiore (PR)   55
Samarate (VA)   170
Sampierdarena (GE)   74
San Benedetto del Tronto (AP)   111
San Benedetto Po (MN)   205
San Bonifacio Strait   47, 120
San Felice sul Panaro (MO)   106
San Martino (RA)   61
San Maurizio (TO)   56
San Severo (FG)   133
San Vito (TE)   165
Santa Maria Capua Vetere (CE)   72
Santerno river   181
Sarajevo (Yugoslavia; now Bosnia Herzegovina)   68
Sarajevo/Rajlovac (Yugoslavia; now Bosnia Herzegovina)   103
Sarsina (FO)   74
Savena river   123
Savigliano (CN)   65
Schongau (Germany)   34, 85
Schwangau (Germany)   112
Scutari (Albania)   32
Semlin (Yugoslavia; Serbia) see also Belgrade-Semlin
Senigallia (AN)   69, 70, 87, 128, 147
Senio river   132, 149, 181
Senj (Yugoslavia; now Croatia)   193
Serchio river   110, 130, 132, 151
Seriate (BG)   183, 202
Siena   16, 22, 30, 33, 55, 65, 66, 165
Sirmione (BS)   57, 62
Sluderno (BZ)   199, 206
Smolensk (Russia)   16
Sondrio   194
St Martin-de-Crau (France)   75
St Trond (France)   47
Ste. Catherine (Corsica)   66
Straubing (Germany)   131
Stubendorf (Germany)   19, 56
Stuttgart-Echterdingen (Germany)   31

Tabiano (PR)   16
Tagliamento river   168, 173
Tangmere (U.K.)   87
Taranto   16, 32, 78, 152, 162
Tarcento (UD)   178
Tarvisio (UD)   129
Termoli (CB)   15, 32, 174
Terni   29, 42
Thiene (VI)   59, 69, 81, 90, 110, 122, 131, 136, 137, 139, 141, 157, 160, 189, 193, 197, 202, 206, 207
Tiber river   20, 41, 43, 61
Tirana (Albania)   68, 71, 84
Tomino (Corsica)   84
Torre Gaia (Roma)   16
Torreano (UD)   168
Torriglia (GE)   75
Tortoreto (TE)   52, 135
Toulon (France)   114, 118, 139, 152
Tradate (VA)   194, 197
Tramonti (PN)   45
Trapani   16, 17
Tremiti Islands   54, 62
Trento   27, 83, 177
Treviso   16, 45, 63, 72, 88, 104, 158, 189
Tricesimo (UD)   58

Trieste   44, 45, 51, 160, 178, 179
Tulln/Vienna (Austria)   65, 68, 72
Turin   20, 21, 27, 39, 56, 71, 83, 84, 90, 146, 199, 210
Tuscania (VT)   20, 31

Udine   19, 23, 45, 47, 58, 69, 78, 84, 90, 98, 99, 104, 105, 108, 117, 125, 127, 129, 135, 142, 150, 151, 152, 153, 154, 160, 161, 162, 163, 165, 168, 177, 182, 185, 190, 191, 193, 200, 206, 207

Valdagno (VI)   157
Valeggio sul Mincio (Valeggio) (MN)   69, 90, 100, 201
Valmontone (Roma)   29
Varese   47
Varsi (PR)   69
Venaria Reale (TO)   24, 25, 27 171
Venegono (VA)   26, 34, 44, 51, 90, 91, 170
Venice   45, 47, 64, 72, 85, 105, 108, 111, 113, 117, 121, 136, 148, 168, 174, 190, 199, 205, 206
Vercelli   83, 191
Vergiate (VA)   34, 62, 110
Verona   16, 30, 41, 63, 64, 83, 84, 87, 95, 99, 105, 106, 108, 111, 129, 134, 136, 144, 145, 148, 149, 153, 165, 175, 178, 185, 189, 191, 200, 206, 207
Viadana (MN)   205
Vicenza   4, 39, 47, 59, 62, 63, 64, 69, 75, 80, 82, 89, 90, 98, 110, 111, 114, 115, 125, 126, 129, 131, 148, 149, 157, 162, 163, 205, 216, 219
Vienna (Austria)   83, 97, 142
Vigatto (PR)   80, 98
Villacidro (CA)   67
Villafontana (VR)   75
Villafranca di Verona (Villafranca) (VR) 20, 30, 39, 40, 41, 44, 45, 46, 47, 50, 59, 62, 65, 66, 67, 70, 71, 72, 75, 75, 77, 78, 82, 83, 86, 87, 88, 89, 90, 91, 94, 95, 97, 98, 99, 104, 105, 106, 107, 108, 110, 112, 113, 114, 114, 115, 118, 119, 119, 121, 122, 123, 124, 125, 126, 127, 129, 130, 131, 133, 134, 135, 136, 136, 138, 139, 141, 145, 148, 149, 153, 154, 157, 160, 162, 163, 164, 165, 168, 174, 177, 182, 183, 185, 186, 187, 188, 189, 193, 194, 195, 197, 200, 200, 201, 202, 204, 206, 210, 216
Villaorba (UD)   30, 31, 69, 82, 99, 109
Vipiteno (BZ)   175, 191
Viterbo   16, 19, 21, 30, 31, 40, 43, 44, 46, 47
Vizzola Ticino (VA)   59, 70, 215
Volturno river   72

Wien-Aspern (Austria)   104
Wiener Neustadt (Germany)   30
Worms (Germany)   152
Wright Field (U.S.A.)   134, 208
Würzburg (Germany)   168

Zagreb (Yugoslavia; now Croatia)   48, 51, 53, 67, 167
Zara (Yugoslavia; now Zadar, Croatia)   134
Zell-am-See (Austria)   65
Zeltweg (Austria)   179